A-Level
Physics

Exam Board: Edexcel

Revising for Physics exams is stressful, that's for sure — even just getting your notes sorted out can leave you needing a lie down. But help is at hand...

This brilliant CGP book explains **everything you'll need to learn** (and nothing you won't), all in a straightforward style that's easy to get your head around. We've also included **exam questions** to test how ready you are for the real thing.

There's even a free Online Edition you can read on your computer or tablet!

How to get your free Online Edition

Go to **cgpbooks.co.uk/extras** and enter this code...

0AA1 5610 0698 2899

This code only works for one person. If somebody else has used
this book before you, they might have already claimed the Online Edition.

A-Level revision? It has to be CGP!

Published by CGP

Editors:
Emily Garrett, David Maliphant, Rachael Marshall, Sam Pilgrim, Charlotte Whiteley and Sarah Williams.

Contributors:
Tony Alldridge, Jane Cartwright, Peter Cecil, Peter Clarke, Mark Edwards, Barbara Mascetti, John Myers and Andy Williams.

ISBN: 978 1 78294 305 1

With thanks to Ian Francis for the proofreading.
With thanks to Jan Greenway for the copyright research.

Photographs used on page 128 © Professor Peter Watkins

Clipart from Corel®
Printed by Elanders Ltd, Newcastle upon Tyne.

Based on the classic CGP style created by Richard Parsons.

Contents

If you're revising for the **AS exams**, you'll need Topics 1-5.
If you're revising for the **A-level exams**, you'll need the whole book.

Topic 1 — Working as a Physicist

Topic 2 — Mechanics

Topic 3 — Electric Circuits

Topic 4 — Materials

Topic 12 — Gravitational Fields

Do Well in Your Exams

Topic 13 — Oscillations

The Scientific Process

You'll need the skills covered in Topic 1 throughout your course, so make sure you're clear on everything that comes up on the next 12 pages, and can apply it to the physics you meet in the rest of your A-level.

Scientists Come Up with **Theories** — Then **Test Them**...

Science tries to explain **how** and **why** things happen — it **answers questions**. It's all about seeking and gaining **knowledge** about the world around us. Scientists do this by **asking** questions, **suggesting** answers and then **testing** their suggestions to see if they're correct — this is the **scientific process**.

1) **Ask** a question about **why** something happens or **how** something works. E.g. what is the nature of light?

2) **Suggest** an answer, or part of an answer, by forming a **theory** (a possible **explanation** of the observations) — e.g. light is a wave. (Scientists also sometimes form a **model** too — a **simplified picture** of what's physically going on.)

3) Make a **prediction** or **hypothesis** — a **specific testable statement**, based on the theory, about what will happen in a test situation. For example, if light is a wave, it will interfere and diffract when it travels through a small enough gap.

4) Carry out a **test** — to provide **evidence** that will support the prediction (or help to disprove it). E.g. shining light through a diffraction grating to show diffraction and interference (p.84).

The evidence supported Quentin's Theory of Flammable Burps.

\\\\\||||||||||||//
A theory is only scientific if it can be tested.
///||||||||||||\\\

...Then They **Tell** Everyone About Their **Results**...

The results are **published** — scientists need to let others know about their work. Scientists publish their results as reports (similar to the lab write-ups you do in school) written up in **scientific journals**. Scientific journals are just like normal magazines, only they contain **scientific reports** (called papers) instead of the latest celebrity gossip.

1) It's important that the **integrity** (trustworthiness) of the reports published in scientific journals is checked. Scientists (like anyone else) might be **dishonest** or **biased**, or an investigation might have made **invalid** conclusions (see page 13).

2) The report is sent out to **peers** — other scientists that are experts in the **same area**. They examine the data and results, and if they think that the conclusion is reasonable it's **published**. This makes sure that work published in scientific journals is of a **good standard**. This process is known as **peer review**.

3) But peer review **can't guarantee** the science is **correct** — other scientists still need to **reproduce** it.

4) Sometimes **mistakes** are made and bad work is published. Peer review **isn't perfect** but it's probably the best way for scientists to self-regulate their work and to publish **quality reports**.

...Then **Other Scientists** Will **Test** the Theory Too

Other scientists read the published theories and results, and try to **test the theory** themselves. This involves:
* Repeating the **exact same experiments**.
* Using the theory to make **new predictions** and then testing them with **new experiments**.

If the **Evidence** Supports a Theory, It's **Accepted** — **for Now**

1) If all the experiments in all the world provide good evidence to back it up, the theory is thought of as **scientific 'fact'** (for now).

2) But it will never become **totally indisputable** fact. Scientific **breakthroughs or advances** could provide new ways to question and test the theory, which could lead to **new evidence** that **conflicts** with the current evidence. Then the testing starts all over again...

And this, my friend, is the **tentative nature of scientific knowledge** — it's always **changing** and **evolving**.

The Scientific Process

So scientists need evidence to back up their theories. They get it by carrying out experiments, and when that's not possible they carry out studies.

Evidence Comes From Controlled Lab Experiments...

1) Results from **controlled experiments** in **laboratories** are **great**.
2) A lab is the easiest place to **control variables** so that they're all **kept constant** (except for the one you're investigating).

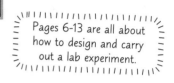
Pages 6-13 are all about how to design and carry out a lab experiment.

...That You can Draw Meaningful Conclusions From

1) You always need to make your experiments as **controlled** as possible so you can be confident that any effects you see are linked to the variable you're changing.
2) If you do find a relationship, you need to be careful what you conclude. You need to decide whether the effect you're seeing is **caused** by changing a variable (this is known as a **causal relationship**), or whether the two are just **correlated**. There's more about drawing conclusions on page 13.

Society Makes Decisions Based on Scientific Evidence

1) Lots of scientific work eventually leads to **important discoveries** or breakthroughs that could **benefit humankind**.
2) These results are **used by society** (that's you, me and everyone else) to **make decisions** — about the way we live, what we eat, what we drive, etc.
3) All sections of society use scientific evidence to make decisions, e.g. politicians use it to devise policies and individuals use science to make decisions about their own lives.

Other factors can **influence** decisions about science or the way science is used:

1) **Economic factors:**
   Society has to consider the **cost** of implementing changes based on scientific conclusions — e.g. the cost of reducing the UK's carbon emissions to limit the human contribution to **climate change**.
   Scientific research is often **expensive**. E.g. in areas such as astronomy, the Government has to **justify** spending money on a new telescope rather than pumping money into, say, the **NHS** or **schools**.

2) **Social factors:**
   Decisions affect **people's lives** — e.g. when looking for a site to build a **nuclear power station**, you need to consider how it would affect the lives of the people in the **surrounding area**.

3) **Environmental factors:**
   Many scientists suggest that building **wind farms** would be a **cheap** and **environmentally friendly** way to generate electricity in the future. But some people think that because **wind turbines** can **harm wildlife** such as birds and bats, other methods of generating electricity should be used.

Practice Questions

Q1 What is peer review?

Q2 Explain why a theory supported by a paper published in a scientific journal is not necessarily scientific 'fact'?

Q3 Explain why considering scientific evidence alone is not enough when making decisions in society.

Exam Question

Q1* A scientist has developed a proposal for a power station which generates electricity renewably from the energy of the tides, without producing greenhouse gases that can lead to climate change. The proposed location of the power station is off a stretch of scenic coastline that attracts a lot of tourism. She claims that her evidence suggests that if built in this location, the power station would produce sufficient electricity to entirely replace a nearby coal-fired power station that uses non-renewable fossil fuels and produces greenhouse gases. Discuss the economic, social and environmental factors that need to be considered by decision-makers considering her proposal. [6 marks]

* The quality of your extended response will be assessed in this question.

No. Borrowing your friend's homework to 'check' it is not peer review...

Hopefully these pages have given you a nice intro to the scientific process, e.g. what scientists do to provide you with 'facts'. You need to understand this, as you're expected to know how science works yourself — for the exam and for life.

Quantities and Units

Learning Physics is a lot like building a house — both involve drinking a lot of tea. Also, both have important foundations — if you skip this stuff everything else is likely to go a bit wrong. So, here goes brick-laying 101...

A *Physical Quantity* has both a *Numerical Value* and a *Unit*

1) Every time you measure or calculate a quantity you need to give the **units**.

2) There are seven **base quantities** from which all the other quantities you'll meet can be **derived**. These other quantities are called **derived quantities**.

3) The **Système International** (SI) includes a set of **base units** for the seven base quantities. The base quantities and their SI base units are:

Quantity	SI base unit
mass	kilogram, kg
length	metre, m
time	second, s
current	ampere, A
temperature	kelvin, K
amount of a substance	mole, mol
luminous intensity	candela, cd

Kilograms are a bit odd — they're the only SI unit with a scaling prefix (see the next page).

You might also see temperatures given in °C.

4) The units for **derived quantities** can be derived from these base units. E.g. **force** is a derived quantity, with the SI derived unit of newtons, N. **1 N is defined as equivalent to 1 kgms^{-2}.**

Remembering how SI derived units are defined will help you make sure the other quantities in your equations are in the right units.

5) The derived quantities and SI derived units you'll need will be covered throughout the book and you need to remember them.

6) You also need to have a rough idea of the size of each SI base unit and SI derived unit in this book, so that you can **estimate quantities** using them.

> **Example:** A man drops a ball from the first floor window of his house. It takes 1 s to hit the ground. Estimate the average speed of the ball.
>
> A first floor window of a normal house is about 6 m above the ground, so $s = 6$ m.
>
> speed = distance ÷ time = 6 m ÷ 1 s = 6 ms^{-1}

You Can *Work Out* Derived Units *Mathematically*

The units in any equation must always be the **same on both sides**.
You can use this rule to work out some of the simpler SI derived units, like speed:

> **Example:** Show that the SI derived unit for speed is ms^{-1} (speed = distance ÷ time).
>
> Distance is a length, so its SI base unit is the metre, m. The base unit of time is the second, s.
> To find the unit for speed, just put the units for distance and time into the equation for speed: **m ÷ s = ms^{-1}**

Some SI derived units have **special names**, like the newton. You can work out what they're **equivalent** to in **SI base units** using the same method as above.

> **Example:** Charge, Q, is measured in coulombs, C, and given by the equation charge = current × time. What is one coulomb equivalent to in SI base units?
>
> The SI base unit for current is the ampere, A, and the SI base unit for time is the second, s.
> Charge = current × time, so 1 C = 1 A × 1 s = **1 As**

Quantities and Units

Prefixes Let You Scale Units

Physical quantities come in a **huge range** of sizes. Prefixes are scaling factors that let you write numbers across this range without having to put everything in standard form.

These are the most common prefixes you'll come across:

prefix	femto (f)	pico (p)	nano (n)	micro (μ)	milli (m)	centi (c)	deci (d)	kilo (k)	mega (M)	giga (G)	tera (T)
multiple of unit	1×10^{-15}	1×10^{-12}	1×10^{-9}	1×10^{-6}	0.001 (1×10^{-3})	0.01 (1×10^{-2})	0.1 (1×10^{-1})	1000 (1×10^{3})	1×10^{6}	1×10^{9}	1×10^{12}

If you're a bit uncertain about moving directly between these scaling factors, then convert quantities into the standard unit before you do anything else with them:

> **Example 1:** Convert 1869 picometres into nanometres.
>
> First, convert the value to metres: $1869 \text{ pm} = 1869 \times 10^{-12} \text{ m}$
>
> Then divide by 1×10^{-9} to convert to nanometres: $1869 \times 10^{-12} \div 1 \times 10^{-9} = \textbf{1.869 nm}$

Or, you can convert between prefixes directly:

> **Example 2:** Convert 0.247 megawatts into kilowatts.
>
> $1 \text{ MW} = 1 \times 10^{6} \text{ W}$ and $1 \text{ kW} = 1 \times 10^{3} \text{ W}$
>
> So the scaling factor to move between MW and kW is:
>
> $(1 \times 10^{6}) \div (1 \times 10^{3}) = 1 \times 10^{3}$.
>
> So $0.247 \text{ MW} = 0.247 \times 1 \times 10^{3} = \textbf{247 kW}$

It's really easy to get muddled up when you're converting between prefixes. The rule is, if you're moving to the right in the table above, your number should get smaller, and if you're moving to the left the number should get larger. If your answer doesn't match the rule, you've made a mistake.

Don't use these prefixes in the middle of calculations — they'll change the units of your final answer, and could get you in a mess. You should generally convert to the units you need to use before you do any calculations, or once you've got a final answer.

Practice Questions

Q1 What is meant by a base quantity and a derived quantity?

Q2 What is the SI unit of mass?

Q3 What is meant by an SI base unit and an SI derived unit?

Q4 What is: a) 20 000 W in kilowatts
b) 2×10^{-6} W in milliwatts
c) 1.23×10^{7} W in gigawatts?

Aliona preferred scaling frozen waterfalls.

Exam Question

Q1 The density, ρ, of a material gives its mass per unit volume. It is given by $\rho = m/V$, where $m = $ mass and $V = $ volume.

a) Express the units of density in terms of SI base units. [1 mark]

b) Calculate the density of a cube of mass 9.8 g, and side length 11 mm. Give your answer in the units stated in part a). [2 marks]

c) A bath tub is filled with water. Given that the density of water is approximately 1000 kg m⁻³, estimate the mass of the water in the bath tub. [2 marks]

What's the SI base unit for boring...

Not the most exciting pair of pages these, I'll admit, but it's important that you have the basics down, or else you're leaving yourself open to simple little mistakes that'll cost you marks. So make sure you've memorised all the SI base units in the table, then try and write down all the prefixes and their scaling factors. If you don't get them all first time, keep trying until you can. Remember, you need to know the units for every derived quantity you meet in this book, too.

Planning and Implementing

Science is all about getting good evidence to support (or disprove) your theories, so scientists need to be able to spot a badly designed experiment, interpret the results of an experiment or study, and design their own experiments too...

You Might have to **Design an Experiment** to Answer a **Question**

1) You might be asked to design a physics experiment to **investigate** something or answer a question.

2) It could be a **lab experiment** that you've seen before, a **new experiment** you aren't familiar with, or it could be something **applied**, like deciding which building material is best for a particular job.

3) Whatever you're asked, you'll be able to use the physics you know and the skills covered on the next few pages to figure out the best way to do the investigation.

A **Variable** is Anything that has the Potential to **Change** in an Experiment

1) First, you need to identify your **independent** and **dependent variables**:

> The **independent** variable is the thing you **change**.
> The **dependent** variable is the thing you **measure**.

Example 1: If you're investigating how changing the potential difference across a component affects the current through it, the **independent variable** is the **potential difference**, and the **dependent variable** is the **current**.

2) Apart from the independent and dependent variables, **all other variables** should stay the same during your experiment. If not, you can't tell whether or not the independent variable is responsible for any changes in your dependent variable, so your results won't be **valid** (p.12). This is known as **controlling variables**. It might be worth **measuring control variables** that are likely to change during your experiment to check that they really are under control.

Example 1 (continued): In the example above, you need to use the same **circuit components**, and to keep the **temperature** of the apparatus **constant** — e.g. by letting the circuit cool down between readings.

Example 2: If you're investigating the value of **acceleration due to gravity** by dropping an object and timing its fall, **draughts** in the room could really mess up your results. Picking an object that is more **resistant** to being blown about (like a ball-bearing) will help make your results more **precise** (p.12).

Select Appropriate **Apparatus** and **Techniques**

1) You need to think about what **units** your measurements of the independent and dependent variables are likely to be in before you begin (e.g. millimetres or metres, milliseconds or hours).

2) Think about the **range** you plan on taking measurements over too — e.g. if you're measuring the effect of increasing the force on a spring, you need to know whether you should increase the force in steps of 1 newton, 10 newtons or 100 newtons. Sometimes, you'll be able to **estimate** what effect changing your independent variable will have, or sometimes a **pilot experiment** might help.

3) Considering your measurements before you start will also help you choose the most appropriate **apparatus** and **techniques** for the experiment:

There's a whole range of apparatus and techniques that could come up in your exam. Make sure you know how to use all the ones you've come across in class.

Example:
- If you're measuring the length of a **spring** that you're applying a force to, you might need a **ruler**. If you're measuring the diameter of a **wire**, you'd be better off with a set of **callipers**.

  If the wire **doesn't stretch** easily, you may need to use a **very long wire** to get an extension that's big enough to measure, so you might need to use a **pulley** like in the Young modulus experiment on p.60.

- If you're measuring a **time interval**, you could use a **stopwatch**. If the time is **really short** (for example if you're investigating acceleration due to gravity), you might need something more sensitive, like **light gates**.

4) Whatever apparatus and techniques you use, make sure you use them **correctly**. E.g. if you're measuring a length, make sure your eye is level with the ruler when you take the measurement.

5) While you're planning, you should also think about the **risks** involved in your experiment and how to manage them — e.g. if you're investigating a material that might snap, wear safety goggles to protect your eyes.

Planning and Implementing

Figure Out how to Record your Data Before you Start

Before you get going, you'll need a **data table** to record your results in.

1) It should include space for your **independent variable** and your **dependent variable**. You should specify the **units** in the headers, not within the table itself.

2) The readings of the **independent variable** should be taken at **evenly spaced intervals**.

3) Your table will need enough room for repeated measurements. You should aim to **repeat** each measurement at least **three times**. Taking repeat measurements can reduce the effect of random errors in your results (see p.12) and makes spotting **anomalous** results, like this one, much easier. If there's no way to take repeat readings, then you should **increase** the **total number** of readings that you take.

P.d. / V	Current / A			
	Trial 1	Trial 2	Trial 3	Average
1.00	0.052	0.047	0.050	0.050
1.50	0.079	0.075	0.077	0.077
2.00	0.303	0.098	0.097	...
2.50	0.129	0.125	0.130	...
3.00	0.149	0.151	0.145	...
...	...	...	...	...

4) There should be space in your table for any data processing you need to do, e.g. calculating an **average** from repeated measurements, or calculating speed from measurements of distance and time.

5) Most of the time, your data will be **quantitative** (i.e. you'll be recording numerical values). Occasionally, you may have to deal with **qualitative** data (data that can be observed but not measured with a numerical value). It's still best to record this kind of data in a table, to keep your results **organised**, but the layout may be a little **different**.

You Could be Asked to Evaluate An Experimental Design

If you need to evaluate an experimental design, whether it's your own or someone else's, you need to think about these sorts of things:

- Does the experiment **actually test** what it sets out to test?
- Is the method **clear** enough for someone else to follow?
- Apart from the **independent** and **dependent variables**, is everything else going to be **properly controlled**?
- Are the **apparatus** and **techniques appropriate** for what's being measured? Will they be used correctly?
- Are enough **repeated measurements** going to be taken?
- Is the experiment going to be conducted **safely**, for those involved and those **nearby**?
- Are there any other **ethical considerations**? For example, does the experiment produce **harmful waste products**? Is the apparatus being used in a way that won't **damage it**?

Greta was paying the price for not planning her experiment properly.

Practice Questions

Q1 What is meant by the term independent variable? What is a dependent variable?

Q2 Why do you need to plan to control all of the other variables in an experiment?

Q3 What do you need to consider when selecting your apparatus?

Q4 Why should you take repeated measurements in an experiment?

Exam Question

Q1 A student is investigating the effect of the light level on the resistance of an LDR (light-dependent resistor). The student connects the LDR to a power supply, and measures the resistance of the LDR at various distances from a light source using a multimeter.

a) State the independent and dependent variables for this experiment. [1 mark]

b) State two variables that the student needs to control in order to ensure his results are valid. [2 marks]

The best-planned experiments of mice and men...

...often get top marks. The details of planning and carrying out an experiment will vary a lot depending on what you're investigating, but if all this stuff is wedged in your brain you shouldn't go far wrong, so make sure you've got it learned.

Analysing Results

You've planned an experiment, and you've got some results (or you've been given some in your exam).
Now it's time to look into them a bit more closely...

Do any **Calculations** You Need to **First**

1) Before you calculate anything, check for any **anomalous results**. If there's something in the results that's **clearly wrong**, then don't include it in your calculations — it'll just **muck everything up**. Be careful though, you should only exclude an anomalous result if you have **good reason** to think it's wrong, e.g. it looks like a decimal point is in the **wrong place**, or you suspect that one of the control variables **changed**. And you should talk about any anomalous results when you're evaluating the experiment (pages 12-13).

2) For most experiments, you'll at least need to calculate the mean (average) of some **repeated measurements**:

$$\text{mean (average) of a measurement} = \frac{\text{sum of your repeated measurements}}{\text{number of repeats taken}}$$

In class, you could use a spreadsheet to process your data (and plot graphs), but it's important that you know how to do it by hand for the exam.

3) Calculate any quantities that you're interested in that you haven't **directly measured** (e.g. pressure, speed).

You should try to give any values you calculate to the **same number of significant figures** as the data value with the **fewest significant figures** in your calculation. If you give your result to too many significant figures, you're saying your final result is more **precise** than it actually is (see p.12).

Present Your Results on a **Graph**

Make sure you know how to plot a graph of your results:

If you need to use your graph to measure something, select axes that will let you do this easily (e.g. by measuring the gradient or the intercept, see the next page).

1) Usually, the **independent variable** goes on the *x*-axis and the **dependent variable** goes on the *y*-axis. Both axes should be **labelled** clearly, with the quantity and **units**. The **scales** used should be sensible (i.e. they should go up in sensible steps, and should spread the data out over the full graph rather than bunching it up in a corner).

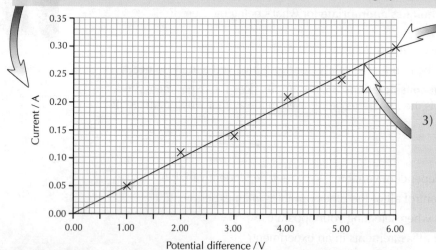

2) Plot your points using a **sharp pencil**, to make sure they're as **accurate** as possible.

3) Draw a **line of best fit** for your results. Around **half** the data points should be above the line, and half should be below it (you should ignore anomalous results). Depending on the data, the line might be **straight**, or **curved**.

Graphs can Show Different Kinds of **Correlation**

Remember, correlation does not necessarily mean cause — p.3.

The **correlation** describes the relationship between the variables. Data can show:

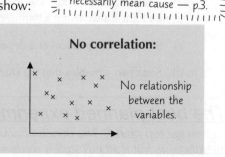

Positive correlation:
As one variable increases the other increases.

Negative correlation:
As one variable increases the other decreases.

No correlation:
No relationship between the variables.

Analysing Results

You Might Need to Find a Gradient or Intercept

If the line of best fit is **straight**, then the graph is **linear**. This means a change in one always leads to a change in the other. The **line of best fit** for a linear graph has the **equation:** $y = mx + c$ — Where m is the **gradient** of the line and c is the **y-intercept**.

If the line of best fit goes through the origin (c is 0), you can say the variables are **directly proportional** to each other: $y \propto x$ — $\propto$ just means 'is directly proportional to'.

Example: This graph shows displacement against time for a motorbike travelling west. Find the bike's velocity.

For a displacement-time graph, the gradient gives the velocity (as velocity = displacement ÷ time).

$\Delta y = 1000 - 400 = 600$ m

$\Delta x = 56 - 16 = 40$ s — Δ means 'change in'.

The y intercept is 160. This means the bike's displacement was 160 m at time 0 s.

$$\text{velocity} = \frac{\text{displacement}}{\text{time}} = \frac{\Delta y}{\Delta x} = 600 \div 40 = 15 \text{ ms}^{-1} \text{ west}$$

If a graph has a **curved** line of best fit, you can find the gradient of a given point on the line by drawing a **tangent** to the curve (see page 23). It's sometimes helpful to choose axes that turn a curved graph into a straight one:

Example:

For a given force, the graph of **pressure** applied against the **area** that the force is applied over looks like this:

If you plot pressure against **1 ÷ area**, the graph looks like this:

pressure = force ÷ area.

The **gradient** is:
pressure ÷ (1 ÷ area)
= pressure × area
= force applied (p.64)

Practice Questions

Q1 Describe what you should do with anomalous results when processing data.

Q2 How do you calculate an average of repeated results?

Q3 Sketch a graph showing a negative correlation.

Exam Question

Q1 An engineer is investigating the performance of a prototype car with a new kind of environmentally-friendly engine. The data below shows the speed of the car, going from stationary to over 70 kilometres per hour.
(In this question, you may use the formula: acceleration = change in speed ÷ time taken to change speed.)

Time / s	0.0	1.0	2.0	3.0	4.0	5.0	6.0	7.0
Speed / km per hour	0	3	8	22	40	54	66	70

a) Draw a graph showing speed against time for this data. [4 marks]

b) State the times, to the nearest second, between which the graph is linear. [1 mark]

c) Using the graph, calculate the maximum acceleration of the car. [4 marks]

My level of boredom is proportional to the time I've spent on this page...

This stuff can get a bit fiddly, especially measuring the gradient of a curved line, but for the most part it's not too bad, and you should have seen a lot of it before. So dust off your pencil sharpener, and get to work...

Measurements and Uncertainties

There are errors and uncertainties in every measurement. You need to be aware of them.

All Results have Some *Uncertainty*

The smallest measuring interval on an instrument gives you its resolution.

1) **Every** measurement you take has an **experimental uncertainty**.

2) The smallest uncertainty you can have in a measurement is the uncertainty due to the **resolution** of your equipment. It's ± **half** of one division on the measuring instrument used. E.g. using a thermometer with a scale where each division represents 2 °C, a measurement of 30 °C will at **best** be measured to be 30 ± 1 °C. And that's without taking into account any other errors that might be in your measurement.

3) The ± sign gives you the **range** in which the **true** length (the one you'd really like to know) probably lies. 30 ± 0.5 cm tells you the true length is very likely to lie in the range of 29.5 to 30.5 cm. The maximum difference between your value and the true value (here 0.5 cm) is sometimes called the **margin of error**.

4) There are two measures of uncertainty you need to know about:

> **Absolute uncertainty** — the **total uncertainty** for a measurement.
> **Percentage uncertainty** — the uncertainty given as a **percentage** of the measurement.
>   Measuring **larger** values reduces the percentage uncertainty.

If you measure a length of something with a ruler, you actually take two measurements, one at each end of the object you're measuring. E.g. 17.0 cm measured using a mm ruler will have an uncertainty of 0.05 + 0.05 = ± 0.1 cm.

5) An uncertainty should also include a level of **confidence** or probability, to indicate how **likely** the true value is to lie in the interval. The **more variation** there is in your results, and the **fewer repeats** you have done, the **less confident** you can be.

6) The uncertainty on a **mean** (see p.8) of repeated results is the **largest difference** between the mean and any of the values used to calculate it. So if you take repeated measurements of a current and get values of 0.1 A, 0.4 A and 0.4 A, the mean current is 0.3 A, and the uncertainty on the mean is 0.3 – 0.1 = ± 0.2 A. You can estimate the uncertainty on the mean as **half the range** — e.g. (0.4 – 0.1) ÷ 2 = **0.15 A**.

7) If no uncertainty is given for a value, the **assumed uncertainty** is **half the increment** of the **last** significant figure that the value is **given** to. E.g. 2.0 is given to 2 **significant figures**, so you would assume an uncertainty of 0.05. You should always assume the **largest** amount of uncertainty when doing an experiment.

Sometimes You Need to *Combine Uncertainties*

You have to combine the uncertainties of different measured values to find the uncertainty of a calculated result:

Adding or *Subtracting* Data — *ADD* the *Absolute Uncertainties*

> **Example:** A wire is stretched from 4.3 ± 0.1 cm to 5.5 ± 0.1 cm. Calculate the extension of the wire.

1) First subtract the lengths without the uncertainty values: 5.5 – 4.3 = 1.2 cm
2) Then find the total uncertainty by adding the individual absolute uncertainties: 0.1 + 0.1 = 0.2 cm
   So, the extension of the wire is **1.2 ± 0.2 cm**.

Multiplying or *Dividing* Data — *ADD* the *Percentage Uncertainties*

> **Example:** A force of 15 N ± 3% is applied to a stationary object which has a mass of 6.0 ± 0.3 kg. Calculate the acceleration of the object and state the percentage uncertainty in this value.

1) First calculate the acceleration without uncertainty: $a = F \div m = 15 \div 6.0 = 2.5 \text{ ms}^{-2}$

2) Next, calculate the percentage uncertainty in the mass: % uncertainty in $m = \frac{0.3}{6.0} \times 100 = 5\%$

3) Add the percentage uncertainties in the force and mass values to find the total uncertainty in the acceleration: Total uncertainty = 3% + 5% = 8%
   So, the acceleration = **2.5 ms⁻² ± 8%**

Raising to a Power — *MULTIPLY* the *Percentage Uncertainty* by the *Power*

> **Example:** The radius of a circle is r = 40 cm ± 2.5%. Find the percentage uncertainty in the circle's area (πr^2).

The radius is raised to the power of **2** to calculate the area. So, the percentage uncertainty is 2.5% × 2 = **5%**

Measurements and Uncertainties

Error Bars *Show the* Uncertainty *of Individual Points*

1) Most of the time, you work out the **uncertainty** in your **final** result using the uncertainty in **each measurement** you make.

2) When you're plotting a **graph**, you can show the uncertainty in **each measurement** by using **error bars** to show the **range** the point is likely to lie in.

3) You can have error bars for just one variable (see below), or **both** the dependent and the independent variable. Error bars on both variables give you an '**error box**' for each point.

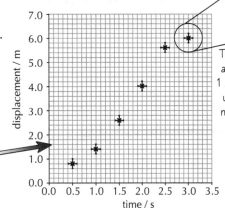

This is an 'error box'. The true value of the data point could lie anywhere in this area.

The error bars extend 1 square right and left for each measurement, and 1 square up and down. This gives an uncertainty of ± O.1 s in each time measurement, and ± O.2 m in each displacement measurement.

Your line of best fit (p.8) should always go through all of the error bars (see below) or boxes.

You Can Calculate *the* Uncertainty *of* Final Results *from a* Line of Best Fit

Normally when you draw a graph you'll want to find the **gradient** or **intercept** (p.9). For example, you can calculate k, the **force constant** of the object being stretched, from the **gradient** of the graph on the right — here it's about $20\,000$ Nm^{-1}. You can find the **uncertainty** in that value by using **worst lines**:

1) Draw lines of best fit which have the **maximum** and **minimum** possible slopes for the data and which should go through all of the **error bars** (see the pink and blue lines on the right). These are the **worst lines** for your data. If your data has errors in **both** the independent and dependent variables, then the worst lines should go through the **corners** of the **error boxes**.

2) Calculate the **gradients** of the worst lines. The blue line's gradient is about $21\,000$ Nm^{-1} and the pink line's gradient is about $19\,000$ Nm^{-1}.

When the force is O N the extension is O mm — this is a measurement with no uncertainty.

3) The **uncertainty** in the gradient is given by half the **difference** between the **worst gradients** — here it's 1000 Nm^{-1}. So this is the uncertainty in the value of the force constant. For this object, the force constant is $20\,000 \pm 1000$ Nm^{-1} (or $20\,000$ Nm^{-1} $\pm 5\%$).

4) Similarly, the uncertainty in the **y-intercept** is just half the **difference** between the **worst** intercepts (although there's no uncertainty here since the worst lines both go through the origin).

Practice Questions

Q1 What is meant by experimental uncertainty? How does it relate to an instrument's resolution?

Q2 What are the rules for combining uncertainties?

Q3 What are worst lines? How could you use them to find the uncertainty in the intercept of a graph?

Exam Question

Q1 A student is investigating the acceleration of a remote controlled car. The car has an initial velocity of 0.52 ± 0.02 ms^{-1} and accelerates to 0.94 ± 0.02 ms^{-1} over an interval of 2.5 ± 0.5 s.

    a) Calculate the percentage uncertainty in the car's initial speed.   [1 mark]

    b) Calculate the percentage uncertainty in the car's final speed.   [1 mark]

    c) Calculate the car's average acceleration over this interval. Include the absolute uncertainty of the result in your answer. (acceleration = change in velocity ÷ time taken).   [4 marks]

My percentage uncertainty about these pages is 0.99%...

Uncertainties are a bit of a pain, but they're really important. Learn the rules for combining uncertainties, and make sure you know how to draw those pesky error bars, and what to do with them when you've got them.

Evaluating and Concluding

Once you've drawn your graphs and analysed your results, you need to think about your conclusions.

Evaluate the Quality of Your Results

Before you draw any conclusions, you should think about the quality of the results — if the quality's not great you won't be able to have much confidence in your conclusion. Good results are **valid**, **precise**, **repeatable**, **reproducible** and **accurate**.

Quality control — also important in construction.

1) **Valid measurements** measure what they're supposed to be measuring. If you haven't **controlled** all the variables (p.6) then your **results** won't be valid, because you won't just be testing the effect of the independent variable.

2) You can say your results are **precise** if the **range** that your repeated data is spread over is small. The precision of a result is only influenced by **random errors** (see below).

3) Results are **repeatable** if **you** can **repeat** an experiment multiple times and get the **same results**. You can measure the repeatability of your results by looking at their **precision**, and by comparing them to the results of other students in your class who have used exactly the same method and equipment.

4) For a result to be **reproducible**, it needs to be obtained by **different experimenters**, using **different equipment** and **different methods**. Testing whether a result is reproducible is a better test of its quality than testing whether it is repeatable, as it's less likely that the same **systematic errors** could have affected both methods (see below).

5) An **accurate result** is one that's really close to the **true value**. You often **can't know** the accuracy of a result, since you can never know the true value of what you're measuring. The exception to this is if you're measuring a **known constant**, like *g*, which has been **tested many times**, and is known to a good degree of certainty. In cases like this, you can assess how accurate your results are by **comparing** them to this known value. One way of doing this is by calculating the **percentage difference** — the difference between your result and the true value, expressed as a **percentage** of the **true value**.

You'll Need to Think About Random and Systematic Errors

An error is the difference between your **measured value** and the **true value** of whatever you're trying to measure. There are two different kinds of error that could affect the quality of your results — **random errors** and **systematic errors**. You should think about these when you're planning your experiment (so you can minimise them) and when you're evaluating your results.

Systematic Errors

1) **Systematic errors** (including **zero errors**) are the same every time you repeat the experiment (they shift all the values by the same amount). They may be caused by the **equipment** you're using or how it's **set-up**, e.g. not lining up a ruler correctly when measuring the extension of a spring.

2) Systematic errors are really **hard to spot**, and they affect the **accuracy** of your results, but not the **precision** — so it can look like you've measured something **really well**, even if your results are actually **completely off**. Systematic errors might show up when you **compare results** with other people in your class who have done the **same experiment** if they're caused by a mistake you made, or when you compare your results with someone else who used a **different method** if there is something wrong with the procedure itself (i.e. when you check the reproducibility of your results).

3) It's always worth **checking your apparatus** at the start of an experiment, e.g. measure a few known masses to check that a mass balance is **calibrated** properly to make systematic errors less likely.

Random Errors

1) **Random errors** vary — they're what make the results a bit different each time you repeat an experiment. For example, if you measured the length of a wire 20 times, the chances are you'd get a slightly different value each time, e.g. due to your head being in a slightly different position when reading the scale. It could be that you just can't keep controlled variables (p.6) exactly the same throughout the experiment.

2) Unlike systematic errors, you can at least generally tell when random errors are there, as they affect your precision.

3) Using apparatus with a **better resolution** (p.10) can reduce the size of random errors in **individual measurements**.

4) Doing more **repeats** can also reduce the effect of random errors on **calculated results** like the mean (p.8).

Evaluating and Concluding

Draw **Conclusions** that Your Results **Support**

1) A conclusion **explains** what the data shows.
   You can only draw a valid conclusion if you have valid data **supporting** it.

2) Your conclusion should be limited to the **circumstances you've tested** it under —
   if you've been investigating how the current flowing through a resistor changes with the
   potential difference across it, and have only used potential differences between 0 and 6 V, you can't claim to
   know what would happen if you used a potential difference of 100 V, or if you used a different resistor.

3) You also need to think about how much you can **believe** your conclusion, by evaluating the quality of
   your results (see previous page). If you can't believe your results, you can't form a **strong conclusion**.

> Your conclusion can't
> be more precise than
> the margin given by the
> uncertainty in your results.

Think About how the Experiment Could be **Improved**

Having collected the data, is there anything you think should have been done **differently**?
Were there any **limitations** to your method?

1) If the results aren't **valid**, could you change the experiment to fix this, e.g. by changing the data you're collecting?

2) If the results aren't **accurate**, what could have caused this?
   If there are **systematic errors** in your results, what could you do to prevent them?

3) Are there any changes you could make to the **apparatus** or **procedure** that would make the results more **precise**?

   - There are some simple ways to reduce **random errors** or their effects (see p.12), including
     using the most **appropriate** equipment, (e.g. swapping a millimetre ruler for a micrometer to
     measure the diameter of a wire) and **increasing** the number of **repeats**.

   - You can also use a **computer** to collect data — e.g. using light gates to measure a time
     interval rather than a **stopwatch**. This makes results more **precise** by reducing **human error**.

4) Are there any other ways you could have **reduced the errors** in the measurements?

Practice Questions

Q1 What is a valid result?

Q2 What is the difference between a repeatable result and a reproducible result?

Q3 What is the difference between saying the results of an experiment are precise and saying that they are accurate?

Q4 Give two examples of possible sources of random error and one example of a possible source of systematic
error in an experiment. Which kind of error won't affect the precision of the results?

Q5 What should you think about when you are trying to improve an experimental design?

Exam Question

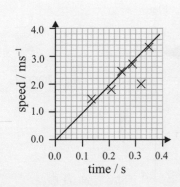

Q1 A student is investigating how the speed of a falling object is affected by
how long it has been falling for. He drops an object from heights between
10 cm and 60 cm and measures its speed at the end of its fall, and the time
the fall takes, using light gates. He plots a graph of the final speed of the
object against the time it took to fall, as shown on the left.

a) Identify the anomalous result. [1 mark]

b) The student concludes that the speed of any falling object is
always proportional to the time it has been falling for.
Explain whether or not the results support this conclusion. [2 marks]

In conclusion, Physics causes headaches...

Valid, precise, repeatable, reproducible and accurate... you'd think they all mean the same thing, but they really don't.
Make sure you know the difference, and are careful about which one you use, or you'll be throwing marks away.

Scalars and Vectors

And now time to draw some lovely triangles. Please, don't all thank me at once...

Scalars Only Have Size, but Vectors Have Size and Direction

1) A **scalar** has **no direction** — it's **just an amount** of something, like the **mass** of a **sack of meaty dog food**.

2) A **vector** has magnitude (**size**) and **direction** — like the **speed and direction** of next door's **cat** running away.

3) **Force, velocity and momentum** are all **vectors** — you need to know **which way** they're going as well as **how big** they are. Here are some of the common scalars and vectors that you'll come across in your exams:

Scalars	Vectors
mass, time, energy temperature, length, speed	displacement, force, velocity, acceleration, momentum

4) Vectors are drawn as **arrows** (to show their direction) with their **size** written next to them (see Example 1 below). In the exam, you might see quantities written with **arrows** above them, e.g. $\vec{v}$, to show that they're vectors.

*Sometimes vectors are printed in bold, e.g. **v**, but it's quite hard to handwrite in bold, so the arrow is used too.*

You can Add Vectors to Find the Resultant

1) Adding two or more vectors is called finding the **resultant** of them.

2) You should always start by drawing a **diagram**. Draw the vectors '**tip to tail**'. If you're doing a **vector subtraction**, draw the vector you're subtracting with the same magnitude but pointing in the **opposite direction**.

3) If the vectors are at **right angles** to each other, then you can use **Pythagoras** and **trigonometry** to find the resultant.

4) If the vectors aren't at right angles, you may need to draw a **scale diagram**.

Example 1: Jemima goes for a walk. She walks 3.0 m north and 4.0 m east. She has walked 7.0 m but she isn't 7.0 m from her starting point. Find the magnitude and direction of her displacement.

First, draw the vectors **tip-to-tail**. Then draw a line from the **tail** of the first vector to the **tip** of the last vector to give the **resultant**:

Because the vectors are at right angles, you get the **magnitude** of the resultant using Pythagoras:

$R^2 = 3.0^2 + 4.0^2 = 25.0$ So $R = \textbf{5.0 m}$

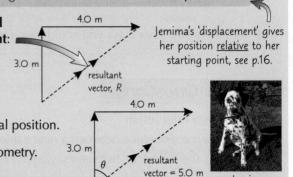

Jemima's 'displacement' gives her position relative to her starting point, see p.16.

Now find the **bearing** of Jemima's new position from her original position.

You use the triangle again, but this time you need to use trigonometry. You know the opposite and the adjacent sides, so you can use:

$\tan \theta = 4.0 / 3.0$ So $\theta = \textbf{053° (to 2 s.f.)}$

Jemima

Example 2: A van is accelerating north, with a resultant force of 510 N. A wind begins to blow on a bearing of 150°. It exerts a force of 200 N (to 2 s.f.) on the van. What is the new resultant force acting on the van?

A bearing is just an angle measured clockwise from the north line, represented by three digits, e.g. 10° = 010°.

The vectors **aren't** at right angles, so you need to do a scale drawing. Pick a sensible scale. Here, 1 cm = 100 N seems good.

Using a really sharp pencil, draw the initial resultant force on the van. As the van is going north, this should be a 5.1 cm long line going straight up.

The force of the wind acts on a bearing of 150°, so add this to your diagram. Using the same scale, this vector has a length of 2.0 cm.

Then you can draw on the new resultant force and measure its length. Measure the angle carefully to get the bearing.

The resultant force has a magnitude of 350 N (to 2 s.f.), acting on a bearing of 017° (to 2 s.f.).

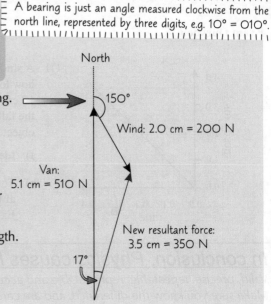

North

150°

Wind: 2.0 cm = 200 N

Van: 5.1 cm = 510 N

New resultant force: 3.5 cm = 350 N

17°

Scalars and Vectors

It's Useful to Split a Vector into Horizontal and Vertical Components

This is the opposite of finding the resultant — it's called **resolving**. You start from the resultant vector and split it into two **components** at right angles to each other. You're basically **working backwards** from Example 1 on the last page.

Resolving a vector *v* into horizontal and vertical components:

You get the **horizontal** component v_h like this:

$$\cos \theta = v_h / v$$

$$\boxed{v_h = v \cos \theta}$$

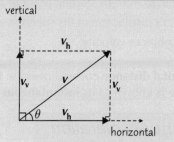

...and the **vertical** component v_v like this:

$$\sin \theta = v_v / v$$

$$\boxed{v_v = v \sin \theta}$$

Where θ is the angle from the horizontal.

Example: Charley's amazing floating home is travelling at a speed of 5.0 ms⁻¹ at an angle of 60° (to 2 s.f.) up from the horizontal. Find the vertical and horizontal components.

The **horizontal** component v_h is:

$v_h = v \cos \theta = 5.0 \cos 60° = \textbf{2.5 ms}^{-1}$

The **vertical** component v_v is:

$v_v = v \sin \theta = 5.0 \sin 60° = \textbf{4.3 ms}^{-1}$ **(to 2 s.f.)**

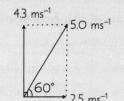

Charley's mobile home was the envy of all his friends.

You can also resolve vectors using **scale drawings**. It's easiest to do this on **squared paper**. Just draw the vector to **scale** in the **correct direction**, then draw a **horizontal** line and **vertical** line from the tip and tail of the vector to form a **right-angled triangle**. Then measure the **lengths** of the lines and use the **scale** to convert them — this gives you the **horizontal** and **vertical** components of the vector.

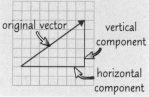

Resolving is dead useful because the two components of a vector **don't affect each other**. This means you can deal with the two directions **completely separately** (there's more on this on page 20).

Practice Questions

Q1 What is the difference between a vector and a scalar? Give three vector quantities and three scalar quantities.

Q2 Describe how to draw a vector, and how to use vector notation.

Q3 Describe how to use a scale diagram to: a) find a resultant vector
b) resolve a vector into components at right angles to each other.

Exam Questions

Q1 The wind applies a horizontal force of 20.0 N on a falling rock of weight 75 N.
Calculate the magnitude and direction of the resultant force. [2 marks]

Q2 A glider is travelling at a velocity of 20.0 ms⁻¹ at an angle of 15.0° below the horizontal.
Calculate the horizontal and vertical components of the glider's velocity. [2 marks]

Q3 A remote controlled boat is placed in a river. The boat produces a driving speed of 1.54 ms⁻¹ at an angle of 60.0° to the current (travelling with the current). The river is flowing at 0.20 ms⁻¹. By resolving the vectors into their horizontal and vertical components, show that the resultant velocity of the boat is 1.6 ms⁻¹ at an angle of 54° to the current. [4 marks]

I think I'm a scalar quantity, my Mum says I'm completely direction-less...

Lots of different ways to solve vector problems on these pages, it must be your lucky day. Trigonometry comes up all over the shop in physics, so make sure you're completely okay with it. Remember: Sin θ = Opposite ÷ Hypotenuse, Cos θ = Adjacent ÷ Hypotenuse, and Tan θ = Opposite ÷ Adjacent. Or SOH CAH TOA.

Motion with Uniform Acceleration

All the equations on this page are for motion with constant acceleration. It makes life a whole lot easier, trust me.

Learn the **Definitions** of **Speed**, **Displacement**, **Velocity** and **Acceleration**

Displacement, velocity and acceleration are all **vector** quantities (page 14), so the **direction** matters.

> **Speed** — How fast something is moving, regardless of direction.
> **Displacement (s)** — How far an object's travelled from its starting point in a given direction.
> **Velocity (v)** — The rate of change of an object's displacement (its speed in a given direction).
> **Acceleration (a)** — The rate of change of an object's velocity.

During a journey, the **average speed** is just the **total distance** covered over the **total time** elapsed.
The speed of an object at any given point in time is known as its **instantaneous** speed.

Uniform Acceleration is Constant Acceleration

> *Acceleration could mean a change in speed or direction or both.*

Uniform means constant here. It's nothing to do with what you wear.
There are **four main equations** that you use to solve problems involving **uniform acceleration**. You need to be able to **use them**, but you don't have to know how they're **derived** — we've just put it in to help you learn them.

1) **Acceleration is the rate of change of velocity.**
   From this definition you get:

   $$a = \frac{(v - u)}{t} \quad \text{so} \quad \boxed{v = u + at}$$

   where:
   u = initial velocity a = acceleration
   v = final velocity t = time taken

2) **s = average velocity × time**
   If acceleration is constant, the average velocity is just the average of the initial and final velocities, so:

   $$\boxed{s = \frac{(u + v)t}{2}} \quad s = \text{displacement}$$

3) Substitute the expression for v from equation 1 into equation 2 to give:

   $$s = \frac{(u + u + at) \times t}{2}$$
   $$= \frac{2ut + at^2}{2}$$

   $$\boxed{s = ut + \tfrac{1}{2}at^2}$$

4) You can **derive** the fourth equation from equations **1** and **2**:

   Use equation **1** in the form: $a = \frac{v - u}{t}$ Multiply both sides by s, where: $s = \frac{(u + v)}{2} \times t$

   This gives us: $as = \frac{(v - u)}{t} \times \frac{(u + v)t}{2}$

   The t's on the right cancel, so: $2as = (v - u)(v + u)$
   $2as = v^2 - uv + uv - u^2$

   so: $\boxed{v^2 = u^2 + 2as}$

Example: A tile falls from a roof 25.0 m high. Calculate its speed when it hits the ground and how long it takes to fall. Take $g = 9.81$ ms^{-2}.

First of all, write out what you know:
$s = 25.0$ m
$u = 0$ ms^{-1} since the tile's stationary to start with
$a = 9.81$ ms^{-2} due to gravity
$v = ?$ $t = ?$

> Usually you take upwards as the positive direction. In this question it's probably easier to take downwards as positive, so you get $g = +9.81$ ms^{-2} instead of $g = -9.81$ ms^{-2}.

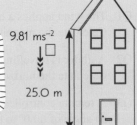
9.81 ms^{-2}

25.0 m

Then, choose an equation with only **one unknown quantity**.
So start with $v^2 = u^2 + 2as$
$v^2 = 0 + 2 \times 9.81 \times 25.0$
$v^2 = 490.5$ $v = $ **22.1 ms^{-1} (to 3 s.f.)**

Now, find t using:
$s = ut + \tfrac{1}{2}at^2$
$25.0 = 0 + \tfrac{1}{2} \times 9.81 \times t^2$
$t^2 = \frac{25.0}{4.905}$

Final answers:
$t = $ **2.26 s (to 3 s.f.)**
$v = $ **22.1 ms^{-1} (to 3 s.f.)**

Motion with Uniform Acceleration

Example: A car accelerates steadily from rest at a rate of 4.2 ms^{-2} for 6.5 seconds.
  a) Calculate the final speed.
  b) Calculate the distance travelled in 6.5 seconds.

4.2 ms^{-2}

Remember — always start by writing down what you know.

a) $a = 4.2$ ms^{-2} choose the right equation... $v = u + at$
   $u = 0$ ms^{-1} $v = 0 + 4.2 \times 6.5$
   $t = 6.5$ s   **Final answer:** $v = 27.3$ ms^{-1}
   $v = ?$ $= 27$ ms^{-1} **(to 2 s.f.)**

b) $s = ?$ **you can use:** $s = \dfrac{(u+v)t}{2}$ **or:** $s = ut + \frac{1}{2}at^2$
   $t = 6.5$ s
   $u = 0$ ms^{-1}
   $a = 4.2$ ms^{-2} $s = \dfrac{(0 + 27.3) \times 6.5}{2}$ $s = 0 + \frac{1}{2} \times 4.2 \times (6.5)^2$
   $v = 27.3$ ms^{-1}

   Final answer: $s = 89$ m **(to 2 s.f.)** $s = 89$ m **(to 2 s.f.)**

Practice Questions

Q1 Write down definitions for speed, displacement, average velocity, instantaneous velocity and acceleration.
Q2 Write out the four constant acceleration equations.

Mona's experiments into uniform acceleration had gone a bit far.

Exam Questions

Q1 A skydiver jumps from an aeroplane when it is flying horizontally. She accelerates due to gravity for 5.0 s.

  a) Calculate her maximum vertical velocity. (Assume no air resistance.) [2 marks]

  b) Calculate how far she falls in this time. [2 marks]

Q2 A motorcyclist slows down uniformly as he approaches a red light.
He takes 3.2 seconds to come to a halt and travels 40 m (to 2 s.f.) in this time.

  a) Calculate how fast he was travelling initially. [2 marks]

  b) Calculate his acceleration. (N.B. a negative value shows a deceleration.) [2 marks]

Q3 A stream provides a constant acceleration of 6 ms^{-2}. A toy boat is pushed directly against the current and then released from a point 1.2 m upstream from a small waterfall. Just before it reaches the waterfall, it is travelling at a speed of 5 ms^{-1}.

  a) Calculate the initial velocity of the boat. [2 marks]

  b) Calculate the maximum distance upstream from the waterfall the boat reaches. [2 marks]

Constant acceleration — it'll end in tears...

If a question talks about "uniform" or "constant" acceleration, it's a dead giveaway they want you to use one of these equations. The tricky bit is working out which one to use — start every question by writing out what you know and what you need to know. That makes it much easier to see which equation you need. To be sure. Arrr.

TOPIC 2 — MECHANICS

Free Fall

Free fall is all about objects falling — no really, that's all that the next two pages are about. Have fun.

Free Fall is when there's Only Gravity and Nothing Else

1) All objects on Earth experience a **force** due to the Earth's **gravitational field** that depends on their **mass**.

2) The **gravitational field strength** near the surface of the Earth is called **g** and is equal to **9.81 Nkg⁻¹**. **g** is given by the equation:

$$g = \frac{F}{m}$$

Where m is the mass of the object and F is the force due to gravity.

3) The force on an object due to gravity is called its **weight** (see page 38).

4) When the only force acting on an object is its weight, it will undergo **free fall**, and will **accelerate towards the ground**.

Force and acceleration are both vector quantities (p.14). In free fall, they act vertically downwards.

5) Acceleration and force are related by **F = ma**.
So, for an object in free fall, $a = \frac{F}{m} = g$.

Objects undergoing free fall on Earth have an acceleration of **g = 9.81 ms⁻²**.

6) Objects can have an initial velocity in any direction and still undergo **free fall** as long as the **force** providing the initial velocity is **no longer acting**.

It seems weird that g is both a gravitational field strength, in Nkg⁻¹, and an acceleration, in ms⁻² However, if you break down Nkg⁻¹ into SI units, they are actually the same as ms⁻².

You can Replace a with g in the Equations of Motion

You need to be able to work out **speeds**, **distances** and **times** for objects in **free fall**. Since g is a **constant acceleration** you can use the **constant acceleration equations**.
g acts **downwards**, so you need to be careful about directions. To make it clear, there's a sign convention: **upwards is positive, downwards is negative**.

$$v = u + gt \qquad s = ut + \tfrac{1}{2}gt^2$$
$$v^2 = u^2 + 2\,gs \qquad s = \frac{(u + v)\,t}{2}$$

g is always **downwards** so it's **usually negative**   **t** is **always positive**
u and **v** can be **positive or negative**   **s** can be **positive or negative**

If an object is dropped, not thrown, u is zero.

You Can Calculate g By Performing an Experiment...

See pages 6-13 for more on doing experiments.

This is just one way of **measuring** g, there are loads of different experiments you could do — just make sure you know **one** method for your exams.

1) Set up the equipment shown in the diagram on the right.

2) Measure the height **h** from the **bottom** of the ball bearing to the **trapdoor**.

3) Flick the switch to simultaneously **start the timer** and **disconnect the electromagnet**, releasing the ball bearing.

4) The ball bearing falls, knocking the trapdoor down and **breaking the circuit** — which **stops the timer**. Record the time **t** shown on the timer.

5) **Repeat** this experiment three times and **average** the time taken to fall from this height. Repeat this experiment but drop the ball from several **different heights**.

6) You can then use these results to find g using a **graph** (see the next page).

- Using a **small** and **heavy** ball bearing means you can assume air resistance is so small you can **ignore it**.

- Having a computer **automatically release** and **time** the ball-bearing's fall can measure times with a **smaller uncertainty** than if you tried to drop the ball and time the fall using a stopwatch.

- The most significant source of **error** in this experiment will be in the measurement of **h**. Using a ruler, you'll have an uncertainty of about ±1 mm. This dwarfs any error from switch delay or air resistance. By making the values of **h** as **large** as possible, you can reduce the **percentage uncertainty** in your measurement of the height, (see p.10) as well as the percentage uncertainty caused by the **resolution** of the **timer** (as the bigger h is, the longer the ball-bearing will take to fall).

Free Fall

...and Plotting a *Graph* of Your *Results*

1) Use your data from the experiment on the last page to plot a graph of **height** (s) against the **time** it takes the ball to fall, **squared** (t^2). Then draw a **line of best fit**.

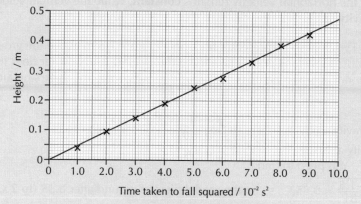

> You could plot error bars on your data graph to find the error in your final value for g. See page 11 for more on error bars.

> In the exam you might be asked to find g from a displacement-time graph (see p.22-23). g is an acceleration and the gradient of the graph will be velocity, so you can find g by finding the change in gradient between two points on the graph (as $a = \Delta v \div \Delta t$).

2) You know that with constant acceleration, $s = ut + \frac{1}{2}at^2$. If you drop the ball, initial speed $u = 0$, so $s = \frac{1}{2}at^2$.

3) Rearranging this gives $\frac{1}{2}a = \frac{s}{t^2}$, or $\frac{1}{2}g = \frac{s}{t^2}$ (remember the acceleration is all due to gravity).

4) So the gradient of the line of best fit, $\frac{\Delta s}{\Delta t^2}$, is equal to $\frac{1}{2}g$:

$$g = 2 \times \frac{\Delta s}{\Delta t^2} = 2 \times \frac{0.43}{0.090} = 9.555...$$
$$= 9.6 \text{ ms}^{-2} \text{ (to 2 s.f.)}$$

5) As you know g (9.8 ms^{-2} to 2 s.f.) you can calculate the **percentage difference** (see p.12) between your value of g and the true value, and use this to evaluate the **accuracy** of your results.

$$\% \text{ difference} = \frac{9.6 - 9.8}{9.8} \times 100\% = -2.040...$$
$$= -2.0\% \text{ (to 2 s.f.)}$$

Practice Questions

Q1 State the equation linking gravitational field strength, force due to gravity, and mass.

Q2 What is the value of the acceleration of a free-falling object on Earth?

Q3 Describe how you would find a value for g by using a trapdoor and electromagnet set-up.

Exam Questions

Q1 A student has designed a device to estimate the value of 'g'. It consists of two narrow strips of card joined by a piece of transparent plastic. The student measures the widths of the strips of card then drops the device through a light gate connected to a computer. As the device falls, the strips of card break the light beam.

a) Give three pieces of data that the student will need from the computer to estimate g. [3 marks]

b) Explain how these measurements can be used to estimate 'g'. [3 marks]

c) Give one reason why the student's value of 'g' will not be entirely accurate. [1 mark]

Q2 Jan bounces on a trampoline, reaching a point 5.0 m above the trampoline's surface. Assume there is no air resistance.

a) Calculate the speed with which she leaves the trampoline surface. [2 marks]

b) Calculate how long it takes Jan to reach her highest point. [2 marks]

c) State her velocity as she lands back on the trampoline. [1 mark]

It's not the falling that hurts — *it's the* being pelted with rotten vegetables... okay, okay...

The hardest bit with free fall questions is getting your signs right. Draw yourself a little diagram before you start doing any calculations, and label it with what you know and what you want to know.

Projectile Motion

Any object given an initial velocity then left to move freely under gravity is a projectile. Time to resolve some vectors...

You have to think of **Horizontal** and **Vertical** Motion **Separately**

In projectiles, the **horizontal** and **vertical** components of the object's motion are **completely independent**. Projectiles follow a **curved path** because the horizontal velocity remains **constant**, while the vertical velocity is affected by the **acceleration due to gravity**, g.

Example: Jane fires a scale model of a TV talent show presenter horizontally from 1.5 m above the ground with a velocity of 100 ms^{-1} (to 2 s.f.). How long does it take to hit the ground, and how far does it travel horizontally? Assume the model acts as a particle, the ground is horizontal and there's no air resistance.

Think about vertical motion first:

1) It's **constant acceleration** under gravity...

2) You know $u = 0$ (no vertical velocity at first), $s = -1.5$ m and $a = g = -9.81$ ms^{-2}. You need to find t.

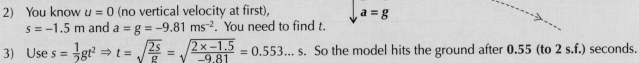
$a = 0$
$u = 0$
$a = g$

3) Use $s = \frac{1}{2}gt^2 \Rightarrow t = \sqrt{\frac{2s}{g}} = \sqrt{\frac{2 \times -1.5}{-9.81}} = 0.553...$ s. So the model hits the ground after **0.55 (to 2 s.f.)** seconds.

Then do the horizontal motion:

1) The horizontal motion isn't affected by gravity or any other force, so it moves at a **constant speed**. That means you can just use good old **speed = distance / time**.

2) Now $v_h = 100$ ms^{-1}, $t = 0.553...$ s and $a = 0$. You need to find s_h.

3) $s_h = v_h t = 100 \times 0.553... = $ **55 m (to 2 s.f.)**

Where v_h is the horizontal velocity, and s_h is the horizontal distance travelled (rather than the height fallen).

It's **Slightly Trickier** if it **Starts Off** at an **Angle**

If something's projected at an **angle** (e.g. a javelin) you'll start with **horizontal** and **vertical velocity**. Here's what to do:

1) **Resolve** the initial velocity into **horizontal** and **vertical** components:

2) Often you'll use the vertical component to work out **how long** it's in the air and/or **how high** it goes, and the horizontal component to work out **how far** it goes while it's in the air.

If an object has velocity v, at an angle of θ to the horizontal:

The horizontal component of its velocity is: $\boxed{v_h = v \cos\theta}$

The vertical component of its velocity is: $\boxed{v_v = v \sin\theta}$

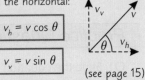

(see page 15)

Example: An athlete throws a javelin from a height of 1.8 m with a velocity of 21 ms^{-1} at an upward angle of 45° to the ground. How far is the javelin thrown? Assume the javelin acts as a particle, the ground is horizontal and there is no air resistance.

1) Draw a quick sketch of the information given in the question.

2) Start by resolving the velocity into horizontal and vertical components:
$u_h = \cos 45° \times 21 = 14.84...$ ms^{-1}
$u_v = \sin 45° \times 21 = 14.84...$ ms^{-1}

3) Then find how long it's in the air for — start by finding v_v. The javelin starts from a height of 1.8 m and finishes at ground level, so its final vertical distance $s_v = -1.8$ m:

$v_v^2 = u_v^2 + 2gs$
$v_v = \sqrt{14.84...^2 + 2 \times (-9.81) \times (-1.8)} = -15.99...$ ms^{-1}

You need the negative square root, as this is a velocity towards the ground.

Now you can use this v_v value and $s = \frac{(u+v)t}{2}$ to find the time it stays in the air:

$s_v = \frac{(u_v + v_v)t}{2} \Rightarrow t = \frac{s_v}{(u_v + v_v)} \times 2 = \frac{-1.8}{14.84... - 15.99...} \times 2 = 3.144...$ s

4) Finally, as $a_h = 0$, you can use **speed = distance / time** to work out how far it travels horizontally in this time. The horizontal velocity is just u_h, so: $s_h = u_h t = 14.84... \times 3.144... = 46.68... = $ **47 m (to 2 s.f.)**

Projectile Motion

You can Investigate Projectile Motion Using a *Video Camera*...

If you **video** a projectile moving, you can use **video analysis software** to investigate its motion:

1) You can **plot the course** taken by an object by recording its **position** in **each frame**.

2) If you know the **frame rate**, and your video includes a metre ruler or grid lines that you can use as a scale, you can calculate the **velocity** of the projectile between **different points** in its motion, by looking at how far it travels **between frames**.

A video camera records a series of pictures, or frames (typically around 25 frames per second). Video analysis software lets you view videos frame by frame.

... or *Strobe Photography*

In strobe photography, a camera is set to take a **long exposure**. While the camera is taking the photo, a **strobe light** flashes repeatedly and the projectile is released. The strobe light **lights up** the projectile at regular intervals. This means that the projectile appears **multiple times** in the same photograph, in a **different position** each time.

Again, if you've got a **reference object** in the photo (for example, you might throw an object in front of a **screen** with a **grid** drawn on it), you can calculate **how far** the object travels **between flashes** of the strobe, and use the **time** between flashes to calculate the **velocity** of the projectile between the flashes.

The motion of a typical projectile captured with strobe photography is shown below.

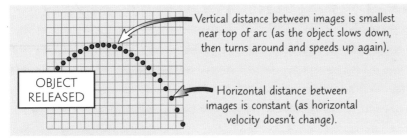

Vertical distance between images is smallest near top of arc (as the object slows down, then turns around and speeds up again).

Horizontal distance between images is constant (as horizontal velocity doesn't change).

Strobe photography and video cameras give you more information than using light-gates to study an object's projectile motion. They can be used whatever the size of the object, unlike a light-gate.

Practice Questions

Q1 What is the initial vertical velocity for an object projected horizontally with a velocity of 5 ms^{-1}?

Q2 How does the horizontal velocity of a projectile change with time?

Q3 What is the horizontal component of the velocity of a stone, hurled at 30 ms^{-1} at 35° to the horizontal?

Q4 Explain how you might use video analysis software to analyse the motion of a projectile.

Exam Questions

Q1 Jason stands on a vertical cliff edge throwing stones into the sea below.
He throws a stone horizontally with a velocity of 20 ms^{-1} (to 2 s.f.), 560 m above sea level.

a) Calculate how long it takes for the stone to hit the water from leaving Jason's hand.
Use $g = 9.81$ ms^{-2} and ignore air resistance.

[2 marks]

b) Calculate the distance of the stone from the base of the cliff when it hits the water.

[2 marks]

Q2 Robin fires an arrow into the air with a vertical velocity of 30.0 ms^{-1}, and a horizontal velocity of 20.0 ms^{-1}, from 1.0 m above horizontal ground. Choose the correct option which shows the maximum height from the ground (to 2 significant figures) reached by his arrow. Use $g = 9.81$ ms^{-2} and ignore air resistance.

A	45 m	C	47 m
B	46 m	D	48 m

[1 mark]

All this physics makes me want to create projectile motions...

...by throwing my revision books out of the window. The maths on these two pages can be tricky, but take it step by step and all will be fine. On the plus side, the next page is full of lovely graphs. Who doesn't love a good graph?

Displacement-Time Graphs

Drawing graphs by hand — oh joy. You'd think examiners had never heard of the graphical calculator.
Ah well, until they manage to drag themselves out of the Dark Ages, you'll just have to grit your teeth and get on with it.

Acceleration Means a Curved Displacement-Time Graph

A graph of displacement against time for an **accelerating object** always produces a **curve**.
If the object is accelerating at a **uniform rate**, then the **rate of change** of the **gradient** will be constant.

Example: Plot a displacement-time graph for a lion who accelerates constantly from rest at 2 ms^{-2} for 5 seconds.

You want to find *s*, and you know that:
$a = 2$ ms^{-2}
$u = 0$ ms^{-1}

Use $s = ut + \frac{1}{2}at^2$

If you substitute in *u* and *a*, this simplifies to:
$s = 0 \times t + \frac{1}{2} \times 2t^2$
$s = t^2$

Do a **table of values**:

t / s	s / m
0	0
1	1
2	4
3	9
4	16
5	25

...then plot the **graph**:

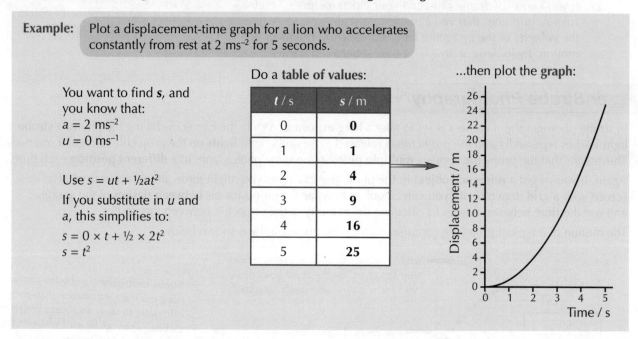

Different Accelerations Have Different Gradients

In the example above, if the lion has a **different acceleration** it'll change the **gradient** of the curve like this:

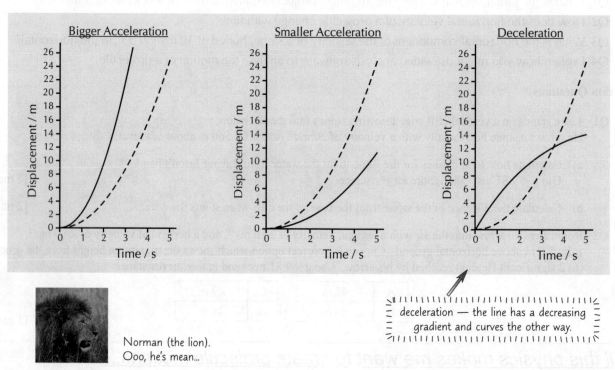

Bigger Acceleration · Smaller Acceleration · Deceleration

deceleration — the line has a decreasing gradient and curves the other way.

Norman (the lion).
Ooo, he's mean...

Displacement-Time Graphs

The *Gradient* of a *Displacement-Time Graph* Tells You the Velocity

When the velocity is constant, the graph's a **straight line**.
Velocity is defined as...

$$\text{velocity} = \frac{\text{change in displacement}}{\text{change in time}}$$

On the graph, this is $\frac{\text{change in } y \, (\Delta y)}{\text{change in } x \, (\Delta x)}$, i.e. the gradient.

So to get the velocity from a displacement-time graph, just find the gradient.

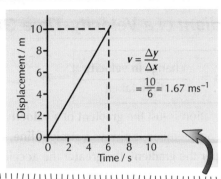

$$v = \frac{\Delta y}{\Delta x}$$
$$= \frac{10}{6} = 1.67 \text{ ms}^{-1}$$

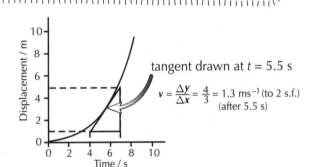

Acceleration is $\frac{\text{change in velocity } (\Delta v)}{\text{change in time } (\Delta t)}$, so it is the rate of change of this gradient. If the gradient is constant (straight line) then there is no acceleration, and if it's changing (curved line) then there's acceleration or deceleration.

It's the Same with *Curved Graphs*

If the gradient **isn't constant** (i.e. if it's a curved line), it means the object is **accelerating**.

> To find the **instantaneous velocity** at a certain point you need to draw a **tangent** to the curve at that point and find its gradient.

To find the **average velocity** over a period of time, just divide the final (change in) displacement by the final (change in) time — it doesn't matter if the graph is curved or not.

tangent drawn at $t = 5.5$ s

$$v = \frac{\Delta y}{\Delta x} = \frac{4}{3} = 1.3 \text{ ms}^{-1} \text{ (to 2 s.f.)}$$
(after 5.5 s)

Practice Questions

Q1 What is given by the slope of a displacement-time graph?
Q2 Sketch a displacement-time graph to show: a) constant velocity,   b) acceleration,   c) deceleration

Exam Questions

Q1 Describe the motion of the cyclist as shown by the graph below.   [4 marks]

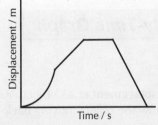

Q2 A baby crawls 5 m in 8 seconds at a constant velocity. She then rests for 5 seconds before crawling a further 3 m in 5 seconds at a constant velocity. Finally, she makes her way back to her starting point in 10 seconds, travelling at a constant speed all the way.

a) Draw a displacement-time graph to show the baby's journey.   [4 marks]

b) Calculate her velocity at all the different stages of her journey.   [2 marks]

Be ahead of the curve, get to grips with this stuff now...

Whether it's a straight line or a curve, the steeper it is, the greater the velocity. There's nothing difficult about these graphs — the problem is that it's easy to confuse them with velocity-time graphs (next page). If in doubt, think about the gradient — is it velocity or acceleration, is it changing (curve), is it constant (straight line), is it 0 (horizontal line)...

Velocity-Time and Acceleration-Time Graphs

Speed-time graphs and velocity-time graphs are pretty similar. The big difference is that velocity-time graphs can have a negative part to show something travelling in the opposite direction:

The **Gradient** of a **Velocity-Time Graph** tells you the **Acceleration**

$$\text{acceleration} = \frac{\text{change in velocity}}{\text{time taken}}$$

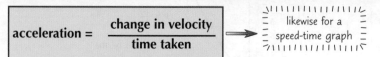
likewise for a speed-time graph

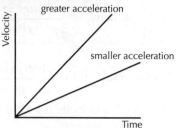

So the acceleration is just the **gradient** of a **velocity-time graph**.

1) **Uniform** acceleration is always a **straight line**.

2) The **steeper** the **gradient**, the **greater** the **acceleration**.

When the **acceleration** is **constant**, you get a **straight-line** *v-t* graph. The equation for a straight line is *y = mx + c*. You can rearrange the acceleration equation into the same form, getting **v = u + at**. So on a linear *v-t* graph, **acceleration**, *a*, is the **gradient** (*m*) and the **initial speed**, *u*, is the **y-intercept** (*c*).

Example: A lion strolls along at 1.5 ms⁻¹ for 4 s and then accelerates uniformly at a rate of 2.5 ms⁻² for 4 s. Plot this information on a velocity-time graph.

So, for the first four seconds, the velocity is 1.5 ms⁻¹, then it increases by **2.5 ms⁻¹ every second**:

time / s	0-4	5	6	7	8
velocity / ms⁻¹	1.5	4.0	6.5	9.0	11.5

You can see that the **gradient of the line** is **constant** between 4 s and 8 s and has a value of 2.5 ms⁻², representing the **acceleration of the lion**.

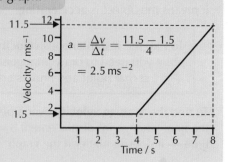

$$a = \frac{\Delta v}{\Delta t} = \frac{11.5 - 1.5}{4}$$
$$= 2.5 \text{ ms}^{-2}$$

Acceleration isn't Always **Uniform**

1) If the acceleration is changing, the gradient of the velocity-time graph will also be changing — so you **won't** get a **straight line**.

2) **Increasing acceleration** is shown by an **increasing gradient** — like in curve ①.

3) **Decreasing acceleration** is shown by a **decreasing gradient** — like in curve ②.

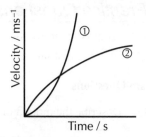

Displacement = **Area** under **Velocity-Time Graph**

You know that: | **displacement = velocity × time** |

Similarly, the area under a speed-time graph is the total distance travelled.

The **area** under a velocity-time graph tells you the **displacement** of an object. Areas under any **negative** parts of the graph count as negative areas, as they show the object moving **back** to its **start point**.

Example: A racing car on a straight track accelerates uniformly from rest to 40 ms⁻¹ in 10 s. It maintains this speed for a further 20 s before coming to rest by decelerating at a constant rate over the next 15 s. Draw a velocity-time graph for this journey and use it to calculate the total displacement of the racing car.

Split the **graph** up into **sections**: A, B and C. Calculate the **area** of each and **add** the three results together.

A: Area = ½ base × height = ½ × 10 × 40 = 200 m

B: Area = *b* × *h* = 20 × 40 = 800 m

C: Area = ½ *b* × *h* = ½ × 15 × 40 = 300 m

Total displacement = 1300 m

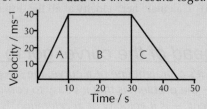

Velocity-Time and Acceleration-Time Graphs

Acceleration-Time (a-t) Graphs are Useful Too

An **acceleration-time graph** shows how an object's **acceleration** changes over time.

1) The **height** of the graph gives the object's **acceleration** at that time.
2) The **area** under the graph gives the object's **change in velocity**.
3) A negative acceleration is a **deceleration**.
4) If $a = 0$, then the object is moving with **constant velocity**.

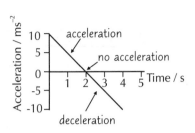

You Have to Estimate the Area Under a Curved Graph

If an object's acceleration **isn't constant**, you won't get a straight line a-t graph. You need to know how to **estimate** the area under a curved graph. If the graph is on **squared paper**, you can work out the value represented by the **area** of **one** square and multiply by the approximate **number of squares** under the curve. Another way is to split the area approximately into simple shapes, calculate the value of the **area** of each of them, and then **add** them all up.

> **Example:** The acceleration of a car in a drag race is shown in this acceleration-time graph. Calculate its change in velocity.
>
> Change in velocity = area under graph
>
> Split the area under the curve up into trapeziums and a triangle.
>
> 0-1 s — estimate the area using a trapezium. Area = $\frac{1}{2}(a + b) \times h$
> a is the length of the first side, $a = 10$
> b is the length of the second side, $b = 9$
> h is the width of each strip, so $h = 1$. Area = $\frac{1}{2}(10 + 9) \times 1 = 9.5 \text{ ms}^{-1}$
>
> 1-2 s — this can also be estimated with another trapezium. $a = 9$, $b = 3.6$, $h = 1$.
>   So area = $\frac{1}{2}(9 + 3.6) \times 1 = 6.3 \text{ ms}^{-1}$
>
>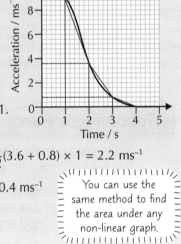
>
> 2-3 s — estimated with another trapezium. $a = 3.6$, $b = 0.8$, $h = 1$. So area = $\frac{1}{2}(3.6 + 0.8) \times 1 = 2.2 \text{ ms}^{-1}$
>
> 3-4 s — this estimation uses a triangle. Area = $\frac{1}{2}(\text{base} \times \text{height}) = \frac{1}{2}(0.8) \times 1 = 0.4 \text{ ms}^{-1}$
>
>   *You can use the same method to find the area under any non-linear graph.*
>
> Now add the areas together — Total area = $9.5 + 6.3 + 2.2 + 0.4 = 18.4 \text{ ms}^{-1}$
> The estimated change in velocity of the car is 18.4 ms^{-1} = **20 ms⁻¹ (to 1 s.f.)**

Practice Questions

Q1 How do you calculate acceleration from a velocity-time graph?
Q2 How do you calculate the displacement travelled from a velocity-time graph?
Q3 Sketch velocity-time graphs for constant velocity and constant acceleration.
Q4 Sketch velocity-time and acceleration-time graphs for a boy bouncing on a trampoline.
Q5 What does the area under an acceleration-time graph tell you?

Exam Question

Q1 A skier accelerates uniformly from rest at 2 ms^{-2} down a straight slope for 5 seconds. He then reaches the bottom of the slope and continues along the flat ground, decelerating at 1 ms^{-2} until he stops.

    a) Sketch the velocity-time and acceleration-time graphs for his journey.   [4 marks]

    b) Use your v-t graph from part a) to find the distance travelled by the skier during the first 5 seconds.   [2 marks]

Still awake — I'll give you five more minutes...

There's a really nice sunset outside my window. It's one of those ones that makes the whole landscape go pinky-yellowish. And that's about as much interest as I can muster on this topic. Normal service will be resumed on page 27.

Forces

Remember the vector stuff from the beginning of the section? Good, you're going to need it...

Free-Body Force Diagrams show All Forces on a Single Body

1) **Free-body force** diagrams show a **single body** on its own.
2) The diagram should include all the **forces** that **act on** the body, but **not the forces it exerts** on the rest of the world.
3) Remember **forces** are **vector quantities** and so the **arrow labels** should show the **size** and **direction** of the forces.
4) If a body is in **equilibrium** (i.e. not accelerating) the **forces** acting on it will be **balanced**.

Drawing free-body force diagrams isn't too hard — you just need to practise them. Here are a few **examples**:

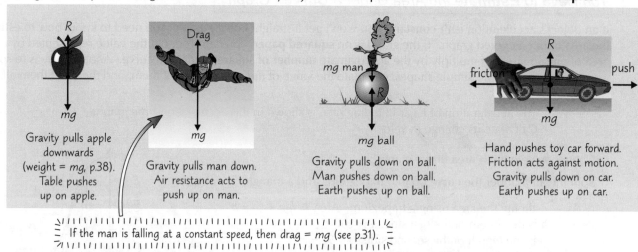

Gravity pulls apple downwards (weight = *mg*, p.38). Table pushes up on apple.

Gravity pulls man down. Air resistance acts to push up on man.

Gravity pulls down on ball. Man pushes down on ball. Earth pushes up on ball.

Hand pushes toy car forward. Friction acts against motion. Gravity pulls down on car. Earth pushes up on car.

If the man is falling at a constant speed, then drag = *mg* (see p.31).

Resolving a Force means Splitting it into Components

See p.15 for a reminder on resolving vectors.

1) Forces can be in **any direction**, so they're not always at right angles to each other. This is sometimes a bit **awkward** for **calculations**.

2) To make an 'awkward' force easier to deal with, you can think of it as two **separate, independent** forces, acting at **right angles** to each other.

The force *F* has exactly the same effect as the horizontal and vertical forces, F_H and F_V.

Replacing *F* with F_H and F_V is called **resolving the force F**.

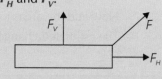

3) These two forces have **no effect** on each other as they are **perpendicular**. E.g. a horizontal force will have no vertical effect, and vice-versa.

4) To find the **size** of a **component** force in a particular **direction**, you need to use trigonometry. Forces are vectors, so you treat them in the same way as velocity or displacement — put them end to end.

So this... 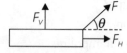 ...could be drawn like this:

Using trigonometry you get:

$$\frac{F_H}{F} = \cos\theta \quad \text{or} \quad F_H = F\cos\theta$$

And:

$$\frac{F_V}{F} = \sin\theta \quad \text{or} \quad F_V = F\sin\theta$$

Remember that $\cos 90° = 0$, so forces which act at an angle of **90°** to each other are **independent** (i.e. they have **no effect** on each other).

Example: A tree trunk is pulled along the ground by an elephant exerting a force of 1200 N at an angle of 25° to the horizontal. Calculate the components of this force in the horizontal and vertical directions.

Horizontal force:
$1200 \times \cos 25° = 1087.5...$
= **1100 N** (to 2 s.f.)

Vertical force:
$1200 \times \sin 25° = 507.1...$
= **510 N** (to 2 s.f.)

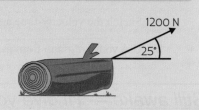

Forces

You Add the Components Back Together to get the Resultant Force

1) If **two forces** act on an object, you can find the **resultant** (total) **force** by adding the **vectors** together and creating a **closed triangle**, with the resultant force represented by the **third side**.

2) Forces are vectors (as you know), so use **vector addition** — draw the forces as vector arrows 'tip-to-tail'.

3) Then it's yet more trigonometry and Pythagoras to find the **angle** and the **length** of the third side.

Example: Two dung beetles roll a dung ball along the ground at a constant velocity. Beetle A applies a force of 0.50 N northwards while beetle B exerts a force of 0.20 N eastwards. What is the resultant force on the dung ball?

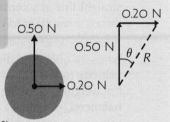

By Pythagoras, $R^2 = 0.50^2 + 0.20^2 = 0.29$
$R = \sqrt{0.29} = 0.538... = \textbf{0.54 N (to 2 s.f.)}$

$\tan\theta = \dfrac{0.20}{0.50}$ so $\theta = \tan^{-1}\left(\dfrac{0.20}{0.50}\right) = 21.8°... = \textbf{22° (to 2 s.f.)}$

So the resultant force is **0.54 N** at an angle of **22° to the vertical** (i.e. a bearing of 022°).

Choose Sensible Axes for Resolving

Use directions that **make sense** for the situation you're dealing with. If you've got an object on a slope, choose your directions **along the slope** and **at right angles to it**. You can turn the paper to an angle if that helps.

Always choose sensible axes.

```
Examiners like to call a
slope an "inclined plane".
```

Example:

The component of the bone's weight down the slope is 2.5 N so you'd need 2.5 N of friction (see p.30) to stop it sliding down.

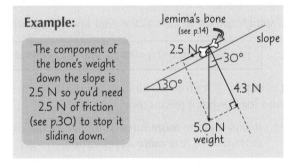

Jemima's bone (see p.14)

Practice Questions

Q1 Sketch a free-body force diagram for an ice hockey puck moving horizontally across a flat sheet of ice at a constant speed (assuming it is not being pushed and there is no friction).

Q2 What are the horizontal and vertical components of a force F if it is applied at an angle of θ to the horizontal?

Q3 Use trigonometry to explain why perpendicular components of a force are independent of each other.

Exam Questions

Q1 An 8 kg picture is suspended from a hook as shown in the diagram. Calculate the tension force, T, in the string.

[2 marks]

Q2 Two dogs pull a frisbee as shown in the diagram. Both values given are correct to 3 significant figures. Calculate the resultant force on the frisbee.

[2 marks]

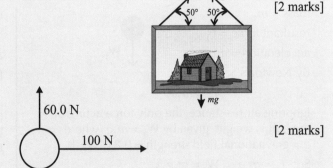

Free-body force diagram — sounds like a dance competition...

Remember those $F\cos\theta$ and $F\sin\theta$ bits. Write them on bits of paper and stick them to your wall. Scrawl them on your pillow. Tattoo them on your brain. Whatever it takes — you just have to learn them.

Newton's Laws of Motion

You did most of this at GCSE, but that doesn't mean you can just skip over it now. You'll be kicking yourself if you forget this stuff in the exam — it's easy marks...

Newton's **1st Law** Says That a **Force** is Needed to Change Velocity

1) **Newton's 1st law of motion** states that the **velocity** of an object will **not change** unless a **resultant force** acts on it.

2) In plain English this means a body will stay still ('at rest') or move in a **straight line** at a **constant speed**, unless there's a **resultant force** acting on it.

An apple sitting on a table won't go anywhere because the **forces** on it are **balanced**.

$$\text{reaction } (R) = \text{weight } (mg)$$
(force of table pushing apple up) = (force of gravity pulling apple down, see p.38)

3) An example of constant velocity is when an object reaches its **terminal velocity** (see p.30). This occurs when the **weight** of a **falling** object is exactly **balanced** by **drag** (e.g. air resistance). Since there is **no resultant force**, there is **no acceleration**, and the object falls at a **constant velocity**.

4) If the forces **aren't balanced**, the **overall resultant force** will make the body **accelerate**. This could be a change in **direction**, or **speed**, or both. (See Newton's 2nd law, below.)

Newton's **2nd Law** Says That **Acceleration** is **Proportional** to the Force

...which can be written as the well-known equation:

resultant force (N) = mass (kg) × acceleration (ms⁻²)

$$\Sigma F = ma$$

The resultant force is the vector sum of all the forces on an object. Σ is the symbol for 'sum of', but you'll often see resultant force as just F.

Learn this — it crops up all over the place in Physics. And learn what it means too:

1) It says that the **more force** you have acting on a certain mass, the **more acceleration** you get.

2) It says that for a given force, the **more mass** you have, the **less acceleration** you get.

REMEMBER:
1) The **resultant force** is the **vector sum** of all the forces.
2) The force is **always** measured in **newtons**.
3) The mass is always measured in **kilograms** and is a **constant**.
4) The **acceleration** is always in the **same direction** as the **resultant force** and is measured in **ms⁻²**.

3) If you have **no resultant force**, then $\Sigma F = 0$. You can see from $\Sigma F = ma$ that this happens when $a = 0$. And as if by magic (or physics), this **matches** what was said above in Newton's 1st law — **no resultant force** means **no acceleration**.

4) There's more on this most excellent law on p.33.

Galileo said: **All Objects Fall** at the **Same Rate** (if You **Ignore Air Resistance**)

You need to understand **why** this is true. Newton's 2nd law explains it neatly — consider two balls dropped at the same time — ball **1** being heavy, and ball **2** being light. Then use Newton's 2nd law to find their acceleration.

mass = m_1
resultant force = F_1
acceleration = a_1
$\downarrow W_1$
By Newton's Second Law:
$$F_1 = m_1 a_1$$
Ignoring air resistance, the only force acting on the ball is weight, given by $W_1 = m_1 g$ (where g = gravitational field strength = 9.81 Nkg⁻¹).
So: $F_1 = m_1 a_1 = W_1 = m_1 g$
So: $m_1 a_1 = m_1 g$, then m_1 cancels out to give: $a_1 = g$

mass = m_2
resultant force = F_2
acceleration = a_2
$\downarrow W_2$
By Newton's Second Law:
$$F_2 = m_2 a_2$$
Ignoring air resistance, the only force acting on the ball is weight, given by $W_2 = m_2 g$ (where g = gravitational field strength = 9.81 Nkg⁻¹).
So: $F_2 = m_2 a_2 = W_2 = m_2 g$
So: $m_2 a_2 = m_2 g$, then m_2 cancels out to give: $a_2 = g$

...in other words, the **acceleration** is **independent of the mass**. It makes **no difference** whether the ball is **heavy or light**. And I've kindly **hammered home the point** by showing you two almost identical examples.

Newton's Laws of Motion

Newton's **3rd Law** Says Each Force has an **Equal**, Opposite Reaction Force

There are a few different ways of stating Newton's 3rd law, but the clearest way is:

> **If an object A exerts a FORCE on object B, then object B exerts AN EQUAL BUT OPPOSITE FORCE on object A.**

You'll also hear the law as "every action has an equal and opposite reaction". But this confuses people who wrongly think the forces are both applied to the same object. (If that were the case, you'd get a resultant force of zero and nothing would ever move anywhere...)

The two forces actually represent the **same interaction**, just seen from two **different perspectives**:

1) If you **push against a wall**, the wall will **push back** against you, **just as hard**. As soon as you stop pushing, so does the wall. Amazing...

2) If you **pull a cart**, whatever force **you exert** on the rope, the rope exerts the **exact opposite** pull on you (unless the rope's stretching).

3) When you go **swimming**, you push **back** against the water with your arms and legs, and the water pushes you **forwards** with an equal-sized force.

This looks like Newton's 3rd law...

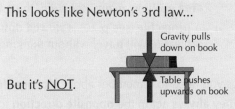

But it's <u>NOT</u>.

Gravity pulls down on book

Table pushes upwards on book

...because both forces are acting on the book, and they're not of the same type. They are two separate interactions. The forces are equal and opposite, resulting in zero acceleration, so this is showing Newton's 1st law.

Newton's 3rd law applies in **all situations** and to all **types of force**. But the pairs of forces are always the **same type**, e.g. both gravitational or both electrical, and they act along the same line.

Practice Questions

Q1 State Newton's 1st, 2nd and 3rd laws of motion, and explain what they mean.

Q2 Explain how you can demonstrate Newton's 1st law using Newton's 2nd law.

Q3 What are the two equal and opposite forces acting between an orbiting satellite and the Earth?

Exam Questions

Q1 A boat is moving across a river. The engines provide a force of 500 N at right angles to the flow of the river and the boat experiences a drag of 100 N in the opposite direction. The force on the boat due to the flow of the river is 300 N. The mass of the boat is 250 kg.

    a) Calculate the magnitude of the resultant force acting on the boat.   [2 marks]

    b) Calculate the magnitude of the acceleration of the boat.   [1 mark]

Q2 John's bike, which has a mass of m, breaks and he has to push it home. The bike has a constant acceleration a and a frictional force F opposes the motion. What force is John using to push his bike?

A	ma
B	$ma + F$
C	$m(a - F)$
D	$ma - F$

[1 mark]

Q3 Michael and Tom are both keen on diving. They notice that they seem to take the same time to drop from the diving board to the water. Use Newton's second law to explain why this is the case. (Assume no air resistance.)   [3 marks]

Newton's three incredibly important laws of motion...

These laws may not really fill you with a huge amount of excitement (and I could hardly blame you if they don't)... but it was pretty fantastic at the time — suddenly people actually understood how forces work, and how they affect motion. I mean arguably it was one of the most important scientific discoveries ever...

Drag and Terminal Velocity

If you jump out of a plane at 1500 m, you want to know that you're not going to be accelerating all the way.

Friction is a Force that Opposes Motion

There are two main types of friction — **friction** between **solid surfaces** and **friction** in a **fluid**. Friction in a fluid is known as **drag** or fluid resistance. **Air resistance** is a type of fluid resistance.

Fluid Friction or Drag:
1) 'Fluid' is a word that means either a **liquid or a gas** — something that can **flow**.
2) The force depends on the thickness (or **viscosity**) of the fluid (see p.64).
3) It **increases** as the **speed increases** (for simple situations it's directly proportional, but you don't need to worry about the mathematical relationship).
4) It also depends on the **shape** of the object moving through it — the larger the **area** pushing against the fluid, the greater the resistance force.
5) A **projectile** (see p.20) is **slowed down** by air resistance. If you calculate how far a projectile will travel without thinking about air resistance, your answer will be **too large**.

Things you need to remember about frictional forces:
1) They **always** act in the **opposite direction** to the **motion** of the object.
2) They can **never** speed things up or start something moving.
3) They convert **kinetic energy** into **heat** and **sound**.

Terminal Velocity — When the Friction Force Equals the Driving Force

You will reach a **terminal (maximum) velocity** at some point, if you have:
1) a **driving force** that stays the **same** all the time
2) a **frictional** or **drag force** (or collection of forces) that increases with velocity

There are **three main stages** to reaching terminal velocity:

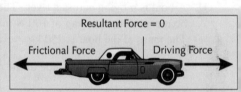

The car **accelerates** from **rest** using a constant driving force.

As the **velocity increases**, the **frictional forces increase** (because of things like turbulence — you don't need the details). This **reduces the resultant force** on the car and hence **reduces its acceleration**.

Eventually the car reaches a velocity at which the **frictional forces are equal to the driving force**. There is now **no resultant force** and **no acceleration**, so the car carries on at **constant velocity**.

Different factors affect a vehicle's maximum velocity

As you just saw, a vehicle reaches maximum velocity when the driving force is equal to the frictional force. So there are two main ways of increasing a vehicle's maximum velocity:
1) **Increasing the driving force**, e.g. by increasing the engine size.
2) **Reducing the frictional force**, e.g. making the body more streamlined.

Drag and Terminal Velocity

Things **Falling** through **Air** or **Water** Reach a **Terminal Velocity** too

When something's falling through air, the weight of the object (p.38) is a constant force accelerating the object downwards. Air resistance is a frictional force opposing this motion, which increases with speed.
So before a parachutist opens the parachute, exactly the same thing happens as with the car example:

1) A skydiver leaves a plane and will **accelerate** until the **air resistance** equals his **weight**.

2) He will then be travelling at a **terminal velocity**.

But... the terminal velocity of a person in free fall is too great to land without dying a horrible death.
The **parachute increases** the **air resistance massively**, which slows him down to a lower terminal velocity:

3) Before reaching the ground he will **open his parachute**, which immediately **increases the air resistance** so it is now **bigger** than his **weight**.

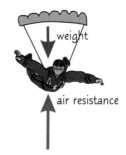

4) This **slows him down** until his speed has dropped enough for the **air resistance** to be **equal to his weight** again. This new terminal velocity is small enough for him to land safely.

A v-t graph of the skydiver looks like this. He reaches terminal velocity twice during his fall — the second one is much slower than the first.

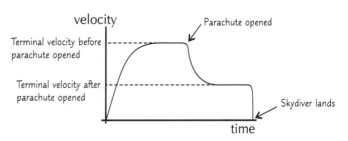

Practice Questions

Q1 What forces limit the velocity of a skier going down a slope?

Q2 Suggest two ways in which the maximum velocity of a car can be increased.

Q3 What conditions cause a terminal velocity to be reached?

Exam Question

Q1 A space probe free-falls towards the surface of a planet.
The graph on the right shows the velocity of the probe as it falls.

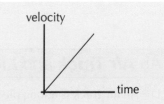

a) The planet does not have an atmosphere. Explain how you can tell this from the graph. [2 marks]

b) Sketch the velocity-time graph you would expect to see if the planet did have an atmosphere. [2 marks]

c) Explain the shape of the graph you have drawn. [3 marks]

You'll never understand this without going parachuting...*

When you're doing questions about terminal velocity, remember the frictional forces reduce acceleration, not speed. They usually don't slow an object down, apart from in the parachute example, where the skydiver is travelling faster just before the parachute opens than the terminal velocity for the open parachute-skydiver combination.

* No. 37 in a series of the 100 least convincing excuses for an interesting holiday.

TOPIC 2 — MECHANICS

Momentum

These pages are about linear momentum — that's momentum in a straight line (not a circle).

Understanding **Momentum** Helps You Do **Calculations** for **Collisions**

The **momentum** of an object depends on two things — its **mass** and **velocity**.
The **product** of these two values is the momentum of the object:

$$p = mv$$

where p is the momentum in kg ms^{-1},
m is the mass in kg, and v is the velocity in ms^{-1}.

*Remember, momentum is a vector quantity, so it has size **and** direction.*

Momentum is Always **Conserved**

You might see momentum referred to as 'linear momentum'. The other kind is 'angular momentum', but you don't need to know about that for now.

1) Assuming **no external forces** act, momentum is always **conserved**.

2) This means the **total momentum** of two objects **before** they collide **equals** the total momentum **after** the collision.

3) This is really handy for working out the **velocity** of objects after a collision (as you do...):

Example: A skater of mass 75 kg and velocity 4.0 ms^{-1} collides with a stationary skater of mass 50 kg (to 2 s.f.). The two skaters join together and move off in the same direction. Calculate their velocity after impact.

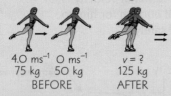

4.0 ms^{-1} 0 ms^{-1}
75 kg   50 kg
BEFORE

v = ?
125 kg
AFTER

Before you start a momentum calculation, always draw a quick sketch.

Momentum of skaters before = Momentum of skaters after
$$(75 \times 4.0) + (50 \times 0) = 125v$$
$$300 = 125v$$
So v = **2.4 ms^{-1}**

4) The same principle can be applied in **explosions**. E.g. if you fire an **air rifle**, the **forward momentum** gained by the pellet **equals** the **backward momentum** of the rifle, and you feel the rifle recoiling into your shoulder.

Example: A bullet of mass 0.0050 kg is shot from a rifle at a speed of 200 ms^{-1} (to 2 s.f.). The rifle has a mass of 4.0 kg. Calculate the velocity at which the rifle recoils.

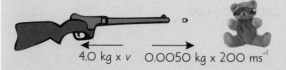

4.0 kg x v 0.0050 kg x 200 ms^{-1}

Momentum before explosion = Momentum after explosion
$$0 = (0.0050 \times 200) + (4.0 \times v)$$
$$0 = 1 + 4v$$
So v = **−0.25 ms^{-1}**

An **Air Track** and **Light Gates** are Used to **Investigate** Momentum

1) An **air track** is a long piece of metal with a series of **small holes** along its surfaces. Air is blown through the holes.

2) This air **reduces friction** between the **track** and the **trolleys** that move on top of it.

3) Momentum is only conserved if **no external forces act**, so air tracks are useful for studying conservation of momentum as you can assume there is **no friction**.

4) **Two** trolleys are pushed towards each other on an air track, so that they **collide** between the **light gates**. The light gates measure the **speed** of each trolley as they pass through them.

5) If the speed of each trolley is measured **before** and **after** the collision, the **initial** and **final** momentum of each trolley can be calculated using $p = mv$.

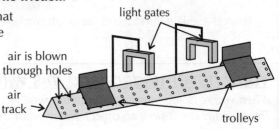

light gates

air is blown through holes

air track →

trolleys

Momentum

Newton's 2nd Law Says That Force is the Rate of Change in Momentum

Newton's second law (p.28) can also be expressed in terms of momentum. The **rate of change of momentum** of an object is **directly proportional** to the **resultant force** which acts on the object.

So: $$F = \frac{\Delta(mv)}{\Delta t} \quad \text{or} \quad F\Delta t = \Delta(mv)$$

where F is the resultant force in N,
m is the mass in kg, v is the velocity in ms^{-1},
and t is the time taken for the velocity to change in s.

If the force is changing, F gives the average force over the time interval Δt.

Remember that acceleration is equal to the rate of change of velocity (page 16), so if mass is constant then this formula gives you that mechanics favourite, $F = ma$ (or $\Sigma F = ma$) (p.28).

1) You can also relate this formula to **conservation of momentum** by considering **Newton's 3rd law**.

2) If object A **collides** with object B and **exerts** a force F on B for a time Δt, Newton's 3rd law says that object B will also exert a force $-F$ on A for a time Δt.

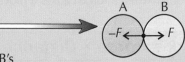

3) The **change** in A's **momentum** is equal to $-F\Delta t$, and the change in B's momentum is $F\Delta t$, so the **overall** change in momentum is $(-F\Delta t) + F\Delta t = 0$. So momentum is **conserved**.

Example: A snooker ball that is initially at rest is hit with a cue.
The cue is in contact with the ball for 0.0040 s and the speed of the ball immediately after being hit is 0.80 ms^{-1}. The mass of the snooker ball is 0.16 kg.
Calculate the average force exerted on the snooker ball by the cue.

Use the equation $F = \frac{\Delta(mv)}{\Delta t}$ and substitute in the values:

$$F = \frac{\Delta(mv)}{\Delta t} = \frac{(0.16 \times 0.80) - (0.16 \times 0)}{0.0040} = \textbf{32 N}$$

Practice Questions

Q1 Give two examples of conservation of momentum in practice.

Q2 Explain how light gates and an air track can be used to investigate conservation of momentum.

Q3 Explain how Newton's 2nd law and Newton's 3rd law can be used to demonstrate conservation of momentum.

Exam Questions

Q1 A ball of mass 0.60 kg moving at 5.0 ms^{-1} collides with a larger stationary ball of mass 2.0 kg.
The smaller ball rebounds in the opposite direction at 2.4 ms^{-1}.

a) Calculate the velocity of the larger ball immediately after the collision. [3 marks]

b) The collision lasts for 0.0055 s. Calculate the average force acting on the smaller ball in this time. [2 marks]

Q2 A toy train of mass 0.7 kg, travelling at 0.3 ms^{-1}, collides with a stationary toy carriage of mass 0.4 kg.
The two toys couple together. Calculate their new velocity. [3 marks]

Momentum'll never be an endangered species — it's always conserved...

...unlike record stores, which are quite the opposite and could probably do with your help. You can't match the excitement of running home with a shiny new CD, spending 20 minutes trying to pick through the shrink wrap then sitting back and enjoying 12 glorious new tracks... Speaking of (air) tracks, there's a lot of important stuff here — make sure you know how Newton's laws relate to conservation of momentum.

Work and Power

As everyone knows, work in Physics isn't like normal work. It's harder. Work also has a specific meaning that's to do with movement and forces. You'll have seen this at GCSE — it just comes up in more detail here.

Work is Done Whenever Energy is Transferred

This table gives you some examples of **work being done** and the **energy changes** that happen.

1) Usually you need a force to move something because you're having to **overcome another force**.

2) The thing being moved has **kinetic energy** while it's **moving**.

3) The kinetic energy is transferred to **another form of energy** when the movement stops.

ACTIVITY	WORK DONE AGAINST	FINAL ENERGY FORM
Lifting up a box.	gravity	gravitational potential energy
Pushing a chair across a level floor.	friction	heat
Pushing two magnetic north poles together.	magnetic force	magnetic energy
Stretching a spring.	stiffness of spring	elastic potential energy

The word **'work'** in Physics means the **amount of energy transferred** from one form to another when a force causes a movement of some sort. It's measured in **joules** (J).

Work = Force × Distance

When a car tows a caravan, it applies a force to the caravan to move it to where it's wanted. To **find out** how much **work** has been **done**, you need to use the **equation**:

> **work done (ΔW) = force causing motion (F) × distance moved (Δs), or $\Delta W = F\Delta s$**
> ...where ΔW is measured in joules (J), F is measured in newtons (N) and Δs is measured in metres (m).

Points to remember:

1) **Work** is the **energy** that's been **changed** from one form to another — it's not necessarily the **total** energy. E.g. moving a book from a low shelf to a higher one will increase its gravitational potential energy, but it had some potential energy to start with.
   Here, the **work done** would be the **increase** in potential energy, **not the total** potential energy.

2) Remember the distance needs to be measured in metres — if you have a **distance in centimetres or kilometres**, you need to **convert** it to metres first.

3) The force F will be a **fixed** value in any calculations, either because it's **constant** or because it's the **average** force.

4) The equation assumes that the **direction of the force** is the **same** as the **direction of movement**.

5) The equation gives you the **definition** of the joule (symbol J):
   'One joule is the work done when a force of 1 newton moves an object through a distance of 1 metre'.

The Force isn't always in the Same Direction as the Movement

Sometimes the **direction of movement** is **different** from the **direction of the** force.

Example:

1) To **calculate the work done** in a situation like the one on the right, you need to consider the **horizontal** and **vertical components** of the force.

2) The only **movement** is in the **horizontal** direction. This means the **vertical force** is not causing any motion (and hence not doing any work) — it's just **balancing** out some of the **weight**, meaning there's a **smaller reaction force**.

direction of force on sledge

direction of motion

3) The horizontal force is causing the motion — so to **calculate** the **work done**, this is the **only force** you need to consider. Which means we get:

$$\Delta W = F\Delta s \cos\theta$$

Where θ is the **angle** between the **direction of the force** and the **direction of motion**. See page 26 for more on resolving forces.

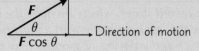

F

θ

F cos *θ*

Direction of motion

Work and Power

Power = Work Done per Second

Power means many things in everyday speech, but in physics (of course!) it has a special meaning. Power is the **rate of doing work** — in other words it is the **amount of energy transferred** from one form to another **per second**. You **calculate power** from the equation:

> **Power** (P) = **energy transferred** (E) ÷ **time** (t), or $P = \dfrac{E}{t}$ ...where P is measured in watts (W), E is measured in joules (J) and t is measured in seconds (s).

Since **work done** is **equal** to the **energy transferred**, you can also write this as:

> **Power** (P) = **work done** (W) ÷ **time** (t), or $P = \dfrac{W}{t}$ ...where P is measured in watts (W), W is measured in joules (J) and t is measured in seconds (s).

The **watt** (symbol W) is defined as a **rate of energy transfer** equal to **1 joule per second** (Js^{-1}). Yep, that's more **equations and definitions** for you to **learn**.

In the equations on this page, W stands for watts (the unit of power) — don't get it confused with W, work done.

Example: A light bulb transfers 230 kJ of electrical energy into light and heat in one hour. Calculate the power of the bulb.

Energy transferred = 230 kJ = 230 000 J
Time taken to transfer the energy = 1 hour = 3600 s
So $P = \dfrac{E}{t} = \dfrac{230\,000}{3600} = 63.888... = \mathbf{64\ W}$ **(to 2 s.f.)**

Remember — 1 kJ = 1000 J

Alice always took a long time to transfer any energy.

Practice Questions

Q1 Write down the equation used to calculate work if the force and motion are in the same direction.
Q2 Write down the equation for work if the force is at an angle to the direction of motion.
Q3 Write down the equations relating: a) power and work done   b) power and energy transferred.

Exam Questions

Q1 A traditional narrowboat is drawn by a horse walking along a canal towpath. The horse pulls the boat at a constant speed between two locks which are 1500 m apart. The tension in the rope is 100 N at 40° to the direction of motion.

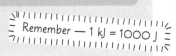

direction of motion
40°
direction of force on boat

   a) Calculate the work done on the boat. [2 marks]

   b) It take 31 minutes for the horse to pull the boat between the two locks. Calculate the power supplied to the boat. [2 marks]

Q2 A motor is used to lift a 20.0 kg load a height of 3.0 m. ($g = 9.81\ ms^{-2}$)

   a) Calculate the work done in lifting the load. [2 marks]

   b) The speed of the load as it is lifted is 0.25 ms^{-1}. Calculate the power delivered by the motor. [3 marks]

Work — there's just no getting away from it...

Loads of equations to learn. Well, that's what you came here for, after all. Can't beat a good bit of equation-learning, as I've heard you say quietly to yourself when you think no one's listening. Aha, can't fool me. Ahahahahahahahahahaha.

Conservation of Energy and Efficiency

Energy cannot be created or destroyed (don't forget that). Which is basically what I'm about to take up two whole pages saying. But that's, of course, because you need to do exam questions on this as well as understand the principle.

Learn the Principle of Conservation of Energy

The **principle of conservation of energy** says that:

> Energy **cannot be created** or **destroyed**. Energy **can be transferred** from one form to another but the total amount of energy in a closed system will not change.

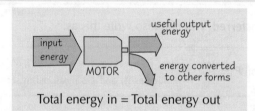

Total energy in = Total energy out

Greg started panic-buying when he heard that more energy couldn't be created.

You need it for Questions about Kinetic and Potential Energy

The principle of conservation of energy nearly always comes up when you're doing questions about **changes** between **kinetic** and **potential energy**. A quick reminder:

1) **Kinetic energy** is the energy of anything due to its **motion**, which you work out from:
$$E_K = \frac{1}{2}mv^2$$
m is the mass of the object (kg) and v is its velocity (ms^{-1})

2) There are **different types of potential energy** — e.g. gravitational potential energy and elastic strain (see page 58).

3) **Gravitational potential energy** is the energy something gains if you lift it up. The **equation** for the change in gravitational potential energy close to the **Earth's surface** is:

> change in gravitational potential energy = ΔE_{grav} = $mg\Delta h$

g is the acceleration due to gravity, g = 9.81 ms^{-2} and Δh is the change in height (m)

Example: A pendulum has a mass of 700 g and a length of 50 cm. It is pulled out to an angle of 30° from the vertical.

a) Find the gravitational potential energy stored in the pendulum bob.

Start by drawing a diagram.
You can work out the increase in height, Δh, of the end of the pendulum using trig.
$\Delta E_{grav} = mg\Delta h = 0.7 \times 9.81 \times (0.5 - 0.5 \cos30°) = 0.460... = $ **0.5 J (to 1 s.f.)**

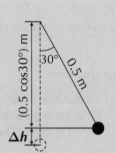

b) The pendulum is released. Find the maximum speed of the pendulum bob as it passes the vertical position. Assume there is no air resistance.

When travelling at its maximum speed, all of the gravitational potential energy has been transferred to kinetic energy, so $mg\Delta h = \frac{1}{2}mv^2 = 0.460...$

$\frac{1}{2}mv^2 = 0.460...$, so $v = \sqrt{\frac{2 \times 0.460...}{0.7}} = 1.146... = $ **1 ms^{-1} (to 1 s.f.)**

Or, you could cancel the 'm's and rearrange to give: $v = \sqrt{2g\Delta h}$
$$= \sqrt{2 \times 9.81 \times (0.5 - 0.5 \cos 30°)}$$
$$= \textbf{1 ms}^{-1} \textbf{ (to 1 s.f.)}$$

Conservation of Energy and Efficiency

All Energy Transfers Involve Losses

You saw on the last page that **energy can never be created or destroyed**. But whenever **energy** is **converted** from one form to another, some is always **'lost'**. It's still there (i.e. it's **not destroyed**) — it's just not in a form you can **use**.

Most often, **energy** is lost as **heat** — e.g. **computers** and **TVs** are always **warm** when they've been on for a while. In fact, **no device** (except possibly a heater) is ever **100% efficient** (see below) because some energy is **always** lost as **heat**. (You want heaters to give out heat, but in other devices the heat loss isn't useful.) Energy can be **lost** as other forms too (e.g. **sound**) — the important thing is the lost energy **isn't** in a **useful** form and you **can't** get it back.

Energy is often lost as **heat** due to **friction**. For example, imagine pushing a **box** along a **table**. **Frictional forces** between the box and the table surface act in the **opposite direction** to the **motion** of the box (see p.30). Work has to be done to **overcome** this friction — energy is transferred to **heat**. Luckily you can usually assume that **friction** is **zero** in exams.

Efficiency is the Ratio of Useful Energy Output to Total Energy Input

Efficiency is one of those words we use all the time, but it has a **specific meaning** in Physics. It's a measure of how well a **device** converts the **energy** you put **in** into the energy you **want** it to give **out**. So, a device that **wastes** loads of **energy** as heat and sound has a really **low efficiency**.

$$\text{Efficiency} = \frac{\text{useful energy output}}{\text{total energy input}} \quad \text{Or} \quad \text{Efficiency} = \frac{\text{useful power output}}{\text{total power input}}$$

You can multiply either of these equations by 100 to find the efficiency as a percentage.

Some questions will be kind and **give you** the **useful output energy** — others will tell you how much is **wasted**. You just have to **subtract** the **wasted energy** from the **total input energy** to find the **useful output energy**, so it's not too tricky if you keep your wits about you.

Energy, as always, is measured in joules (J). Efficiency has no units because it's a fraction (or a percentage).

Practice Questions

Q1 State the principle of conservation of energy.
Q2 Show that, if there's no air resistance and the mass of the string is negligible, the speed of a pendulum is independent of the mass of the bob.
Q3 Why can a device never be 100% efficient?
Q4 Give an equation for efficiency in terms of a) energy and b) power.

Exam Questions

acceleration of free fall, g = 9.81 ms⁻²

Q1 A skateboarder is skating on a half-pipe. He lets the board run down one side of the ramp and up the other. The height of the ramp is 2.0 m.

  a) Calculate his speed at the lowest point of the ramp. Assume friction is negligible. [3 marks]

  b) State how high he will rise up the other side of the half-pipe. [1 mark]

  c) Real ramps are not frictionless. Describe what the skater must do to reach the top on the other side. [1 mark]

Q2 A 20.0 g rubber ball is released from a height of 8.0 m. Assume that the effect of air resistance is negligible.

  a) Calculate the kinetic energy of the ball just before it hits the ground. [2 marks]

  b) The ball strikes the ground and rebounds to a height of 6.5 m. Calculate the amount of energy that is converted to heat and sound in the impact with the ground. [2 marks]

Q3 Calculate the efficiency (as a fraction) of a device that wastes 65 J for every 140 J of input energy. [1 mark]

Eat, sleep, state the principle of conservation of energy, repeat...

Remember to check your answers — I can't count the number of times I've forgotten to square the velocities or to multiply by the ½... I reckon it's definitely worth the extra minute to check. You never know what you might find.

Mass, Weight and Centre of Gravity

I'm sure you know all this 'mass', 'weight' and 'centre of gravity' stuff from GCSE. But let's just make sure...

The Mass of a Body makes it Resist Changes in Motion

1) The **mass** of an object is the **amount of 'stuff'** (or **matter**) in it. It's measured in **kg**.
2) The greater an object's mass, the greater its **resistance** to a **change in velocity**.
3) The **mass** of an object **doesn't change** if the strength of the **gravitational field** changes.
4) As you've already seen in this topic, weight is a **force**. It's measured in **newtons** (N), like all forces.
5) Weight is the **force experienced by a mass** due to a **gravitational field**.
6) The weight of an object **does vary** according to the size of the **gravitational field** acting on it.

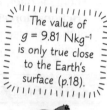
The value of $g = 9.81$ Nkg^{-1} is only true close to the Earth's surface (p.18).

> **weight = mass × gravitational field strength** ($W = mg$) where $g = 9.81$ Nkg^{-1} on Earth.

This table shows a lion's mass and weight on the Earth and the Moon.

Name	Quantity	Earth ($g = 9.81$ Nkg^{-1})	Moon ($g = 1.6$ Nkg^{-1})
Mass	Mass (scalar)	150 kg	150 kg
Weight	Force (vector)	1470 N (to 3 s.f.)	240 N (to 2 s.f.)

Weight 240 N

Weight 1470 N

Centre of Gravity — Assume All the Mass is in One Place

1) The **centre of gravity** of an object is the **single point** that you can consider its **whole weight** to **act through** (whatever its orientation).
2) The object will always **balance** around this **point**, although in some cases the **centre of gravity** will **fall outside** the object.

You might come across the phrase 'extended body' when dealing with the centre of gravity. This is just another name for an object that isn't a single point.

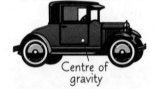
Centre of gravity

Centre of gravity

Centre of gravity

Find the Centre of Gravity either by Symmetry...

1) To find the centre of gravity for a **regular** object you can just use **symmetry**.
2) The centre of gravity of any regular shape is at its **centre** — where the lines of symmetry will cross.
3) The centre of gravity is **halfway** through the **thickness** of the object at the point the lines meet.

The symmetry in this picture shows the centre of cuteness.

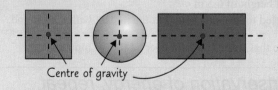
Centre of gravity

Mass, Weight and Centre of Gravity

... Or By Experiment

Experiment to find the Centre of Gravity of an Irregular Object

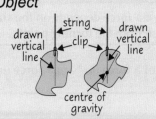

1) **Hang** the object freely from a point (e.g. one corner).
2) Draw a **vertical line** downwards from the point of suspension — use a plumb bob to get your line exactly vertical.
3) Hang the object from a different point.
4) Draw another vertical line down.
5) The centre of gravity is where the two lines **cross**.

A plumb bob is just a weight on a string — when suspended, the string will be exactly vertical.

How High the Centre of Gravity is tells you How Stable the Object is

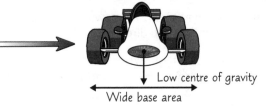

1) An object will be nice and **stable** if it has a **low centre** of **gravity** and a **wide base area**. This idea is used a lot in design, e.g. racing cars.

2) The **higher** the **centre of gravity**, and the **smaller** the **base area**, the **less stable** the object will be. Think of unicyclists...

Low centre of gravity

Wide base area

3) An object will topple over if a **vertical line** drawn **downwards** from its **centre of gravity** falls **outside** its **base area**. This is because the object's weight is causing a turning force (a moment — see p.40) around a pivot.

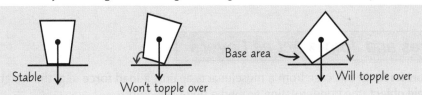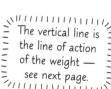

Stable

Won't topple over

Base area

Will topple over

The vertical line is the line of action of the weight — see next page.

Practice Questions

Q1 A lioness has a mass of 200 kg. What would be her mass and weight on Earth and on the Moon (where g = 1.6 Nkg^{-1})?

Q2 Define centre of gravity.

Exam Questions

Q1 Joanne weighs X N on Earth. Which of the following statements are correct?

A She will weigh the same on the Moon as on Earth.

B Her mass is equal to $\frac{X}{g}$ kg.

C Her mass depends on the gravitational field strength.

D Her acceleration due to gravity will be the same on Earth as the Moon. [1 mark]

Q2 a) Describe an experiment to find the centre of gravity of an object of uniform density with a constant thickness and irregular cross-section. [3 marks]

b) Identify one major source of uncertainty for this method and suggest a way to reduce its effect on the accuracy of the result. [2 marks]

The centre of gravity of this book should be round about page 98...

This is a really useful area of physics. To would-be nuclear physicists it might seem a little dull, but if you want to be an engineer — then things like centre of gravity and weight are dead important things to understand. You know, for designing things like cars and submarines... yep, pretty useful I'd say.

Moments

This is not a time for jokes. There is not a moment to lose. Oh ho ho ho ho *bang*. (Ow.)

A **Moment** is the **Turning Effect** of a **Force**

The **moment** of a **force** depends on the **size** of the force and **how far** the force is applied from the **turning point** (also called the **axis of rotation**):

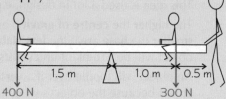
The line of action of a force is a line along which it acts.

| moment of a force (in Nm) = force (in N) × | perpendicular distance from the line of action of the force to the axis of rotation (in m) | $M = Fx$ |

Moments Must be **Balanced** or the **Object** will **Turn**

The **principle of moments** states that for a body to be in **equilibrium**, the **sum of the clockwise moments** about any point **equals** the **sum of the anticlockwise moments** about the same point.

Remember ∑ means "the sum of".

Example:
Two children sit on a seesaw as shown in the diagram. An adult balances the seesaw at one end. Find the size and direction of the force that the adult needs to apply.

In equilibrium, $\sum$ anticlockwise moments = $\sum$ clockwise moments

$$400 \times 1.5 = (300 \times 1.0) + 1.5F$$
$$600 = 300 + 1.5F$$

Final answer: F = **200 N downwards**

1.5 m   1.0 m   0.5 m
400 N   300 N

Muscles, **Bones** and **Joints** Act as **Levers**

1) In a lever, an **effort force** (in this case from a muscle) acts against a **load force** (e.g. the weight of your arm) by means of a **rigid object** (the bone) rotating around a **pivot** (the joint).

2) You can use the **principle of moments** to answer lever questions:

Example:
Find the force, E, exerted by the biceps in holding a bag of gold still. The bag of gold weighs 100 N and the forearm weighs 20 N.

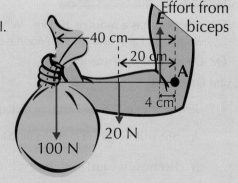
Effort from biceps
40 cm
20 cm
A
4 cm
20 N
100 N

Take moments about **A**.
In equilibrium:

$$\sum \text{anticlockwise moments} = \sum \text{clockwise moments}$$
$$(100 \times 0.4) + (20 \times 0.2) = 0.04E$$
$$40 + 4 = 0.04E$$

Final answer: E = 1100 = **1000 N (to 1 s.f.)**

The Principle of Moments can **Explain** why Things **Fall Over**

1) As you saw on page 39, you can assume that **all** the weight of an object **acts through** its **centre of gravity**. This is important when dealing with moments.

2) Imagine you are trying to balance a broomstick on a pivot.
If the **centre of gravity** is to one side of the **pivot** (as shown here) then there will be a **clockwise** moment due to the **weight** of the broomstick acting at a **distance x** from the pivot. There is **no anticlockwise** moment, so the broomstick will **rotate** clockwise (fall off the pivot).

3) However, if the centre of gravity is **directly above** the pivot, then there are no clockwise or anticlockwise **moments** and so the broomstick is in **equilibrium**.

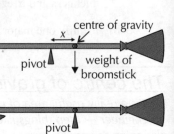
centre of gravity
x
pivot   weight of broomstick
pivot

Moments

Sometimes you Need to Resolve Forces to Calculate Moments

Example: Jamie Band is trying to save some top secret documents falling from a plank which is hanging precariously over a cliff. The diagram shows the plank pivoting at the edge of the cliff, labelled point P. He has tied a rope to one end of the plank and attached the other end of the rope to the ground. Jamie edges towards the top secret documents, but gets scared and stops at the point shown in the diagram below. Jamie has a mass of 75 kg and the top secret documents have a mass of 12 kg.

The distances and angles have been drawn to scale on the diagram below. Assuming the mass of the plank is negligible, calculate the tension, T, in the rope.

First you need to resolve all the forces (see p.26) acting perpendicular to the plank by measuring the angle between the line of action of Jamie's weight and the plank.

Angle $\theta = 60°$, so the force exerted by Jamie's weight acting perpendicular to the plank = $m_{Jamie}g \times \sin60°$ and the force exerted by the documents acting perpendicular to the plank = $m_{doc}g \times \sin60°$.

The angle between the rope and plank is 90°, so the tension acting perpendicular to the plank is just T.

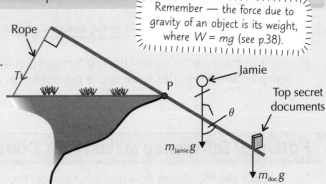

Remember — the force due to gravity of an object is its weight, where $W = mg$ (see p.38).

You then need to measure all the distances: from P to rope = 3.6 cm, from P to Jamie = 1.2 cm, from P to documents = 2.8 cm. Using these values and the values for the forces, you can use the principle of moments to give:

Σ anticlockwise moments = Σ clockwise moments

$T \times 3.6 = (m_{Jamie}g \times \sin60° \times 1.2) + (m_{doc}g \times \sin60° \times 2.8)$

Which gives: $T = \dfrac{(75 \times 9.81 \times \sin60° \times 1.2) + (12 \times 9.81 \times \sin60° \times 2.8)}{3.6} = 291.68... = $ **290 N (to 2 s.f.)**

Practice Questions

Q1 A force of 54 N acts at a perpendicular distance of 84 cm from a pivot. Calculate the moment of the force.

Q2 A girl of mass 40 kg sits 1.5 m from the middle of a seesaw.
Show that her brother, mass 50 kg, must sit 1.2 m from the middle if the seesaw is to balance.

Q3 Explain why a ruler will only balance on a narrow pivot if it is positioned so the pivot is exactly halfway along the ruler.

Exam Questions

Q1 A driver is changing his flat tyre. The moment required to undo the nut is 60 Nm (to 2 s.f.).
He uses a 0.40 m long spanner. Calculate the force that he must apply at the end of the spanner. [2 marks]

Q2 A diver of mass 60 kg stands on the end of a diving board 2.0 m from the pivot point.
Calculate the downward force exerted on the board by the retaining spring 30 cm from the pivot.

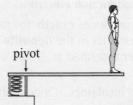

pivot

[2 marks]

It's all about balancing — just ask a tightrope walker...

They're always boring questions aren't they — seesaws or bicycles. It'd be nice if just once, they'd have a question on... I don't know, rotating knives or something. Just something unexpected. It'd make physics a lot more fun, I'm sure.

Charge, Current and Potential Difference

Electricity's brilliant, I love it. It's what gets me out of bed in the morning. (Not literally of course, that'd be quite painful.)

Current is the Rate of Flow of Charge

1) The **current** in a **wire** is like **water** flowing in a **pipe**. The **amount** of water that flows depends on the **flow rate** and the **time**. It's the same with electricity — **current is the rate of flow of charge**.

$$I = \frac{\Delta Q}{\Delta t}$$ Where I is the current in amperes, ΔQ is the charge in coulombs, and Δt is the time taken in seconds.

Remember that conventional current flows from + to −, the opposite way from electron flow.

2) The **coulomb** is the **unit of charge**.

> **One coulomb** (C) is defined as the **amount of charge** that passes in **1 second** when the **current** is **1 ampere**.

3) You can measure the current flowing through part of a circuit using an **ammeter**. This is the circuit symbol for an ammeter:  (A)

Attach an ammeter in series with the component you're investigating.

Potential Difference is the Work Done per Unit Charge

1) To make electric charge flow through a conductor, you need to do **work** on it.

2) **Potential difference** (p.d.), or **voltage**, is defined as the **work done per unit charge moved**: $V = \frac{W}{Q}$ W is the work done in joules (see p.34). It's the energy transferred in moving the charge.

> The **potential difference** across a component is **1 volt** (V) when you do **1 joule** of work moving **1 coulomb** of charge through the component. This **defines** the volt.

$$1\,V = 1\,J\,C^{-1}$$

Back to the 'water analogy' again. The p.d. is like the pressure that's forcing water along the pipe.

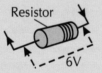
Resistor

Here you do 6 J of work moving each coulomb of charge through the resistor, so the p.d. across it is 6 V. The energy gets converted to heat.

3) You can measure the potential difference across a component using a **voltmeter**. This is the circuit symbol for a voltmeter: (V)

The maximum value that a voltmeter or ammeter can measure is called the full scale deflection.

4) Remember, the potential difference across components in parallel is **the same**, so the **voltmeter** should be connected in **parallel** with the component you're investigating.

Charge Carriers in Liquids and Gases are Ions

1) A current is the **rate of flow of charged particles** (called **charge carriers**). In a circuit, the charge carriers are free electrons (sometimes called **conduction electrons**), but there are **other types** of charge carrier.

2) A flow of **positively-charged** particles produces **exactly** the **same current** as an **equal** flow of negatively-charged particles in the **opposite direction**. This is why we use **conventional current**, defined as 'in the same direction as a flow of positive charges'.

3) **Ionic crystals** like sodium chloride are **insulators**. Once **molten**, though, the liquid **conducts**. Positive and negative **ions** are the **charge carriers**. The **same thing** happens in an **ionic solution** like copper sulfate solution.

4) **Gases** are **insulators**, but if you apply a **high enough voltage** electrons get **ripped out** of **atoms**, giving you **ions** along a path. You get a **spark**.

Uses of ions in air include creating a dramatic backdrop to a Gothic horror story, and bringing the creations of mad scientists to life.

Charge, Current and Potential Difference

The **Mean Drift Velocity** is the **Average** Velocity of the **Charge Carriers**

When **current** flows through a wire, you might imagine the **electrons** all moving uniformly in the **same direction**. In fact, they move **randomly** in **all directions**, but tend to **drift** one way. The **mean drift velocity** is just the **average velocity** and it's **much, much less** than the electrons' **actual speed**. (Their actual speed is about 10^6 ms^{-1}.)

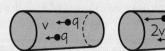
The charge on an electron, e, is -1.60×10^{-19} C.

The Current Depends on the Mean Drift Velocity:

The **current** is given by the equation:

$$I = nqvA$$

where: I = electrical current (A)
n = number density of charge carriers (m^{-3}) (number per unit volume)
q = charge on each charge carrier (C)
v = mean drift velocity (ms^{-1})
A = cross-sectional area (m^2)

So...

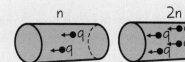

1) Double the number of charge carriers and the current doubles.

 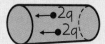

2) If the carriers move twice as fast you get twice the charge in the same time — twice the current.

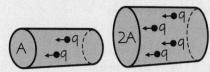

3) Doubling the area also doubles the current.

4) Doubling the charge carried by each carrier gives you twice the charge in the same time — twice the current.

Different Materials have Different Numbers of Charge Carriers

1) In a **metal**, the **charge carriers** are **free electrons** — they're the ones from the **outer shell** of each atom. Thinking about the formula $I = nqvA$, there are **loads** of charge carriers per unit volume, making n **big**. The **drift velocity** is **small**, even for a **high current**.

2) **Semiconductors** have **fewer charge carriers**, so the **drift velocity** needs to be **higher** to give the **same current**.

3) A **perfect insulator** wouldn't have **any charge carriers**, so $n = 0$ in the formula and you'd get **no current**. **Real** insulators have a **very small** n.

Practice Questions

Q1 Describe in words and symbols how current and charge are related.
Q2 Define potential difference.
Q3 What happens to the current in a wire if the mean drift velocity of the electrons is halved?
Q4 Describe how metals, semiconductors and insulators differ in terms of n.

Exam Questions

Q1 A battery delivers 4500 C of electric charge to a circuit in 10 minutes. Calculate the average current. [1 mark]

Q2 A kettle runs off the mains supply (230 V) and has an overall efficiency of 88%. Calculate how much electric charge will pass through the kettle if it transfers 308 J of energy to the water it contains. [2 marks]

Q3 Copper has 1.0×10^{29} free electrons per m^3. Calculate the mean drift velocity of the electrons in a copper wire of cross-sectional area 5.0×10^{-6} m^2 when it is carrying a current of 13 A. [2 marks]

I can't even be bothered to make the current joke...

Talking of currant jokes, I saw this bottle of wine the other day called 'raisin d'être' — 'raison d'être' meaning 'reason for living', but spelled slightly differently to make 'raisin', meaning 'grape'. Ho ho. Chuckled all the way home.

Resistance and Resistivity

Resistance and resistivity. Not quite the same word, not quite the same thing. Make sure you know which is which...

Everything has Resistance

1) If you put a **potential difference** (p.d.) across an **electrical component**, a **current** will flow.
2) **How much** current you get for a particular **p.d.** depends on the **resistance** of the component.
3) You can think of a component's **resistance** as a **measure** of how **difficult** it is to get a **current** to **flow** through it.

Mathematically, **resistance** is: This equation really **defines** what is meant by resistance.

$$R = \frac{V}{I}$$

This is the **circuit symbol** for a resistor: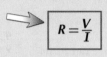

4) **Resistance** is measured in **ohms** (Ω).

A component has a resistance of **1 Ω** if a **potential difference** of **1 V** makes a **current** of **1 A** flow through it.

Three Things Determine Resistance

If you think about a nice, **simple electrical component**, like a **length of wire**, its **resistance** depends on:

1) **Length (*l*)**. The **longer** the wire the **more difficult** it is to make a **current flow**.
2) **Area (*A*)**. The **wider** the wire the **easier** it is to make a current flow.
3) **Resistivity (ρ)**. This **depends** on the **material** the wire's made from, as the **structure** of the material may make it easy or difficult for charge to flow. In general, resistivity depends on **environmental factors** as well, like **temperature**.

ρ is the Greek letter rho, the symbol for resistivity.

The **resistivity** of a material is defined as the **resistance** of a **1 m length** with a **1 m² cross-sectional area**, so $\rho = \frac{RA}{l}$. Resistivity is measured in **ohm metres** (Ωm).

In your exams, you'll be given this equation in the **form**:
Typical values for the **resistivity** of **conductors** are **really small**.
However, if you **calculate** a **resistance** for a **conductor** and end up with something **really small** (e.g. 1 × 10⁻⁷ Ω), go back and **check** that you've **converted** your **area** into **m²**.

$$R = \frac{\rho l}{A}$$

where A = cross-sectional area in m², and l = length in m

The resistivity of a material is related to the **number density of charge carriers**, (and their **mean drift velocity**, which often varies with temperature, p.46). The higher the number of charge carriers, (and the higher their mean drift velocity), the higher the current at a given p.d. (as $I = nqvA$, see p.43), and so the lower the resistance and therefore the lower the material's resistivity.

The number density of charge carriers **varies greatly** between different materials (see p.43), which means there can be a **huge variation** in their resistivities.

For an Ohmic Conductor, R is a Constant

A chap called **Ohm** did most of the early work on resistance. He developed a rule to **predict** how the **current** would **change** as the applied **potential difference increased**, for **certain types** of conductor.
The rule is now called **Ohm's law** and the conductors that **obey** it (mostly metals) are called **ohmic conductors**.

Provided the **temperature** is **constant**, the **current** through an ohmic conductor is **directly proportional** to the **potential difference** across it (that's $I \propto V$).

1) As you can see from the graph, **doubling** the **p.d. doubles** the **current**.
2) What this means is that the **resistance** is **constant**.
3) Often **external factors**, such as **temperature** will have a **significant effect** on resistance, so you need to remember that Ohm's law is **only** true for **ohmic conductors** at **constant temperature**.

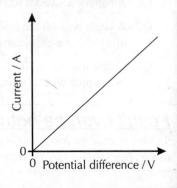

Resistance and Resistivity

To Find the **Resistivity** of a **Wire** You Need to Find its **Resistance**

Before you start, you need to know the **cross-sectional area** of your test wire.
Assume that the wire is **cylindrical**, and so the cross-section is **circular**.

Then you can find its **cross-sectional area** using: $\boxed{\text{area of a circle} = \pi r^2}$

Use a **micrometer** to measure the **diameter** of the test wire for at least **three**
different points along the wire. Take an **average** value of the diameter and
divide by **2** to get the **radius** (make sure this is in m). Plug it into the equation for
cross-sectional area and... **ta da**. Now you can get your teeth into the electricity bit...

A micrometer, sometimes called a micrometer caliper, is used to precisely measure very small distances.

1) The **test wire** should be **clamped** to a ruler and connected to
   the rest of the circuit at the point where the ruler reads zero.

2) Attach the **flying lead** to the test wire — the lead is
   just a wire with a crocodile clip at the end to allow
   connection to any point along the test wire.

3) Record the **length** of the test wire **connected** in the circuit,
   the **voltmeter reading** and the **ammeter reading**.

4) Use your readings to calculate the
   resistance of the length of wire, using: $\Rightarrow$ $R = \dfrac{V}{I}$

5) Repeat for several **different** lengths within
   a sensible range, e.g. at 0.10 m intervals
   from 0.10 m to 1.00 m.

6) Plot your results on a graph of **resistance** against
   length, and draw a **line of best fit** (see page 8).

You could also use a digital multimeter to measure the resistance of the wire directly — you'd connect it in parallel with the length of wire you're investigating and set it to measure resistance.

The **gradient** of the line of best fit is equal to $\dfrac{R}{l} = \dfrac{\rho}{A}$. So **multiply** the **gradient** of the line
of best fit by the **cross-sectional area** of the wire to find the resistivity of the wire material.

7) The **resistivity** of a material depends on its **temperature**, so you can only find the resistivity of a material **at a certain temperature**. Current flowing in the test wire can cause its temperature to increase, so failing to keep the wire at a **constant temperature** could invalidate your results (see p.12). Try to keep the temperature of the test wire constant by e.g. only having small currents flow through the wire.

Practice Questions

Q1 State the equation that links the resistance of a wire to its resistivity.

Q2 The resistivity of a piece of glass is 1×10^{11} Ωm at 20 °C. The resistivity of aluminium at 20 °C is around 3×10^{-8} Ωm. Explain this difference in terms of charge carriers.

Q3 What is Ohm's law?

Q4 Describe an experiment to find the resistivity of a metal.

Exam Questions

Q1 Aluminium has a resistivity of 2.8×10^{-8} Ω m at 20 °C.
   Calculate the resistance of a pure aluminium wire of length 4.0 m and diameter 1.0 mm, at 20 °C. [3 marks]

Q2 The table on the right shows some measurements taken by a student
   during an experiment investigating an unknown electrical component.
   The temperature of the circuit is held constant throughout the experiment.

P.d. / V	3.00	7.00	11.00
Current /mA	4.00	9.33	14.67

   a) Calculate the resistance of the component when a p.d. of 7.00 V is applied. [1 mark]

   b) State whether the component is an ohmic conductor. Explain your answer. [3 marks]

I find the resistivity to my chat-up lines is very high...

Examiners love to ask questions about this experiment, so make sure you learn it well. Make sure you can think of some ways to reduce random errors too — e.g. by repeating measurements and by using more sensitive equipment.

I-V Characteristics

Woohoo — real physics. This stuff's actually kind of interesting.

Make sure you learn all the circuit symbols that come up in this section, and know how to design and use circuits using them.

I-V Graphs Show How Resistance Varies

The term '*I-V characteristic*' refers to a **graph** which shows how the **current** (*I*) flowing through a **component changes** as the **potential difference** (*V*) across it is increased.

You can investigate the *I-V* characteristic of a component using a **test circuit** like this one:

1) Use the **variable resistor** to alter the **potential difference** across the component and the **current** flowing through it, and record *V* and *I*.

2) **Repeat** your measurements and take **averages** to reduce the effect of random errors on your results.

3) **Plot a graph** of current against potential difference from your results. This graph is the *I-V* **characteristic** of the component.

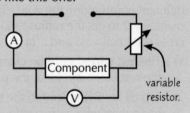

variable resistor.

The I-V Characteristic for a Metallic Conductor is a Straight Line

1) At **constant temperature**, the **current** through a **metallic conductor**, e.g. a **wire** or a **resistor**, is **directly proportional** to the **potential difference**.

2) The fact that the characteristic graph is a **straight line through the origin** tells you that the **resistance doesn't change** — it's equal to 1 / gradient.

3) The **shallower** the **gradient** of the characteristic *I-V* graph, the **greater** the **resistance** of the conductor.

4) **Metallic conductors** are **ohmic** — they have **constant resistance provided** their temperature doesn't change (see below).

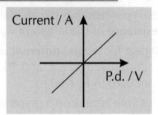

The I-V Characteristic for a Filament Lamp is Curved

Filament lamp circuit symbol:

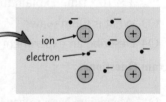

1) The characteristic graph for a **filament lamp** is a curve, which starts **steep** but gets **shallower** as the **potential difference rises**.

2) The **filament** in a lamp is just a **coiled up** length of **metal wire**, so you might think it should have the **same characteristic graph** as a **metallic conductor**.

3) However, **current** flowing through the lamp **increases** its **temperature**, so its **resistance increases** (see below).

The Resistivity of a Metal Increases with Temperature

1) **Charge** is carried through **metals** by **free electrons** in a **lattice** of **positive ions**.

2) Heating up a metal makes it **harder** for electrons to **move about**. The **lattice of ions vibrates more** when heated, meaning the electrons **collide** with them more frequently, **transferring** some of their **kinetic energy** into other forms.

ion

electron

3) When kinetic energy is **lost** by the individual electrons, their speed and therefore the **mean drift velocity** (see page 43) decreases. As current is proportional to drift velocity, ($I = nqvA$) this means the **current** in the wire **decreases** so its **resistance** (and its resistivity, as it's dimensions haven't changed) **increases**.

Semiconductors are Used in Sensors

1) **Semiconductors** have a **higher resistivity** than **metals** because there are fewer **charge carriers** available (see page 43).

2) However, if **energy** is supplied to some types of semiconductor (e.g. by increasing their temperature), **more charge carriers** are **released**, so the current increases (as $I = nqvA$) and their resistance and resistivity **decrease**.

3) This means that they can make **excellent sensors** for detecting **changes** in their **environment**. You need to know about **three** semiconductor components — **thermistors**, **LDRs** and **diodes** (see the next page).

Like metals, increasing the temperature of semiconductors increases their lattice vibrations, reducing the mean drift velocity of electrons. But this effect is dwarfed by the effect of releasing more charge carriers with increasing temperature.

I-V Characteristics

The **Resistance** of a **Thermistor** Depends on **Temperature**

Thermistor circuit symbol:

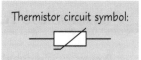

A **thermistor** is a **resistor** with a **resistance** that depends on its **temperature**. You only need to know about **NTC** thermistors — NTC stands for 'Negative Temperature Coefficient'. This means that the **resistance decreases** as the **temperature goes up**.

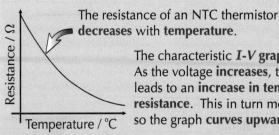

The resistance of an NTC thermistor **decreases** with **temperature**.

The characteristic **I-V graph** for an NTC thermistor looks like this: As the voltage **increases**, the current **increases**. More current leads to an **increase in temperature** and so a **decrease in resistance**. This in turn means more current can flow, so the graph **curves upwards**.

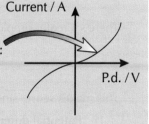

Warming the thermistor gives more **electrons** enough **energy** to **escape** from their atoms. This means that there are **more charge carriers** available, so the **current increases** and the **resistance decreases** ($R = V/I$).

The **Resistance** of an **LDR** Depends on **Light Intensity**

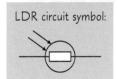

LDR circuit symbol:

LDR stands for **Light-Dependent Resistor**. The **greater** the intensity of **light** shining on an LDR, the **lower** its **resistance**.

The explanation for this is similar to that for the thermistor. In this case, **light** provides the **energy** that releases more electrons. This means more charge carriers, which means a higher current and a lower resistance.

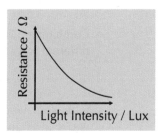

Diodes Only Let **Current Flow** in **One Direction**

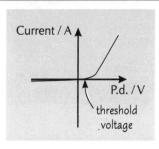

Diodes (including light-emitting diodes (LEDs)) are designed to let **current flow** in **one direction** only. You don't need to be able to explain how they work, just what they do.

1) **Forward bias** is the **direction** in which the **current** is **allowed to flow**. It's the direction of the arrow in the circuit symbol.

Diode circuit symbol:

2) **Most** diodes require a **threshold voltage** of about **0.6 V** in the **forward direction** before they will conduct.

LED circuit symbol:

3) In **reverse bias**, the **resistance** of the diode is **very high** and the current that flows is **very tiny**.

Practice Questions

Q1 If an *I-V* graph is a straight line through the origin, what does this tell you about the resistance?
Q2 Draw an *I-V* characteristic graph for a resistor.
Q3 What is an LDR?
Q4 Draw an *I-V* characteristic graph for a diode. Label the areas of forward bias and reverse bias.

Exam Question

Q1 a) Sketch a characteristic *I-V* graph for a filament lamp. [1 mark]

b) Explain how increasing the voltage across a filament lamp affects its resistance, with reference to the mean drift velocity of electrons in the lamp. [4 marks]

c) Explain how the resistance of an NTC thermistor changes with temperature. [3 marks]

You light up my world like an LED — with One-Directional current...

Make sure you learn all these graphs and can explain them all. It's all about energy — for metals, more energy means more heat and a higher resistance. For semiconductors, more energy means more charge carriers and lower resistance.

Electrical Energy and Power

Power and energy are pretty familiar concepts — and here they are again. Same principles, just different equations.

Power is the Rate of Transfer of Energy

Power (*P*) is **defined** as the **rate** of **doing work**. It's measured in **watts (W)**, where **1 watt** is equivalent to **1 joule of work done per second**.

in symbols: $P = \dfrac{W}{t}$

There's a really simple formula for **power** in **electrical circuits**:

$$P = VI$$

In an electrical circuit, W is the work done moving a charge.

This makes sense, since:

1) **Potential difference** (*V*) is defined as the **work done** per **coulomb**.
2) **Current** (*I*) is defined as the **number** of **coulombs** transferred per **second**.
3) So **p.d.** × **current** is **work done per second**, i.e. **power**.

You also know (from the definition of **resistance**) that *V* = *IR* (see p.44). **Combining** this with the equation above gives you loads of **different ways** to **calculate power**.

$$P = VI \qquad P = \dfrac{V^2}{R} \qquad P = I^2R$$

Obviously, which equation you should use depends on what **quantities** you're given in the **question**.

Arnold had a pretty high resistance to doing work.

Example: A robotic mutant Santa from the future converts 750 J of electrical energy into heat every second.

a) What is the operating power of the robotic mutant Santa?

b) All of the robotic mutant Santa's components are connected in series, with a total resistance of 30 Ω. What current flows through his wire veins?

a) Power = $W \div t$ = 750 ÷ 1 = **750 W**   b) $P = I^2R$ so $I = \sqrt{\dfrac{P}{R}} = \sqrt{\dfrac{750}{30}} = \sqrt{25} = $ **5.0 A**

Energy is Easy to Calculate if you Know the Power

Sometimes it's the **total energy** transferred that you're interested in. In this case you simply need to **multiply** the **power** by the **time**. So:

$W = VIt$ (or $W = \dfrac{V^2}{R}t$ or $W = I^2Rt$)

Make sure that the time is in seconds before you use these equations.

Example: The circuit diagram on the right is part of an electric kettle. A current of 4.0 A flows through the kettle's heating element once it is connected to the mains (230 V).

The kettle takes 4.5 minutes to boil the water it contains. How much energy does the kettle's heating element transfer to the water in the time it takes to boil?

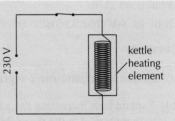

kettle heating element

Time the kettle takes to boil in seconds = 4.5 × 60 = 270 seconds.

Use the equation *W* = *VIt* = 230 × 4.0 × 270 = 248 400 J = **250 kJ (to 2 s.f.)**

Remember, this is the circuit symbol for an open switch:

This is a closed switch:

Electrical Energy and Power

You can Investigate the Power Output of an Electric Motor

1) Attach a mass, **m**, to a motor, as shown on the right, and connect the motor to the **circuit** shown. When you close the switch, the motor will **turn on**, winding the string around the axle and **raising the mass**.

2) Record the **time taken**, **t**, for the motor to raise the mass a **set distance**, **Δh**, e.g. 50 cm, using a **stopwatch** and the metre ruler.

3) Calculate the **work done against gravity** by the motor to raise the mass using the equation: $\Delta E_{grav} = mg\Delta h$ (see p.36).

4) You can then calculate the **power output** of the motor, using the equation $P = W/t$ (p.48).

5) You could also investigate the **efficiency** of the motor when lifting a given mass using this equipment. You'd need to measure the **potential difference** across the motor, and the **current** through it, as it lifts the load (see the circuit diagram on the right). You could then calculate the input power using $P = VI$.

6) You could then calculate the efficiency of the motor using the equation: **Efficiency = (useful power output ÷ total power input)** (see page 37). The motor won't be **100% efficient** as some energy will be lost, e.g. as heat to **resistance** in the circuit components.

7) You could also use this apparatus to investigate whether the power input and power output of the motor **varies** with the **load** attached to it by **varying the mass** attached to it.

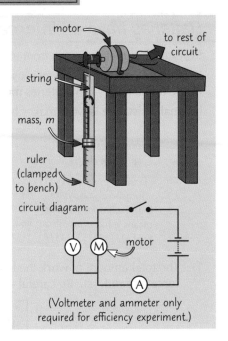

(Voltmeter and ammeter only required for efficiency experiment.)

Practice Questions

Q1 Power is measured in watts. What is 1 watt equivalent to?

Q2 What equation links power, voltage and resistance?

Q3 Write down the equation linking power, current and resistance.

Q4 Describe how you could investigate the power output of an electric motor when raising different loads.

Exam Questions

Q1 The circuit diagram for a mains-powered hairdryer is shown below.

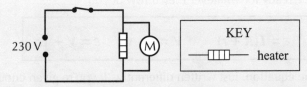

a) The heater has a power of 920 W in normal operation. Calculate the current in the heater. [1 mark]

b) The motor's resistance is 190 Ω. Calculate the current through the motor when the hairdryer is used. [1 mark]

c) Show that the total power of the hairdryer in normal operation is just under 1.2 kW. [2 marks]

Q2 A 12 V car battery supplies a current of 48 A for 2.0 seconds to the car's starter motor. The total resistance of the connecting wires is 0.010 Ω.

a) Calculate the energy transferred by the battery in this time. [1 mark]

b) Calculate the energy wasted as heat in the wires. [1 mark]

Ultimate cosmic powers...

Another load of equations on these pages to add to your collection, oh joy. Make sure you learn the circuit symbol for a heater in exam question 1 — you won't get a key in the exam (I gave you one because I'm nice).

E.m.f and Internal Resistance

There's resistance everywhere — inside batteries, in all the wires (although it's very small) and in the circuit components themselves. Who said current had it easy?

Batteries have an Internal Resistance

Resistance in metals comes from **electrons colliding** with **atoms** (or ions) and **losing energy** (see p.46).

In a **battery**, **chemical energy** is used to make **electrons move**. As they move, they collide with atoms inside the battery — so batteries **must** have resistance. This is called **internal resistance**.

Internal resistance is what makes **batteries** and **cells warm up** when they're used.

Because the resistance of wires is so small, on these two pages I'm assuming they have zero resistance.

Chemical reactions in the battery produce electrical energy.

Internal resistance (*r*)

In general, r is typically less than 1 ohm for a battery. This means a high current can flow.

Load resistance is the total resistance of all the components in the external circuit. You might see it called 'external resistance'.

Load resistance (**R**)

1) The total amount of **work** the battery does on each **coulomb** of charge is called its **electromotive force** or **e.m.f.** (ε). Be careful — e.m.f. **isn't** actually a force. It's measured in **volts**.

$$W = \varepsilon Q \quad \text{or} \quad \varepsilon = \frac{W}{Q}$$

W is the work done on the charge (i.e. the energy transferred to the charge) in joules.

2) The **potential difference** across the **load resistance** (*R*) is the **work done** when **one coulomb** of charge flows through the **load resistance**. This potential difference is called the **terminal p.d.** (*V*).

3) If there was **no internal resistance**, the **terminal p.d.** would be the **same** as the **e.m.f.** However, in **real** power supplies, there's **always some energy lost** overcoming the internal resistance.

4) The **energy wasted per coulomb** overcoming the internal resistance is called the **lost volts** (*v*).

Conservation of energy tells us:

| energy per coulomb supplied by the source | = | energy per coulomb used in load resistance | + | energy per coulomb wasted in internal resistance |

There are Loads of Calculations with E.m.f. and Internal Resistance

Examiners can ask you to do **calculations** with **e.m.f.** and **internal resistance** in loads of **different** ways. You've got to be ready for whatever they throw at you.

$$\varepsilon = V + v \qquad \varepsilon = I(R + r) \qquad V = \varepsilon - v \qquad \varepsilon = V + Ir$$

These are all basically the **same equation**, just written differently. If you're given enough information you can calculate the e.m.f. (ε), terminal p.d. (*V*), lost volts (*v*), current (*I*), load resistance (*R*) or internal resistance (*r*). Which equation you should use depends on what information you've got, and what you need to calculate.

You Can Work Out the E.m.f. of Multiple Cells in Series or Parallel

For cells **in series**, you can calculate the **total e.m.f.** of the cells by **adding** their individual e.m.f.s.

$$\varepsilon_{total} = \varepsilon_1 + \varepsilon_2 + \varepsilon_3 + ...$$

This makes sense if you think about it, because each charge goes through each of the cells and so gains e.m.f. from each one.

For identical cells **in parallel**, the **total e.m.f.** of the combination of cells is the **same size** as the e.m.f. of each of the individual cells.

See p.52 for all the rules for parallel and series circuits.

$$\varepsilon_{total} = \varepsilon_1 = \varepsilon_2 = \varepsilon_3 = ...$$

This is because the current will split equally between identical cells. The charge only gains e.m.f. from the cells it travels through — so the overall e.m.f. in the circuit doesn't increase.

E.m.f and Internal Resistance

Time for an Example *E.m.f. Calculation Question*...

Example Three identical cells each with an e.m.f. of 2.0 V and an internal resistance of 0.20 Ω are connected in parallel in the circuit shown to the right. A current of 0.90 A is flowing through the circuit. Calculate the total p.d. across the cells.

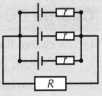

First calculate the lost volts, v, for 1 cell using $v = Ir$.

Since the current flowing through the circuit is split equally between each of the three cells, the current through one cell is $I/3$. So for 1 cell: $v = I/3 \times r = 0.90/3 \times 0.20 = 0.30 \times 0.20 = 0.06$ V

Then find the terminal p.d. across 1 cell using the equation: $V = \varepsilon - v = 2 - 0.06 = 1.94$

So the total p.d. across the cells combined = **1.9 V (to 2 s.f.)**

Investigate *Internal Resistance* and *E.m.f.* With This *Circuit*

1) **Vary** the **current** in the circuit by changing the value of the **load resistance** (*R*) using the variable resistor. **Measure** the **p.d.** (*V*) for several different values of **current** (*I*).

2) Record your data for *V* and *I* in a table, and **plot the results** in a graph of *V* against *I*.

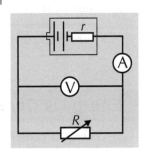

To find the **e.m.f.** and **internal resistance** of the cell, start with the equation: $\boxed{\varepsilon = V + Ir}$

1) Rearrange to give $V = -rI + \varepsilon$

2) Since ε and *r* are constants, that's just the equation of a **straight line**:

> **Equation of a straight line**
> $$y = mx + c$$
> gradient   y-intercept

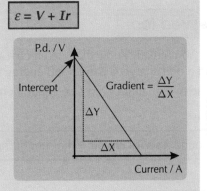

3) So the intercept on the vertical axis is ε.

4) And the gradient is $-r$.

You probably don't need to take repeated readings in an experiment like this one, but make sure you get plenty of data points to draw your line.

An **easier** way to **measure** the **e.m.f.** of a **power source** to just connect a **voltmeter** across its **terminals**. Voltmeters have a very **high resistance**, but a **small current** will still flow through them. This means there must be some **lost volts**, which means you measure a value **very slightly less** than the **e.m.f.** (Although in practice the difference isn't usually significant.)

Practice Questions

Q1 What causes internal resistance? Write down the equation linking work, e.m.f. and charge.

Q2 What is the difference between e.m.f. and terminal p.d.?

Q3 What is meant by 'lost volts'?

Q4 Give an example of a source of e.m.f and describe an experiment to find the value of its e.m.f.

Exam Questions

Q1 A battery with an internal resistance of 0.8 Ω and an e.m.f. of 24 V powers a dentist's drill with resistance 4.0 Ω.

    a) Calculate the current in the circuit when the drill is connected to the power supply. [1 mark]

    b) Calculate the voltage across the drill while it is being used. [1 mark]

Q2 A bulb of resistance *R* is powered by two cells connected in series, each with internal resistance *r* and e.m.f. ε. Which expression represents the current flowing through each cell? [1 mark]

    A $\dfrac{\varepsilon}{R+r}$ **B** $\dfrac{\varepsilon}{2(R+2r)}$ **C** $\dfrac{2\varepsilon}{R+2r}$ **D** $\dfrac{\varepsilon}{R+2r}$

Why'd the physicist swallow a multimeter? To find his internal resistance...

Thank you, thank you, I'm here all week. A jam-packed pair of pages here, but it's all stuff you need to know. Make sure you know the difference between terminal p.d. and e.m.f., and that you've got a handle on all those equations.

Conservation of Charge & Energy in Circuits

There are some things in Physics that are so fundamental that you just have to accept them. Like the fact that there's loads of Maths in it. And that energy is conserved. And that Physicists get more homework than everyone else.

Charge Doesn't 'Leak Away' Anywhere — it's Conserved

1) As **charge flows** through a circuit, it **doesn't** get **used up** or **lost**.

2) This means that whatever charge flows **into** a junction will flow **out** again.

3) Since **current** is **rate of flow of charge**, it follows that whatever current flows **into** a junction is the same as the current flowing **out** of it.

> **Example:** 6 coulombs of charge flow into a junction in 1 second, and split in the ratio 1:2.
>
> $$Q_1 = 6\,C \Rightarrow I_1 = 6\,A$$
> at junction, current branches in two
> $$Q_2 = 2\,C \Rightarrow I_2 = 2\,A$$
> $$Q_3 = 4\,C \Rightarrow I_3 = 4\,A$$
> $$I_1 = I_2 + I_3$$

Kirchhoff's first law says:

> The total **current entering a junction** = the total **current leaving it.**

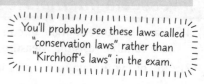
You'll probably see these laws called "conservation laws" rather than "Kirchhoff's laws" in the exam.

Energy is Conserved too

1) **Energy is conserved.** You already know that. In **electrical circuits**, **energy** is **transferred round** the circuit. Energy **transferred to** a unit charge is **e.m.f.**, and energy **transferred from** a unit charge is **potential difference**.

2) In a **closed loop**, these two quantities must be **equal** if energy is conserved (which it is).

Kirchhoff's second law says:

> The **total e.m.f.** around a **series circuit** = the **sum** of the **p.d.**s across each component. (or $\varepsilon = \Sigma IR$ in symbols)

The Conservation Laws Apply to Different Combinations of Resistors

A **typical exam question** will give you a **circuit** with bits of information missing, leaving you to fill in the gaps. Not the most fun... but on the plus side you get to ignore any internal resistance stuff (unless the question tells you otherwise)... hurrah. You need to remember the **following rules:**

Series Circuits:

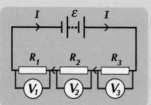

1) **same current** at **all points** of the circuit (since there are no junctions)

2) **e.m.f. split** between **components** (by Kirchhoff's 2nd law), so:
$$\varepsilon = V_1 + V_2 + V_3$$

3) $V = IR$, so if I is constant:
$$IR_{total} = IR_1 + IR_2 + IR_3$$

4) cancelling the Is gives:

> $$R_{total} = R_1 + R_2 + R_3$$

Parallel Circuits:

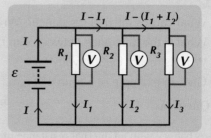

1) **current** is split at each **junction**, so: $I = I_1 + I_2 + I_3$

2) **same p.d.** across **all components** (remember that within a loop the e.m.f. equals the sum of individual p.d.s)

3) so, $V/R_{total} = V/R_1 + V/R_2 + V/R_3$

4) cancelling the Vs gives:

> $$\frac{1}{R_{total}} = \frac{1}{R_1} + \frac{1}{R_2} + \frac{1}{R_3}$$

...and there's an example on the next page to make sure you know what to do with all that...

Conservation of Charge & Energy in Circuits

Worked Exam Question

Example:

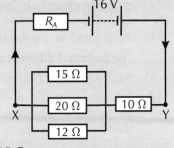

A battery with an e.m.f. of 16 V and negligible internal resistance is connected in a circuit as shown on the right. The resistances are all correct to 2 s.f..

a) Show that the group of resistors between X and Y could be replaced by a single resistor of resistance 15 Ω.

You can find the combined resistance of the 15 Ω, 20 Ω and 12 Ω resistors using:

$1/R = 1/R_1 + 1/R_2 + 1/R_3 = 1/15 + 1/20 + 1/12 = 1/5 \Rightarrow R = 5 \Omega$

So overall resistance between X and Y can be found by: $R = R_1 + R_2 = 5 + 10 = \mathbf{15\ \Omega}$

b) If $R_A = 20 \Omega$ (to 2 s.f.):
   i) calculate the potential difference across R_A.

Careful — there are a few steps here. You need the p.d. across R_A, but you don't know the current through it. So start there: total resistance in circuit $= 20 + 15 = 35 \Omega$,
so current through R_A can be found using $I = V_{total}/R_{total} = 16/35$ A
then you can use $V = IR_A$ to find the p.d. across R_A: $V = 16/35 \times 20 = \mathbf{9.1\ V\ (to\ 2\ s.f.)}$

   ii) calculate the current in the 15 Ω resistor.

You know the current flowing into the group of three resistors and out of it, but not through the individual branches. But you know that their combined resistance is 5 Ω from part a), so you can work out the p.d. across the group:

$V = IR = 16/35 \times 5 = 16/7$ V

The p.d. across the whole group is the same as the p.d. across each individual resistor, so you can use this to find the current through the 15 Ω resistor:

$I = V/R = (16/7) / 15 = \mathbf{0.15\ A\ (to\ 2\ s.f.)}$

Practice Questions

Q1 State Kirchhoff's first and second laws and state what quantity is conserved in each case.

Q2 Show how conservation of charge leads to the rule for combining resistors in series: $R_{total} = R_1 + R_2 + R_3$.

Q3 Show how conservation of energy leads to the rule for combining resistors in parallel: $\frac{1}{R_{total}} = \frac{1}{R_1} + \frac{1}{R_2} + \frac{1}{R_3}$.

Q4 Find the current through and potential difference across each of two 5 Ω resistors when they are placed in a circuit containing a 5 V battery, and are wired: a) in series, b) in parallel.

Exam Question

Q1 For the circuit on the right:

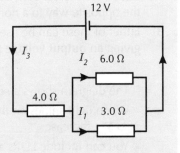

a) Calculate the total effective resistance of the three resistors in this combination. [2 marks]

b) Calculate the main current, I_3. [1 mark]

c) Calculate the potential difference across the 4.0 Ω resistor. [1 mark]

d) Calculate the potential difference across the parallel pair of resistors. [1 mark]

e) Calculate the currents I_1 and I_2. [2 marks]

Conservation of energy is really important — time for a nap I think...

$V = IR$ is the formula you'll use most often in these questions. Make sure you know whether you're using it on the overall circuit, or just one specific component. It's amazingly easy to get muddled up — you've been warned.

The Potential Divider

I remember the days when potential dividers were pretty much the hardest thing they could throw at you.
Then along came A level Physics. Hey ho. Anyway, in context this doesn't seem too hard now, so get stuck in.

Use a **Potential Divider** to get a **Fraction** of a **Source Voltage**

1) At its simplest, a **potential divider** is a circuit with a **voltage source** and a couple of **resistors** in series.

2) The **potential difference** across the voltage source (e.g. a battery) is **split** in the **ratio** of the **resistances** (p.52).

3) So, if you had a **2 Ω** resistor and a **3 Ω** resistor, you'd get **2/5** of the p.d. across the **2 Ω** resistor and **3/5** across the **3 Ω**

4) You can use potential dividers to supply a potential difference, V_{out}, between **zero** and the potential difference across the voltage source. This can be useful, e.g. if you need a **varying** p.d. supply or one that is at a **lower p.d.** than the voltage source.

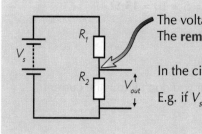

The voltage has **dropped** by V_1 (the voltage across R_1) by the time it gets to here. The **remaining voltage** that can be supplied, e.g. to another component, is V_{out}.

In the circuit shown, R_2 has $\dfrac{R_2}{R_1 + R_2}$ of the total resistance. So: $\boxed{V_{out} = \dfrac{R_2}{R_1 + R_2} V_s}$

E.g. if $V_s = 9$ V and you want V_{out} to be 6 V, then you need:

$$\frac{R_2}{R_1 + R_2} = \frac{2}{3} \text{ which gives } R_2 = 2R_1$$

So you could have, say, $R_1 = 100\ \Omega,\ R_2 = 200\ \Omega$

5) This circuit is mainly used for **calibrating voltmeters**, which have a **very high resistance**.

6) If you put something with a **relatively low resistance** across R_2 though, you start to run into **problems**. You've **effectively** got **two resistors** in **parallel**, which will **always** have a **total** resistance **less than** R_2. That means that V_{out} will be **less** than you've calculated, and will depend on what's connected across R_2. Hrrumph.

Use a **Variable Resistor** to Vary the **Voltage**

If you replace R_1 with a **variable resistor**, you can change V_{out}. When $R_1 = 0$, $V_{out} = V_s$. As you increase R_1, V_{out} gets smaller.

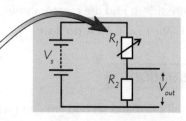

Add an **LDR** or **Thermistor** for a **Light** or **Temperature Sensor**

1) A **light-dependent resistor** (LDR) has a very **high resistance** in the **dark**, but a **lower resistance** in the **light**.

2) An **NTC thermistor** has a **high resistance** at **low temperatures**, but a much **lower resistance** at **high temperatures** (it varies in the opposite way to a normal resistor, only much more so).

3) Either of these can be used as one of the **resistors** in a **potential divider**, giving an **output voltage** that **varies** with the **light level** or **temperature**.

See page 47 for why the resistances of LDRs and NTC thermistors change like this.

The diagram shows a **sensor** used to detect **light levels**.

When light shines on the LDR its **resistance decreases**, so V_{out} increases.

You can include LDRs and thermistors in circuits that control **switches**, e.g. to turn on a light or a heating system.

If you replace the LDR with an NTC thermistor, V_{out} will increase with temperature.

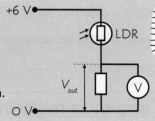

The Potential Divider

A *Potentiometer* uses a *Variable Resistor* to give a *Variable Voltage*

1) Imagine you have a long length of wire connected to a power supply. If the wire is **uniform** (i.e. same cross-sectional area and material throughout), then its **resistance** is **proportional** to its **length**.

2) This means that if you were to connect a voltmeter across different lengths of the wire, the **potential difference** you'd record would be **proportional** to the **length** you'd connected it over — you're measuring across a bigger share of the total resistance so you get a bigger potential difference.

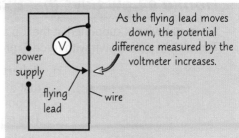

As the flying lead moves down, the potential difference measured by the voltmeter increases.

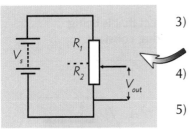

3) This is the basis of how a **potentiometer** works. A **potentiometer** is basically a potential divider, with a variable resistor replacing R_1 and R_2 (it's even sometimes **called** a potential divider just to confuse things).

4) You move a **slider** or turn a knob to **adjust** the **relative sizes** of R_1 and R_2. That way you can vary V_{out} from **0 V** up to the source voltage.

5) This is dead handy when you want to be able to **change** a **voltage continuously**, like in the **volume control** of a stereo:

I've often wished bagpipes had a volume control. Or just an off switch.

Example:
Here, V_s is replaced by the input signal (e.g. from a CD player) and V_{out} is the output to the amplifier and loudspeaker.

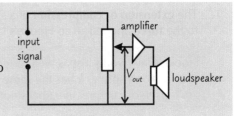

Practice Questions

Q1 Look at the light sensor circuit on page 54.
How could you change the circuit so that it could be used to detect temperature changes?

Q2 The LDR in the circuit on page 54 has a resistance of 300 Ω when in light conditions, and 900 Ω in dark conditions. The fixed resistor has a value of 100 Ω. Show that V_{out} (light) = 1.5 V and V_{out} (dark) = 0.6 V.

Exam Questions

Q1 In the circuit on the right, all the resistors have the same value. Calculate the p.d. between:

a) A and B. [1 mark]

b) A and C. [1 mark]

c) B and C. [1 mark]

Q2 Look at the circuit on the right. All the resistances are given to 2 significant figures.

a) Calculate the p.d. between A and B as shown by a high resistance voltmeter placed between the two points. [1 mark]

b) A 40.0 Ω resistor is now placed between points A and B. Calculate the p.d. across AB and the current flowing through the 40.0 Ω resistor. [4 marks]

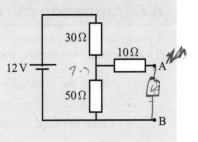

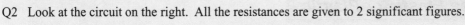

OI... YOU... [bang bang bang]... turn that potentiometer down...

You'll probably have to use a potentiometer in every experiment you do with electricity from now on in, so you'd better get used to them. I can't stand the things myself, but then lab and me don't mix — far too technical.

Hooke's Law

Hooke's law applies to all materials, but only up to a point. For some materials that point is so tiny you wouldn't notice...

Hooke's Law *Says that* Extension *is* Proportional *to* Force

If a **metal wire** is supported at the top and then a weight attached to the bottom, it **stretches**.
The weight pulls down with force **F**, producing an equal and opposite force at the support.

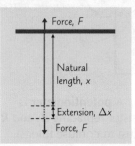

1) **Robert Hooke** discovered in the 17th century that the extension of a stretched wire, Δx, is proportional to the change in load or force, ΔF. This relationship is now called **Hooke's law**.

2) Hooke's law can be written:

$$\Delta F = k\Delta x$$

Where k is the stiffness of the object that is being stretched. k is also called the **spring constant**. It has units of Nm^{-1}.

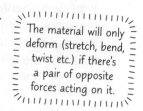

The material will only deform (stretch, bend, twist etc.) if there's a pair of opposite forces acting on it.

Hooke's Law *Also Applies to* Springs

A metal spring also changes length when you apply a **pair of opposite forces**.

1) The **extension** or **compression** of a spring is **proportional** to the **force** applied — so Hooke's law applies.

Hooke's law works just as well for **compressive** forces as **tensile** forces. For a spring, k has the **same value** whether the forces are tensile or compressive (that's not true for all materials).

2) **Hooke's Law** doesn't just apply to metal **springs** and **wires** — most **other materials** obey it up to a point.

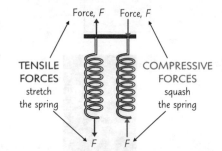

TENSILE FORCES
stretch the spring

COMPRESSIVE FORCES
squash the spring

Tensile forces create <u>tension</u> in a stretched spring. Compressive forces create compression in a squashed spring. Tensile or compressive forces in the spring act in the opposite direction to the tensile or compressive forces stretching or squashing it.

Hooke's Law *Stops Working* when the *Load is* Great Enough

There's a **limit** to the force you can apply for Hooke's law to stay true.

1) The graph shows force against extension for a **typical metal wire** or **spring**.

2) The first part of the graph (up to point P) shows Hooke's law being obeyed — there's a **straight-line relationship** between **force** and **extension**.

3) When the force becomes great enough, the graph starts to **curve**. **Metals** generally obey Hooke's law up to the **limit of proportionality, P**.

4) The point marked **E** on the graph is called the **elastic limit**. If you exceed the elastic limit, the material will be **permanently stretched**. When all the force is removed, the material will be **longer** than at the start.

5) Be careful — there are some materials, like **rubber**, that only obey Hooke's law for **really small** extensions.

A Deformation *can be* Elastic *or* Plastic

A material will show elastic deformation **up to** its **elastic limit**, and plastic deformation **beyond** it.
If a **deformation** is **elastic**, the material returns to its **original shape** once the forces are removed.

1) When the material is put under **tension**, the **atoms** of the material are **pulled apart** from one another.

2) Atoms can **move** slightly relative to their **equilibrium positions**, without changing position in the material.

3) Once the **load** is **removed**, the atoms **return** to their **equilibrium** distance apart.

If a deformation is **plastic**, the material is **permanently stretched**.

1) Some atoms in the material move position relative to one another.

2) When the load is removed, the **atoms don't return** to their original positions.

Extension and compression are sometimes called <u>tensile deformation</u> and <u>compressive deformation</u>.

Hooke's Law

Investigating Extension

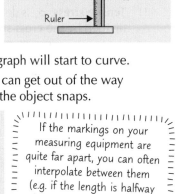
Object being tested — Clamp and clamp stand — Weights — Ruler

1) Set up the experiment shown in the diagram. Support the object being tested at the top (e.g. with a clamp) and measure its original (natural) length with a ruler.

2) Add weights one at a time to the bottom of the object.

3) After each weight is added, measure the new length of the object, then **calculate the extension**:

> **extension = new length – original length**

4) Plot a graph of **force** (weight) against **extension** for your results. Where the line of best fit is **straight**, then the object obeys Hooke's law and the gradient = **k** (as $\Delta F = k\Delta x$). If you've loaded the object beyond its limit of proportionality, the graph will start to curve.

5) Make sure you carry out the experiment **safely**. You should be **standing up** so you can get out of the way quickly if the weights fall, and wearing **safety goggles** to protect your eyes in case the object snaps.

Example: A student investigates extension using the set-up shown above, and plots their results on the graph below. Find the stiffness of the object being stretched.

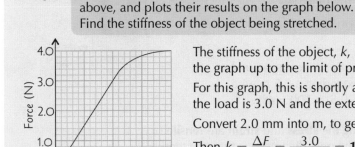
Graph: Force (N) on y-axis (1.0 to 4.0), Extension (mm) on x-axis (1.0 to 4.0)

If the markings on your measuring equipment are quite far apart, you can often interpolate between them (e.g. if the length is halfway between the markings for 2 mm and 3 mm you could record it as 2.5 mm). But it's better to use something with a finer scale if you can.

The stiffness of the object, k, is the gradient of the graph up to the limit of proportionality.

For this graph, this is shortly after the point where the load is 3.0 N and the extension is 2.0 mm.

Convert 2.0 mm into m, to get 0.0020 m.

Then $k = \dfrac{\Delta F}{\Delta x} = \dfrac{3.0}{0.0020} = $ **1500 Nm^{-1}**.

To measure an extension as accurately as possible, make sure you fix a ruler close to the extending object and take readings with your eye close to the ruler. It's a good idea to use a 'fiducial marker' (a thin tag on the object that marks where you're measuring) and a set square to ensure the ruler is vertical. Make sure the marker and ruler are both at eye level when you take readings.

Practice Questions

Q1 State Hooke's law and explain what is meant by the elastic limit of a material.

Q2 Define tensile forces and compressive forces.

Q3 From studying the force-extension graph for a material as it is loaded and unloaded, how can you tell:
   a) if Hooke's law is being obeyed,   b) if the elastic limit has been reached?

Q4 What is meant by plastic deformation of a material?

Q5 Describe how you could determine the stiffness of an object being stretched, k, experimentally.

Exam Questions

Q1 A metal guitar string stretches 4.0 mm when a 10.0 N force is applied.

   a) If the string obeys Hooke's law, calculate how far the string will stretch when a 15 N force is applied.   [1 mark]

   b) Calculate the stiffness for this string in Nm^{-1}.   [1 mark]

   c) The string is then stretched beyond its elastic limit. Describe the effect this will have on the string.   [1 mark]

Q2 A rubber band is 6.0 cm long. When it is loaded with 2.5 N, its length becomes 10.4 cm. Further loading increases the length to 16.2 cm when the force is 5.0 N.

   State whether the rubber band obeys Hooke's law when the force on it is 5.0 N. Explain your answer.   [2 marks]

Sod's Law — if you don't learn it, it'll be in the exam...

Three things you didn't know about Robert Hooke — he was the first person to use the word 'cell' (as in biology, not prisons), he helped Christopher Wren with his designs for St. Paul's Cathedral and no-one's sure what he looked like. I'd like to think that if I did all that stuff, then someone would at least remember what I looked like — poor old Hooke.

Stress, Strain and Elastic Strain Energy

How much a material stretches for a particular applied force depends on its dimensions. If you want to compare it to another material, you need to use stress and strain instead. A stress-strain graph is the same for any sample of a particular material — the size of the sample doesn't matter.

A Stress Causes a Strain

A material subjected to a pair of **opposite forces** might **deform** (i.e. **change shape**).
If the forces **stretch** the material, they're **tensile**. If the forces **squash** the material, they're **compressive**.

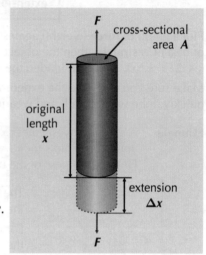

1) **Tensile stress**, σ, is defined as the **force applied**, F,
   divided by the **cross-sectional area**, A:

   $$\sigma = \frac{F}{A}$$

   The **units** of stress are **Nm⁻²** or pascals, **Pa**.

2) **Tensile strain**, ε, is defined as the **change in length** (i.e. the
   extension), divided by the **original length** of the material:

   $$\varepsilon = \frac{\Delta x}{x}$$

   Strain has **no units**, it's just a **ratio** and is usually written as a **number**.
   It can also be written as a **percentage**, e.g. extending a 0.5 m wire
   by 0.02 m would produce a strain of $(0.02 \div 0.5) \times 100 = 4\%$.

3) It doesn't matter whether the forces producing the **stress** and **strain** are **tensile** or
   compressive — the **same equations** apply. The only difference is that you tend to
   think of **tensile** forces as **positive**, and **compressive** forces as **negative**.

A Stress Big Enough to Break the Material is Called the Breaking Stress

As a greater and greater tensile **force** is applied to a material, the **stress** on it **increases**.

1) The effect of the **stress** is to start to **pull** the
   atoms apart from one another.

2) Eventually the stress becomes **so great** that atoms
   separate completely, and the **material breaks**.
   This is shown by point **B** on the graph. The stress
   at which this occurs is called the **breaking stress**.

3) The point marked **UTS** on the graph is called the **ultimate tensile
   stress**. This is the **maximum stress** that the material can withstand.

4) Both **UTS** and **B** depend on conditions e.g. **temperature**.

5) **Engineers** have to consider the **UTS** and **breaking stress** of materials
   when designing a **structure** — e.g. they need to make sure the stress
   on a material won't reach the **UTS** when the **conditions change**.

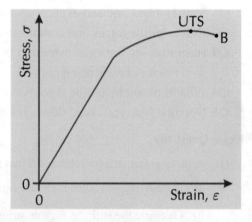

Elastic Strain Energy is the Area under a Force-Extension Graph

1) **Work** has to be done to **stretch** a material.

2) **Before** the **elastic limit** is reached, **all** this **work done** in
   stretching is **stored** as **elastic strain energy** in the material.

3) On a **graph** of **force against extension**, the elastic
   strain energy is given by the **area under the graph**.

4) If the force-extension graph is **non-linear**, you'll
   need to **estimate** the area by **counting squares** or
   dividing the curve into **trapeziums** (see page 25).

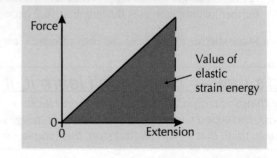

Stress, Strain and Elastic Strain Energy

You can Calculate the Energy Stored in a Stretched Material

Provided a material obeys Hooke's law, the **potential energy** stored inside it can be **calculated** quite easily.

1) The work done on the material in stretching it is equal to the energy stored.

2) **Work done** equals **force × displacement**.

3) However, the **force** on the material **isn't constant**. It rises from zero up to force F. To calculate the **work done**, use the **average force** between zero and F, i.e. $\frac{1}{2}F$: ➡ | **work done = $\frac{1}{2}F\Delta x$** |

4) So the **elastic strain energy** stored, E_{el}, is: | $\Delta E_{el} = \frac{1}{2}F\Delta x$ | ⬅ 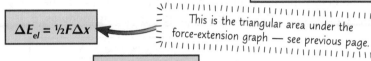 This is the triangular area under the force-extension graph — see previous page.

5) Because Hooke's law is being obeyed, $\Delta F = k\Delta x$, which means F can be replaced in the equation to give: | $\Delta E_{el} = \frac{1}{2}k\Delta x^2$ |

> **Example:** A metal wire is 55.0 cm long. A force of 550 N is applied to the wire, and the wire stretches. The length of the stretched wire is 56.5 cm. Calculate the elastic strain energy stored in the wire.
>
> The extension of the wire is $\Delta x = 56.5$ cm $- 55.0$ cm $= 1.5$ cm $= 0.015$ m
> So the elastic strain energy $\Delta E_{el} = \frac{1}{2} \times F \times \Delta x$
> $\qquad\qquad\qquad\qquad = \frac{1}{2} \times 550 \times 0.015 = 4.125$ J $= $ **4.1 J (to 2 s.f.)**

Practice Questions

Q1 Write a definition for tensile stress.

Q2 Explain what is meant by the tensile strain on a material.

Q3 What is meant by the breaking stress of a material?

Q4 How can the elastic strain energy in a material under load be found from its force-extension graph?

Q5 The work done is usually calculated as force multiplied by displacement.
Explain why the work done in stretching a wire is $\frac{1}{2}F\Delta x$.

Exam Questions

Q1 A steel wire is 2.00 m long. When a 300 N (to 3 s.f.) force is applied to the wire, it stretches by 4.0 mm.
The wire has a circular cross-section with a diameter of 1.0 mm.
a) Calculate the tensile stress in the wire. [2 marks]
b) Calculate the tensile strain of the wire. [1 mark]

Q2 A copper wire (which obeys Hooke's law) is stretched by 3.0 mm when a force of 50.0 N is applied.
a) Calculate the stiffness of this wire in Nm⁻¹. [2 marks]
b) Calculate the value of the elastic strain energy in the stretched wire. [1 mark]

Q3 A force is applied to stretch an unknown material.
The graph shows the force-extension graph for this stretch.
Estimate the elastic strain energy stored in the material as a
result of this stretch.

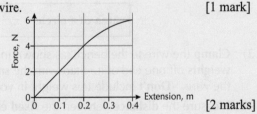

[2 marks]

Q4 A pinball machine contains a spring which is used to fire a small, light metal ball to start the game.
The spring has a stiffness of 40.8 Nm⁻¹. It is compressed by 5.00 cm and then released to fire the ball. Calculate
the maximum possible kinetic energy of the ball. [3 marks]

UTS a laugh a minute, this stuff...

...or it would be, if there were more jokes. But you know what they say — a stress causes a strain, and nobody likes strained jokes. So you'd better just get on with learning this stuff proper good like. And before you ask, no — grabbing a slingshot and shooting the neighbours' begonias __doesn't__ count as 'revising the energy stored in a stretched material'.

The Young Modulus

Busy chap, Thomas Young. He did this work on tensile stress as something of a sideline. Light was his main thing.
He proved that light behaved like a wave, explained how we see in colour and worked out what causes astigmatism.

The **Young Modulus** is Stress ÷ Strain

When you apply a **load** to stretch a material, it experiences a **tensile stress** and a **tensile strain**.

1) Up to the **limit of proportionality** (see p.56), the stress and strain of a material are proportional to each other.

2) So below this limit, for a particular material, stress divided by strain is a **constant**. This constant is called the **Young modulus**, **E**.

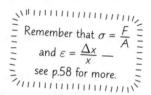
Remember that $\sigma = \frac{F}{A}$
and $\varepsilon = \frac{\Delta x}{x}$ —
see p.58 for more.

$$\text{Young modulus} = E = \frac{\text{stress}}{\text{strain}} = \frac{\sigma}{\varepsilon}$$
Where σ = stress and ε = strain

3) The **units** of the Young modulus are the same as stress (**Nm⁻²** or pascals), since strain has no units.

4) The Young modulus is a measure of the **stiffness** of a material. It is used by **engineers** to make sure the materials they are using can withstand sufficient forces.

To **Find** the Young Modulus, You need a **Very Long Wire**

This is the experiment you're most likely to do in class:

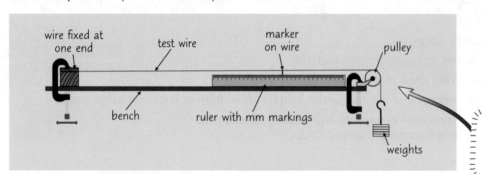

wire fixed at one end | test wire | marker on wire | pulley | bench | ruler with mm markings | weights

"Okay, found one. Now what?"

1) The test wire should be thin, and as long as possible. The **longer and thinner** the wire, the more it **extends** for the same force — this reduces the percentage uncertainty in your measurements.

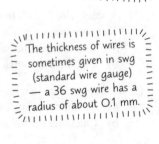
Mum moment: if you're doing this experiment, wear safety goggles — if the wire snaps, it could get very messy...

2) First you need to find the **cross-sectional area** of the wire. Use a **micrometer** to measure the **diameter** of the wire in several places and take an **average** of your measurements. By assuming that the cross-section is **circular**, you can use the formula for the area of a circle:

$$\text{area of a circle} = \pi r^2$$

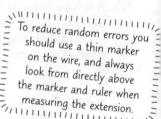
The thickness of wires is sometimes given in swg (standard wire gauge) — a 36 swg wire has a radius of about 0.1 mm.

3) **Clamp** the wire to the bench (as shown in the diagram above) so you can hang **weights** off one end of it. Start with the **smallest weight** necessary to **straighten** the wire. (**Don't** include this weight in your final calculations.)

4) Measure the **distance** between the **fixed end of the wire** and the **marker** — this is your unstretched length.

To reduce random errors you should use a thin marker on the wire, and always look from directly above the marker and ruler when measuring the extension.

5) Then if you increase the weight, the **wire stretches** and the **marker moves**.

6) **Increase** the **weight** in equal steps (e.g. 100 g intervals), recording the marker reading each time — the **extension** is the **difference** between this reading and the **unstretched length**. Because you can't take repeat readings (the wire might snap or be permanently stretched), you should take more readings than usual.

7) You can use your results from this experiment to calculate the **stress** and **strain** of the wire and plot a stress-strain curve (see next page).

(The other standard way of measuring the Young modulus in the lab is using **Searle's apparatus**. This is a bit more accurate, but it's harder to do and the equipment's more complicated.)

TOPIC 4 — MATERIALS

The Young Modulus

Use a *Stress-Strain Graph* to Find *E*

You can plot a **graph** of **stress against strain** from your results.

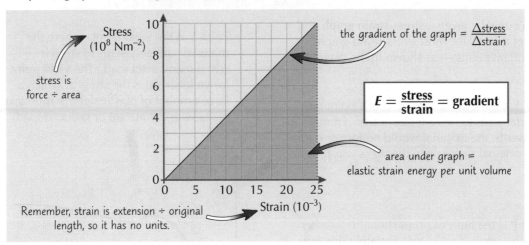

Stress (10⁸ Nm⁻²) ... stress is force ÷ area ... the gradient of the graph = $\frac{\Delta stress}{\Delta strain}$

$$E = \frac{\text{stress}}{\text{strain}} = \text{gradient}$$

area under graph = elastic strain energy per unit volume

Remember, strain is extension ÷ original length, so it has no units. Strain (10⁻³)

1) The **gradient** of the graph gives the Young modulus, **E**.

2) The **area under the graph** gives the **strain energy** (or energy stored) per unit volume, i.e. the energy stored per 1 m³ of wire.

3) The stress-strain graph is a **straight line** provided that Hooke's law is obeyed, so you can also calculate the energy per unit volume (Jm⁻³) as:

| energy per unit vol = ½ × stress × strain |

Example: The stress-strain graph above is for a thin metal wire. Find the Young modulus of the wire from the graph.

E = stress ÷ strain = gradient

The gradient of the graph = $\frac{\Delta \text{stress}}{\Delta \text{strain}} = \frac{10 \times 10^8}{25 \times 10^{-3}}$

$= 4 \times 10^{10} \text{ Nm}^{-2}$

Practice Questions

Q1 Define the Young modulus for a material. What are the units for the Young modulus?

Q2 Describe an experiment to find the Young modulus of a test wire. Explain why a thin test wire should be used.

Q3 What is given by the area contained under a stress-strain graph?

Exam Questions

Q1 A steel wire is stretched elastically. For a load of 80.0 N, the wire extends by 3.6 mm.
The original length of the wire was 2.50 m and its average diameter is 0.60 mm.
Calculate the value of the Young modulus for steel. [4 marks]

Q2 Two wires, A and B, are stretched elastically under a load of 50.0 N. The original length and the extension of both wires under this load are the same. The Young modulus of wire A is found to be 7.0×10^{10} Nm⁻².
The cross-sectional area of wire B is half that of wire A. Calculate the Young modulus of wire B. [2 marks]

Q3 The Young modulus for copper is 1.3×10^{11} Nm⁻².

a) The stress on a copper wire is 2.6×10^8 Nm⁻². Calculate the strain on the wire. [2 marks]

b) The load applied to the copper wire is 100 N (to 3 s.f.). Calculate the cross-sectional area of the wire. [2 marks]

c) Calculate the strain energy per unit volume for this loaded wire. [2 marks]

Learn that experiment — it's important...

Getting back to the good Dr Young... As if ground-breaking work in light, the physics of vision and materials science wasn't enough, he was also a well-respected physician, a linguist and an Egyptologist. He was one of the first to try to decipher the Rosetta stone (he didn't get it right, but nobody's perfect). Makes you feel kind of inferior, doesn't it...

Stress-Strain and Force-Extension Graphs

I hope the stresses and strains of this section aren't getting to you too much.

There are **Three Important Points** on a **Stress-Strain Graph**

In the exam you could be given a **stress-strain graph** and asked to **interpret** it. Luckily, most stress-strain graphs share **three** important points — as shown in the **diagram**.

Point **Y** is the **yield point** — here the material suddenly starts to **stretch** without any extra load. The **yield point** (or yield stress) is the **stress** at which a large amount of **plastic deformation** takes place with a **constant** or **reduced load**.

Point **E** is the **elastic limit** — at this point the material starts to behave **plastically**. From point E onwards, the material would **no longer** return to its **original shape** once the stress was removed.

Point **P** is the **limit of proportionality** — after this, the graph is no longer a straight line but starts to **bend**. At this point, the material **stops** obeying **Hooke's law**, but would still **return** to its **original shape** if the stress was removed.

Before point **P**, the graph is a **straight line** through the **origin**. This shows that the material is obeying Hooke's law (page 56). The **gradient** of the line is constant — it's the **Young modulus** (see pages 60-61).

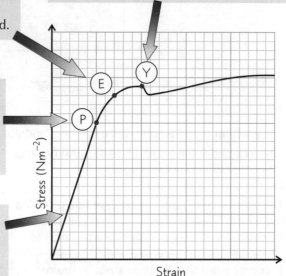

You might see the x-axis labelled as percentage strain instead — this is just the strain (a ratio) expressed as a percentage.

Stronger Materials can Withstand **More Stress** Before they **Break**

The graph below shows the stress-strain curves for materials of different strengths and stiffnesses.

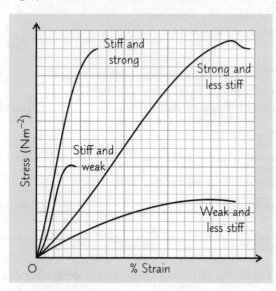

1) Different materials have different **breaking stresses** (p.58).
2) The **stronger** the material, the higher the breaking stress.
3) **Stiff** materials are difficult to stretch or compress. They have a **large** Young's modulus.
4) For a given stress, a stiff material will have a lower strain (i.e. a smaller extension) than a less stiff material.
5) A stiff material **doesn't** have to be strong (and vice versa). Some stiff materials **break** under a low stress, and some strong materials **aren't** very stiff.

When a line on a stress-strain graph just stops, you can assume the material has reached its breaking extress and fractured (unless the question says otherwise).

Steve took a break after a stressful day at the office

Stress-Strain and Force-Extension Graphs

Force-Extension Graphs Are Similar to Stress-Strain Graphs

You first met force-extension graphs on page 56.

1) Force-extension graphs look a lot like **stress-strain** graphs, but they show slightly different things.

2) Force-extension graphs are **specific** for the tested **object** and **depend on its dimensions**. Stress-strain graphs describe the **general behaviour** of a **material**, they are **independent of the dimensions**.

3) You can plot a force-extension graph of what happens when you gradually **remove** a **force** from an object. The **unloading** line doesn't always match up with the **loading** line though.

A force-extension graph for a metal wire

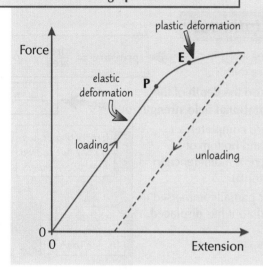

1) This graph is for a metal wire that has been stretched beyond its **limit of proportionality** (**P**) so the graph starts to **curve**.

2) When the load is **removed**, the **extension decreases**.

3) The unloading line is **parallel** to the loading line because the stiffness of the wire, k, is still the same (since the forces between the atoms are the same as they were during the loading).

4) But because the wire was stretched beyond its **elastic limit** (**E**) and deformed **plastically**, it has been **permanently stretched**. This means the unloading line doesn't go through the origin.

5) The **area** between the two lines is the **work done** to permanently deform the wire.

Of course, if you apply a big enough load to <u>fracture</u> the object, you can't draw an unloading line — you just get a force-extension graph like one of these graphs.

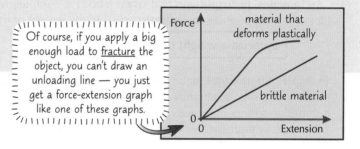

Practice Questions

Q1 What is the difference between the limit of proportionality and the elastic limit?

Q2 Describe what happens at the yield point.

Q3 A metal wire is stretched beyond its elastic limit. Why does the unloading line on the force-extension graph for the wire not go through the origin?

Exam Questions

Q1 Sketch a stress-strain graph to show (use the same axes):

a) A stiff and weak material being stretched to its breaking point. [1 mark]

b) A strong and less stiff material being stretched to its breaking point. [1 mark]

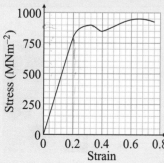

Q2 The diagram shows a stress-strain graph for a nylon thread.

a) State the yield stress for nylon. [1 mark]

b) Calculate how much energy per unit volume is stored in the thread when the limit of proportionality is reached. [2 marks]

I don't want to stress you, but this page can strain even the strongest brains...

The trick to revising is realising when you've really reached your yield point. That's when you need to take a break and get up and go for a walk. (It's not when you get the urge to have a quick check of your FaceTwittFeed or whatnot...)

Density, Upthrust and Viscosity

Yikes, three whole things in one go. Grab a coffee, take a deep breath and put on your snazziest learning hat...

Density *is* Mass *per* Unit Volume

Density is a measure of the '**compactness**' (for want of a better word) of a substance. It relates the **mass** of a substance to how much **space** it takes up.

1) The density of an object depends on what it's made of. Density **doesn't vary** with **size or shape**.

2) The **average density** of an object determines whether it **floats** or **sinks**. A solid object will **float** on a fluid if it has a **lower density** than the **fluid**.

> The symbol for density is a Greek letter rho (ρ) — it looks like a p but it isn't.

$$\text{density} = \frac{\text{mass}}{\text{volume}} \qquad \rho = \frac{m}{V}$$

The units of density are $g\,cm^{-3}$ or $kg\,m^{-3}$
$1\,g\,cm^{-3} = 1000\,kg\,m^{-3}$

Bodies *in* Fluids *Experience* Pressure *and* Upthrust

1) Pressure is the **amount of force** applied per **unit area**. It is measured in **pascals (Pa)**, which are equivalent to newtons per square metre (Nm^{-2}).

$$\text{pressure} = \frac{\text{force}}{\text{area}} \qquad p = \frac{F}{A}$$

2) The extra pressure acting on an object due to a fluid depends on the **depth** of the object in the fluid (h), the **density** of the fluid (ρ) and the **gravitational field strength** (g).

$$p = h\rho g$$

3) Upthrust is an **upward force** that fluids exert on objects that are **completely** or **partially submerged** in the fluid. It's caused because the top and bottom of a submerged object are at different depths. Since $p = h\rho g$, there is a difference in pressure which causes an overall upwards force known as upthrust.

4) **Archimedes' principle** says that when a body is completely or partially immersed in a fluid, it experiences an **upthrust** equal to the **weight** of the fluid it has **displaced**.

> **upthrust = weight of fluid displaced**

This is just because
$(h_2 - h_1)\rho gA = V\rho g = mg = W$

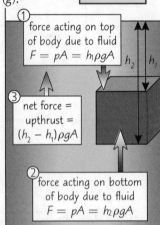

① force acting on top of body due to fluid
$F = pA = h_1\rho gA$

③ net force = upthrust = $(h_2 - h_1)\rho gA$

② force acting on bottom of body due to fluid
$F = pA = h_2\rho gA$

Example: **Submarines** make use of upthrust to dive underwater and return to the surface. To sink, large tanks are filled with water to **increase** the weight of the submarine so that it **exceeds** the upthrust. To rise to the surface, the tanks are filled with compressed air to **reduce** the weight so that it's **less** than the upthrust.

Viscous Drag *Acts on* Objects Moving Through Fluids

When an object moves through a fluid, or a fluid moves past an object, you get **friction** between the surface of the **object** and the **fluid**. This is **viscous drag**. You can calculate the force due to viscous drag on a **spherical** object moving through a fluid using **Stokes's law**.

$$F = 6\pi\eta rv$$

Viscous drag depends on the **viscosity** (or "thickness") of a fluid, η. Viscosity is **temperature-dependent** — liquids get **less viscous** as temperature **increases**, but **gases** (like **dry air**) get **more viscous** as temperature **increases**.

F is the viscous drag (N), η (eta) is the viscosity of the fluid (Nsm^{-2} or $Pa\,s$), r is the radius of the object (m) and v is the speed the object is moving at (ms^{-1})

Stokes's Law *Only* Applies to *Small* Objects *Moving Slowly with* Laminar Flow

1) **Laminar flow** is a flow **pattern** where all the parts of the fluid are flowing in the **same direction** — the layers in the fluid **do not mix**.

2) Laminar flow usually occurs when a fluid is **flowing slowly**, or when an object is **moving slowly** through a fluid. The diagram shows a ball falling slowly with laminar flow.

3) **Turbulent flow** is a different flow **pattern**. You don't get nice layers like you do with laminar flow, all the parts of the **fluid** get **mixed up**.

4) Turbulent flow usually occurs when a **fluid** is flowing **quickly**, or an object is **moving quickly** through a fluid.

5) **Stokes's law only** applies to **small, spherical** objects moving **slowly** with **laminar flow**. It **doesn't** apply to **turbulent flow**.

Fluid 'layers'

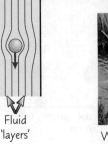

What do you get if you cross a baby sheep with a river? A lamb in a flow.

Density, Upthrust and Viscosity

Measure the Viscosity of a Liquid

You don't have to use elastic bands — you could also use insulation tape or another marker for your intervals.

You can calculate the **viscosity** of a liquid by timing the **fall** of different sizes of ball bearings (little steel balls) of **known density**, ρ. using an experiment like this:

1) Fill a wide, clear tube with the liquid you want to investigate (e.g. washing up liquid). Make sure you know the **density** of the liquid, σ.

2) Put one rubber band about halfway down the tube at a position such that the ball bearings will have achieved **terminal velocity** (see page 30) when they reach it.

3) Place two more elastic bands **below** the first so that the distance between each band is **equal** and the lowest band is near the **bottom** of the tube. Record the distance between them. These are the points at which you will record t_1 and t_2.

4) Measure the diameter of your ball bearing and halve it to get the **radius**.

5) **Drop** the ball bearing into the tube. Start a **stopwatch** when the ball reaches the first band, and record the time at which it reaches each of the other bands. Record your results in a **table** (see below).

6) **Repeat** this at least three times for each ball bearing to reduce the effect of **random errors** on your results, then repeat the whole thing for different sizes of ball bearing. You can use a **strong magnet** to remove the ball bearings from the tube.

7) If the ball falls **close** to the **wall**, **re-do the reading** — the flow will no longer be laminar and Stokes's law will not apply.

8) **Calculate** the **average time taken** for each size of ball bearing to fall between the elastic bands. Use the **average time** and the **distance between bands** to calculate the **average (terminal) velocity** of the ball bearing between the elastic bands.

9) You can then calculate the **viscosity**, η, of the liquid. The ball bearings are falling at terminal velocity, so the **sum** of the forces acting on the ball is **zero**:

glass tube
viscous liquid e.g. washing up liquid or glycerol
ball bearing
start timer here
d
t_1
d
t_2

weight − drag − upthrust = 0

Substituting the equation for each force and rearranging gives $\eta = \dfrac{2r^2 g(\rho - \sigma)}{9v}$, where r is the radius of the ball bearing, g is the gravitational field strength due to gravity, ρ is the density of the ball bearing, σ is the density of the liquid and v is the average terminal velocity between the elastic bands.

10) Your table could look like this:

radius of ball bearing /mm	density of ball bearing / kg m^{-3}	time to t_1 / s	velocity at t_1 / ms^{-1}	time between t_1 and t_2 / s	velocity at t_2 / ms^{-1}	average velocity / ms^{-1}	viscosity / Nsm^{-2}	average viscosity / Nsm^{-2}
2.0		1		1				
		2		2				
		3		3				
3.0		1						
		2						

If the velocities at t_2 are consistently larger than those at t_1, the ball bearing might not have reached terminal velocity when you started timing — move the elastic bands down the tube a bit and try again.

Practice Questions

Q1 Show that the mass of 3.8 m³ of a liquid with density 1.5 kg m^{-3} is 5.7 kg.

Q2 State Archimedes's principle and explain how it is used by submarines.

Q3 What is meant by laminar flow?

Q4 Describe an experiment you could carry out to determine the viscosity of a liquid using ball bearings.

Exam Question

Q1 a) State Stokes's law and explain what each term represents. [1 mark]
   b) State three conditions that must be true for Stokes's law to be apply. [3 marks]
   c) A ball bearing of radius 3.0 mm is falling at a constant speed of 0.040 ms^{-1} through a liquid of viscosity 3.0 Pa s. The density of the liquid is 1400 kg m^{-3}. Calculate the weight of the ball bearing. ($V_{sphere} = \frac{4}{3}\pi r^3$) [5 marks]

My discoscity increases with temperature — warm me up, I'll dance for hours...

Sorry about the 'lamb-in-a-flow' joke — it really is awful. My boss Joe thought it up, I'm just not that funny. If you're struggling to remember this page, try explaining it to someone else (little brothers are useful for this) — it really helps.

The Nature Of Waves

Aaaah... waggling ropes about. It's all good clean fun as my mate Richard used to say...

A **Wave** Transfers **Energy** Away From Its **Source**

A **progressive** (moving) wave carries **energy** from one place to another **without transferring any material**. The transfer of energy is in the **same direction** as the wave is **travelling**. Here are some ways you can tell waves carry energy:

1) Electromagnetic waves cause things to **heat up**.
2) **X-rays** and **gamma rays** knock electrons out of their orbits, causing **ionisation**.
3) Loud **sounds** cause large oscillations in air particles which can make things **vibrate**.
4) **Wave power** can be used to **generate electricity**.

Since waves carry energy away, the **source** of the wave **loses energy**.

You Need to Know These **Bits** of a **Wave**

1) **Displacement**, *x*, metres — how far a **point** on the wave has **moved** from its **undisturbed position**.
2) **Amplitude**, *A*, metres — the **maximum magnitude** of the **displacement**.
3) **Wavelength**, λ, metres — the **length** of **one whole wave cycle**, e.g. from **crest** to **crest** or **trough** to **trough**.

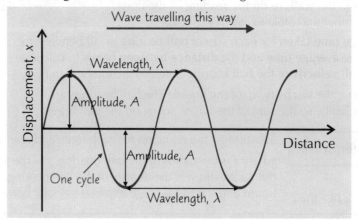

4) **Period**, *T*, seconds — the **time taken** for a **whole cycle** (vibration) to complete.
5) **Frequency**, *f*, hertz — the **number** of **cycles** (vibrations) **per second** passing a given **point**.
6) **Phase** — a measurement of the **position** of a certain **point** along the wave cycle.
7) **Phase difference** — the amount one wave lags behind another.

Phase and phase difference are measured in angles (in degrees or radians). See p.74.

The **Frequency** is the **Inverse** of the **Period**

$$\text{Frequency} = \frac{1}{\text{Period}} \qquad f = \frac{1}{T}$$

It's that simple.
Get the **units** straight: **1 Hz = 1 s⁻¹**.

The **Wave Equation** Links **Wave Speed, Frequency** and **Wavelength**

1) **Wave speed** can be measured just like the speed of anything else:

$$\text{Wave speed } (v) = \frac{\text{Distance } (d)}{\text{Time } (t)}$$

2) You can use this equation to derive the **wave equation** (but thankfully you don't have to do that, you just need to be able to use it).

$$\text{Speed of wave } (v) = \text{frequency } (f) \times \text{wavelength } (\lambda) \qquad v = f\lambda$$

> Remember, you're not measuring how fast a physical point (like one molecule of rope) moves. You're measuring how fast a point on the **wave pattern** moves.

The Nature Of Waves

Oscilloscopes Display Waves

1) A cathode ray **oscilloscope** (CRO) measures **voltage**. It **displays** waves from a **signal generator** as a function of **voltage** over **time**.

2) The displayed wave is called a **trace**.

3) The screen is split into squares called **divisions**.

4) The vertical axis is in **volts**. The **volts per division** shown on this axis is controlled by the **gain dial**.

5) The horizontal axis is in **seconds** — also called the **timebase**. The **seconds per division** shown on this axis is controlled by the **timebase** dial.

6) You can alter the gain and timebase to make it **easy to read** off measurements.

Screen split into divisions

Gain dial in volts/div

Timebase dial in ms/div

The period of a wave is found from: the no. of divisions in one complete wave × the timebase setting.

If you plug an **AC** (**alternating current**) **supply** into an oscilloscope, you get a trace that goes up and down in a regular pattern — some of the time it's positive and some of the time it's negative.
A **microphone** converts **sound waves** into **electrical signals** which can be seen on an **oscilloscope**.

An Oscilloscope Can be Used to Find the Speed of Sound

1) Set up the experiment as shown in the diagram below and set the **frequency** of the signal generator to around 2-6 kHz. A **2-beam oscilloscope** must be used as this can display **two waves** — one for the **signal generator** generating a **sound wave** and one for the **same sound wave** being **received** by the **microphone**.

2) A 2-beam oscilloscope has **three dials** — two are the gain dials for **each** input signal and the other dial is the timebase dial for **both** input signals. Adjust the **dials** so that you can see at least one **complete cycle** of each wave.

3) **Change** the **distance** between the microphone and loudspeaker so that the **peaks** of one wave **line up** with the **troughs** of the other wave (i.e. the waves are **out of phase** — see p.74) and then **measure** the distance between the microphone and loudspeaker.

4) Calculate the **frequency** of the wave by measuring the **period** of the wave from the oscilloscope display and using it in $f = \frac{1}{T}$ (see p.66). The **resolution** of the oscilloscope will be **better** than the resolution of the signal generator, so measuring and calculating the frequency this way will give you a **smaller uncertainty** than just reading the frequency from the signal generator.

2-beam Oscilloscope

Signal generator

Microphone

Loudspeaker

Ruler

5) Move the microphone **away from** (or **towards**) the loudspeaker so that the microphone's corresponding wave on the oscilloscope **moves** one **full wavelength** along the signal generator's wave — the peaks of one wave and the troughs of the other wave will **line up** again. Measure the **new** distance between the microphone and loudspeaker.

6) The **difference** in your two recorded distances is equal to the **wavelength** of the sound wave.

7) Repeat steps 5-6 and use your results to find a **mean value** for the distance moved by the microphone each time (i.e. the **wavelength**). Then use the equation $v = f\lambda$ to find the value for the **speed of sound**.

Practice Questions

Q1 Define and give the units of the frequency, displacement, amplitude, speed and period of a wave.
Q2 Write down the wave equation.
Q3 Describe an experiment involving a 2-beam oscilloscope, a loudspeaker and a microphone to measure the speed of sound.

Exam Question

Q1 An oscilloscope has the gain set to 2.0 volts/div and a timebase set to 3.0 ms/div.
It is displaying the trace of a wave that has a wave speed of 280 ms⁻¹.
a) State the maximum voltage of the trace. [1 mark]
b) Calculate the frequency and wavelength of the wave. [5 marks]

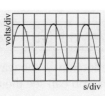

volts/div

s/div

Hope you haven't phased out...

Make sure you know what all the waves terms (amplitude, frequency etc.) mean — or this section could get confusing...

Types of Wave

Get a long spring and have a go at making different waves. Or sit there beeping pretending to be a microwave.

In **Transverse Waves**, **Vibration** is at Right Angles to the **Direction** of Travel

1) All **electromagnetic waves** are **transverse**. Other examples of transverse waves are ripples on water or waves on strings.

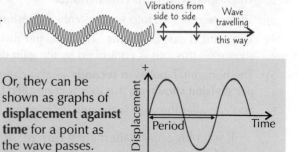

Vibrations from side to side

Wave travelling this way

2) There are **two** main ways of **drawing** transverse waves:

They can be shown as **graphs** of **displacement** against **distance along the path of the wave**.

crest

Displacement

λ Distance

trough

Or, they can be shown as graphs of **displacement against time** for a point as the wave passes.

Displacement

Period   Time

Displacements **upwards** from the centre line are given a **+ sign**. Displacements downwards are given a **– sign**.

3) Both sorts of graph often give the **same shape** (a **sine wave**), so make sure you check out the label on the **x-axis**.

4) You can work out what **direction** a point on a wave is moving in when given a snapshot of the wave.

Example: Look at the snapshot of the wave on the right. Which direction is point A on the wave moving in?

1) Look at which **direction** the wave is **travelling** in — here the wave is moving from **left** to **right**.

2) The displacement of the wave **just to the left** of point A is **greater** than point A's. So as the wave travels along, point A will need to move **upwards** to have that displacement. (If the displacement to the left was less than point A's, point A would need to move down.)

A

Direction of travel

In **Longitudinal Waves** the **Vibrations** are **Along** the Direction of Travel

The most **common** example of a **longitudinal wave** is **sound**. A sound wave consists of alternate **compressions** and **rarefactions** of the **medium** it's travelling through. (That's why sound can't go through a vacuum.)

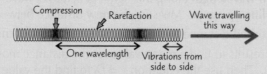

Compression   Rarefaction   Wave travelling this way

One wavelength   Vibrations from side to side

Some types of earthquake shock waves are also longitudinal.

The compressions and rarefactions create **pressure variations** in the medium the wave is travelling through — at the points of compression, the **molecules** of the medium are **closer** together, **increasing** the pressure at that point. At the points of rarefaction, the molecules are **further apart**, which means a **lower** pressure at that point.

It's hard to **represent** longitudinal waves **graphically**. You'll usually see them plotted as **displacement** against **time**. These can be **confusing** though, because they look like a **transverse wave**.

Waves Can Be **Reflected** and **Refracted**

Reflection — the wave is **bounced back** when it **hits a boundary**. E.g. you can see the reflection of light in mirrors. The reflection of water waves can be demonstrated in a ripple tank.

Refraction — the wave **changes direction** as it enters a **different medium**. The change in direction is a result of the wave slowing down or speeding up.

Tim refused to accept that his long lost twin was just a reflection at an air-water boundary.

Types of Wave

Intensity is a Measure of How Much Energy a Wave is Carrying

1) When you talk about "**brightness**" for light or "**loudness**" for sound, what you really mean is **how much light** or **sound** energy hits your eyes or your ears **per second**.

2) The scientific measure of this is **intensity**.

> Intensity is the **rate of flow** of **energy** per **unit area** at **right angles** to the **direction of travel** of the wave. It's measured in **Wm⁻²**.

$$\text{Intensity} = \frac{\text{Power}}{\text{Area}} \qquad I = \frac{P}{A}$$

> **Example:** Light is hitting a 12 cm² piece of paper at right angles to its surface. The power received at the paper is 0.26 W. Calculate the intensity of the light received.

The area of the piece of paper = 12 cm² = 0.0012 m²

Using the equation for intensity:

$$I = \frac{P}{A} = \frac{0.26}{0.0012} = 216.6... = 220 \text{ Wm}^{-2} \text{ (to 2 s.f.)}$$

Don't forget to convert from cm² to m² — 1 cm² = 0.0001 m².

Intensity is Proportional to Amplitude Squared

1) This comes from the fact that **intensity** is **proportional** to **energy**, and the energy of a wave depends on the square of the **amplitude**.

$$\text{Intensity} \propto (\text{Amplitude})^2$$

2) From this you can tell that for a **vibrating source** it takes four times as much energy to double the size of the vibrations.

All Electromagnetic (EM) Waves Have Some Properties In Common

1) All EM waves travel in a **vacuum** at a **speed** of **3.00 × 10⁸ ms⁻¹** (to 3 s.f.), and at **slower** speeds in other media.

2) They are **transverse** waves consisting of **vibrating electric** and **magnetic fields**. The **electric** and **magnetic** fields are at **right angles** to each other and to the **direction of travel**.

3) Like all waves, EM waves can be **refracted** (p.78), **reflected** and **diffracted** (p.82-83) and can undergo **interference** (p.74). They also obey $v = f\lambda$ (v = velocity, f = frequency, λ = wavelength).

4) Like all progressive waves, progressive EM waves **carry energy**.

5) EM waves are transverse so, like all transverse waves, they can be **polarised** (see page 70).

Practice Questions

Q1 Draw a displacement-time graph for a transverse wave. Label a point of maximum displacement and the wavelength of the wave on the graph.

Q2 Draw a displacement-time graph for a point on a longitudinal wave as the wave passes.

Q3 Describe the difference between the vibrations in a transverse wave and a longitudinal wave.

Q4 Describe a longitudinal wave in terms of pressure variations in the medium through which the wave is travelling.

Q5 Give the equation relating power, intensity and area.

Exam Question

Q1 a) A 10.0 W light beam is shone onto a screen with an area of 0.002 m². Calculate the intensity of the light beam on the screen. [1 mark]

b) The intensity of the light on the screen is increased until it is exactly triple the original beam intensity. Which of the following describes the amplitude of the light waves in the beam compared to their original amplitude?

A It is 3 times larger.   B It has halved.   C It is 9 times larger.   D It is √3 times larger.   [1 mark]

So many waves — my arms are getting tired...

Make sure you know the difference between transverse and longitudinal waves — one is up-y down-y and the other is forward-y backward-y. There's nothing quite like a hand-wavey explanation of something (no pun intended...no, really).

Polarisation of Waves

Light waves shake about all over the place. Polarisation is just getting rid of the directions that you don't want.

A *Polarised Wave* Only *Oscillates* in One Direction

1) If you **shake a rope** to make a **wave** you can move your hand **up and down** or **side to side** or in a **mixture** of directions — it still makes a **transverse wave**.

2) But if you try to pass **waves in a rope** through a **vertical fence**, the wave will only get through if the **vibrations** are **vertical**. The fence filters out vibration in other directions. This is called **polarising** the wave.

3) The **plane** in which a wave **vibrates** is called the **plane of polarisation** — e.g. the rope wave was polarised in the **vertical** plane by the fence.

4) Polarising a wave so that it only oscillates in one direction is called **plane polarisation**.

5) Ordinary **light waves** are a mixture of **different directions** of vibration. (The things vibrating are electric and magnetic fields).

Polarisation can only happen for **transverse waves**. So polarising light is one piece of **evidence** that it's a transverse wave.

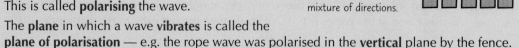

Vertical fence — Only up and down vibrations make it through

Vibrations in a mixture of directions.

The wave is polarised.

For polarised light, the direction of the vibrations (or the plane of polarisation) is always perpendicular to the direction of the propagation of light.

Polarising Filters Only *Transmit* Vibrations in *One Direction*

1) Ordinary **light waves** can be **polarised** using a **polarising filter**.

2) When the transmission axes of the two filters are **aligned**, **all** of the light that passes through the first filter also passes through the second.

3) As you rotate the second filter, the amount of light that passes through the second filter **varies**.

4) As the second filter is rotated, **less** light will get through it as the **vertical** component of the second filter's transmission axis **decreases**. This means the **intensity** of the light getting through the second filter will gradually **decrease**.

5) When the two transmission axes are at **45°** to each other, the intensity will be **half** that getting through the first filter. When they're at **right angles** to each other **no** light will pass through — **intensity** is **0**.

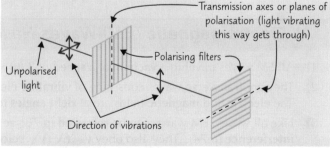

Transmission axes or planes of polarisation (light vibrating this way gets through)

Polarising filters

Unpolarised light

Direction of vibrations

3D films use polarised light to create depth — the filters in each lens are at right angles to each other so each eye gets a slightly different picture.

6) As you continue turning, the intensity should then begin to **increase** once again.

7) When the two axes **realign** (after a 180° rotation), **all** the light will be able to pass through the second filter again.

Maximum

Light intensity

0

0   90   180   270   360

Angle of rotation of filter from the plane of polarisation, °

When *Light Reflects* it is *Partially Polarised*

1) If you direct a beam of unpolarised light at a reflective surface then view the **reflected ray** through a polarising filter, the intensity of light leaving the filter **changes** with the **orientation** of the filter.

2) The intensity changes because at certain **angles**, light is **partially polarised** when it is **reflected**.

3) This effect is used to remove **unwanted reflections** in photography and in **Polaroid sunglasses** to remove **glare**.

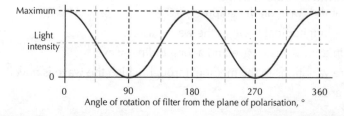

Unpolarised light

Glass block

Partially polarised light

As the polarising filter is rotated, the intensity of light leaving it changes.

When the light reaches the glass block, it is reflected and partially polarised.

Polarisation of Waves

Television and Radio Signals are Polarised

If you look up at the **TV aerials** on people's houses, you'll see that the **rods** (the sticky-out bits) on them are all **horizontal**. This is because **TV signals** are **polarised** by the orientation of the **rods** on the **broadcasting aerial**. To receive a strong signal, you have to **line up** the **rods** on the **receiving aerial** with the **rods** on the **transmitting aerial** — if they aren't aligned, the signal strength will be lower.

It's the **same** with **radio** — if you try **tuning a radio** and then **moving** the **aerial** around, your signal will **come and go** as the transmitting and receiving aerials go in and out of **alignment**.

Metal Grilles are Used to **Polarise Microwaves**

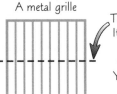

A metal grille

This is the plane of polarisation. It's at right-angles to the wires, unlike with polarising filters where it's parallel to the slits. You don't need to worry about why they're different though.

Polarising filters don't work on **microwaves** — their **wavelength** is too long. Instead, **metal grilles** (squares full of metal wires which are all aligned) are used to polarise them.

You can investigate the polarisation of microwaves using a **microwave transmitter** and a **microwave receiver** linked to a **voltmeter**.

1) Place a metal **grille** between the microwave **transmitter** and **receiver** as shown on the right. (Handily, microwave transmitters transmit **polarised** microwaves, so you only need one metal grille.)

2) The intensity of microwaves passing through the grille is at a **maximum** when the direction of the vibration of the microwaves and the plane of polarisation of the grille are **parallel** to each other.

3) As you rotate the grille, the **intensity** of polarised microwaves able to pass through the grille **decreases**, so the reading on the voltmeter **decreases**.

4) When the plane of polarisation of the metal grille is **perpendicular** with the direction of the vibration of the microwaves, **no signal** will be shown on the voltmeter.

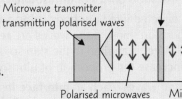

Metal grille - the planes of polarisation of the grille and the microwaves are parallel

Microwave transmitter transmitting polarised waves

Microwave receiver (receives polarised waves)

Voltmeter

Polarised microwaves (direction of vibrations)

Microwaves with slightly reduced amplitudes

The **intensity** drops to **zero** when the plane of polarisation of the metal grille is at **right angles** to the plane of polarisation of the microwaves, because the grille is **absorbing their energy**.

Make sure all of your electrical equipment is safely connected before you turn it on — microwave transmitters operate at very high voltages.

Practice Questions

Q1 What is plane polarisation?

Q2 Why can't you polarise sound waves?

Q3 Why do you have to line up transmitting and receiving television aerials?

Exam Question

Q1 Two polarising filters are placed on top of each other and held in front of a source of white unpolarised light.

a) No light can be seen through the filters. State the angle between the transmission axes of the two filters.

[1 mark]

b) The filters are rotated so that the angle between their transmission axes is 45°. Describe the difference in the intensity of the light once it has passed through both filters compared to the light once it has only passed through the first filter.

[1 mark]

Forget polarisation, I need a mental filter...

...to stop me talking rubbish all the time. Polarisation isn't too bad once you get your head around it. It's just a case of filtering out different directions of wave vibrations. Make sure you really know it though as you'll have to be able to explain how both the experiments for polarising light and microwaves work. Doesn't that sound like a barrel of laughs.

Ultrasound Imaging

I wrote these next two pages for you, because I know what you're thinking — 'This is great, but I want to learn about waves in medical imaging. Also, as a side note, I think CGP books are brilliant.' Oh stop, no really, I'm blushing...

Waves are **Reflected** and **Transmitted** at **Interfaces**

1) The **boundary** between two different media is called an **interface**.

2) When a wave passes from one medium to another, some of its **energy** is **reflected** and some of it is **transmitted** — as shown in the diagram.

3) The proportion of energy reflected or transmitted depends on the two media involved. If the media have very **different** **densities**, most of the energy is **reflected**. If they are quite **similar**, most of the energy is **transmitted**.

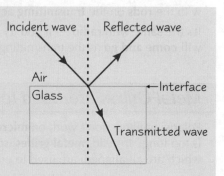

The **Reflection** of **Ultrasound Waves** is Used in **Ultrasound Scans**

1) **Ultrasound waves** are **sound waves** that have too high a **frequency** for humans to **hear**.

2) Ultrasound scans use short pulses of **ultrasound radiation** to form images of the inside of your body.

3) The ultrasound is directed into your body using a **transducer**. If you have air between the transducer and your skin, most of the waves are **reflected** because air has a very **different** density from skin. A **gel** is applied to the skin so there is no air between the transducer and your skin to **increase** the proportion of ultrasound waves that **enter** your body.

4) When the ultrasound waves reach an **interface** inside your body — e.g. between different types of tissue — some of them are **reflected**. A computer attached to the transducer calculates how far from the surface of your skin the interface is by **timing** how long it takes for the reflected waves to **return**.

Sending out ultrasound waves and detecting the reflections is known as a pulse-echo technique.

5) The computer uses the information about the **location** of the boundaries between different tissues to build up an **image** of the inside of your body.

A similar technique is used in **sonar** — e.g. ships send sonar pulses (**ultrasound waves**) down towards the seabed and the pulses are **reflected** back from any **submerged** objects. It can also be used to measure the **speed** of objects.

Shorter Pulses Produce Clearer Images

Ultrasound transducers cannot **transmit** and **receive** pulses at the same time. If **reflected** waves reach the transducer while it is **transmitting**, the information they contain will be **lost** and image **quality** will be reduced. This means:

1) The **pulses** of ultrasound transmitted must be **very short** (a few microseconds long) so that the reflections from nearby interfaces don't reach the transducer before the pulse has ended.

2) The gap between pulses must be **long** (at least 1 millisecond) so that all the reflected waves from one pulse return to the transducer **before** the next pulse is transmitted.

Jack didn't know how to tell Joanna that most of the image quality had been lost.

Ultrasound Imaging

Shorter Wavelengths Produce Clearer Images

Ultrasound scanning can be a really useful technique — but only if the images are **clear**.
The **properties** of the ultrasound **radiation** used has a big effect on the clarity of the images produced.

1) **Shorter** wavelengths **diffract** much **less** than longer wavelengths.
2) This means that the shorter the **wavelength** of the ultrasound, the less the waves **spread out** as they travel and the more **precisely** the location of the interfaces between tissues can be mapped.
3) So ultrasound scanners use waves with a **high frequency** and **short wavelength**.

For more on diffraction of waves, see page 82.

In order for an **object** to be **resolved** (distinguished from other objects), the **wavelength** of the ultrasound wave must be of a **similar size** to the width of the object being resolved.

Example: Ultrasound of frequency 0.95 MHz is used to image a spherical tumour with a diameter of 3.2 mm. If the speed of ultrasound waves in the body is 1540 ms^{-1}, will the tumour be resolved in the ultrasound image?

Find the wavelength of the ultrasound by rearranging $v = f\lambda$:

$$\lambda = \frac{v}{f} = \frac{1540}{0.95 \times 10^6} = 962\ 500$$
$$= 1.6210... \times 10^{-3} \text{ m}$$
$$= 1.6210... \text{ mm}$$

Take a look back at p.66 for a reminder on the wave equation.

The wavelength used is approximately half the size of the tumour, so the wavelength and tumour are similar in size. This means it is reasonable to assume that **the tumour will be resolved**.

Practice Questions

Q1 What is an interface?

Q2 What happens to a wave when it reaches an interface?

Q3 How is sonar similar to ultrasound scanning?

Q4 State and explain two things you can do to improve the clarity of an ultrasound image.

Q5 How long does the wavelength of ultrasound used to form an image need to be compared to the size of the object in order to be able to resolve it?

Exam Questions

Q1 Explain how pulse-echo techniques are used to image the inside of a patient's body, including what happens when waves meet an interface between media. [5 marks]

Q2 Explain why a transducer used in medical imaging produces pulses of ultrasound waves with the following properties:

a) A short wavelength. [3 marks]

b) A short pulse length and a long time between pulses. [4 marks]

Ultrasound — Mancunian for 'très bien'

Next time you're watching TV and they show a pregnant woman having her unborn baby scanned, turn to the person you're sat next to and explain how the procedure works. You'll also be able to explain why they put a gel on their stomach first. Just make sure you know the person first before you launch into an explanation about transducers.

Superposition and Coherence

When two waves get together, it can be either really impressive or really disappointing.

Superposition Happens When Two or More Waves Pass Through Each Other

1) At the **instant** the waves **cross**, the displacements due to each wave **combine**. Then **each wave** goes on its merry way. You can **see** this if **two pulses** are sent **simultaneously** from each end of a rope.

2) The **principle of superposition** says that when two or more **waves cross**, the **resultant** displacement equals the **vector sum** of the **individual** displacements.

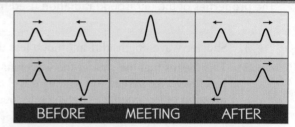

"**Superposition**" means "one thing on top of another thing". You can use the same idea in **reverse** — a **complex wave** can be separated out mathematically into **several simple** sine waves of various sizes.

Interference can be Constructive or Destructive

1) When two or more waves **superpose** with each other, the effect is called **interference**.

2) A **crest** plus a **crest** gives a **bigger crest**. A **trough** plus a **trough** gives a **bigger trough**. These are both examples of **constructive interference**.

3) A **crest** plus a **trough** of **equal size** gives... **nothing**. The two displacements **cancel each other out** completely. This is called **destructive interference**.

4) If the **crest** and the **trough** aren't the **same size**, then the destructive interference **isn't total**. For the interference to be **noticeable**, the two **amplitudes** should be **nearly equal**.

Graphically, you can superimpose waves by adding the individual displacements at each point along the x-axis, and then plotting them.

In Phase Means In Step — Two Points In Phase Interfere Constructively

1) Two points on a wave are **in phase** if they are both at the **same point** in the **wave cycle**. Points in phase have the **same displacement** and **velocity**.

2) On the graph on the right, points **A** and **B** are **in phase**; points **A** and **C** are **out of phase**.

3) It's mathematically **handy** to show one **complete cycle** of a wave as an **angle of 360° (2π radians)**.

4) **Two points** with a **phase difference** of **zero** or a **multiple of 360°** are **in phase**.

5) **Points** with a **phase difference** of **odd-number multiples** of **180° (π radians)** are **exactly out of phase**.

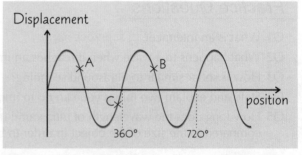

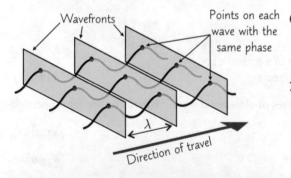

6) You can also talk about two **different waves** being **in phase**. **In practice** this usually happens because **both** waves came from the **same oscillator**. In **other** situations there will nearly always be a **phase difference** between two waves.

7) Two or more waves that are **coherent** (see below), **in phase** and travelling in the **same direction** will have **wavefronts**. These are imaginary planes that cut **across** all the waves, joining up all the **points** that are **in phase** with each other. The **distance** between each wavefront is equal to one **wavelength**, i.e. each wavefront is at the same point in the **cycle**.

To Get Interference Patterns the Two Sources Must Be Coherent

Interference **still happens** when you're observing waves of **different wavelength** and **frequency** — but it happens in a **jumble**. In order to get clear **interference patterns**, the two or more sources must be **coherent**.

Coherent sources — they have the **same wavelength** and **frequency** and a **fixed phase difference** between them.

Superposition and Coherence

Constructive or Destructive Interference Depends on the Path Difference

1) Whether you get **constructive** or **destructive** interference at a **point** depends on how **much further one wave** has travelled than the **other wave** to get to that point (assuming the sources are coherent and in phase).

2) The **amount** by which the path travelled by one wave is **longer** than the path travelled by the other wave is called the **path difference**.

3) At **any point an equal distance** from both sources you will get **constructive interference**. You also get constructive interference at any point where the **path difference** is a **whole number of wavelengths**, because the waves arrive at the same point **in phase**. At points where the path difference is an odd number of **half wavelengths**, the waves arrive **out of phase** and you get **destructive interference**.

Constructive interference
occurs when:

> path difference = $n\lambda$ (where n is an integer)

Destructive interference
occurs when:

> path difference $= \dfrac{(2n+1)\lambda}{2} = (n + \frac{1}{2})\lambda$

If the sources are not in phase but are coherent, there will be constructive and destructive interference, but they will not occur at these path differences.

You Can Observe Interference With Sound Waves

1) Connect two **speakers** to the same oscillator (so the sound waves from them are **coherent** and **in phase**) and place them in line with each other.

2) Walk slowly across the room in front of them.

3) You will hear varying volumes of sound. At the points where the sound is **loudest**, the **path difference** is a **whole** wavelength.

4) The sound will be quietest at points where the path difference is an **odd** number of **half wavelengths**.

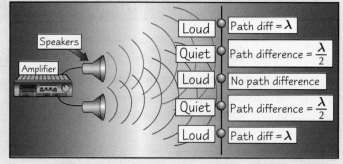

You may still hear some sound at the quietest points due to sound being reflected off walls and around the room.

Practice Questions

Q1 What is the principle of superposition?

Q2 If two points on a wave have a phase difference of 1440°, are they in phase?

Q3 What is a wavefront?

Q4 If there was a path difference of 5λ between two coherent, in phase waves, what kind of interference would occur?

Exam Questions

Q1 a) Two wave sources are coherent. Explain what this means. [2 marks]

   b) Explain why you might have difficulty in observing interference patterns in an area affected by two waves from two sources even though the two sources are coherent. [1 mark]

Q2 Two waves from coherent sources meet and interfere. Which row of the table shows the correct type of interference that would occur with the stated phase and path difference? [1 mark]

	Phase Difference	Path Difference	Type of Interference
A	180°	λ	Constructive
B	180°	λ/2	Constructive
C	360°	λ	Destructive
D	360°	λ/2	Constructive

Learn this and you'll be in a super position to pass your exam... *...I'll get my coat.*

A few crucial concepts here: a) interference can be constructive or destructive, b) you get constructive interference when the path difference is a whole number of wavelengths (for sources in phase), c) the sources must be coherent.

Stationary (Standing) Waves

Stationary waves are waves that... er... stand still... well, not still exactly... I mean, well... they don't go anywhere... um...

You get Stationary Waves When a **Progressive Wave** is **Reflected** at a **Boundary**

A stationary wave is the **superposition** of **two progressive waves** with the **same wavelength**, moving in **opposite directions**.

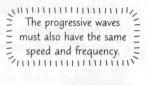
The progressive waves must also have the same speed and frequency.

1) Unlike progressive waves, **no energy** is transmitted by a stationary wave.

2) You can demonstrate stationary waves by attaching a **vibration transducer** at one end of a **stretched string** with the other end fixed. The transducer is given a wave frequency by a **signal generator** and creates that wave by vibrating the string.

3) The wave generated by the vibration transducer is **reflected** back and forth.

4) For most frequencies the resultant **pattern** is a **jumble**. However, if you alter the **signal generator** so the **transducer** produces an **exact number of waves** in the time it takes for a wave to get to the **end** and **back again**, then the **original** and **reflected** waves **reinforce** each other.

5) At these **"resonant frequencies"** you get a **stationary** (or **standing**) **wave** where the **pattern doesn't move** — it just sits there, bobbing up and down. Happy, at peace with the world...

A sitting wave.

Stationary Waves in **Strings** Form **Oscillating "Loops"** Separated by **Nodes**

1) Each particle vibrates at **right angles** to the string.

2) **Nodes** are where the **amplitude** of the vibration is **zero**.

3) **Antinodes** are points of **maximum amplitude**.

4) At resonant frequencies, an **exact number** of **half wavelengths** fits onto the string.

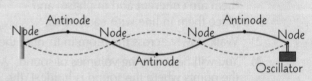

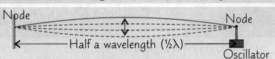

The standing wave above is vibrating at the **lowest possible** resonant frequency (the **fundamental mode of vibration** — also called the **first harmonic**). It has **one "loop"** with a **node at each end**.

This is the **second harmonic**. It is **twice the fundamental mode of vibration**. There are two **"loops"** with a **node** in the **middle** and **one at each end**.

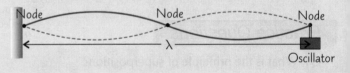

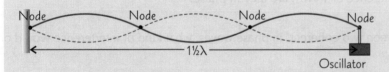

The **third harmonic** is **three times** the fundamental mode of vibration. **1½ wavelengths** fit on the string.

You can **Demonstrate Stationary Waves** with Microwaves and Sounds

Microwaves Reflected Off a Metal Plate Set Up a Stationary Wave

Microwave stationary wave apparatus

You can find the **nodes** and **antinodes** by moving the **probe** between the **transmitter** and **reflecting plate**.

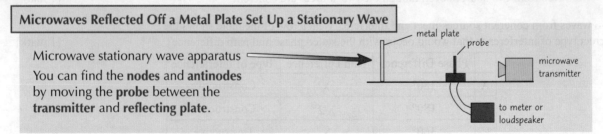

Powder Can Show Stationary Waves in a Tube of Air

Stationary **sound** waves are produced in the **glass tube**.

The lycopodium **powder** (don't worry, you don't need to know what that is) laid along the bottom of the tube is **shaken away** from the **antinodes** but left **undisturbed** at the **nodes**.

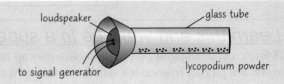

Stationary (Standing) Waves

You Can Investigate **Factors** Affecting the **Resonant Frequencies** of a String

1) Start by measuring the **mass** (M) and **length** (L) of strings of different types using a **mass balance** and a ruler. Then find the **mass per unit length** of each string (μ) using:

$$\mu = \frac{M}{L}$$ The units of μ are kgm⁻¹

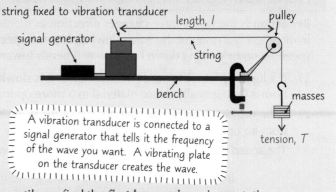

string fixed to vibration transducer — length, l — pulley

signal generator

string

bench

masses

tension, T

2) Set up the apparatus shown in the diagram with one of your strings. Record μ, measure and record the **length** (l) and work out the **tension** (T) using:

$$T = mg$$ where m is the total mass of the masses in kg

A vibration transducer is connected to a signal generator that tells it the frequency of the wave you want. A vibrating plate on the transducer creates the wave.

3) Turn on the **signal generator** and vary the frequency until you find the **first harmonic** — i.e. a stationary wave that has a **node** at each end and a single **antinode**. This is the **frequency** of the first harmonic, f.

4) The **wavelength** of the wave, λ, is given by λ = 2l for the **fundamental mode frequency**. The **frequency**, f, and the **velocity** of the wave, v, for the first harmonic are:

You can investigate how the **length, tension** or **mass per unit length** of the string affects the **resonant frequency** by:

$$f = \frac{1}{2l}\sqrt{\frac{T}{\mu}}$$ $$v = \sqrt{\frac{T}{\mu}}$$

The equation for v is true for <u>any</u> transverse wave on a string.

1) Keeping the string **type** (μ) and the **tension** (T) in it the same and altering the **length** (l). Do this by moving the **vibration transducer** towards or away from the pulley. Find the **first harmonic** again, and record f against l.

2) Keeping the string **type** (μ) and **length** (l) the same and **adding** or **removing masses** to change the tension (T). Find the first harmonic again and record f against T.

3) Keeping the **length** (l) and **tension** (T) the same, but using **different string** samples to vary μ. Find the first harmonic and record f against μ.

You can do this experiment with a different harmonic — just remember to use the same one throughout the experiment. You won't be able to use the equation for f though — this is just for the fundamental mode of vibration.

You should find the following from your investigation:

1) The **longer** the string, the **lower** the resonant frequency — because the **half wavelength** at the resonant frequency is longer.

2) The **heavier** (i.e. the more mass per unit length) the string, the **lower** the resonant frequency — because waves travel more **slowly** down the string. For a given **length** a **lower** wave speed, v, makes a **lower** frequency, f.

3) The **looser** the string the **lower** the resonant frequency — because waves travel more **slowly** down a **loose** string.

Practice Questions

Q1 How do stationary waves form?

Q2 Sketch the first three fundamental modes of vibration of a standing wave on three different diagrams.

Q3 At four times the frequency of the first harmonic, how many half wavelengths would fit on a violin string?

Q4 How does the displacement of a particle at one antinode compare to that of a particle at another antinode?

Exam Questions

Q1 A string of fixed length 2.8 m is oscillating at its fundamental mode of vibration. Calculate the mass of the string if the standing wave has velocity 16 ms⁻¹ and the tension on the string is 3.2 N. [2 marks]

Q2 A stationary wave at the first harmonic frequency, 10 Hz (to 2 s.f.), is formed on a stretched string of length 1.2 m.

a) Calculate the wavelength of the wave. [2 marks]

b) The tension is doubled whilst all other factors remain constant. The frequency is adjusted to once more find the first harmonic of the string. Calculate the new frequency of the first harmonic. [3 marks]

c) Explain how the variation of amplitude along the string differs from that of a progressive wave. [2 marks]

Don't get tied up in knots...

Remember — the lowest frequency at which a standing wave is formed is the fundamental mode of vibration.

Refractive Index

The stuff on the next two pages explains why your legs look short in a swimming pool.

Refraction Occurs When the Medium a Wave is Travelling in Changes

Refraction is the way a wave **changes direction** as it enters a **different medium**. The change in direction is a result of the wave **slowing down** or **speeding up**. You can tell if the wave is speeding up or slowing down by the way it **bends towards** or **away** from the normal.

1) If a light ray bends **towards** the normal — it is **slowing** down. The ray is going from a **less** optically dense material to a **more** optically dense material.

2) If the ray bends **away** from the normal — the wave is **speeding up**. It is going from an optically **denser** material to a **less** optically dense material.

The more optically dense material will have a higher refractive index (see below).

3) The speed changes because the **wavelength** of the wave is changing and the **frequency** stays **constant** ($v = f\lambda$).

> If light travels from a **less** optically dense material to a **more** optically dense material, the wave **slows down**, the wavelength **decreases** and the frequency stays the **same**.

The Refractive Index of a Material Measures How Much It Slows Down Light

Light goes fastest in a **vacuum**. It **slows down** in other materials, because it **interacts** with the particles in them. The more **optically dense** a material is, the more light **slows down** when it enters it.

> The **refractive index** of a material, n, is the **ratio** between the **speed of light** in a vacuum, c, and the speed of light in that **material**, v.

$$n = \frac{c}{v}$$

$c = 3.00 \times 10^8$ ms^{-1}.

The speed of light in air is only a tiny bit smaller than c. So you can assume the refractive index of air is 1.

Snell's Law uses Angles to Calculate the Refractive Index

1) The **angle** the **incoming light** makes to the **normal** is called the **angle of incidence**, θ_1. The **angle** the **refracted ray** makes with the **normal** is the **angle of refraction**, θ_2.

2) The light is crossing a **boundary**, going from a medium with **refractive index** n_1 to a medium with refractive index n_2.

3) When light enters an **optically denser** medium it is refracted **towards** the normal.

4) n_1, n_2, θ_1 and θ_2 are related by **Snell's law**: $\boxed{n_1 \sin\theta_1 = n_2 \sin\theta_2}$

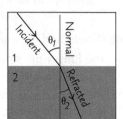

You can use a **ray box** to find the **refractive index** of a glass block:

You can do this experiment to find the refractive index of any solid, transparent material.

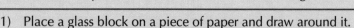

1) Place a glass block on a piece of paper and draw around it.

2) Use the ray box to shine a beam of light into the glass block. Turn off any other lights so you can see the path of the light beam through the block clearly.

3) **Trace** the path of the **incoming** and **outgoing** beams of light either side of the block.

4) Remove the block and join up the two paths you've drawn with a **straight line** that follows the path the light beam took through the glass block. You should be able to see from your drawing how the path of the ray **bent** when entering and leaving the block.

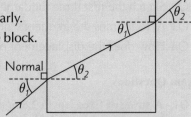
Outline of block
Normal

5) Measure the angles of incidence (θ_1) and refraction (θ_2) where the light enters and exits the block. Air is **less** optically dense than glass, so as the light **enters** the glass block it **bends towards** the normal ($\theta_1 > \theta_2$) as it **slows down**. The beam should **bend away** from the normal as it **exits** the block ($\theta_2 > \theta_1$) and **speeds up**.

6) Rearrange **Snell's law** to make the refractive index of the **material** the subject, and substitute in $n = 1$ for **air** and the values you found for θ_1 and θ_2 to calculate a value for n.

Alternatively, you could plot a graph of $\sin\theta_1$ against $\sin\theta_2$. The gradient of the graph will be equal to the refractive index of the material.

7) The **percentage uncertainty** (see p.10) in your measurements for θ_1 and θ_2 will be **smaller** for **larger angles**, so it's better to do the experiment at large angles and then **repeat** the experiment to find an **average** of your results.

8) Your result should be more **precise** (see p.12) if you use a **narrower** beam of light as the **uncertainty** in the **position** of the beam will be lower.

Refractive Index

When the Angle of **Refraction** is a **Right Angle**, the Angle of **Incidence** is **Critical**

When light **goes from** an optically dense material into an optically **less dense** material (e.g. glass to air), interesting things can start to happen.

Shine a ray of light at a **glass to air** boundary, then gradually **increase** the angle of incidence. As you increase the angle of incidence, the angle of **refraction** gets closer and closer to **90°**. Eventually the angle of incidence, θ_1 reaches a **critical angle C** for which the angle of refraction, $\theta_2 = 90°$. The light is refracted **along the boundary**.

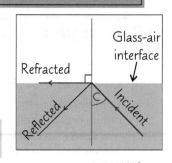

At angles of incidence **greater than C**, refraction is **impossible**. That means **all** the light is reflected back into the material. This effect is called **total internal reflection**.

For light hitting a **material-to-air boundary** (assuming the material is more optically **dense**) at the critical angle, **Snell's law** simplifies to become:

$$\sin C = \frac{1}{n}$$

This happens because $n_{air} = 1$ and $\sin(90°) = 1$. n is the refractive index of the material.

You can Investigate **Critical Angles** and **Total Internal Reflection** with **Glass Blocks**

1) Shine a light ray into the **curved face** of a semi-circular glass block so that it always enters at **right angles** to the edge — this means the ray won't **refract** as it enters the block, just when it leaves from the straight edge.

2) Vary the angle of **incidence**, θ_1, until the light beam refracts so much that it exits the block along the **straight edge**. This angle of incidence is the **critical angle**, C, for glass-air boundary.

You can rearrange the formula for the critical angle above and put in your value for C to find the refractive index of the block.

3) If you increase the angle of incidence so it's **greater** than C, you'll find the ray is reflected from the straight edge of the block.

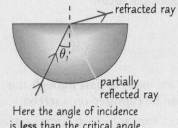 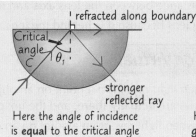 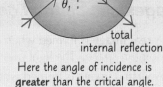

Here the angle of incidence is **less** than the critical angle

Here the angle of incidence is **equal** to the critical angle

Here the angle of incidence is **greater** than the critical angle.

Practice Questions

Q1 What happens to the wavelength of light as it passes from water into air?
Q2 Why does light go fastest in a vacuum and slow down in other media?
Q3 Diamond has a higher refractive index than sapphire. Is total internal reflection possible for light travelling in sapphire when it meets a sapphire-diamond interface?
Q4 Describe an experiment you could do to determine the critical angle of a boundary between a material and air.

Exam Questions

Q1 a) Light travels in diamond at 1.24×10^8 ms^{-1}. What is the refractive index of diamond? [1 mark]

b) Calculate the angle of refraction if light strikes a facet of a diamond ring at an angle of exactly 50° to the normal of the air/diamond boundary. [2 marks]

Q2 An adjustable underwater spotlight is placed on the floor of an aquarium tank. When the light points upwards at a steep angle a beam comes through the surface of the water into the air, and the tank is dimly lit. When the spotlight is placed at a shallower angle, no light comes up through the water surface, and the tank is brightly lit.

a) Explain what is happening. [2 marks]

b) It is found that the beam into the air disappears when the spotlight is pointed at any angle of less than 41.25° to the floor. Calculate the refractive index of water. [2 marks]

Critical angles are never happy...

Total internal reflection doesn't sound like the most riveting subject, but it's super useful. Optical fibres wouldn't work without it, and we use them for all sorts of things — broadband connections, telephone cables, making things sparkly...

Lenses

Lenses are pretty useful — they're used in glasses to help you see, they're used in telescopes to help you see, they're used in magnifying glasses to help you see, they're used in your eyes to help... you get the picture.

Converging Lenses Bring Light Rays Together

1) **Lenses** change the **direction** of light rays by **refraction**.
2) **Converging** lenses bulge **outwards**.
3) Rays **parallel** to the **principal axis** of the lens converge onto a point called the **principal focus**. Parallel rays that **aren't** parallel to the principal axis converge somewhere else on the **focal plane** (see diagram).
4) The **focal length**, *f*, is the distance between the **lens axis** and the **focal plane**.
5) *f* is **positive** for a **converging** lens because it is **in front of** the lens.

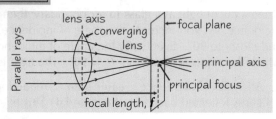

Diverging Lenses Spread Light Rays Out

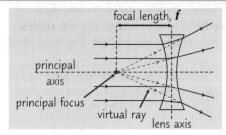

1) **Diverging** lenses cave **inwards**.
2) The **principal focus** of a diverging lens is at a point **behind** the lens.
3) The principal focus is the point that rays from a **distant** object, assumed to be parallel to the principal axis, **appear** to have come from. The dotted lines in the diagram show **virtual rays**. The light **doesn't** actually follow this path, but **appears** to have done so.
4) The **focal length**, *f*, is the distance between the **lens axis** and the **principal focus**.
5) *f* is **negative** for a **diverging** lens because it is **behind** the lens.

Images can be Real or Virtual

1) A **real image** is formed when light rays from a point on an object are made to **pass through** another point in space. The light rays are **actually there**, and the image can be **captured** on a **screen**.
2) A **virtual image** is formed when light rays from a point on an object **appear** to have come from another point in space. The light rays **aren't really where the image appears to be**, so the image **can't** be captured on a screen.
3) Converging lenses can form both **real** and **virtual** images, depending on where the object is. If the object is **further** than the **focal length** away from the lens, the image is **real**. If the object's **closer**, the image is **virtual**.
4) To work out where an image formed by a converging lens will appear, you can draw a **ray diagram**. Draw **two rays** from the same point on the object (the top is best) one **parallel** to the principal axis that passes through the **principal focus**, and one passing through the **centre** of the lens that **doesn't get refracted** (bent). The image will form where the **two rays meet** if the image is real. If the rays don't meet, the image is **virtual**. **Extend** the rays back (draw **virtual rays**) to locate where the two rays appear to have **come from**:

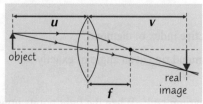

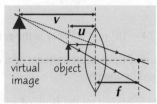

If an object sits on the principal axis, so will the image.

In the diagram, **u** = distance between object and lens axis, **v** = distance between image and lens axis (**positive** if image is **real**, **negative** if image is **virtual**), **f** = focal length.

5) A diverging lens will **always** form a virtual image — the **position** of the **object** in relation to the **focal length** will not affect the **type** of image formed.
6) To draw a **ray diagram** for a diverging lens, draw **two rays** from the same point on the object. One must pass through the **centre** of the lens without getting refracted. The other travels **parallel** to the **principal axis** until it meets the centre of the lens. Then it **refracts** so that it **appears** to come from the **principal focus**. The image will form where the real and virtual rays **meet**.
7) The values **u**, **v** and **f** are related by the **lens equation**:

$$\frac{1}{f} = \frac{1}{u} + \frac{1}{v}$$

This equation only works for thin lenses.

Lenses

Power Tells You How Much a Lens Bends Light

1) You can calculate the **power** of a lens, which tells you the lens' ability to **bend light**. The higher the power, the more the lens will **refract** light.

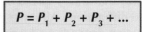

$$P = \frac{1}{f}$$

where P is the power of the lens in dioptres (D).

2) Imagine you have two or more **thin** lenses in a line, with their principal axes lined up. If the lenses are **touching** or are very **close together**, the **total power** of the lenses is found by just **adding** all the powers together — how simple.

$$P = P_1 + P_2 + P_3 + \ldots$$

Example: An image of Mabel the cow is being projected onto a screen 80 cm from a 3.25 D converging lens. How far must the picture slide of Mabel be from the lens?

$P = \frac{1}{f} = 3.25$ D, and the image must be real as it is captured on a screen, so $v = 80$ cm $= 0.8$ m.

Rearrange the lens equation: $\frac{1}{u} = \frac{1}{f} - \frac{1}{v} = 3.25 - \frac{1}{0.8}$

$$= 3.25 - 1.25 = 2$$

$u = \frac{1}{2} = 0.5$ m,

so the slide must be **0.5 m** from the lens.

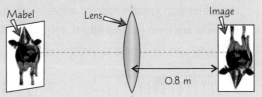

A Lens Can Produce a Magnified Image

The magnification, m, of an image can be calculated in two different ways. They are:

$$m = \frac{\text{image height}}{\text{object height}} \qquad m = \frac{v}{u}$$

Magnification is a ratio and so has no units.

Practice Questions

Q1 Define the focal length and power of a converging lens.

Q2 Draw a ray diagram for the converging lens and object shown on the right. State whether the image formed is real or virtual.

Q3 State whether real or virtual images are produced by diverging lenses.

Q4 Write an equation to show how the object distance (u), image distance (v) and focal length of a thin lens (f) are related.

Q5 A diverging lens has a magnification of 3.4. An image of an object created by the lens is 12.8 cm wide. How wide is the object?

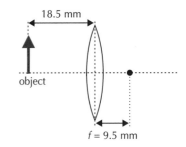

Exam Questions

Q1 a) Define the principal focus of a converging lens. [1 mark]

b) An object was placed 0.20 m in front of a converging lens of focal length 0.15 m. Calculate how far behind the lens the image was formed. [2 marks]

Q2 The length of a seed is 12.5 mm. A lens is placed in front of the seed, so that the principal axis of the lens is parallel to the seed. An image of the seed is projected onto a screen. The image has a length of 47.2 mm.

a) Calculate the linear magnification of the lens. [1 mark]

b) If the seed is 4.0 mm from the lens, calculate how far the screen is from the lens. [2 marks]

c) Calculate the power of the lens in dioptres. [2 marks]

d) A second lens is placed directly after the first lens. The focal length of the combined lenses is 0.22 cm. Calculate the power of the second lens. [2 marks]

The physics is real, the fun is virtual...

Ray diagrams might look complicated, but once you've practised them a few times it'll all be a doddle. Or a doodle...

Diffraction

Diffraction is some funky stuff — it's all about waves squeezing through spaces and then spreading out.
Kind of like whipped cream from a can. Actually, it's nothing like that... read the pages and learn some stuff.

Waves Go **Round Corners** and **Spread out** of **Gaps**

The way that **waves spread out** as they come through a **narrow gap** or go round obstacles is called **diffraction**. **All** waves diffract, but it's not always easy to observe. The amount of diffraction depends on the **size of the gap** in comparison to the **wavelength** of the wave.

You Can Use a **Ripple Tank** to Investigate **Diffraction**

1) **Ripple tanks** are shallow tanks of water that you can generate a wave in.

2) This is done by an **oscillating paddle**, which continually dips into the water and creates regular waves with straight, parallel wavefronts.

Take a look back at p.74 for a reminder on what a wavefront is.

3) Objects are then placed into the ripple tank to create a **barrier** with a **gap** in the middle of it.

4) This gap can be varied to see the effects this has on how the waves spread through the tank.

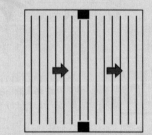

When the gap is **a lot bigger** than the **wavelength**, diffraction is **unnoticeable**.

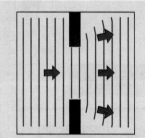

You get **noticeable diffraction** through a gap **several** wavelengths wide.

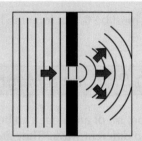

You get the **most** diffraction when the gap is **the same** size as the **wavelength**.

As the gap decreases, the diffraction becomes more noticeable until the gap becomes too small and the water waves cannot pass through it anymore. The waves are then **reflected** back on themselves.

When **sound** passes through a **doorway**, the **size of gap** and the **wavelength** are usually roughly **equal**, so **a lot** of **diffraction** occurs. That's why you have no trouble **hearing** someone through an **open door** to the next room, even if the other person is out of your **line of sight**. The reason that you can't **see** him or her is that when **light** passes through the doorway, it is passing through a **gap** around a **hundred million times bigger** than its wavelength — the amount of diffraction is **tiny**.

Diffraction can be **Explained** Using **Huygens' Construction**

1) Huygens developed a **general model** of the propagation of **waves** in what is now known as **Huygens' construction**

HUYGENS' CONSTRUCTION: Every point on a wavefront may be considered to be a **point source** of **secondary wavelets** that spread out in the forward direction at the speed of the wave. The **new wavefront** is the surface that is **tangential** to all of these **secondary wavelets**.

This diagram shows how this works:

2) Huygens' construction can be used to explain the shape of the wavefronts as light travels through a **slit**. The **secondary wavelets** that pass through the slit are what produce the curve of the **new wavefront** emerging from the slit.

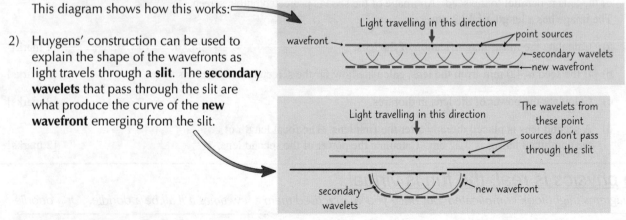

Diffraction

You Get *Diffraction* Around an *Obstacle* Too

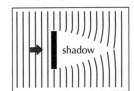

When a wave meets an **obstacle**, you get diffraction around the edges. Behind the obstacle is a '**shadow**', where the wave is blocked. The **wider** the obstacle compared with the wavelength of the wave, the less diffraction you get, and so the **longer** the shadow.

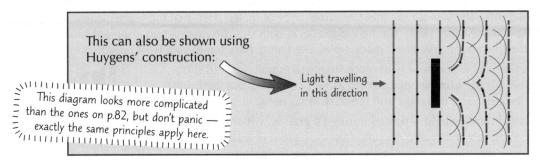

This can also be shown using Huygens' construction:

This diagram looks more complicated than the ones on p.82, but don't panic — exactly the same principles apply here.

Light travelling in this direction →

With *Light Waves* you get a Pattern of *Light* and *Dark Fringes*

1) If the **wavelength** of a **light wave** is roughly similar to the size of the **aperture**, you get a **diffraction pattern** of light and dark fringes.

2) The pattern has a **bright central fringe** with alternating **dark and bright fringes** on either side of it.

3) The **spread** of the diffraction pattern depends on the **relative sizes** of the wavelength and the slit width. The **longer** the wavelength is **compared** to the **width** of the slit, the **wider** the diffraction pattern.

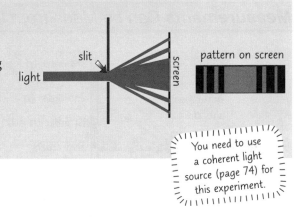

You need to use a coherent light source (page 74) for this experiment.

Practice Questions

Q1 What is diffraction?

Q2 For a long time some scientists argued that light couldn't be a wave because it did not seem to diffract. Suggest why they might have got this impression.

Q3 Light passes through a slit that is a few wavelengths wide. Use Huygens' construction to explain the shape of the wavefronts of the light as they emerge from the other side of the slit.

Q4 Sketch what happens when plane waves meet an obstacle about as wide as one wavelength.

Q5 Light passing through a slit produces a diffraction pattern. State what effect decreasing the wavelength of the light would have on the width of the diffraction pattern.

Exam Questions

Q1 A mountain lies directly between you and a radio transmitter.
Explain, with the use of a diagram, why you can pick up long-wave radio broadcasts
from the transmitter but not short-wave radio broadcasts.   [3 marks]

Q2 Describe how you would use a ripple tank to investigate how the wavelength of a
wave and the size of the gap a wave travels through relates to the amount of
diffraction which occurs. Comment on when maximum diffraction will be seen.   [3 marks]

Even hiding behind a mountain, you can't get away from long-wave radio...

Unfortunately "Bay FM" don't transmit using long wave radio. So as I'm giving the singing-in-the-car performance of my life, I go over a hill and the signal cuts out. Where's diffraction when I need it then hmm? How will I ever become famous? Diffraction crops up again in stuff like quantum physics so make sure you really understand it.

Diffraction Gratings

What could possibly be more exciting than shining a laser through two slits? Shining a laser through more than two slits of course. Jeez, ask a stupid question...

Interference Patterns Get **Sharper** When You Diffract Through **More Slits**

1) You saw on pages 74-75 that **two sources** that produce waves that are **coherent** and **in phase** will result in an **interference pattern** (alternating bands of constructive and destructive interference). If you are using **light waves**, you can pass one **monochromatic** (one wavelength) **beam of light** through **two slits**. The slits are cut into the **same** piece of material, so that the wave passes through them at the **same** time. The light **diffracts** at both slits, producing two coherent sources of light. The interference pattern is made up of alternating **dark bands** and **light bands**.

2) You can repeat this experiment with **more than two equally spaced** slits. You get basically the **same shaped** pattern as for two slits — but the **bright bands** are **brighter** and **narrower** and the **dark areas** between are **darker**.

3) When **monochromatic light** is passed through a **grating**, which has **hundreds** of slits per millimetre, the interference pattern is **really sharp** because there are so **many beams reinforcing the pattern**.

4) Sharper fringes make for more **precise** measurements as they are easier to tell apart and so are **easier** to measure.

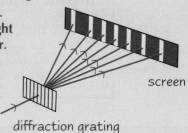

screen

diffraction grating

Measurements Can be Made from Interference Patterns

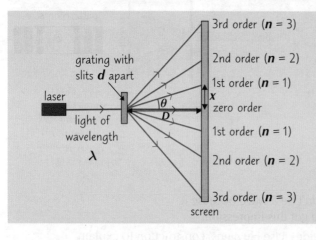

3rd order (**n** = 3)

2nd order (**n** = 2)

1st order (**n** = 1)

x

zero order

1st order (**n** = 1)

2nd order (**n** = 2)

3rd order (**n** = 3)

screen

grating with slits **d** apart

laser

light of wavelength

λ

θ

D

1) For monochromatic light, all of the maxima are sharp lines. (It's different for white light — see the next page).

2) This means the distance between the maxima can be easily measured (**fringe width**).

3) There's a line of **maximum brightness** at the centre called the **zero order** line.

4) The lines just **either side** of the central one are called **first order lines**. The **next pair out** are called **second order** lines and so on.

If the grating has N slits per metre, then the slit spacing, d, is just 1/N metres.

Measuring the Wavelength of Light using a Diffraction Grating

1) Position a **laser** (or other monochromatic light source) in front of a **diffraction grating** so that the light travels through the grating and creates an interference pattern on a **flat wall** or **screen** a few metres away.

2) Measure the **distance, D**, between the diffraction grating and the wall.

3) Measure the **distance, x**, between the **zero order maximum** and the **1st order maximum** for both sides and take an **average** of the two readings.

Make sure the light is travelling at right angles to the diffraction grating and wall.

4) Using the **fringe width, x**, and the distance to the wall, **D**, the angle the 1st order fringe makes with the zero order line can be calculated using **small angle approximations**.

Don't forget to set your calculator to radians when using this equation.

$$\tan\theta \approx \theta \text{ and } \tan\theta = \frac{x}{D}, \text{ so } \theta \approx \frac{x}{D}$$

The value for d is usually given on the grating. Don't forget that n = 1 for the zero order line.

5) You can then use the following **equation** to **calculate** the wavelength of light: $\boxed{d \sin\theta = n\lambda}$

6) **Repeat** the measurements for more **order lines** to find an **average** for the wavelength.

7) Repeat the experiment for a diffraction grating that has a **different distance** between the **slits**.

Diffraction Gratings

You can Draw General Conclusions from $d \sin \theta = n\lambda$

1) If λ is **bigger**, $\sin \theta$ is **bigger**, and so θ is **bigger**. This means that the larger the **wavelength**, the more the pattern will **spread out**.

2) If d is **bigger**, $\sin \theta$ is **smaller**. This means that the **coarser** the grating, the **less** the pattern will **spread out**.

3) Values of $\sin \theta$ greater than **1** are **impossible**. So if for a certain n you get a result of **more than 1** for $\sin \theta$ you know that that order **doesn't exist**.

Shining White Light Through a Diffraction Grating Produces Spectra

1) **White light** is really a **mixture** of **colours**. If you **diffract** white light through a **grating** then the patterns due to **different wavelengths** within the white light are **spread out** by **different** amounts.

2) Each **order** in the pattern becomes a **spectrum**, with **red** on the **outside** and **violet** on the **inside**. The **zero order maximum** stays **white** because all the wavelengths just pass straight through.

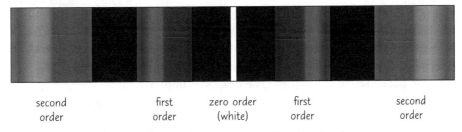

| second order | first order | zero order (white) | first order | second order |

3) **Astronomers** and **chemists** often need to study spectra to help identify elements. They use diffraction gratings rather than prisms because they're **more accurate**.

4) Another example of white light being **split** into a spectrum due to diffraction can be seen on **CDs** and **DVDs**. There are **grooves** etched into the **reflective surface**, which causes the light to **diffract**. Constructive interference occurs at different points for light with different wavelengths, so you end up seeing a **rainbow pattern**.

Practice Questions

Q1 Why do more slits in a diffraction grating lead to a sharper diffraction pattern?

Q2 What is the formula for finding the wavelength of light incident on a diffraction grating?

Q3 A beam of light is diffracted through a diffraction grating. State what will happen to the diffraction pattern if the wavelength of the light decreases.

Q4 Describe an experiment to find the wavelength of monochromatic light using a diffraction grating.

Exam Questions

Q1 Yellow laser light of wavelength 6.00×10^{-7} m is transmitted through a diffraction grating of 4.0×10^5 lines per metre.

a) State the angle to the normal where the first and second order bright lines are seen. [4 marks]

b) State whether there is a fifth order line. Explain your answer. [1 mark]

Q2 Visible, monochromatic light is transmitted through a diffraction grating of 3.70×10^5 lines per metre. The first order maximum is at an angle of $14.2°$ to the incident beam.

Calculate the wavelength of the incident light. [2 marks]

Ooooooooooooo — pretty patterns...

Yes, it's the end of another beautiful topic. Three important points for you to take away — the more slits you have, the sharper the image, monochromatic light leads to sharp fringes and one lovely equation to get to know. Make sure you get everything in this topic — there's some good stuff waiting in the next one and I wouldn't want you to be distracted.

Light — Wave or Photon?

You probably already thought light was a bit weird — but oh no... being a wave that travels at the fastest speed possible isn't enough for light — it has to go one step further and act like a particle too...

Light Behaves Like a **Wave**... or a **Stream of Particles**

1) In the **late nineteenth century**, if you asked what light was, scientists would happily show you lots of nice experiments showing how light must be a **wave**.

2) Light produces **interference** and **diffraction** patterns — **alternating bands** of **dark** and **light**. These patterns can **only** be explained using **waves**.

Take a look back at p.82-85 for a reminder on interference and diffraction.

3) That was all fine and dandy... until the **photoelectric effect** (p.88), which mucked up everything. The only way you could explain this effect was if light acted as a **particle** — called a **photon**.

A **Photon** is a **Quantum** of **EM Radiation**

1) When Max Planck was investigating **black body radiation** (don't worry — you don't need to know about that right now), he suggested that **EM waves** can **only** be **released** in **discrete packets**, called **quanta**. A single packet of **EM radiation** is called a **quantum**.

The **energy carried** by one of these **wave-packets** had to be:

$$E = hf = \frac{hc}{\lambda}$$

where h = Planck constant = 6.63×10^{-34} Js, f = frequency (Hz), λ = wavelength (m) and c = speed of light in a vacuum = 3.00×10^8 ms^{-1}

2) So, the **higher** the **frequency** of the electromagnetic radiation, the more **energy** its wave-packets carry.

3) **Einstein** went **further** by suggesting that **EM waves** (and the energy they carry) can only **exist** in discrete packets. He called these wave-packets **photons**.

4) He believed that a photon acts as a **particle**, and will either transfer **all** or **none** of its energy when interacting with another particle, e.g. an electron.

5) Photons have **no charge** — they are **neutral**, like neutrons.

Electrons in **Atoms** Exist in **Discrete Energy Levels**

1) **Electrons** in an **atom** can **only exist** in certain **well-defined energy levels**. Each level is given a **number**, with **n = 1** representing the **ground state**.

The ground state is the lowest energy state of the atom.

2) Electrons can **move down** energy levels by **emitting** a **photon**.

3) Since these **transitions** are between **definite energy levels**, the **energy** (and therefore the **frequency**) of **each photon** emitted can **only** take a **certain allowed value**.

4) The diagram on the right shows the **energy levels** for **atomic hydrogen**.

5) The **energies involved** are **so tiny** that it makes sense to use a more **appropriate unit** than the **joule**. When you **accelerate** an electron between two electrodes, it transfers some electrical potential energy (eV) into kinetic energy.

$$eV = \frac{1}{2}mv^2$$

e is the size of the charge on an electron: 1.60×10^{-19} C. See page 43.

6) The **electronvolt (eV)** is defined as:

> The **kinetic energy carried** by an **electron** after it has been **accelerated** through a **potential difference** of **1 volt**.

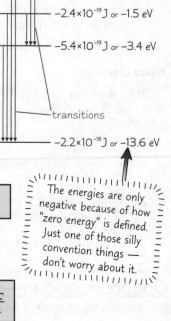

LEVEL	ENERGY
$n = \infty$	zero energy
$n = 5$	-8.6×10^{-20} J or -0.54 eV
$n = 4$	-1.4×10^{-19} J or -0.85 eV
$n = 3$	-2.4×10^{-19} J or -1.5 eV
$n = 2$	-5.4×10^{-19} J or -3.4 eV
$n = 1$	-2.2×10^{-18} J or -13.6 eV

transitions

So 1 electron volt = $e \times V = 1.60 \times 10^{-19}$ C $\times$ 1 JC^{-1}.

$$1 \text{ eV} = 1.60 \times 10^{-19} \text{ J}$$

The energies are only negative because of how "zero energy" is defined. Just one of those silly convention things — don't worry about it.

7) On the diagram, energies are labelled in **both units** for **comparison's** sake.

8) The **energy** carried by each **photon** is **equal** to the **difference in energies** between the **two levels**. The equation below shows a **transition** between a higher energy level n = 2 where the electrons have energy E_2 and a lower energy level n = 1 with electrons of energy E_1:

$$\Delta E = E_2 - E_1 = hf = \frac{hc}{\lambda}$$

9) Electrons can also **move up** energy levels if they **absorb a photon** with the **exact energy difference** between the two levels. The movement of an electron to a higher energy level is called **excitation**.

Light — Wave or Photon?

Continuous Spectra Contain All Possible Wavelengths

1) The **spectrum** of **white light** is **continuous**.

2) If you **split** the **light** up with a **prism**, the **colours** all **merge** into each other — there **aren't** any **gaps** in the spectrum.

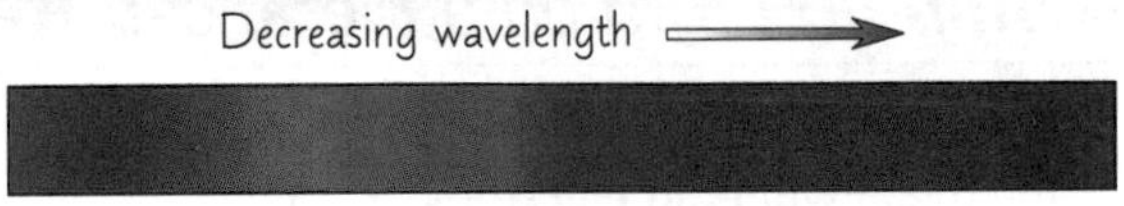

Decreasing wavelength ⟹

Hot Gases Produce Line Emission Spectra

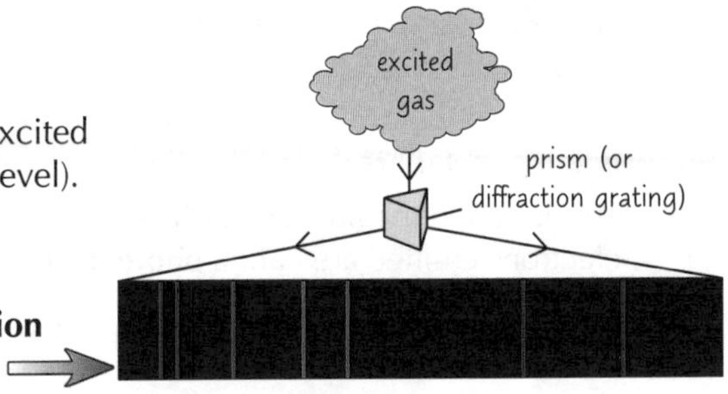

1) If you heat a gas to a **high temperature**, the **atoms** become **excited** (one or more of their **electrons** is moved to a **higher** energy level).

2) As electrons within the atoms **fall** back to the **lower energy levels**, they **emit energy** as **photons** (see previous page).

3) If you **split** the light from a **hot gas** with a **prism** or a **diffraction grating** (see pages 84-85), you get a **line emission spectrum**. ⟹

4) A line emission spectrum is seen as a **series** of **bright lines** against a **black background**, as shown above.

5) Each **line** on the spectrum corresponds to a **particular wavelength** of light **emitted** by the source. Since only **certain photon energies** are **allowed**, you only see the **corresponding wavelengths**.

excited gas

prism (or diffraction grating)

Cool Gases Produce Line Absorption Spectra

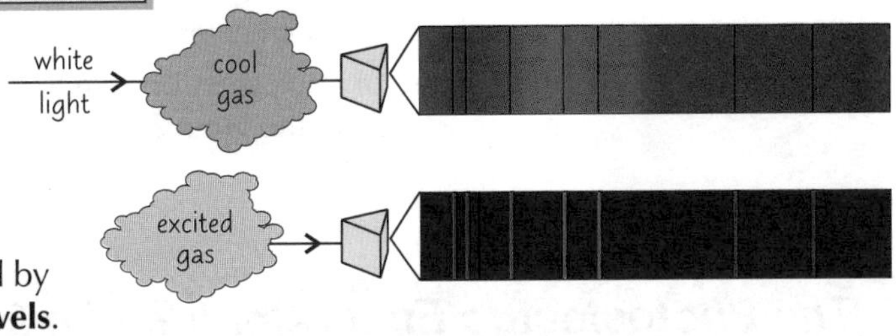

1) You get a **line absorption spectrum** when **white light** passes through a cool gas and then a **diffraction grating** or **prism**.

2) At **low temperatures**, **most** of the **electrons** in the **gas atoms** will be in their **ground states**.

3) **Photons** of the **correct wavelength** are **absorbed** by the **electrons** to **excite** them to **higher energy levels**.

4) These **wavelengths** are then **missing** from the **continuous spectrum** when it **comes out** the other side of the gas.

5) You see a **continuous spectrum** with **black lines** in it corresponding to the **absorbed wavelengths**.

6) If you **compare** the **absorption** and **emission** spectra of a **particular gas**, the **black lines** in the **absorption spectrum** match up to the **bright lines** in the **emission spectrum**.

white light ⟶ cool gas

excited gas

Practice Questions

Q1 Give two different ways to describe the nature of light.
Q2 What is a photon?
Q3 Write down the two formulas you can use to find the energy of a photon. Define all the symbols you use.
Q4 What is an electronvolt? What is 1 eV in joules?
Q5 Describe line absorption and line emission spectra. How are these two types of spectra produced?

Exam Question

Q1 An electron is accelerated through a potential difference of 12.1 V.

a) How much kinetic energy has it gained in i) eV and ii) joules? [2 marks]

b) This electron hits a hydrogen atom in its ground state and excites it.
   i) Explain what is meant by excitation. [1 mark]
   ii) Using the energy values on the right, calculate which energy level the electron from the hydrogen atom is excited to. [1 mark]
   iii) Calculate the energies and frequencies of all the photons that might be emitted as the electron returns to its ground state. [6 marks]

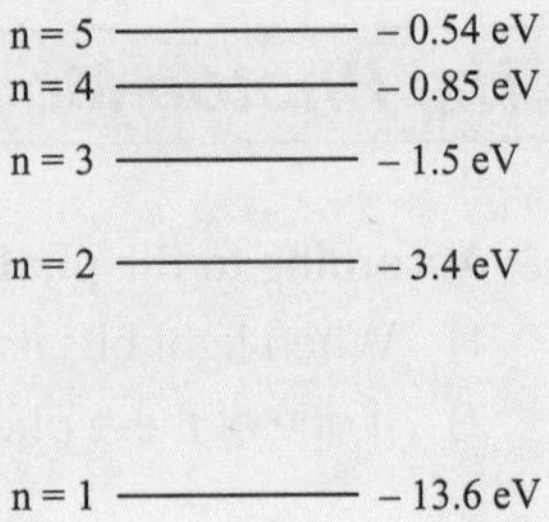

$n = 5$ —— -0.54 eV
$n = 4$ —— -0.85 eV
$n = 3$ —— -1.5 eV
$n = 2$ —— -3.4 eV
$n = 1$ —— -13.6 eV

Light can be a particle — well that's a twist in the tale...
Physics is just ridiculous sometimes. But learn it you must — get your head around those energy levels in atoms folks.

TOPIC 5 — WAVES AND PARTICLE NATURE OF LIGHT

The Photoelectric Effect

I think they should rename 'the photoelectric effect' as 'the piece-of-cake effect' — it's not easy, I just like cake.

Shining Light on a Metal can Release Electrons

If you shine **light** of a **high enough frequency** onto the **surface of a metal**, the metal will **emit electrons**. For **most** metals, this **frequency** falls in the **UV** range.

1) **Free electrons** on the **surface** of the metal **absorb energy** from the light.

2) If an electron **absorbs enough** energy, the **bonds** holding it to the metal **break** and the electron is **released**.

3) This is called the **photoelectric effect** and the electrons emitted are called **photoelectrons**.

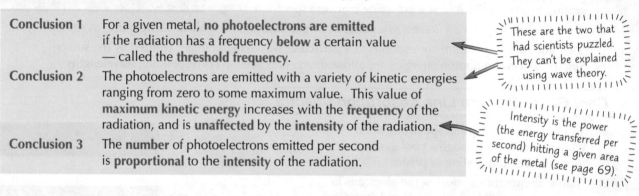

'Light' means any EM radiation — not just visible light.

ultraviolet radiation

electrons

You don't need to know the details of any experiments on this, you just need to learn the three main conclusions:

Conclusion 1	For a given metal, **no photoelectrons are emitted** if the radiation has a frequency **below** a certain value — called the **threshold frequency**.
Conclusion 2	The photoelectrons are emitted with a variety of kinetic energies ranging from zero to some maximum value. This value of **maximum kinetic energy** increases with the **frequency** of the radiation, and is **unaffected** by the **intensity** of the radiation.
Conclusion 3	The **number** of photoelectrons emitted per second is **proportional** to the **intensity** of the radiation.

These are the two that had scientists puzzled. They can't be explained using wave theory.

Intensity is the power (the energy transferred per second) hitting a given area of the metal (see page 69).

The Photoelectric Effect Couldn't be Explained by Wave Theory...

According to wave theory:

1) For a particular frequency of light, the **energy** carried is **proportional** to the **intensity** of the beam.

2) The energy carried by the light would be **spread evenly** over the wavefront.

3) **Each** free electron on the surface of the metal would gain a **bit of energy** from each incoming wave.

4) Gradually, each electron would gain **enough energy** to leave the metal.

Charlotte thought that landing on her head would get her top marks for beam intensity.

SO... The **higher the intensity** of the wave, the **more energy** it should transfer to each electron — the kinetic energy should increase with intensity. There's **no explanation** for the **kinetic energy** depending only on the **frequency**.

There is also **no explanation** for the **threshold frequency**. According to **wave theory**, the electrons should be emitted **eventually**, no matter what the **frequency** is.

The Photon Model Explained the Photoelectric Effect Nicely

According to the photon model (see page 86):

1) When light hits its surface, the metal is **bombarded** by photons.

2) If one of these photons is **absorbed** by a free electron, the electron will gain energy equal to *hf*.

Before an electron can **leave** the surface of the metal, it needs enough energy to **break the bonds holding it there**. This energy is called the **work function energy** (symbol ϕ, phi) and its **value** depends on the **metal**.

The Photoelectric Effect

The **Photon Model** Explains the **Threshold Frequency**...

1) If the energy **gained** by an electron (on the surface of the metal) from a photon is **greater** than the **work function**, the electron is **emitted**.

2) If it **isn't**, the metal will heat up, but **no electrons** will be emitted.

3) Since, for **electrons** to be released, $hf \geq \phi$, the **threshold frequency** must be:

$$f = \frac{\phi}{h}$$

...and the **Maximum Kinetic Energy**

1) The **energy transferred** to an electron is hf.

2) The **kinetic energy** the electron will be carrying when it **leaves** the metal is hf **minus** any energy it's **lost** on the way out. Electrons **deeper** down in the metal lose more energy than the electrons on the **surface**, which explains the **range** of energies.

3) The **minimum** amount of energy it can lose is the **work function**, so the **maximum kinetic energy** of a photoelectron, $E_{k\,(max)}$, is hf minus the work function, which gives the photoelectric equation:

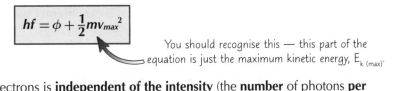

$$hf = \phi + \frac{1}{2}mv_{max}^2$$

You should recognise this — this part of the equation is just the maximum kinetic energy, $E_{k\,(max)}$.

4) The **kinetic energy** of the electrons is **independent of the intensity** (the **number** of photons **per second** on an **area**), as they can **only absorb one photon** at a time. Increasing the **intensity** just means **more photons per second** on an **area** — each photon has the **same energy** as before.

Practice Questions

Q1 Explain what the photoelectric effect is.

Q2 What three conclusions were drawn from experimentation on the photoelectric effect?

Q3 What is meant by the term threshold frequency?

Q4 Write down the equation that relates the work function of a metal and the threshold frequency.

Q5 Write down an equation that relates the maximum kinetic energy of a photoelectron released from a metal surface and the frequency of the incident light on the surface.

Exam Questions

$h = 6.63 \times 10^{-34}\ Js;\ e = 1.60 \times 10^{-19}\ C$

Q1 The work function of calcium is 2.9 eV. Calculate the threshold frequency of radiation needed for the photoelectric effect to take place. [2 marks]

Q2 The surface of a copper plate is illuminated with monochromatic ultraviolet light, with a frequency of 2.0×10^{15} Hz. The work function for copper is 4.7 eV.

a) Calculate the energy in eV carried by one photon of the ultraviolet light. [2 marks]

b) Calculate the maximum kinetic energy of a photoelectron emitted from the copper surface. [2 marks]

Q3 Explain why the photoelectric effect only occurs after the incident light has reached a certain frequency. [2 marks]

I'm so glad we got that all cleared up...

Yep, the photoelectric effect is a bit tricky. The most important bits here are why wave theory doesn't explain the phenomenon, and why the photon theory does. A good way to learn conceptual stuff like this is to try to explain it to someone else. You'll get most formulas in your handy data sheet, but it's probably a good idea to learn them too...

Wave-Particle Duality

Is it a wave? Is it a particle? No, it's a wave. No, it's a particle. No it's not, it's a wave. No don't be daft, it's a particle. (etc

There's Evidence for Light Being a **Wave** and for Light Being a **Particle**

Towards the end of the **17th century**, two important **theories of light** were published — one by Isaac Newton and the other by Huygens. Newton's theory suggested that light was made up of tiny particles, which he called "**corpuscles**", and Huygens put forward a theory using **waves**.

Interference and Diffraction show Light as a Wave

The **corpuscular** theory could explain **reflection** and **refraction**, but **diffraction** and **interference** (p.84-85) are both uniquely wave properties. Over 100 years later, it was shown that light could interfere and diffract, so that settled the argument... for now.

The Photoelectric Effect Shows Light Behaving as a Particle

After another 100 years or so, the debate was raging once again after the photoelectric effect was observed (p.88).

1) **Einstein** explained the results of **photoelectricity experiments** by thinking of the **beam of light** as a series of **particle-like photons** (see p.86). He published his particle theory of light in **1905**.

2) If a **photon** of light is a **discrete** bundle of energy, then it can **interact** with an **electron** in a **one-to-one way**.

3) **All** the **energy** in the **photon** is **given** to one **electron**.

De Broglie Came up With the Wave-Particle Duality Theory

1) In **1924**, Louis de Broglie made a **bold suggestion** in his **PhD thesis**:

> If 'wave-like' light showed particle properties (photons), 'particles' like electrons should be expected to show wave-like properties.

2) The **de Broglie equation** relates a **wave property** (**wavelength**, λ) to a **moving particle property** (momentum, p). h = Planck constant = 6.63×10^{-34} Js.

$$\lambda = \frac{h}{p}$$

I'm not impressed — this is just speculation. What do you think Dad?

3) The de Broglie wave of a particle can be interpreted as a '**probability wave**' — the **likelihood** of finding a particle at a point is **directly proportional** to the **square** of the **amplitude** of the wave at that point.

4) Many physicists at the time **weren't very impressed** — his ideas were just **speculation**. But later experiments **confirmed** the wave nature of electrons.

Electron Diffraction shows the Wave Nature of Electrons

1) In **1927**, two American physicists, **Clinton Davisson** and **Lester Germer**, succeeded in diffracting **electrons**.

2) **Diffraction patterns** are observed when **accelerated electrons** in a vacuum tube **interact** with the **spaces** between **carbon atoms** in **polycrystalline graphite**.

3) This **confirms** that electrons show **wave-like** properties.

4) According to wave theory, the **spread** of the **lines** in the diffraction pattern **increases** if the **wavelength** of the wave is **greater**.

5) In electron diffraction experiments, a **smaller accelerating voltage**, i.e. **slower** electrons, gives **widely spaced** rings.

6) **Increase** the **electron speed** and the diffraction pattern circles **squash together** towards the **middle**. This fits in with the **de Broglie** equation above — if the **momentum** is **higher**, the **wavelength** is **shorter** and the **spread** of lines is **smaller**.

7) Electron diffraction was a **huge** discovery — this was the first **direct evidence** for de Broglie's theory.

> In general, λ for **electrons** accelerated in a **vacuum tube** is about the **same size** as **electromagnetic waves** in the **X-ray** part of the spectrum.

Wave-Particle Duality

Particles Don't show Wave-Like Properties All the Time

1) You **only** get **diffraction** if a particle interacts with an object of about the **same size** as its **de Broglie wavelength**.
2) A **tennis ball**, for example, with **mass 0.058 kg** and **speed 100 ms⁻¹** has a **de Broglie wavelength** of 10^{-34} m. That's 10^{19} **times smaller** than the **nucleus** of an **atom**! There's nothing that small for it to interact with.

> **Example:** An electron of mass 9.11×10^{-31} kg is fired from an electron gun at 7.00×10^6 ms⁻¹. What size object will the electron need to interact with in order to diffract?
>
> Momentum of electron $= p = mv = (9.11 \times 10^{-31}) \times (7.00 \times 10^6) = 6.377 \times 10^{-24}$ kg ms⁻¹
>
> $$\lambda = \frac{h}{p} = \frac{6.63 \times 10^{-34}}{6.377 \times 10^{-24}} = \mathbf{1.04 \times 10^{-10}} \text{ m (to 3 s.f.)}$$

> Electrons with a wavelength of around 1×10^{-10} m are **likely** to be diffracted by the atoms in **polycrystalline structures**.

3) A **shorter wavelength** gives **less diffraction effects**. This fact is used in the **electron microscope**.
4) **Diffraction** effects **blur detail** on an image. If you want to **resolve tiny detail** in an **image**, you need a **shorter wavelength**. **Light** blurs out detail more than 'electron-waves' do, so an **electron microscope** can resolve **finer detail** than a **light microscope**. They can let you look at things as tiny as a single strand of DNA... which is nice.

Practice Questions

Q1 Which observations show light to have a 'wave-like' character?

Q2 Which observations show light to have a 'particle' character?

Q3 What happens to the de Broglie wavelength of a particle if its velocity increases?

Q4 Describe the experimental evidence that shows electrons have a 'wave-like' character.

Exam Questions

proton mass, $m_p = 1.673 \times 10^{-27}$ kg; electron mass, $m_e = 9.11 \times 10^{-31}$ kg

Q1 a) State what is meant by the wave-particle duality of electromagnetic radiation. [1 mark]

  b) Calculate the momentum of an electron with a de Broglie wavelength of 590 nm. [2 marks]

Q2 Electrons travelling at a speed of 3.50×10^6 ms⁻¹ exhibit wave properties.

  a) Calculate the wavelength of these electrons. [2 marks]

  b) Calculate the speed of protons which would have the same wavelength as these electrons. [2 marks]

  c) Some electrons and protons were accelerated from rest by the same potential difference, giving them the same kinetic energy. Explain why they will have different wavelengths. [3 marks]

Q3 Electrons are directed at a thin slice of graphite at high speed and a diffraction pattern is observed. Which of the following statements correctly describe a conclusion that this observation supports? [1 mark]

    1   Electrons can show particle-like behaviour.
    2   Waves can show particle-like behaviour.
    3   Photons can show wave-like behaviour.
    4   Electrons can show wave-like behaviour.

  A   1, 2 and 4   B   4 only   C   3 only   D   1 and 4 only

---

Don't hide your wave-particles under a bushel...

Right — I think we'll all agree that quantum physics is a wee bit strange when you come to think about it. What it's saying is that electrons and photons aren't really waves, and they aren't really particles — they're both... at the same time. It's what quantum physicists like to call a 'juxtaposition of states'. Well they would, wouldn't they...

Momentum and 2D Collisions

You've met linear momentum before, way back on pages 32-33. Time to make things a bit more complicated...

Momentum is Always **Conserved**

1) The linear **momentum** of an object depends on two things — its **mass** and **velocity**:

> **momentum** (in kg ms⁻¹) = **mass** (in kg) × **velocity** (in ms⁻¹)   or   **p = mv**

Remember — momentum is a vector quantity (p.14), so it has size and direction.

2) Assuming **no external forces** act, momentum is always **conserved**. For example, the **total momentum** of two objects **before** they collide **equals** the total momentum **after** the collision.

3) Momentum conservation also applies in **explosions**. E.g. if you fire an **air rifle**, the **forward momentum** gained by the pellet **equals** the **backward momentum** of the rifle, and you feel the rifle recoiling into your shoulder.

4) Collisions and explosions usually happen in more than one dimension. In **two-dimensional (2D) collisions**, momentum is conserved in **both dimensions**. You can solve 2D collision problems by **resolving vectors**.

You can Resolve Momentum **Horizontally** and **Vertically**...

1) Often, the most sensible directions to resolve vectors in are the **horizontal** and **vertical** directions.

2) Vectors at right angles **don't affect** each other, so momentum **must be conserved** in both the **horizontal** and **vertical** directions for momentum to be conserved **overall**.

Example: Ball A collides with stationary ball B, as shown in diagram 1. After the collision, the two balls move off as shown in diagram 2. Ball A has a mass of 40 g. Calculate the mass, m, of ball B.

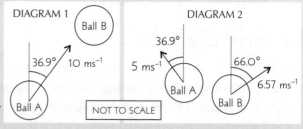

You can work this out by resolving in the horizontal or vertical direction. Here, we'll use the horizontal direction. We'll also take movement to the right to be positive.

horizontal momentum before the collision = horizontal momentum after the collision

$$(0.04 \times 10 \sin 36.9°) + (m \times 0) = (0.04 \times -5 \sin 36.9°) + (m \times 6.57 \sin 66.0°)$$

so, $m = \dfrac{0.04 \times (10 \sin 36.9° + 5 \sin 36.9°)}{6.57 \sin 66.0°} = 0.0600...$ kg = **60 g (to 1 s.f.)**   *You can check your answer by doing the same calculation for the vertical direction.*

...or **Parallel** and **Perpendicular** to the **Line of Impact**

When two objects **collide**, they only transfer momentum **parallel to the line of impact**. For uniform circular or spherical objects, this is a **line** that runs between their **centres**. If one object is **stationary** before the collision, its **final velocity** will be along the **line of impact**.

Example: Ball A is moving at 7.5 ms⁻¹ when it collides with stationary ball B, as shown in the diagram. After the collision, ball B moves off at a speed of 2.5 ms⁻¹. Ball A has a mass of 45 g and ball B has a mass of 25 g. Find the velocity of ball A after the collision, giving its direction relative to the line of the collision.

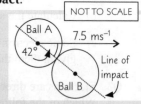

Resolve parallel to the line of impact to find the final velocity of A **parallel** to the line, v_{par}:

parallel component of momentum before	=	parallel component of momentum after

$$0.045 \times 7.5 \cos 42 = (0.045 \times v_{par}) + (0.025 \times 2.5)$$

So $v_{par} = ((0.045 \times 7.5 \cos 42) - (0.025 \times 2.5)) \div 0.045$
$$= 4.184... \text{ ms}^{-1}$$

Resolve perpendicular to line of impact to find the final velocity of A **perpendicular** to the line, v_{perp}:

perpendicular component of momentum before	=	perpendicular component of momentum after

$$0.045 \times 7.5 \sin 42 = (0.045 \times v_{perp}) + (0.025 \times 0)$$

So $v_{perp} = 7.5 \sin 42 = 5.018...$ ms⁻¹

Then you can use Pythagoras to find the magnitude of ball A's final velocity:

$$v_{final} = \sqrt{4.184...^2 + 5.018...^2} = 6.534... = \textbf{6.5 ms}^{-1}\textbf{(to 2 s.f.)}$$

And trigonometry to find its direction relative to the line of impact:

$$\theta = \tan^{-1}(5.018... \div 4.184...) = 50.176...° = \textbf{50° (to 2 s.f.)}$$

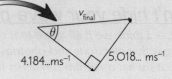

Momentum and 2D Collisions

You can Investigate *Momentum* in 2D Using *Video Analysis Software*

A simple experiment for investigating conservation of momentum involves rolling ball bearings on a flat table top:

1) Weigh **two ball bearings** and note down their **masses**.

2) On a **level table top**, position **two metre rulers** at **right angles** to each other. Put one of the ball bearings on the table and position a **video camera** above the table so it has a **birds-eye view** of the table. The table should look like this from above:

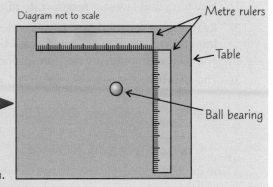
Diagram not to scale — Metre rulers, Table, Ball bearing

3) Start the video camera recording, then **roll** the second ball bearing towards the **stationary** ball bearing so that they **collide**.

4) When both ball bearings have come to **rest**, stop the video recording and use **video analysis software** to study the collision.

5) If you know the time **between** each frame of the video, you can work out how many frames there are in each **0.1 s**.

6) Go through **frame by frame** and use the rulers to find the **distance** travelled by each ball bearing in the horizontal and vertical directions every 0.1 s. Then you can use **Pythagoras** to find the **magnitude** of each ball's velocity **immediately before** and **immediately after** the collision, and **trigonometry** to find the **directions** of these velocities.

7) You can show that **momentum** is **conserved** by calculating the total momentum **before** the collision and the total momentum **after** the collision.

Your video analysis software might be able to track the ball-bearings and calculate their velocities for you.

Practice Questions

Q1 Give the equation for calculating an object's momentum.

Q2 How is calculating the momentum before and after a collision different when objects collide in two dimensions rather than one?

Q3 Which direction will a stationary ball travel in if another ball collides with it?

Q4 Describe an experiment to investigate conservation of momentum in two dimensions using ball bearings and video analysis software.

Exam Questions

Q1 A snooker ball of mass 0.145 kg moving at 1.94 ms^{-1} collides with a stationary snooker ball of mass 0.148 kg. The first ball rebounds along its initial path at 0.010 ms^{-1}, and the second ball moves off in the opposite direction. Calculate the velocity of the second ball immediately after the collision. [2 marks]

Q2 The diagram below shows the velocities of two balls before and after colliding with each other (all angles are given to the nearest degree). Ball A has a mass of 1.00 kg. Calculate the mass of ball B. [2 marks]

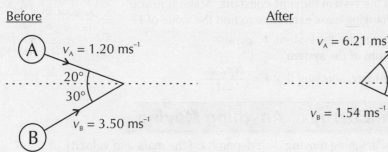

Before — (A) $v_A = 1.20$ ms^{-1}, 20°, 30°, (B) $v_B = 3.50$ ms^{-1}

After — (A) $v_A = 6.21$ ms^{-1}, 45°, 25°, (B) $v_B = 1.54$ ms^{-1}

Life would be a lot easier if all of these balls would stop hitting each other...

There are two key tricks to 2D vector questions — think about which directions make the most sense to resolve along before you start, and make sure you have a clearly labelled diagram to look at so you don't get in a muddle.

Force, Impulse and Energy

Just when you thought you were done with momentum, here it comes again — now with added impulse and energy...

Impulse = Change in Momentum

1) Newton's 2nd law says **force = rate of change of momentum** (see page 33), or $F = \Delta p \div \Delta t$

2) **Rearranging** Newton's 2nd law gives:
   Impulse is defined as **average force × time**, $F\Delta t$.
   The units of impulse are **newton seconds**, Ns.

   > $F\Delta t = \Delta p$
   > so **impulse = change of momentum**

3) The area under a force-time graph is $F \times \Delta t$ = impulse. See p.25 for estimating the area under non-linear graphs.

Example: A golfer hits a golf ball that is initially at rest. The golf club is in contact with the ball for 0.0016 s and the velocity of the ball immediately after it is hit is 6.2 ms⁻¹. The mass of the ball is 0.0044 kg. Calculate the impulse on the ball and find the average force exerted by the golf club on the ball.

The impulse is equal to the change in momentum of the ball during the time it is being hit. It is given by:

$\Delta p = mv_{final} - mv_{initial} = (0.0044 \times 6.2) - (0.0044 \times 0) = 0.02728 = \textbf{0.027 kg ms⁻¹ (to 2 s.f.)}$

Rearrange $F\Delta t = \Delta p$ to give: $F = \dfrac{\Delta p}{\Delta t} = \dfrac{0.02728}{0.0016} = 17.05 = \textbf{17 N (to 2 s.f.)}$

You Can Investigate $F\Delta t = \Delta p$ with an Air Track and Light Gates

1) Set up your apparatus as shown in the diagram on the right, and connect the light gates to a **data logger** and **computer**.

> Make sure you you're aware of any risks associated with this experiment before starting.

2) Hold the **trolley** at one end of the **air track** and then release it. The hanging mass will fall, pulling the trolley along the air track.

3) The **total mass** of the **system** is equal to the sum of the **mass on the trolley** and the **hanging mass**, $m_{system} = m + M$.

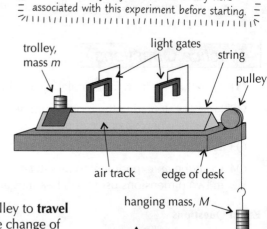

4) Use the **data logger** and **computer** to find the **velocity** of the trolley at each **light gate**. From this calculate the **change in momentum** of the system, $\Delta p_{system} = m_{system}\Delta v$, where Δv is the **change** in velocity between the light gates. (The change in velocity of the trolley is **equal** to the change in velocity of the hanging mass, because the string doesn't stretch. So the **change in velocity of the system** = Δv.)

5) You can also use the data logger to find the **time taken** for the trolley to **travel between** the two light gates, Δt. Using Δt and your value for the change of momentum of the system, you can find the **rate of change of momentum of the system**, $\dfrac{\Delta p_{system}}{\Delta t}$.

6) **Repeat** this three times to find an **average value** of $\dfrac{\Delta p_{system}}{\Delta t}$.

7) The **force** acting on the **system** is equal to the **weight** of the **hanging mass**, $F = Mg$.

8) **Repeat** the experiment for **varying masses** on the end of the string. Each time you remove a mass from the hanging mass, place it on the trolley, so that the mass of the **system** remains **constant**. Make sure you **measure** the mass of the hanging mass **each time** to find the value of F.

> 'The system' in this experiment is the combination of the trolley, the string and the hanging mass. You can assume the mass of the string is negligible.

9) Plot a **graph** of the **force** acting on the system, **F**, against **rate of change of momentum of the system**.

10) The graph will be a **straight line**, showing that $F = \dfrac{\Delta p_{system}}{\Delta t}$.

Kinetic Energy is the Energy of Anything Moving

Kinetic energy is the energy of anything **moving** — it depends on the **mass** and **velocity** of whatever is moving. There are two **equations** for kinetic energy that you need to learn — the **standard one** that you'll know and love, and a form written in terms of **momentum**:

> $E_k = \dfrac{1}{2}mv^2$ and $E_k = \dfrac{p^2}{2m}$

where v is the velocity of the object, m is its mass. and p is its momentum

> These equations can only be used for non-relativistic particles (i.e. particles that aren't travelling close to the speed of light).

Force, Impulse and Energy

Make sure you can **Derive** the Kinetic Energy Equation in terms of **Momentum**

1) You know that: $E_k = \frac{1}{2}mv^2$ and $p = mv$.

2) Substitute p for mv in $E_k = \frac{1}{2}mv^2$ to give $E_k = \frac{pv}{2}$.

3) Rearrange $p = mv$ to give $v = \frac{p}{m}$ and substitute it into $E_k = \frac{pv}{2}$ to give $E_k = \frac{p^2}{2m}$.

Kinetic Energy is Conserved in Elastic Collisions

1) As long as there are **no external forces** (like friction), you know that **momentum is always conserved** in a collision — you have the **same total momentum after** a collision **as you had before** (see p.92-93).

2) **After** a collision, objects sometimes **stick together**, and sometimes **bounce apart**. Either way, momentum is **conserved**.

3) But the **kinetic energy** is **not** always conserved. Usually, some of it gets converted into **sound or heat** energy. A collision where the **total kinetic energy** is the **same** after a collision is called an **elastic collision**. A collision where the **total kinetic energy** is **less** after a collision is called an **inelastic collision**.

4) It's important to remember that overall, **total energy is conserved** though — this is the **principle of conservation of energy** (see p.36). When energy is said to be 'lost', it just means it's **transferred** to another (generally useless) form of energy.

In the real world, some energy's always lost in a collision. Sometimes, if the energy loss is small, it's okay to assume the collision is elastic.

Example: A cart of mass 50 g hurtles at 20 ms⁻¹ towards a stationary cart of mass 60 g. After the collision, both carts move forward in the same direction.

a) If the first cart moves forward at 8 ms⁻¹ after the collision, calculate the speed of the second cart.
b) Calculate the total kinetic energy before and after the collision.
c) State whether the collision is elastic or inelastic, giving a reason for your answer.

a) Using conservation of momentum:
total momentum before = total momentum after
$(0.05 \times 20) + (0.06 \times 0) = (0.05 \times 8) + (0.06 \times v_2)$
$1 = 0.4 + 0.06v_2$
So $v_2 = 0.6 \div 0.06 = \textbf{10 ms}^{-1}$

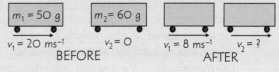

b) $E_k = \frac{1}{2}mv^2$ Before the collision: $E_k = \frac{1}{2} \times 0.05 \times 20^2 = \textbf{10 J}$
After the collision: $E_k = (\frac{1}{2} \times 0.05 \times 8^2) + (\frac{1}{2} \times 0.06 \times 10^2)$
$= 1.6 + 3 = 4.6 = \textbf{5 J (to 1 s.f.)}$

You could also use $E_k = \frac{p^2}{2m}$ to answer b).

c) The collision must be **inelastic**, because the total kinetic energy is reduced in the collision.

Practice Questions

Q1 Define impulse in terms of momentum.

Q2 Describe an experiment to investigate the relation $F\Delta t = \Delta p$.

Q3 State the equation for calculating an object's kinetic energy in terms of its velocity.
Use this equation to derive a second equation for kinetic energy in terms of momentum.

Q4 What is the difference between an elastic and an inelastic collision?

Exam Questions

Q1 A cricket ball travelling at 29 ms⁻¹ is caught by a fielder, and brought to a stop over a period of 0.47 s.
Given that the average force exerted on the ball by the fielder is 9.8 N, calculate the mass of the ball. [2 marks]

Q2 A railway truck of mass 12 000 kg with momentum 16 000 kg ms⁻¹ collides with a stationary truck of mass 15 000 kg.
The two trucks stay together after the collision.

a) Calculate the total kinetic energy before. [1 mark]

b) Calculate the final velocity of the two trucks. [2 marks]

c) State whether the collision is elastic or inelastic, and give a reason for your answer. [2 marks]

Want to revise elastic collisions — ping a rubber band at a friend...

Make sure you're comfortable with how that experiment works — it can be a bit tricky to get your head around.

Circular Motion

*It's probably worth putting a bookmark in here — this stuff is needed **all** over the place.*

Angular Displacement can be Expressed in Radians or Degrees

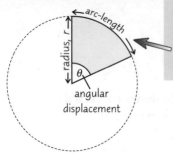

radius, *r*

arc-length

θ

angular displacement

Angular displacement is the **angle** through which a point has been **rotated** in a given direction. The magnitude of the angular displacement in **radians**, θ, is equal to the **arc-length** divided by the radius of the circle, *r*.

For a **complete circle** (360°), the arc-length is just the circumference of the circle, $2\pi r$. Dividing this by the radius gives 2π. So there are 2π radians in a complete circle.

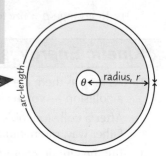

arc-length   *θ*   radius, *r*

Some common angles:

45°
$\frac{\pi}{4}$ rad
θ

90°
$\frac{\pi}{2}$ rad
θ

180°
π rad
θ

To convert from degrees to radians, multiply by $\frac{\pi}{180}$.
To convert from radians to degrees, multiply by $\frac{180}{\pi}$.
1 radian ≈ 57°.

Angular Velocity is the Angle an Object Rotates Through per Second

1) Just as **linear velocity** is defined as displacement ÷ time, the **angular velocity**, ω, is defined as **angular displacement ÷ time**. The unit of angular velocity is rad s^{-1} — radians per second.

$$\omega = \frac{\theta}{t}$$

ω is the angular velocity in rad s^{-1}, θ is the angle in rad turned through in a time, *t* in s.

If you calculate the angular velocity, ω, using the equation on the left, you can then substitute the magnitude of this value into the equation below for ω.

2) The **linear speed**, *v*, (the magnitude of the linear velocity) and the **angular speed**, ω, (the **magnitude** of the angular velocity), of a rotating object are linked by the equation:

$$v = \omega r$$

v is the linear speed in ms^{-1}, *r* is the radius of the circle in m and ω is the magnitude of the angular velocity in rad s^{-1}.

Example: In a cyclotron, a beam of particles spirals outwards from a central point. The angular speed of the particles remains constant. The beam of particles in the cyclotron rotates through 360° in 35 μs.

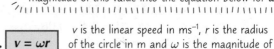

FAST
v = ?
SLOW
r = 1.5 m

a) Explain why the linear speed of the particles increases as they spiral outwards, even though their angular speed is constant.

Linear speed depends on *r*, the radius of the circle being turned as well as ω. So, as *r* increases, so does *v*, even though ω remains constant.

b) Calculate the linear speed of a particle at a point 1.5 m from the centre of rotation.

The linear speed is sometimes called tangential speed.

First, calculate the angular speed:

$$\omega = \frac{\theta}{t} = \frac{2\pi}{35 \times 10^{-6}} = 1.7951... \times 10^{5}\,\text{rad s}^{-1}$$

Then substitute ω into $v = \omega r$:

$$v = \omega r = 1.7951... \times 10^{5} \times 1.5 = 2.6927... \times 10^{5}\,\text{ms}^{-1}$$
$$v = 2.7 \times 10^{5}\,\text{ms}^{-1}\ \textbf{(to 2 s.f.)}$$

You can find out more about cyclotrons on p.117.

Circular Motion has a Frequency and Period

1) The **frequency**, *f*, is the number of complete **revolutions per second** (rev s^{-1} or hertz, Hz). The **period**, *T*, is the **time taken** for a complete revolution (in seconds). Frequency and period are **linked** by the equation:

$$f = \frac{1}{T}$$

2) For a complete circle, an object turns through 2π radians in a time *t*, so frequency and period are related to ω by:

$$\omega = 2\pi f \quad \text{and} \quad T = \frac{2\pi}{\omega}$$

where ω is the angular speed in rad s^{-1}.

Circular Motion

Objects Travelling in Circles are *Accelerating* as their *Velocity is Changing*

1) Imagine a ball is moving at a **constant speed** in a **circle**. The ball is always **changing direction**, so the linear velocity is always changing (it's **accelerating**) but the **magnitude** of the linear velocity (i.e. the **linear speed**), v, is always the **same**.

2) In **time** Δt, the ball moves from **point A to B** and turns through the **angle** θ.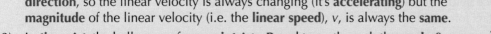

3) The ball travels a **distance** s during this time, which is equal to the ball's linear speed multiplied by the time taken: $s = v\Delta t$.
If θ is **small**, you can approximate the arc-length s to be **equal** to the **straight line AB**.

4) At point A the ball has **linear velocity** v_A and at point B it has **linear velocity** v_B. The **change** in linear velocity, $\Delta v = v_B - v_A$.

5) You can draw a **vector diagram** of the velocity vectors v_A, v_B and Δv. They form a **triangle** that is **similar** to **triangle ABO** — both are **isosceles triangles** with the **same angle** θ between two **sides** of **identical length**.

6) Because the two triangles are similar, the **ratio** of s to r is the **same** as the ratio of Δv to v_A: $\frac{s}{r} = \frac{\Delta v}{v_A} = \frac{\Delta v}{v}$.

7) The previous equation, $s = v\Delta t$, can be **substituted** in to give: $\frac{v\Delta t}{r} = \frac{\Delta v}{v}$ which rearranges to give $\frac{\Delta v}{\Delta t} = \frac{v^2}{r}$.

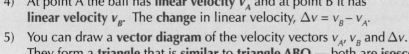
The linear velocity is always at a tangent to the radius, so the angle between v_A and v_B is equal to the angle between A and B, θ.

8) Since **acceleration**, a, is equal to the **change** in **velocity over time**, this gives $a = \frac{\Delta v}{\Delta t} = \frac{v^2}{r}$.

9) This acceleration is called the **centripetal acceleration**, and is always directed towards the **centre** of the circle. It can be written in terms of **linear** or **angular speed**:

$$a = \frac{v^2}{r} \quad \text{and} \quad a = r\omega^2$$

The *Centripetal Acceleration* is produced by a *Centripetal Force*

From Newton's laws (p.28), if there's a **centripetal acceleration**, there must be a resultant force (the **centripetal force**) acting towards the **centre of the circle**.
Since $F = ma$, the centripetal force must be:

$$F = \frac{mv^2}{r} \quad \text{and} \quad F = mr\omega^2$$

The centripetal force is what keeps the object moving in a circle — remove the force and the object would fly off at a tangent.

Practice Questions

Q1 Convert: a) $\pi/4$ radians into degrees, b) 11.25 degrees into radians.

Q2 How is angular velocity defined and what is the relationship between angular speed and linear speed?

Q3 Derive the two equations for centripetal acceleration using vector diagrams.

Exam Questions

Q1 a) Calculate the angular velocity at which the Earth orbits the Sun. (1 year $= 3.2 \times 10^7$ s) [2 marks]

b) Calculate the Earth's linear speed. (Assume radius of orbit $= 1.5 \times 10^{11}$ m) [2 marks]

c) Calculate the centripetal force needed to keep the Earth in its orbit. (Mass of Earth $= 6.0 \times 10^{24}$ kg) [2 marks]

d) State the direction of the centripetal force on the Earth. [1 mark]

Q2 A car is driving in a circle around a roundabout with linear speed 15 ms^{-1}. The radius of the car's circular motion is 12 m.

a) Calculate the centripetal acceleration of the car. [1 mark]

b) Calculate the time taken for the car to drive once around the roundabout. [2 marks]

My head is spinning after all that...

"Centripetal" just means "centre-seeking". The centripetal force is what actually causes circular motion. What you feel when you're spinning, though, is the reaction (centrifugal) force. Don't get the two mixed up.

Electric Fields

Electric fields can be attractive or repulsive — it's all to do with charge, and nothing to do with green spaces full of sheep.

There is an **Electric Field** around a **Charged Object**

An electric field is a force field — it's a region in which a charged particle experiences a non-contact force (either of attraction or repulsion).

1) Electric charge, **Q**, is measured in **coulombs** (C) and can be either positive or negative.
2) **Oppositely** charged particles **attract** each other. **Like** charges **repel**.
3) If a **charged object** is placed in an electric field, then it will experience a **force**.
4) If the charged object is a uniformly charged **sphere**, you can assume all of its **charge** is at its **centre** — it behaves like a **point charge**. Point charges have **radial fields** (see the next page).
5) Just like with gravitational fields, **electric fields** can be represented by **field lines**.

You can **Calculate Forces** using **Coulomb's Law**

Coulomb's law gives the force of attraction or repulsion between two **point charges** in a **vacuum**:

$$F = \frac{Q_1 Q_2}{4\pi\varepsilon_0 r^2}$$

ε_0 ("epsilon-nought") is the permittivity of free space and is equal to 8.85×10^{-12} Fm^{-1} (farads per metre), Q_1 and Q_2 are the charges, r is the distance between Q_1 and Q_2.

1) The force on Q_1 is always **equal** and **opposite** to the force on Q_2 — the **direction** depends on the charges.

If the charges are **opposite** then the force is **attractive**. *F* will be **negative**.

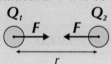

If Q_1 and Q_2 are **alike** then the force is **repulsive**. *F* will be **positive**.

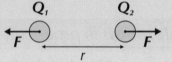

Mr Allan liked to explain Coulomb's law using prairie dogs.

2) Coulomb's law is an **inverse square law**. The **further apart** the charges, the **weaker** the force between them.
3) If the point charges aren't in a vacuum, then ε_0 is replaced by the **permittivity**, ε, of the material between them. **Air** can be treated as a **vacuum** when using Coulomb's law.

You can use an **electronic balance** to measure the **force** between two charges:

1) Fix a charged sphere to a mass balance and **zero** the balance.
2) Clamp another charged sphere carrying the **same charge** directly above the first sphere (take care that the two don't touch).
3) The spheres will **repel** each other, causing the lower sphere to **push down** on the scales, so the scales will register a mass.
4) Convert the mass reading on the scales into a force using $F = W = mg$ (see p.38).
5) If you vary the distance, r, between the spheres, you should find that $F \propto \frac{1}{r^2}$.

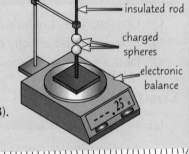

insulated rod

charged spheres

electronic balance

You could charge the spheres by connecting them to a power supply.

Electric Field Strength is Force per Unit Charge

Electric field strength, E, is defined as the **force per unit positive charge**.
It's the force that a charge of +1 C would experience if it was placed in the electric field.

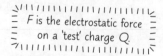
F is the electrostatic force on a 'test' charge *Q*.

$$E = \frac{F}{Q}$$

Where *E* is electric field strength (NC^{-1}, newtons per coulomb), *F* is the force (N) and *Q* is the charge (C).

Electric field strength is a **vector** pointing in the **direction** that a **positive charge** would **move**. Field strength depends on **where you are** in the field for a **radial field**, and is the **same everywhere** in a **uniform field** (see next page).

Electric Fields

In a *Radial Field*, *E* is *Inversely Proportional* to r^2

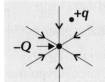

The electric field lines around a uniformly charged sphere would look the same as for a point charge.

1) A **point charge** — or any body that behaves as if all its charge is concentrated at the centre — has a **radial** field.

For a **positive Q**, a small positive 'test' charge *q* would be **repelled**, so the field lines point **away** from **Q**.

For a **negative Q**, a small positive charge *q* would be **attracted**, so the field lines point **towards Q**.

2) In a **radial field**, the electric field strength, **E**, depends on the distance **r** from the point charge **Q**:

$$E = \frac{Q}{4\pi\varepsilon_0 r^2}$$

where *E* is the electric field strength (NC^{-1}), ε_0 is the permittivity of free space (8.85×10^{-12} Fm^{-1}), *Q* is the point charge (C) and *r* is the distance from the point charge (m).

3) This is another **inverse square law**: $E \propto \frac{1}{r^2}$. A graph of *E* against *r* looks like this:

4) Field strength **decreases** as you go **further away** from **Q** — on a diagram, the **field lines** get **further apart**.

In a *Uniform Field*, *E* is the *Same Everywhere*

1) A **uniform field** can be produced by connecting two **parallel plates** to the opposite poles of a battery:

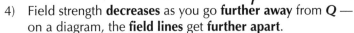

The **field lines** are **parallel** to each other and point **from** the **positive plate towards** the **negative** plate.

This is a parallel plate capacitor (see p.101.)

2) In a **uniform field**, the field lines are **parallel** so they're always the **same distance** apart. This means that the field strength is the **same at all points** within the field — i.e. a test charge would experience the **same force** wherever it was.

3) The **field strength** between two **parallel plates** depends on the **potential difference** between the plates, **V**, and the **distance, d**, between them, according to the equation:

$$E = \frac{V}{d}$$

E can be measured in volts per metre (Vm^{-1}).

Investigating charged drops in a uniform electric field

1) An **atomiser** creates a **fine mist** of oil drops that are **charged** by **friction** as they leave the atomiser.

2) When the circuit is **switched off**, a drop falls from the top plate to the bottom plate due to its **weight**.

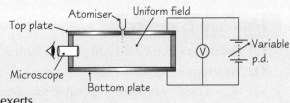

3) When the circuit is **switched on**, the potential difference between the plates creates a **uniform electric field**, which exerts a **force** on the oil drop. A negatively charged oil drop can be made to 'float' between the plates by **balancing** the **upward force** from the electric field with the **downward force** of the oil drop's weight by adjusting the voltage between the plates:

If there's no electric field, the drop will accelerate until it reaches terminal velocity, when drag = the weight of the drop (see pages 30-31).

$$F_{electric} = EQ = \frac{V}{d}Q \text{ and } F_{weight} = mg, \text{ so for a drop to float: } \frac{V}{d}Q = mg$$

4) If you **increase the p.d.** while a drop is **floating** between the plates (i.e. the forces on the drop are **balanced**), you **increase the field strength**. This means the forces on the oil drop will no longer be balanced, so it will **accelerate** towards the **positive top plate** because the force due to the electric field is **greater** than its weight.

5) If you **increase the distance** between the plates or **decrease the p.d.**, you **reduce the field strength** and therefore the electric force on the oil drop. The oil drop will **accelerate** towards the **bottom plate** due to its **weight** being **larger** than the force due to the electric field.

Electric Fields

Electric Potential is Potential Energy per Unit Charge

All points in an **electric field** have an **electric potential, V**. This is the electric **potential energy** that a **unit positive charge** (+ 1 C) would have at that point. The **electric potential** of a point depends on **how far** it is from the **charge** creating the **electric field** and the **size** of that charge.

In a **radial field**, **electric potential** is given by:

$$V = \frac{Q}{4\pi\varepsilon_0 r}$$

where V is electric potential (V),
Q is the size of the charge (C)
and r is the distance from the charge (m).

1) The **sign** of **V** depends on the charge **Q** — i.e. **V** is **positive** when **Q** is positive and the force is **repulsive**, and **negative** when **Q** is negative and the force is **attractive**.

2) The **magnitude** of **V** is **greatest** directly **next to the charge**, and **decreases** as the **distance** from the charge **increases** — **V** will be **zero** at an **infinite distance** from the charge.

Repulsive force

V is initially **positive** and tends to **zero** as **r** increases towards **infinity**.

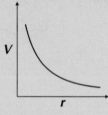

Attractive force

V is initially **negative** and tends to **zero** as **r** increases towards **infinity**.

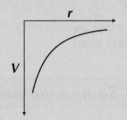

You can also find **ΔV** (the change in electric potential) between two points from the **area** under a graph of **E** (see p.98-99) against **r**.

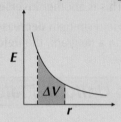

The **gradient** of a **tangent** to either **V-r** graph gives the **field strength** at that point: $E = \frac{\Delta V}{\Delta r}$

Equipotentials Show All Points of Equal Potential in a Field

1) **Equipotentials** are lines joining points where the electric potential is **equal**. For a **radial field**, equipotentials are **surfaces**, where any point on the surface is the same distance from the centre of the charge (i.e. they are spheres centred on the charge). Between **parallel plates**, the equipotentials are **flat planes**.

2) **No work** is done when you travel **along** an equipotential — an electric charge can travel along an equipotential without any **energy** being transferred.

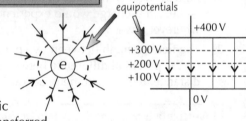

Practice Questions

Q1 Define an electric field and give the formula for electric field strength in terms of force and charge.

Q2 Write down Coulomb's law.

Q3 Sketch field lines and equipotentials for both a radial and a uniform electric field. How would you find E for each

Q4 Define electric potential and write down the equation for electric potential in a radial field.

Exam Questions

Q1 An alpha particle (charge +2e) was deflected while passing through thin gold foil. The alpha particle passed within 5.0×10^{-12} m of a gold nucleus (charge +79e). What was the magnitude and direction of the electrostatic force experienced by the alpha particle at this distance? ($\varepsilon_0 = 8.85 \times 10^{-12}$ Fm^{-1} and $e = 1.60 \times 10^{-19}$ C) [4 marks]

Q2 a) Two parallel plates are connected to a 1500 V dc supply, and separated by an air gap of 4.5 mm. What is the electric field strength between the plates? State the direction of the field. [2 marks]

   b) The plates are now pulled further apart so that the distance between them is doubled. The potential difference across the plates is altered so that the electric field strength remains the same. What is the new voltage between the plates? [1 mark]

Electric fields — one way to roast beef...

Lots of equations and graphs to memorise I'm afraid. Have another read through it all, then treat yourself to a biccie...

Capacitors

Capacitors are things that store electrical charge — like a charge bucket. The capacitance of one of these things tells you how much charge the bucket can hold. Sounds simple enough... ha... ha, ha, ha...

Capacitors Build Up Charge on Plates

1) A **capacitor** is an electrical component that can **store electrical charge**.

2) Capacitors are made up of two **conducting plates** separated by an air **gap** or an insulating material. The **circuit symbol** for a capacitor is two **parallel lines**.

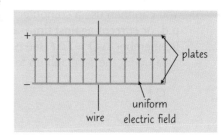

The circuit symbol for a capacitor.

3) When a capacitor is connected to a **power source**, **positive** and **negative** charge build up on **opposite** plates. The insulating material stops charge moving between the two plates, so a **potential difference** is created.

4) This creates a **uniform electric field** (p.99) between the plates.

5) The amount of **charge per unit voltage** stored by a capacitor is called its **capacitance**.

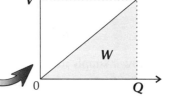

plates

uniform electric field

wire

$$C = \frac{Q}{V}$$

where Q is the charge in coulombs, V is the potential difference in volts and C is the capacitance in farads (F) — 1 farad = 1 CV^{-1}.

6) A farad is a **huge** unit so you'll usually see capacitances expressed in terms of:

μF — microfarads ($\times 10^{-6}$)   **nF** — nanofarads ($\times 10^{-9}$)   **pF** — picofarads ($\times 10^{-12}$)

Capacitors Store Energy

1) In this circuit, when the switch is flicked to the **left**, **charge** builds up on the plates of the **capacitor**. **Electrical energy**, provided by the battery, is **stored** by the capacitor.

2) If the switch is flicked to the **right**, the charge stored on the plates will **discharge** through the **bulb**, converting electrical energy into light and heat.

3) **Work** is done **removing negative charge** from **one plate** and depositing it onto the other plate (to charge the capacitor). The energy for this must come from the **electrical energy** of the **battery**, and is given by **charge × average p.d.**

4) The energy **stored** by a capacitor is **equal** to the **work done** by the **battery**. So, you can find the **energy stored** from the **area** under a **graph** of **p.d.** against **charge stored** on the capacitor.

5) The p.d. across the capacitor is **proportional** to the charge stored on it, so the graph will be a **straight line** through the origin. The **energy stored** is given by the **yellow triangle**.

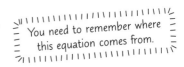

Area of triangle = ½ × base × height, so the energy stored by the capacitor is:

$$W = \frac{1}{2}QV$$

W stands for 'work done', but you can also use *E* for 'energy stored'.

You need to remember where this equation comes from.

There are Three Expressions for the Energy Stored by a Capacitor

Starting from the equation for work above and using $C = \frac{Q}{V}$ you can find two more equations for calculating the energy stored by a capacitor:

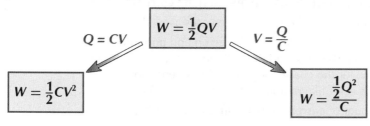

$Q = CV$

$$W = \frac{1}{2}QV$$

$V = \frac{Q}{C}$

$$W = \frac{1}{2}CV^2$$

$$W = \frac{\frac{1}{2}Q^2}{C}$$

Samantha had heard there was energy stored on plates.

Capacitors

You can **Investigate** what Happens when you **Charge** a **Capacitor**

1) Set up the test circuit shown in the circuit diagram.
2) Close the switch to connect the **uncharged** capacitor to the power supply.
3) Let the capacitor **charge** whilst the **data logger** records both the **potential difference** (from the voltmeter) and the **current** (from the ammeter) over time.
4) When the current through the ammeter is **zero**, the capacitor is fully charged.
5) You can then use a computer to plot a graph of **charge**, **p.d.** or **current against time**, as shown below.
(Remember $\Delta Q = I\Delta t$ (see p.42), so the charge transferred in a given time is equal to the area under the I-t graph up to that point — this is how you generate the Q-t graph).

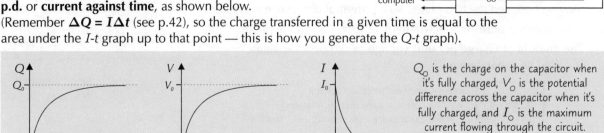

Q_0 is the charge on the capacitor when it's fully charged, V_0 is the potential difference across the capacitor when it's fully charged, and I_0 is the maximum current flowing through the circuit.

1) As soon as the switch closes, current starts to flow. The electrons flow onto the plate connected to the **negative terminal** of the power supply, so a **negative charge** builds up.
2) This build-up of negative charge **repels** electrons off the plate connected to the **positive terminal** of the power supply, making that plate positive. These electrons are attracted to the positive terminal of the power supply.
3) An **equal** but **opposite** charge builds up on each plate, causing a **potential difference** between the plates. Remember that **no charge** can flow **between** the plates because they're **separated** by an **insulator**.
4) Initially the **current** through the circuit is **high**. But, as **charge** builds up on the plates, **electrostatic repulsion** makes it **harder** and **harder** for more electrons to be deposited. When the p.d. across the **capacitor** is equal to the p.d. across the **power supply**, the **current** falls to **zero**. The capacitor is **fully charged**.

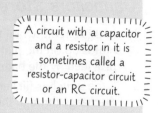

A circuit with a capacitor and a resistor in it is sometimes called a resistor-capacitor circuit or an RC circuit.

To **Discharge** a Capacitor, **Remove** the **Power Supply** and **Close** the **Switch**

1) **Remove the power supply** from the test circuit and close the **switch** to complete the circuit.
2) Let the capacitor **discharge** whilst the data logger records **potential difference** and **current** over time.
3) When the **current** through the ammeter and the **potential difference** across the plates are **zero**, the capacitor is fully discharged.

You can then plot graphs of current, potential difference and charge against time once more.

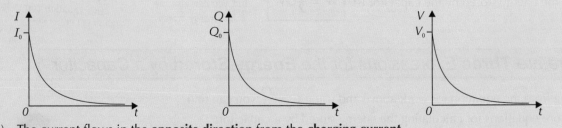

1) The current flows in the **opposite direction** from the **charging current**.
2) As the **potential difference** decreases, the **current** decreases as well.
3) When a capacitor is **discharging**, the amount of **charge** on and **potential difference** between the plates falls **exponentially** with time. That means it always takes the **same length** of time for the charge or potential difference to **halve**, no matter what value it starts at — like radioactive decay (see p.153).
4) The same is true for the amount of **current flowing** around the circuit.

Capacitors

You Could use an **Oscilloscope** Instead of a Data Logger

Rather than using a **voltmeter** and **data logger** to measure and record the potential difference across the capacitor over time, you could use a **cathode ray oscilloscope** (CRO). (You met oscilloscopes on page 67).

1) The screen of an oscilloscope is split into squares called **divisions**.
2) The vertical axis is in **volts**. The **volts per division** shown on this axis is controlled by the **gain dial**.
3) The horizontal axis is in **seconds** — also called the **timebase**. The **seconds per division** shown on this axis is controlled by the **timebase** dial. The time-base can be turned on and off.
4) You can alter the gain and timebase to make it **easy to read** off measurements.
5) There's also a button to freeze whatever's on the screen.

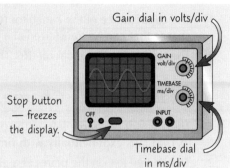

Gain dial in volts/div

Stop button — freezes the display.

Timebase dial in ms/div

If you connect an oscilloscope **across** the capacitor in the circuit on page 102 and turn the **time-base off**, you'll just get a **dot** on the middle of the display, corresponding to the p.d. across the capacitor. If you take regular readings of this p.d. for a charging and discharging capacitor, you'll be able to **plot** the *V-t* graphs on p.102.

Alternatively, if you turn the **time base on**, and **adjust the dial** (this may take some fiddling) you can get the **oscilloscope** to plot the voltage graphs on the previous page for you on its display. Once the capacitor is fully charged, you can then press the **stop button**, and copy down the information from the display.

Practice Questions

Q1 Explain how you get the formula relating work, charge and voltage for a capacitor.
Q2 Write down the three formulas for calculating the energy stored by a capacitor.
Q3 Describe how you could investigate how the potential difference across a charging capacitor varies with time.
Q4 Sketch graphs to show the variation of the current round the circuit and potential difference across the plates of a capacitor with time for: a) charging a capacitor, b) discharging a capacitor.

Exam Questions

Q1 A 250 μF capacitor is fully charged to 1.5 μC and then discharged through a fixed resistor.

a) Calculate the energy stored by the capacitor when it is fully charged. [1 mark]

b) Calculate the voltage of the battery used to charge the capacitor. [2 marks]

c) Sketch the graph of charge against time as the capacitor discharges. [1 mark]

Q2 The graph of current against time for a charging capacitor is shown on the right. Explain the shape of the graph. [1 mark]

Q3 The potential difference across the plates of a capacitor is increased by a factor of two. The capacitance of the capacitor remains the same. Which of the following statements is true? [1 mark]

A The charge on the capacitor will remain the same. B The energy stored by the capacitor will half.
C The energy stored by the capacitor will quadruple. D The energy stored by the capacitor will remain the same.

An analogy — consider the lowly bike pump...

A good way to think of the charging process is like pumping air into a bike tyre. To start with, the air goes in easily, but as the pressure in the tyre increases, it gets harder and harder to squeeze any more air in. The tyre's 'full' when the pressure of the air in the tyre equals the pressure of the pump. The analogy works just as well for discharging...

Discharging Capacitors

You're not out of the capacitor woods yet — it's time for some fun exponential relationships.

The **Time Taken** to **Charge** or **Discharge** Depends on **Two Factors**

The **time** it takes to charge or discharge a capacitor depends on:

1) The **capacitance** of the capacitor (**C**). This affects the amount of **charge** that can be transferred at a given **potential difference**.

2) The **resistance** of the circuit (**R**). This affects the **current** in the circuit.

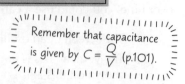

Remember that capacitance is given by $C = \frac{Q}{V}$ (p.101).

You can Calculate **Charge**, **Current**, and **P.d.** for a **Discharging Capacitor**

1) The amount of **charge** left on the plates of a capacitor in a resistor-capacitor circuit (p.102) falls **exponentially with time** as a capacitor discharges.

2) The charge left on the plates at a given time after a capacitor begins discharging from being fully charged is given by the equation:

$$Q = Q_0 e^{-t/RC}$$

where Q_0 is the charge of the capacitor when it's fully charged (C), t is time since charging began (s), R is the resistance (Ω) and C is the capacitance (F).

3) As the **potential difference** and **current** also decrease **exponentially** as a capacitor discharges, the formulas for calculating the current or potential difference at a certain time are similar:

$$I = I_0 e^{-t/RC}$$

$$V = V_0 e^{-t/RC}$$

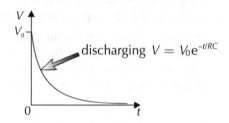

discharging $V = V_0 e^{-t/RC}$

Time Constant τ = RC

τ is the Greek letter 'tau'

If $t = \tau = RC$ is put into the **discharging** equations above, then $Q = Q_0 e^{-1}$, $V = V_0 e^{-1}$ and $I = I_0 e^{-1}$.

So when $t = \tau$: $\frac{Q}{Q_0} = \frac{1}{e} \approx \frac{1}{2.718} \approx 0.37$

1) τ, the time constant, is the time taken for the charge, potential difference or current of a discharging capacitor to fall to 37% of its value when fully charged.

2) It's also the time taken for the charge or potential difference of a charging capacitor to **rise** to **63%** of its value when fully charged.

3) So the **larger** the **resistance** in series with the capacitor, the **longer it takes** to charge or discharge.

4) In practice, the time taken for a capacitor to charge or discharge **fully** is taken to be about 5*RC*.

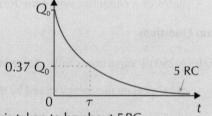

Example: The graph on the right shows how the charge on a capacitor connected in a 10 kΩ circuit falls with time as it discharges. Use the graph to estimate the capacitance of the capacitor.

First, use the graph to estimate the time constant, *RC*.

When the capacitor is fully charged, it holds a charge of 50 mC. The time constant is the time it takes to fall to 37% of this value.

$50 \times (37 \div 100) = 18.5$ mC

From the graph, the charge falls to 18.5 mC after 1.2 s, so *RC* = 1.2 s

So the capacitance of the capacitor is: $1.2 \div (10 \times 10^3) = \textbf{1.2} \times \textbf{10}^{-4}$ **F**

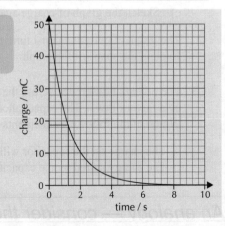

Because charge, potential difference, and current fall **exponentially** with time for a discharging capacitor, it always takes the **same length of time** ($T_{1/2}$) for the charge, current or potential difference in a given *RC* circuit to **halve**, no matter what values they start with. You can show (if you fancy doing some extra algebra) that $T_{1/2} = \textbf{0.69}RC$.

Discharging Capacitors

You Can **Find** the **Time Constant** from **Log-Linear** Graphs

Instead of using $\tau = RC$, you can create **log-linear graphs** from data (p.244-245) to find the time constant.

1) Starting from the equation for Q on a discharging capacitor (p.104).
   take the **natural log** of both sides and rearrange:

   $Q = Q_0 e^{-t/RC}$ becomes $\boxed{\ln Q = \ln Q_0 - \dfrac{t}{RC}}$

   For this you need to use the log rules:
   $\ln(A \times B) = \ln(A) + \ln(B)$ and $\ln(e^A) = A$

2) The equation is now in the form of $y = mx + c$ (see p.9).
   This means if you plotted a graph of **ln(Q)**
   against time, t, you would get a **straight line**.

3) The **gradient** of this line would be $-\dfrac{1}{RC}$ or $-\dfrac{1}{\tau}$
   and the y-intercept would be $\ln(Q_0)$.

4) To get the time constant from the graph, you
   divide –1 by the gradient of the line.

   $\dfrac{\Delta y}{\Delta x} = \dfrac{-1.01}{3.5} = -0.288...$

   $\tau = \dfrac{-1}{-0.288...} = 3.465...$
   $= 3.5\mu s$ (to 2 s.f.)

   graph: ln(Q) vs t (μs); points 5.01, 4.02; 3.5; 5 RC

5) You can do the **same thing** for **current** and **potential difference**:

   $I = I_0 e^{-t/RC}$ becomes $\boxed{\ln I = \ln I_0 - \dfrac{t}{RC}}$

   If you plot $\ln I$ against t, the intercept will be equal
   to $\ln I_0$ and the gradient will be equal to $-\dfrac{1}{RC}$.

   $V = V_0 e^{-t/RC}$ becomes $\boxed{\ln V = \ln V_0 - \dfrac{t}{RC}}$

   If you plot $\ln V$ against t, the intercept will be equal
   to $\ln V_0$ and the gradient will be equal to $-\dfrac{1}{RC}$.

Practice Questions

Q1 What two factors affect how quickly a capacitor charges?

Q2 Write down the formula for calculating potential difference
at a given time for a discharging capacitor.

Q3 Write down the formula for calculating charge at a
given time for a discharging capacitor.

Q4 What is meant by the time constant of a
resistor-capacitor circuit? How is it calculated?

Q5 Describe how you would calculate the time constant
from a plot of $\ln(V)$ against t for a discharging capacitor.

*The dancers felt pretty good
about their cap-acitance.*

Exam Question

Q1 A 250 µF capacitor is fully charged from a 6.0 V battery and then discharged through a 1.0 kΩ resistor.

a) Calculate the time taken for the charge on the capacitor to fall to 37% of its original value. [2 marks]

b) Calculate the percentage of the total charge remaining on the capacitor after 0.7s. [2 marks]

c) The charging voltage is increased to 12 V. Explain the effect this has on the total charge stored on
the capacitor and the time taken to discharge the capacitor from when it is fully charged. [2 marks]

I'll spare you a log cabin joke — it just woodn't be fir...

*You'll be given all the formulas for charge, current and potential difference for discharging capacitors (and their log
forms) in the exam, but it's a good idea to make sure you understand where the log equations come from. Check that
you're sure what the time constant is, and that you're happy with how to find it from a log-linear graph for an RC circuit.*

Magnetic Fields and Forces

Magnetic fields — making pretty patterns with iron filings before spending an age trying to pick them off the magnet.

A **Magnetic Field** is a **Region** Where a **Force** is Exerted on **Magnetic Materials**

1) Magnetic fields can be represented by **field lines** (also called flux lines).
2) Field lines go from the **north** to the **south pole** of a magnet.
3) The **closer** together the lines, the **stronger** the field.
4) The field lines around a bar magnet, or pair of bar magnets, have a characteristic shape:

At a <u>neutral point</u>
magnetic fields <u>cancel out</u>.

There is a **Magnetic Field** Around a **Wire** Carrying **Electric Current**

When **current** flows in a **wire** or any other long straight conductor, a **magnetic field** is induced around it.

1) The **field lines** are **concentric circles** centred on the wire.
2) The **direction** of a magnetic **field** around a current-carrying wire can be worked out with the **right-hand rule**.
3) If you loop the wire into a **coil**, the field is **doughnut-shaped**, while a coil with length (a **solenoid**) forms a **field** like a **bar magnet**.

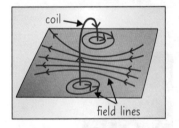

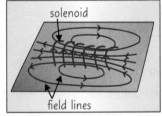

Right-hand Rule

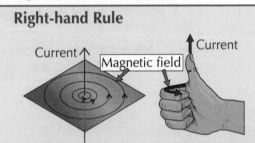

1) Stick your <u>right thumb</u> up, like you're hitching a lift.
2) Your <u>thumb</u> points in the direction of <u>conventional current</u>...
3) ...your curled <u>fingers</u> point in the direction of the <u>field</u>.

A **Wire** Carrying a **Current** in a **Magnetic Field** will **Experience** a **Force**

1) If you put a **current-carrying wire** into an **external** magnetic field (e.g. between two magnets), the field around the wire and the field from the magnets are **added together**. This causes a **resultant field** — lines **closer together** show where the magnetic field is **stronger**. These bunched lines cause a 'pushing' **force** on the wire.

2) The direction of the force is always **perpendicular** to both the current direction and the magnetic field — it's given by **Fleming's left-hand rule**.

3) If the current is **parallel** to the field lines the size of the force is **0 N** — there is **no component** of the magnetic field perpendicular to the current.

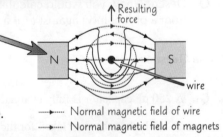

········· Normal magnetic field of wire
········· Normal magnetic field of magnets
───► Resultant magnetic field

Fleming's Left-Hand Rule

The **F**irst finger points in the direction of the external uniform magnetic **F**ield, the se**C**ond finger points in the direction of the conventional **C**urrent. Then your thu**M**b points in the direction of the force (in which **M**otion takes place).

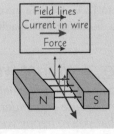

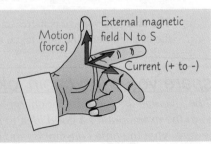

Magnetic Fields and Forces

The **Force** on a Wire is **Proportional** to the **Flux Density**

1) The **force** on a **current-carrying** wire at a **right angle** to an external magnetic field is proportional to the **magnetic flux density**, **B**. Magnetic flux density is sometimes called the **strength** of the magnetic field.

2) **Magnetic flux density**, **B**, is **defined** as:

> The **force** on **one metre** of wire carrying a **current** of **one amp** at **right angles** to the **magnetic field**.

3) When current is at 90° to the magnetic field, the size of the force, F is proportional to the **current**, I, the **length of wire** in the field, l, as well as the **flux density**, B. This gives the equation: $\boxed{F = BIl}$

4) **Flux density** is a **vector** quantity with both a **direction** and **magnitude**. It's measured in **teslas**, **T**:

$$1 \text{ tesla} = \frac{\text{Wb}}{\text{m}^2}$$

It helps to think of flux density as the number of flux lines (measured in webers (Wb), see p.109) per unit area.

Ed's flocks density investigation was a bit unusual.

Example: A current-carrying wire of length 125 mm runs at 90° to a uniform magnetic field with a flux density of 18 mT. Given that the wire experiences a force of 0.013 N, calculate the current in the wire.

Watch out for quantities that aren't in standard units — a tesla is quite a large unit so you may see flux densities given in millitesla (mT).

$F = BIl$, so $I = \dfrac{F}{Bl} = 0.013 \div ((18 \times 10^{-3}) \times (125 \times 10^{-3}))$
$= 5.777... = \textbf{5.8 A (to 2 s.f.)}$

The Force is **Greatest** when the **Wire** and **Field** are **Perpendicular**

1) The **force** on a current-carrying wire in an external magnetic field is caused by the **component** of the magnetic field **perpendicular** to the wire — **B sin θ**.

2) So, for a wire at an **angle** θ to the field, the **force** acting on the wire is given by:

$$F = BIl \sin\theta$$

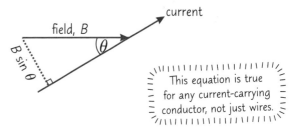

This equation is true for any current-carrying conductor, not just wires.

3) If the current and the field are **parallel**, θ = 0. Sin (0) = 0, so when the current and field are parallel, there's **no force**.

Examples:

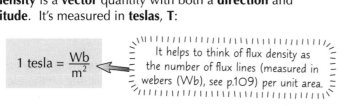

→ current
→ magnetic field

i) If θ = 90°, F = BIl   ii) If θ = 30°, F = BIl×0.5   iii) If θ = 0°, F = 0

Example: A current of 1.64 A is flowing through a wire at an angle of 56° to the field lines of a uniform magnetic field. 25 cm of the wire is within the uniform field and experiences a force of 8.2×10^{-3} N. Calculate the magnetic flux density of the uniform field.

First rearrange the equation to get B. $F = BIl \sin\theta$, so $B = \dfrac{F}{Il \sin\theta}$

Then solve the equation: $B = \dfrac{8.2 \times 10^{-3}}{1.64 \times 0.25 \times \sin 56} = 0.02412... = \textbf{0.024 T (to 2 s.f.)}$

Magnetic Fields and Forces

Forces Act on Charged Particles in Magnetic Fields

A **force** acts on a charged particle **moving** in a **magnetic field**. This is why a **current-carrying wire** experiences a force in a magnetic field (page 106) — electric current in a wire is the **flow** of **negatively charged electrons**.

1) The **force** on a current-carrying **wire** in a **magnetic field** that is **perpendicular** to the **current** is given by $F = BIl$.

2) **Electric current**, I, is the flow of **charge**, Q, per unit time, t. So $I = \frac{Q}{t}$.

3) A **charged** particle which moves a distance l in time t has a **velocity**, $v = \frac{l}{t}$. So $l = vt$.

Putting all these equations together gives the force acting on a single charged particle, with a charge q, moving through a magnetic field, where its velocity is perpendicular to the magnetic field:

$$F = BIl = B\frac{q}{\cancel{t}}v\cancel{t} \implies \boxed{F = Bqv} \quad \text{or more generally:} \quad \boxed{F = Bqv \sin\theta}$$

where F = force in N,
B = magnetic flux density in T,
q = charge on the particle in C,
v = velocity of the particle in ms^{-1},
θ = angle between current and field lines.

> **Example:** An electron travels at a velocity of 2.00×10^4 ms^{-1} perpendicular to a uniform magnetic field with a magnetic flux density of 2.00 T. What is the magnitude of the force acting on the electron?
>
> Just use the equation $F = Bqv$ and put the correct numbers in:
>
> $F = BqV = 2.00 \times (1.60 \times 10^{-19}) \times (2.00 \times 10^4) = \mathbf{6.40 \times 10^{-15}}$ **N**
>
> The magnitude of the charge on an electron $= 1.60 \times 10^{-19}$ C (you will be given the charge on an electron in your exam).

By **Fleming's left-hand rule**, the force on a **moving charge** in a magnetic field is always **perpendicular** to its **direction of travel**. Mathematically, that is the condition for **circular** motion. This effect is used in **particle accelerators** (see p.116).

Practice Questions

Q1 Sketch the magnetic field lines around a long, straight, current-carrying wire. Show the directions of the current and the magnetic field.

Q2 Write the rule that relates the directions of force, current and B field. What is this rule called?

Q3 A copper bar can roll freely on two copper supports, as shown in the diagram. When current is applied in the direction shown, which way will the bar roll?

Q4 What is magnetic flux density? What are its units?

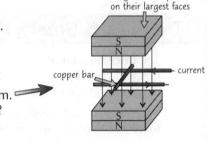
magnets with poles on their largest faces
copper bar
current

Exam Question

Q1 A student plots a graph of force against wire length for a current-carrying wire in a magnetic field. The current-carrying wire is perpendicular to the field. Which of the following statements is true?

    A The flux density is the gradient of the best fit line.

    B The force is inversely proportional to the wire length.

    C The force is proportional to the wire length.

    D The flux density is the y-intercept of the best fit line.

[1 mark]

Q2 A wire carrying a current of 3.00 A runs through a magnetic field of strength 2.00×10^{-5} T. 4.00 cm of the wire is within the field. The wire experiences a force of 1.20×10^{-6} N.

    a) Calculate the angle between the wire and the magnetic field. [2 marks]

    b) The wire is rotated so that it runs parallel to the magnetic field. Give the new force on the wire. Explain your answer. [2 marks]

Q3 An electron is travelling through a uniform magnetic field of flux density 1.10 T at an angle of 30.0° to the field lines. A force of 4.91×10^{-15} N is acting on the electron. Calculate the velocity of the electron. [2 marks]

Left hand rule. Left hand rule. LEFT HAND RULE. **LEFT HAND RULE.**

Fleming's left hand rule is the key to understanding magnetic fields — so make sure you know how to use it and understand what it all means. Remember that the direction of the magnetic field is from N to S, and that the current is from +ve to −ve — this is as important as using the correct hand. You need to get those right or it'll all go to pot...

Electromagnetic Induction

So it turns out that if you waggle a bit of metal around near a magnet you can make your own electricity — don't ever let anybody tell you that physics isn't seriously cool. Chemistry's got nothing on this.

Think of the **Magnetic Flux** as the Total **Number** of **Field Lines**

1) **Magnetic flux density**, **B**, is a measure of the **strength** of a magnetic field. It helps to think of it as the **number** of field lines **per unit area**.

2) The total **magnetic flux**, ϕ, passing through an **area**, **A**, perpendicular to a **magnetic field**, **B**, is defined as:

$$\phi = BA$$

where ϕ is magnetic flux (Wb), B is magnetic flux density (T) and A is area (m^2).

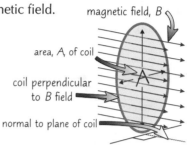

magnetic field, B

area, A of coil

coil perpendicular to B field

normal to plane of coil

An E.m.f is **Induced** in a Conductor when it **Cuts** Magnetic Flux

1) If there is relative motion between a **conducting rod** and a magnetic field, the **electrons in the rod** will experience a **force** (see p.106), which causes them to **accumulate** at one end of the rod.

2) This **induces** an **electromotive force** (**e.m.f.**) across the ends of the rod — this is called **electromagnetic induction**.

3) An e.m.f. will be induced whenever the **magnetic field** (or '**magnetic flux**') that passes through a conductor **changes**.

4) You can induce an e.m.f. in a **flat coil** or **solenoid** by:

   • **moving the coil** towards or away from the poles of a magnet.

   • **moving a magnet** towards or away from the coil.

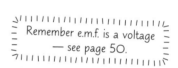

motion

B-field

Remember e.m.f. is a voltage — see page 50.

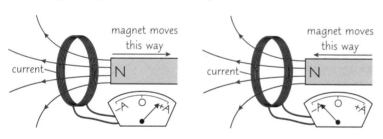

magnet moves this way

magnet moves this way

current

current

Rose's cheap knock-off conductors had induced the wrong sort of force.

5) If the coil is part of a **complete circuit**, an **induced current** will flow through it.

More Turns in a Coil of Wire Mean a Bigger E.m.f. will be Induced

1) When you move a **coil** in a magnetic field, the size of the e.m.f. induced depends on the **magnetic flux** passing through the coil, ϕ, and the **number of turns** in the coil that **cut the flux**, **N**.

2) The product of these is called the **flux linkage**. For a coil with N turns, perpendicular to a field with flux density B, the flux linkage is given by:

$$N\phi = BAN$$

Flux linkage is sometimes given in "weber-turns" or "Wb turns"

The unit of both flux linkage and ϕ is the weber, Wb.

3) The rate of change in flux linkage tells you how **strong** the **electromotive force** will be in **volts** (see next page):

> A **change** in **flux linkage** of **one weber per second** will induce an **electromotive force** of **1 volt** in a loop of wire.

Electromagnetic Induction

Use *Trigonometry* if the Magnetic Flux *Isn't Perpendicular* to the *Area*

When the magnetic flux **isn't perpendicular** to the area you're interested in, you need to use **trigonometry** to resolve the **magnetic field vector** into components that are **parallel** and **perpendicular** to the area.

For a **single loop** of wire when B is **not perpendicular** to the **plane of the loop**, you can find the **magnetic flux** using this equation: $\boxed{\phi = BA\cos\theta}$ where θ is the angle between the field and the normal to the plane of the loop.

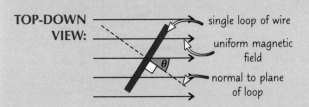

TOP-DOWN VIEW: single loop of wire — uniform magnetic field — normal to plane of loop

3D VIEW:

Pulling the loop out of field B would induce an e.m.f. — see below.

For a **coil** with N turns the **flux linkage** is: $\boxed{N\phi = BAN\cos\theta}$

Remember SOH CAH TOA: $\cos\theta = \text{adjacent} \div \text{hypotenuse}$

Faraday's Law Links the *Rate of Change* of *Flux Linkage* with *E.m.f.*

FARADAY'S LAW: The **induced e.m.f.** is **directly proportional** to the **rate of change of flux linkage**.

1) As an equation, this can be written as: $$\varepsilon = \frac{\text{flux linkage change}}{\text{time taken}} = \frac{d(N\phi)}{dt}$$ where ε (sometimes written as E) is the magnitude of the induced e.m.f. ($N = 1$ if it's just a single loop)

2) This gives you the **magnitude** of the induced e.m.f. (it only tells you the size, not the direction).

3) The term $\frac{d(N\phi)}{dt}$ in this formula means 'the **rate of change** of **flux linkage** over time'. It's the **gradient** of a graph of **flux linkage** against **time**.

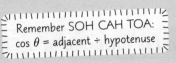

e.m.f. = gradient

If the line on a graph of $N\phi$ against time is flat, then the gradient is zero and no e.m.f. is induced.

4) More generally, **any term** with the form of **dy/dx** tells you the **rate of change of y with respect to x**.

5) $\Delta y/\Delta x$ is the **change in y** divided by the **change in x**. As Δy and Δx get **smaller**, $\Delta y/\Delta x$ gets **closer** to **dy/dx**, and for a **straight line graph** like the one on the right, $\Delta y/\Delta x$ and **dy/dx** are **the same**.

$\Delta(N\phi)$ = area

Remember — Δ is just the symbol that means 'the change in'.

6) You can also plot a graph of the magnitude of the induced e.m.f. against time. The **area under** this graph between two times gives you the **flux linkage change** between the two times.

Example: A 0.60 m long metal rod moves through a perpendicular uniform magnetic field with magnetic flux density 0.24 T, at a constant velocity of 0.50 ms^{-1}. Find the flux cut by the rod in 5.0 seconds, and hence the magnitude of the e.m.f. induced.

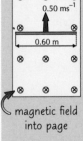

0.50 ms^{-1}

0.60 m

magnetic field into page

Distance travelled, $s = v\Delta t = 0.50 \times 5.0 = 2.5$ m.

The area of flux cut is equal to this distance multiplied by the length of the rod: $A = 2.5 \times 0.60 = 1.5$ m^2

From p.109, you know: $\phi = BA$, so the flux cut in 5 seconds = $0.24 \times 1.5 = $ **0.36 Wb**

Faraday's law gives $\varepsilon = \frac{d(N\phi)}{dt} = \frac{d\phi}{dt}$ (since $N = 1$)

As the rod is moving at a constant speed and the field is uniform, the rate of change of flux linkage will be constant, so you can say: induced e.m.f., $\varepsilon = \frac{d\phi}{dt} = \frac{\Delta\phi}{\Delta t} = 0.36 \div 5.0 = $ **0.072 V**

If you're not given a time period in the question, call the change in time Δt and work through the whole question algebraically. The Δt's will cancel out in the end.

Electromagnetic Induction

The *Direction* of the *Induced E.m.f.* and *Current* are given by *Lenz's Law*

LENZ'S LAW: The **induced e.m.f.** is always in such a **direction** as to **oppose** the **change** that caused it.

1) **Lenz's law** and **Faraday's law** can be **combined** to give one formula that works for both:

2) The **minus sign** shows the direction of the **induced e.m.f.**

3) The idea that an induced e.m.f. will **oppose** the change that caused it agrees with the principle of the **conservation of energy** — the **energy used** to pull a conductor through a magnetic field, against the **resistance** caused by magnetic **attraction**, is what **produces** the **induced current**.

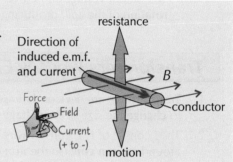

$$\varepsilon = \frac{-\text{flux linkage change}}{\text{time taken}} = \frac{-d(N\phi)}{dt}$$

where ε is the induced e.m.f.

4) **Lenz's law** can be used to find the **direction** of an **induced e.m.f.** and **current** in a conductor travelling at right angles to a magnetic field.

- **Lenz's law** says that the **induced e.m.f.** will produce a force that **opposes** the motion of the conductor — in other words a **resistance**.
- Using **Fleming's left-hand rule** (see p.106), point your thumb in the direction of the force of **resistance** — which is in the **opposite direction** to the motion of the conductor.
- Point your **first finger** in the direction of the **field**. Your **second finger** will now give you the direction of the **induced e.m.f.**
- If the conductor is **connected** as part of a **circuit**, a current will be induced in the **same direction** as the induced e.m.f.

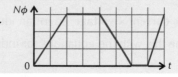

Practice Questions

Q1 What is the difference between magnetic flux density, magnetic flux and magnetic flux linkage?

Q2 A coil consists of N turns, each of area A in magnetic field B. State the equation to calculate the flux linkage if the normal to the plane of the coil is at an angle to a uniform magnetic field.

Q3 State Faraday's law and Lenz's law.

Q4 Describe how to find the direction of an induced e.m.f. in a copper bar moving at right angles to a magnetic field.

Exam Questions

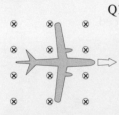

Q1 An aeroplane with a wingspan of 33.9 m flies at a constant speed of 148 ms⁻¹ perpendicular to the Earth's magnetic field, as shown. The Earth's magnetic field at the aeroplane's location is 6.00×10^{-5} T.

a) By considering how far the plane travels in 1 second, calculate the magnitude of the induced e.m.f. between the wing tips of the plane. [3 marks]

b) Copy and complete the diagram to show the direction of the induced e.m.f. between the wing-tips. (Magnetic field is into the page in this diagram.) [1 mark]

Q2 A 0.010 m² coil of 550 turns is perpendicular to a magnetic field of strength 0.92 T.

a) Calculate the magnetic flux linkage in the coil. [1 mark]

b) The coil is rotated until the normal to the plane of the coil is at 90.0° to the magnetic field. The movement is uniform and takes 0.50 s. Calculate the e.m.f. induced by this movement. [2 marks]

Q3 The graph shows how the flux linkage through a coil varies over time. Sketch a graph to show how the magnitude of the induced e.m.f. in the coil varies over this same time period. [3 marks]

Beware — physics can induce extreme confusion...

Make sure you know the difference between flux and flux linkage, and that you can calculate both. The stuff about rates of change at the bottom of page 110 is a bit tricky too, so I'd go over it again if I were you.

Alternating Currents

Faraday's law of electromagnetic induction turns up all over the place — from phone chargers to power stations...

Alternating Current is Constantly Changing

1) An **alternating current** (a.c.) or voltage is one that changes direction with time.

2) This means the voltage across a resistance goes up and down in a **regular pattern** — some of the time it's positive and some of the time it's negative.

alternating currants

An Alternator is a Generator of Alternating Current

1) **Generators**, or dynamos, **convert** kinetic energy into **electrical energy** — they **induce** an electric **current** by rotating a **coil** in a magnetic field.

2) The diagram shows a simple **alternator** — a generator of **a.c.** It has **slip rings** and **brushes** to connect the coil to an external circuit.

3) The output **voltage** and **current** change direction with every **half rotation** of the coil, producing an **alternating current**.

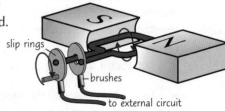

slip rings

brushes

to external circuit

Transformers Work by Electromagnetic Induction

1) **Transformers** are devices that use electromagnetic induction to **change** the size of the **voltage** for an **alternating current**.

2) They consist of **two coils of wire** wrapped around an **iron core** (so the iron core **links** them).

3) An alternating current flowing in the **primary** (or input) **coil** produces a changing **magnetic field** in the **iron core**.

4) The **changing magnetic field** is passed through the **iron core** to the **secondary** (or output) coil, where the changing magnetic flux **induces** an alternating **voltage** (e.m.f.) of the same frequency as the input voltage.

5) The **ratio** of the **number of turns** on each coil along with the voltage across the primary coil determines the **size of the voltage** induced in the secondary coil (see below).

laminated iron core

magnetic field in the iron core

primary coil

secondary coil

> **Step-up** transformers **increase** the **voltage** by having **more turns** on the **secondary** coil than the primary.
>
> **Step-down** transformers **reduce** the voltage by having **fewer** turns on the secondary coil.

6) **Transformers** only work with alternating current — the changing voltage means the **flux linkage** in the iron core is **constantly changing**, which is what causes a voltage to be induced in the secondary coil. If you used **direct current** (d.c.), **not much** would happen.

7) Real-life transformers **aren't 100% efficient** — some power is always lost. Using a **laminated core** reduces losses.

You Can Calculate the Induced E.m.f.s in Each Coil

1) From Faraday's law (page 110), the **induced** e.m.f.s in both the **primary** (p) and **secondary** (s) coils can be calculated:

Primary coil: $\qquad$ Secondary coil:

$$V_p = -\frac{n_p \mathrm{d}\phi}{\mathrm{d}t} \qquad V_s = -\frac{n_s \mathrm{d}\phi}{\mathrm{d}t}$$

Where n is the number of turns in a coil.

2) Ideal transformers are **100% efficient**, so **power in** equals the **power out**.

3) Power is **current × voltage**, so for an ideal transformer $I_p V_p = I_s V_s$, or $\frac{I_p}{I_s} = \frac{V_s}{V_p}$.

4) **Combine** this with the equations for induced e.m.f. in each coil to get the **transformer equation**:

$$\frac{n_s}{n_p} = \frac{V_s}{V_p} = \frac{I_p}{I_s}$$

> **Example:** What is the output voltage for a transformer with a primary coil of 120 turns, a secondary coil of 350 turns and an input voltage of 230 V?
>
> $$\frac{n_s}{n_p} = \frac{V_s}{V_p} \qquad V_s = \frac{V_p \times n_s}{n_p} = \frac{230 \times 350}{120} = 670.83... = \textbf{670 V (to 2 s.f.)}$$

Alternating Currents

Find the **rms**, **Peak** and **Peak-to-Peak Voltages** using an **Oscilloscope**

1) An alternating current is produced by an **alternating voltage**. You can use an **oscilloscope** to show the waveform of an alternating voltage.

See p.103 for more on oscilloscopes.

2) There are three basic pieces of information you can get from a voltage waveform for an a.c. power supply — the **period**, **T**, the **peak voltage**, V_0, and the **peak-to-peak voltage**.

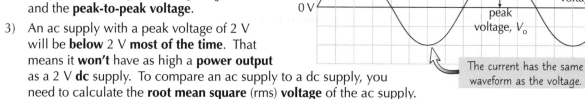

period, T

peak-to-peak voltage

0 V

peak voltage, V_o

3) An ac supply with a peak voltage of 2 V will be **below** 2 V **most of the time**. That means it **won't** have as high a **power output** as a 2 V **dc** supply. To compare an ac supply to a dc supply, you need to calculate the **root mean square** (rms) **voltage** of the ac supply.

The current has the same waveform as the voltage.

4) For a sine wave, you can calculate the rms voltage (V_{rms}) by **dividing** the **peak voltage**, V_0, by $\sqrt{2}$. You do the same to calculate the rms current I_{rms}:

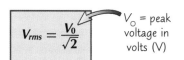

$$V_{rms} = \frac{V_0}{\sqrt{2}}$$

V_o = peak voltage in volts (V)

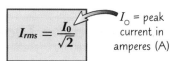

$$I_{rms} = \frac{I_0}{\sqrt{2}}$$

I_o = peak current in amperes (A)

For more about root mean square values, see page 137.

To work out the **average power** for an ac supply, just use the **rms values** of voltage and current: **power**$_{rms}$ = I_{rms} × V_{rms}

5) Measuring the distance **between** successive **peaks** along the **time axis** (the horizontal axis) gives you the **period** (as long as you know the time base setting, see p.103). You can use this to calculate the **frequency**:

$$\text{frequency} = \frac{1}{\text{period}}, \text{ or } f = \frac{1}{T}$$

Where the period is measured in seconds and the frequency is measured in hertz (Hz).

Practice Questions

Q1 What is an alternating current?

Q2 Draw a diagram of a simple transformer. What is meant by a step-down transformer?

Q3 State the transformer equation.

Q4 Describe the waveform of the voltage in an alternating current.

Q5 The frequency of UK mains alternating current is 50 Hz. Show that its time period is 0.02s.

Exam Questions

Q1 A transformer is made up of two coils of wire linked by an iron core.
A particular transformer with 158 turns in the primary coil has an input voltage of 9.30 V.
  a) i) Calculate the number of turns needed in the secondary coil to step up the voltage to 45.0 V. [1 mark]
    ii) The secondary coil actually has 90.0 turns. Calculate the voltage induced in the secondary coil. [1 mark]
  b) The input current for the transformer is 1.50 A.
     Assuming the transformer is ideal, calculate the output current. [1 mark]

Q2 a) The peak current in an ac circuit is 9.13 A. Calculate the root mean square current. [1 mark]
  b) The root mean square voltage of the same alternating supply is 119 V.
     Calculate the peak-to-peak voltage. [2 marks]

Arrrrrrrrrgggggggghhhhhhhh...

Breathe a sigh of relief, pat yourself on the back and make a brew — well done, you've reached the end of the section. That was pretty nasty stuff (the section, not your tea), but don't let all of those equations get you down — once you've learnt the main ones and can use them blindfolded, even the trickiest looking exam question will be a walk in the park...

Atomic Structure

We have a pretty good idea of atomic structure these days — but it's been anything but plain sailing...

The **Thomson Model** said **Electrons** were **Spread Out** Inside an **Atom**

1) The idea of **atoms** has been around since the time of the **Ancient Greeks** in the 5th Century BC. A man called **Democritus** proposed that all matter was made up of little, identical lumps called '**atomos**'.

2) Much later, in 1804, a scientist called **John Dalton** put forward a hypothesis that agreed with Democritus — that matter was made up of **tiny spheres** ('**atoms**') that couldn't be broken up. He reckoned that each element was made up of a **different type** of 'atom'.

3) Nearly 100 years later, **J. J. Thomson** discovered that **electrons** could be **removed** from atoms. So Dalton's theory wasn't quite right (atoms could be **broken up**). Thomson suggested that atoms were **spheres of positive charge** with tiny **negative electrons** stuck in them like fruit in a plum pudding. This "**plum pudding**" model of the atom was known as the **Thomson Model**.

4) The Thomson Model was widely accepted at the time, until the **Rutherford scattering experiment** of 1909. In Rutherford's laboratory, **Hans Geiger** and **Ernest Marsden** studied the scattering of **alpha particles** by **thin metal foils**.

Rutherford's Experiment **Disproved** the **Thomson Model**...

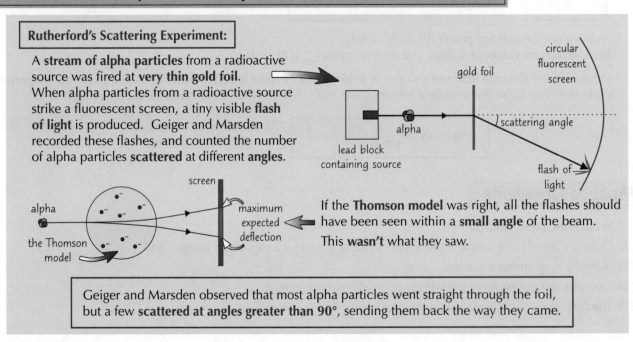

Rutherford's Scattering Experiment:

A **stream of alpha particles** from a radioactive source was fired at **very thin gold foil**. When alpha particles from a radioactive source strike a fluorescent screen, a tiny visible **flash of light** is produced. Geiger and Marsden recorded these flashes, and counted the number of alpha particles **scattered** at different **angles**.

If the **Thomson model** was right, all the flashes should have been seen within a **small angle** of the beam. This **wasn't** what they saw.

Geiger and Marsden observed that most alpha particles went straight through the foil, but a few **scattered at angles greater than 90°**, sending them back the way they came.

...and Supported the Idea of a **Small, Positively Charged Nucleus**

This experiment led Rutherford to some **important conclusions**:

1) Most of the fast, charged alpha particles went **straight through** the foil. So the atom is mainly **empty space**.

2) **Some** of the alpha particles were **deflected** through **large angles**, so the **centre** of the atom must have a **large, positive charge** to repel them. Rutherford named this the **nucleus**.

3) Very few particles were deflected by angles greater than **90 degrees** (and most went straight through), so the diameter of nucleus must be **tiny** in comparison to the diameter of the atom.

4) The alpha particles could only have been deflected by angles greater than **90 degrees** if they were scattered by something **more massive** than themselves, so most of the **mass** must be in the nucleus.

So most of the **mass** and the **positive charge** in a atom must be contained within a **tiny, central nucleus**.

Atomic Structure

The *Nuclear Model* Explained *Rutherford Scattering*

1) Inside **every atom**, there's a **positive nucleus** containing **neutrons** (which have no charge) and **positively charged protons**. Protons and **neutrons** are both known as **nucleons**. **Orbiting** this core are the **negatively charged electrons**.

2) The **charge** on an **electron**, $-e$, is **equal and opposite** to the charge on a **proton**, $+e$. e is the **elementary charge** 1.60×10^{-19} C.

3) The **nucleus** only makes up a tiny proportion of an atom — it's only about **one 10 000th of the size** of the whole atom. The electrons orbit at relatively **vast distances** from the nucleus, so most of the atom is **empty space**.

4) The **proton** and **neutron** are roughly **2000 times** more **massive** than the **electron**, so the nucleus makes up **nearly all** of the **mass** of the atom.

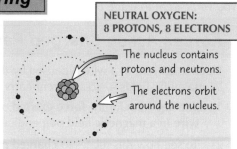

NEUTRAL OXYGEN:
8 PROTONS, 8 ELECTRONS

The nucleus contains protons and neutrons.

The electrons orbit around the nucleus.

The *Proton Number* is the *Number* of *Protons* in the Nucleus

No... really.

The **proton number** is sometimes called the **atomic number**, and has the **symbol Z** (don't ask me why). Z is just the **number of protons** in the nucleus.

It's the **proton number** that **defines** the **element** — **no two elements** will have the **same** number of protons.

In a **neutral atom**, the number of **electrons equals** the number of **protons**. The element's **reactions** and **chemical behaviour** depend on the number of **electrons**. So the **proton number** tells you a lot about its **chemical properties**.

The *Nucleon Number* is the *Total Number* of *Protons* and *Neutrons*

The **nucleon number** is also called the **mass number**, and has the **symbol A** (*shrug*). It tells you how many **protons** and **neutrons** are in the nucleus.

Each **proton or neutron** has a **mass** of (approximately) **1 atomic mass unit** (1.66×10^{-27} kg, see p.155). The mass of an electron compared with a nucleon is virtually nothing, so the **number** of **nucleons** is about the same as the **atom's mass** (in atomic mass units).

Nuclei can be Represented Using *Standard Notation*

Standard notation summarises the important information about an element's **atomic structure**:

The **proton number** or **atomic number** (Z) — there are six protons in a carbon atom.

$$^{12}_{6}\text{C}$$

The **nucleon number** or **mass number** (A) — there are a total of 12 protons and neutrons in a carbon-12 atom.

The symbol for the element carbon.

Practice Questions

Q1 Describe how our understanding of atomic structure has changed since the time of the Ancient Greeks.

Q2 List the particles that make up the atom and give their charges and relative masses.

Q3 Define the proton number and nucleon number.

Exam Questions

Q1 In 1911, Ernest Rutherford proposed the nuclear model of the atom after experiments using alpha-particle scattering.

    a) Describe the nuclear model of the atom. [3 marks]

    b) Explain how the alpha-particle scattering experiment provided evidence for Rutherford's model. [4 marks]

Q2 State how many protons, neutrons and electrons there are in a (neutral) $^{139}_{57}$La atom. [2 marks]

Alpha scattering — it's positively repulsive...

The important things to learn from these two pages are the nuclear model for the structure of the atom (i.e. a large mass nucleus surrounded by orbiting electrons), how our understanding of the atom has changed over time and how the alpha particle scattering experiment provides evidence that supports the nuclear model.

Particle Accelerators

Particle accelerators are devices that (surprisingly) accelerate particles, using electric and magnetic fields. Sadly you've first got to wade through the physics of charged particles in magnetic fields before you get to the juicy bits.

Forces Act on Charged Particles in Magnetic Fields

Electric current in a wire is caused by the **flow** of negatively **charged** electrons. These charged particles are affected by **magnetic fields** — so a current-carrying wire can experience a **force** in a magnetic field (see pages 106-107).

1) The equation for the **force** exerted on a **current-carrying wire** in a **magnetic field** perpendicular to the current is:

   | Equation 1: $F = BIl$ |

   Where B is the magnetic flux density, I is the current through the wire and l is the length of the wire.

2) To see how this relates to **charged particles** moving through a wire, you need to know that electric **current**, I, is the flow of **charge**, Q, per unit **time**, t: $I = \dfrac{Q}{t}$

3) A charged particle which moves a **distance** l in **time** t has a **velocity**, v, given by $v = \dfrac{l}{t}$ (speed = dist ÷ time), so: $t = \dfrac{l}{v}$

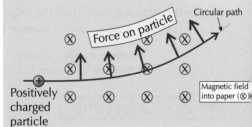

In many exam questions, Q is the size of the charge on the electron, which is 1.60×10^{-19} coulombs.

4) Putting the two equations **together** gives the **current** in terms of the **charge** flowing through the **wire**:

   | Equation 2: $I = \dfrac{Qv}{l}$ |

5) Putting **equation 2** back into **equation 1** gives the **electromagnetic force** on the wire as:

   | $F = BQv$ | Where F is in newtons (N), B is in tesla (T), Q is in coulombs (C), and v is in metres per second (ms⁻¹).

6) You can use this equation to find the **force** acting on a **single charged particle moving through a magnetic field**.

Example: An electron is travelling at 2.00×10^4 ms⁻¹ perpendicular to the field lines of a uniform magnetic field of 2.00 T. Calculate the size of the force acting on the electron. (The magnitude of the charge on an electron is 1.60×10^{-19} C.)

$F = BQv$
so $F = 2.00 \times 1.60 \times 10^{-19} \times 2.00 \times 10^4$
$F = \mathbf{6.40 \times 10^{-15}}$ **N**

Charged Particles in a Magnetic Field are Deflected in a Circular Path

1) By **Fleming's left hand rule** (see p.106) the force on a **moving charge** in a magnetic field is always **perpendicular** to its **direction of travel**. Mathematically, that is the condition for **circular motion** (p.97).

2) This effect is used in **particle accelerators** such as **cyclotrons**, which use **magnetic fields** to accelerate particles to very **high energies** along circular paths (see next page).

3) It's also used for identifying particles in particle accelerators and mass spectrometers (see p.127).

Circular path

Force on particle

Positively charged particle

Magnetic field into paper (⊗)

Centripetal Force Tells Us About a Particle's Path

The centripetal force and the electromagnetic force are equivalent for a charged particle travelling along a circular path.

You might see the charge of a particle denoted by a q, rather than a Q. It's the same thing, so don't panic.

1) For uniform circular motion **Newton's second law** gives: $F = \dfrac{mv^2}{r}$

2) So, for a **charged particle** following a **circular** path in a **magnetic field** (where $F = BQv$): $BQv = \dfrac{mv^2}{r}$

3) Rearranging, cancelling and substituting in $p = mv$ (see p.92) gives:

   | $r = \dfrac{p}{BQ}$ | Where p is the momentum of the particle, r is the radius of the circular path, B is the magnetic flux density and Q is the charge of the particle.

   $F = \dfrac{mv^2}{r}$ $F = BQv$

4) So, different charged particles will have paths with different radii — the higher the ratio of p to Q, the larger the radius of the path.

Centripetal force   Electromagnetic force

Particle Accelerators

Cyclotrons Make Use of Circular Deflection

This is not a cyclotron.

1) Circular deflection is used in particle accelerators such as **cyclotrons**.
2) Cyclotrons have many uses, for example in **medicine**. Cyclotrons are used to produce **radioactive tracers** or high-energy beams of radiation for use in **radiotherapy**.
3) A **cyclotron** is made up of two hollow **semicircular electrodes** with a uniform magnetic field applied perpendicular to the plane of the electrodes, and an **alternating** potential difference (p.d.) applied between the electrodes:

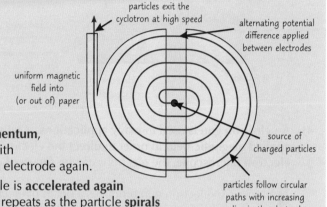

- Charged particles are **fired** into one of the electrodes. The magnetic field makes them follow a (semi)circular path and then **leave** the electrode.
- An applied potential difference between the electrodes **accelerates** the particles across the gap until they enter the next electrode.
- Because the particle's speed, and therefore **momentum**, is **slightly higher**, it will follow a circular path with a **larger** radius (see page 116) before leaving the electrode again.
- The potential difference is **reversed** so the particle is **accelerated again** before entering the next electrode. This process repeats as the particle **spirals outwards**, increasing in momentum, before eventually **exiting** the cyclotron.

The Electronvolt is Defined Using Accelerated Charges

You met electronvolts on p.86.

1) The **kinetic energy** that a particle with charge Q gains when it's **accelerated** through a p.d. of V volts is given by $E_K = QV$. That just comes from the definition of the **volt** (JC^{-1}).
2) You know that $E_K = \frac{1}{2}mv^2$ (p.94) so $\frac{1}{2}mv^2 = QV$. If you replace Q in this equation with the size of the charge of a **single electron**, e, you get: $\boxed{\frac{1}{2}mv^2 = eV}$
3) From this you can define a new **unit of energy** called the **electronvolt (eV)**:

1 electronvolt is the **kinetic energy carried** by an **electron** after it has been **accelerated** through a **p.d. of 1 volt**.

4) So, the **energy in eV** of an electron accelerated by a potential difference is:

energy gained by electron (eV) = accelerating p.d. (V)   **Conversion factor:** $1\ eV = 1.60 \times 10^{-19}\ J$

5) The unit MeV is the mega-electronvolt (equal to 1.60×10^{-13} J) and GeV is the giga-electronvolt (1.60×10^{-10} J).

Linear Particle Accelerators Use Alternating Electric Fields

1) A **linear particle accelerator** (**linac**) is a long, **straight** tube containing a series of tube-shaped **electrodes**. The charge on each electrode alternates along the tube (so a positive electrode is always between two negative electrodes and vice-versa).
2) The electrodes are connected to an **alternating p.d. supply** so that the charge of each **electrode** continuously **changes** between + and −. This means the **electric field** (p.98) between **each pair** of electrodes is continuously **switching direction** over time.
3) The alternating p.d. is **timed** so that the particles are always **attracted** to the **next electrode** in the accelerator and **repelled** from the **previous** one.
4) A particle's **speed increases** each time it **passes** an electrode.
5) To compensate for this increasing speed, the **length** of the electrodes **increases** as the particle travels down the accelerator, so that the particle spends the same amount of time in each electrode.
6) The **high-energy particles** leaving a linac **collide** with a **fixed target** at the end of the tube.

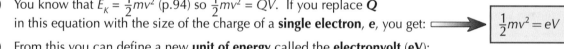
A linear particle accelerator

Particle Accelerators

Electron Guns *Produce Electrons by* Thermionic Emission

1) When you **heat** a **metal**, its **free electrons** gain a load of **thermal energy**.
2) Give them **enough energy** and they **break free** from the surface of the metal — this is called **thermionic emission**.
3) Once they've been emitted, the electrons can be **accelerated** by an **electric field** in an **electron gun**:

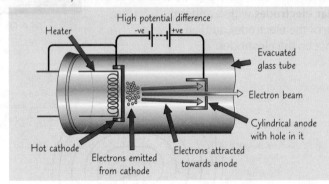

High potential difference
-ve +ve
Heater
Evacuated glass tube
Electron beam
Cylindrical anode with hole in it
Hot cathode
Electrons emitted from cathode
Electrons attracted towards anode

A **heating coil** heats the metal cathode. The electrons that are emitted are **accelerated** towards the **cylindrical anode** by the electric field set up by the high potential difference.

Some electrons pass through a **little hole** in the anode, making a narrow electron beam. The electrons in the beam move at a **constant velocity** because there's **no field** beyond the anode — i.e. there's **no force**.

4) An **electron gun** is used in many **applications**. Quite often, the electron beam passes through an **applied magnetic field** in order to **direct** the electrons towards something. For example, in an **electron microscope**, the electrons can be **focussed** onto a sample using a **magnetic field**.

Example: An electron gun produces a beam of electrons which pass through a magnetic field of 0.080 T, perpendicular to their direction of motion. This causes the electrons to travel in a circular path with a radius of 1.8×10^{-4} m. The speed of the electrons remains constant. Calculate the speed of the electrons.

You met the equation for the radius of the path of a charged particle in a magnetic field on p.116.

A charged particle moving perpendicular to a magnetic field moves in a circle with radius $r = \dfrac{p}{BQ} = \dfrac{mv}{BQ}$, so $v = \dfrac{BQr}{m}$.

The size of the charge on an electron is 1.60×10^{-19} C (only the magnitude of the charge is used here — we're calculating speed, not velocity).

Substitute the values in: $v = \dfrac{0.080 \times (1.60 \times 10^{-19}) \times (1.8 \times 10^{-4})}{9.11 \times 10^{-31}} = 2.52... \times 10^{6} = \mathbf{2.5 \times 10^{6}}$ **ms⁻¹ (to 2 s.f.)**

The mass of an electron is 9.11×10^{-31} kg.

The charge and mass of an electron are given in the data and formulae booklet in the exam.

Practice Questions

Q1 Write an equation to calculate the force on a charged particle, Q, moving perpendicular to a magnetic field, B.

Q2 Derive an equation for the radius of the circular path of a charged particle moving at right angles to a magnetic field, in terms of the magnetic flux density and the particle's momentum and charge.

Q3 Explain how particles are accelerated in a linear accelerator (linac) and in a cyclotron.

Q4 Convert 246 J into: a) eV b) MeV c) GeV

Q5 What is meant by thermionic emission?

Exam Questions

Q1 An electron travels at a velocity of 5.00×10^{6} ms⁻¹ through a perpendicular magnetic field of 0.770 T. Calculate the magnitude of the force acting on the electron.
[2 marks]

Q2 An electron is accelerated to a velocity of 2.3×10^{7} ms⁻¹ by a particle accelerator. The electron moves in a circular path perpendicular to a magnetic field of 0.60 mT. Calculate the radius of the electron's path.
[2 marks]

Hold on to your hats folks — this is starting to get tricky...

Remember, magnetic fields cause an acceleration perpendicular to the field, electric fields cause an acceleration parallel to the field. In cyclotrons and linacs, the field that increases the <u>speed</u> of the charged particle is the electric field — the magnetic field in the cyclotron changes the particle's <u>direction</u> (this still an acceleration, as its a change of velocity).

Classification of Particles

There are loads of different types of particle apart from the ones you get in normal matter (protons, neutrons, etc.).
They only appear in cosmic rays and in particle accelerators, and they often decay very quickly so they're
difficult to get a handle on. Nonetheless, you need to learn about a load of them and their properties.

This stuff is known as the standard quark-lepton model. Stick with it — you'll get there.

Hadrons are Particles that are Made Up of Quarks

1) Hadrons aren't **fundamental** particles. They're made up of **smaller particles** called **quarks** (see pages 124-126).

2) There are **two** types of **hadrons** — **baryons** (and anti-baryons) and **mesons**. They're classified according to the number of **quarks** that make them up, but don't worry about that for now.

Protons and Neutrons are Baryons

1) It's helpful to think of **protons** and **neutrons** as **two versions** of the **same particle** — the **nucleon**. They just have **different electric charges**.

2) **Protons** and **neutrons** are both **baryons**.

3) There are **other baryons** that you don't get in normal matter — like **sigmas** (Σ).

Priscilla and Nora liked to
describe protons and neutrons
through the medium of dance.

The Proton is the Only Stable Baryon

All **baryons** — except the proton — are **unstable**. This means that they **decay** to become other **particles**.
The **particles** a baryon ends up as depends on what it started as, but it **always** includes a **proton**.
Protons are the only **stable baryons** — they don't decay (as far as we know).

> All baryons except protons decay to a **proton**.

*Some theories predict that protons should
decay with a very long half-life, but there's
no evidence for it at the moment.*

Antiprotons and Antineutrons are Antibaryons

The **antiparticles** of protons and neutrons — **antiprotons** and **antineutrons** — are **antibaryons**.
But, as you will see on page 123, **antiparticles** are **annihilated** when they meet the
corresponding **particle** — which means that you **don't** find **antibaryons** in ordinary matter.

Baryon Number is Always Conserved

The **baryon number** is the number of baryons. (A bit like **nucleon number** but including unusual baryons like Σ too.)
The **proton** and the **neutron** each have a baryon number **B = +1**. **Antibaryons** have a baryon number **B = −1**.
Other particles (i.e. things that aren't baryons) are given a baryon number **B = 0**.

Baryon number is a **quantum number** that must be **conserved** in any interaction — that means it can only take on
a **certain set of values** (so you can't have 2.7981 baryons, or 1.991112 baryons... you get the idea).

When an **interaction** happens, the **baryon number** on either side of the interaction has to be the **same**.
You can use this fact to **predict** whether an **interaction** will **happen** — if the numbers don't match, it can't happen.

> The **total baryon number** in **any** particle interaction **never changes**.

Classification of Particles

Mesons are Another Type of Hadron

The second type of hadron you need to know about is the **meson**.

1) **All mesons are unstable** and have **baryon number B = 0** (because they're not baryons).

2) **Pions** (π-mesons) are the **lightest mesons**. You get **three versions** with different **electric charges** — π^+, π^0 and π^-. You get **loads** of pions in **high-energy particle collisions** like those studied at the **CERN** particle accelerator.

3) You get other types of mesons too — for example **kaons** are **heavier** and more **unstable** than **pions**.

4) Pions and kaons were **discovered** in **cosmic rays** — cosmic ray showers are a source of both particles. You can observe the tracks of these particles with a **cloud chamber** (see p.127).

Pies have a short lifetime too, especially in our house.

Summary of Hadron Properties

DON'T PANIC if you don't understand all this yet. For now, just **learn** these properties.

You'll need to work through to the end of page 126 to see how it **all fits together**.

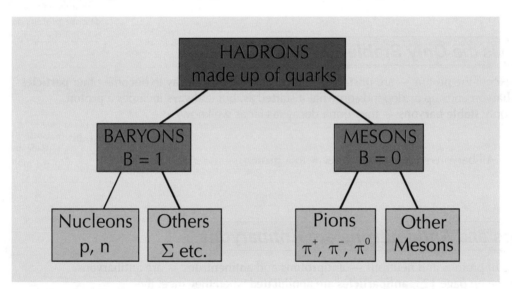

Leptons Are Fundamental Particles

1) **Leptons** are **fundamental particles** — i.e. they're not made up of anything smaller.

2) **Electrons** (e⁻) are **stable** and very **familiar** but — you guessed it — there are also **two more leptons** called the **muon** (μ⁻) and the **tau** (τ⁻) that are just like **heavy electrons**.

3) **Muons and taus** are **unstable**, and **decay** eventually into **ordinary electrons**.

4) The **electron, muon** and **tau** each come with their **own neutrino**: ν_e, ν_μ and ν_τ.

5) **Neutrinos** have **zero** or **almost zero mass** and **zero electric charge** — so they don't do much. In fact, a neutrino can **pass right through the Earth** without **anything** happening to it.

ν is the Greek letter "nu".

Classification of Particles

You Have to **Count** the **Three Types** of Lepton **Separately**

Each lepton is given a **lepton number** of **+1**, but the **electron**, **muon** and **tau** types of lepton have to be **counted separately**.

You get **three different** lepton numbers: L_e, L_μ and L_τ.

Like the baryon number, the lepton number is just the number of leptons.

Name	Symbol	Charge	L_e	L_μ	L_τ
electron	e^-	-1	$+1$	0	0
electron neutrino	ν_e	0	$+1$	0	0
muon	μ^-	-1	0	$+1$	0
muon neutrino	ν_μ	0	0	$+1$	0
tau	τ^-	-1	0	0	$+1$
tau neutrino	ν_τ	0	0	0	$+1$

Nick had just been told he had six more particles to learn.

Photons aren't Made of Quarks or Leptons

1) **Light** can act as a **particle** — these particles are called **photons** (see p.86).

2) A photon has **no mass**, **no charge**, **no baryon number** and **no lepton number**. A photon does have **energy** though, and this is going to be important on the next couple of pages.

3) When photons are involved in interactions (see p.125-126), they are denoted by a γ.

Practice Questions

Q1 What is the difference between a hadron and a lepton?

Q2 Which is the only stable baryon (probably)?

Q3 A particle collision at CERN produces 2 protons, 3 pions and 1 neutron.
What is the total baryon number of these particles?

Q4 Which two particles have lepton number $L_\mu = +1$?

Exam Questions

Q1 Initially, the muon was incorrectly identified as a meson. Explain why the muon is not a meson. [2 marks]

Q2 A sodium atom contains 11 electrons, 11 protons and 12 neutrons. Which row in the table contains the correct numbers of hadrons, baryons, mesons and leptons in a sodium atom? [1 mark]

	Hadrons	Baryons	Mesons	Leptons
A	12	11	12	11
B	23	23	0	11
C	23	0	23	23
D	12	11	0	23

Go back to the top of page 119 — do not pass GO, do not collect £200...

Do it. Go back and read it again. I promise — read these pages a few times and you'll start to see a pattern. There are hadrons that are made of quarks, leptons that aren't. Hadrons are either baryons or mesons, and they're all weird except for those well-known baryons: protons and neutrons. There are loads of leptons, including good old electrons.

Antiparticles

More stuff that seems to laugh in the face of common sense — but actually, antiparticles help to explain a lot in particle physics... (Oh, and if you haven't read p.119-121 yet then go back and read them now — no excuses, off you go...)

Antiparticles were Predicted Before they were Discovered

When **Paul Dirac** wrote down an equation obeyed by **electrons**, he found a kind of **mirror image** solution.

Nice one Paul. Now we've got twice as many things to worry about.

1) It predicted the existence of a particle like the **electron** but with **opposite electric charge** — the **positron**.

2) The **positron** turned up later in a cosmic ray experiment. Positrons are **antileptons** so $L_e = -1$ for them. They have **identical mass** to electrons but they carry a **positive** charge.

Every Particle has an Antiparticle

Each particle type has a **corresponding antiparticle** with the **same mass** but with **opposite charge**, **opposite baryon number** and **opposite lepton number**.

You will be given the mass of a proton and an electron in your data and formulae booklet. The mass of a neutron can be assumed to be the same as the mass of a proton.

For instance, an **antiproton** is a **negatively charged** particle with $B = -1$ and the same mass as the **proton**.

Even the shadowy **neutrino** has an antiparticle version called the **antineutrino** — it doesn't do much either.

Particle	Symbol	Charge	B	L_e	Antiparticle	Symbol	Charge	B	L_e
proton	p	+1	+1	0	antiproton	$\bar{p}$	−1	−1	0
neutron	n	0	+1	0	antineutron	$\bar{n}$	0	−1	0
electron	e	−1	0	+1	positron	e^+	+1	0	−1
electron neutrino	ν_e	0	0	+1	electron antineutrino	$\bar{\nu}_e$	0	0	−1

You can Create Matter and Antimatter from Energy

You've probably heard about the **equivalence** of energy and mass. It all comes out of Einstein's special theory of relativity.

Energy can turn into **mass** and **mass** can turn into **energy** if you know how — all you need is one fantastic and rather powerful formula.

$$\Delta E = c^2 \Delta m$$

where ΔE is the change in energy, c is the speed of light in a vacuum and Δm is the change in mass.

If you've done any chemistry, you'll know that when you carry out a reaction the **mass of your reactants** will always equal the **mass of your products** — i.e. **mass is conserved**. In **nuclear reactions**, the **mass of the particles you start with** might be **more** or **less** than the mass of the particles you end up with. This happens when **energy** is **converted** to mass or mass to energy. This time it's the **total mass and energy** that's **conserved**.

> When **energy** is converted into **mass** you have to make **equal amounts** of **matter** and **antimatter**.

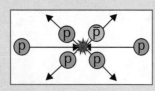

Fire **two protons** at each other at high speed and you'll end up with a lot of **energy** at the point of impact. This energy can form **more particles**.

So this means that particles with a large mass need a large amount of energy to be created.

If an extra **proton** is created, there has to be an **antiproton** made to go with it. It's called **pair production**.

When you're describing nuclear reactions, the SI units of **kilograms** and **joules** are **too big** to be easily used. Instead, the electronvolt, **eV** (p.117), is used for **energy**. **Atomic mass units**, **u** (p.115), or **eV/c²** are used for **mass**. The prefixes mega (M) and giga (G) are often used with eV, since the numbers involved are usually so small.

Conversion factors:

$$1 \text{ eV} = 1.60 \times 10^{-19} \text{ J}$$

$$\frac{1 \text{eV}}{c^2} = \frac{1.60 \times 10^{-19} \text{ J}}{(3.00 \times 10^8 \text{ ms}^{-1})^2} = 1.78 \times 10^{-36} \text{ kg (to 3 s.f.)}$$

1 MeV/c² = 1.78 × 10⁻³⁰ kg and 1 GeV/c² = 1.78 × 10⁻²⁷ kg

Antiparticles

Each *Particle-Antiparticle Pair* is Produced from a *Single Photon*

Pair production only happens if **one photon** has enough energy to produce that much mass. It also tends to happen near a **nucleus**, which helps conserve momentum.

You usually get **electron-positron** pairs produced (rather than any other pair) — because they have a relatively **low mass**.

The **minimum** amount of energy the **photon** must have is the **combined energy** of the **two** particles **due to their masses** (i.e. assuming that the particles have **negligible** kinetic energy).

You can calculate the **minimum** energy, E_γ, using $\Delta E = c^2 \Delta m$:

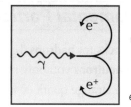

The particle tracks are curved because there's usually a magnetic field present in particle physics experiments. They curve in opposite directions because of the opposite charges on the electron and positron (see p.122).

1) A particle and its antiparticle have the **same mass** (m), which means that: $\Longrightarrow E_\gamma = 2c^2m$
2) You can go further and find the **maximum wavelength** or **minimum frequency** of the photon using the equation for the **energy of a photon** (see p.86): $\Longrightarrow E_\gamma = \dfrac{hc}{\lambda} = hf$

The *Opposite* of *Pair Production* is *Annihilation*

When a **particle** meets its **antiparticle** the result is **annihilation**. All the **mass** of the particle and antiparticle gets converted to **energy**, in the form of a pair of photons. In ordinary matter antiparticles can only exist for a fraction of a second before this happens, so you won't see many of them.

Just like with pair production, you can calculate the **minimum energy** of each photon produced (i.e. assuming that the particles have **negligible** kinetic energy).

The minimum combined energy of the photons will be equal to the combined energy of the particles due to their masses, so $2E_\gamma = 2c^2m$ and so:

$$E_\gamma = c^2m$$

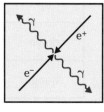

The electron and positron annihilate and their mass is converted into the energy of a pair of identical gamma ray photons.

You can calculate the minimum frequency and maximum wavelength as before.

Practice Questions

Q1 Which antiparticle has zero charge and a baryon number of –1?

Q2 Give the symbol for an electron antineutrino, and describe its properties.

Q3 Write down the charge, mass and lepton number of a positron, given that an electron has a charge of -1.60×10^{-19} C, a mass of 9.11×10^{-31} kg and an electron lepton number of +1.

Q4 Give one similarity and one difference between a proton and an antiproton.

Q5 Convert 2.1×10^{-31} kg into GeV/c^2.

Exam Questions

Q1 Explain why two protons and a neutron cannot be the only products of a collision between two protons. [1 mark]

Q2 Describe what happens when an electron and a positron collide and give the name for this process. [2 marks]

Q3 A neutron has a mass of 0.939375 GeV/c^2. Find the minimum energy (in GeV) required for a photon to produce a neutron-antineutron pair. [2 marks]

Q4 Assuming both particles have negligible kinetic energy, calculate the frequency of the photons produced when a proton and an antiproton annihilate.
($m_p = 1.67 \times 10^{-27}$ kg, $h = 6.63 \times 10^{-34}$ Js, $c = 3.00 \times 10^8$ ms^{-1}) [3 marks]

Pair production — never seems to happen with my socks...

The idea of every particle having an antiparticle might seem a bit strange, but just make sure you know the main points — a) if energy is converted into a particle, you also get an antiparticle, b) an antiparticle won't last long before it bumps into the right particle and annihilates it, c) this releases the energy it took to make them to start with...

Quarks

*If you haven't read pages 119 to 123, do it now! For the rest of you — here are the **juicy bits** you've been waiting for. Particle physics makes **a lot more sense** when you look at quarks. More sense than it did before anyway.*

Quarks are Fundamental Particles

Quarks are the **building blocks** for **hadrons** (baryons and mesons).

1) To make **protons** and **neutrons** you only need two types of quark — the **up** quark (**u**) and the **down** quark (**d**).

2) An extra one called the **strange** quark (**s**) lets you make more particles with a property called **strangeness**.
Antiparticles of hadrons are made from **antiquarks**.

Quarks and Antiquarks have Opposite Properties

The **antiquarks** have **opposite properties** to the quarks — as you'd expect.

QUARKS

Name	Symbol	Charge	Baryon number	Strangeness
up	u	$+\frac{2}{3}$	$+\frac{1}{3}$	0
down	d	$-\frac{1}{3}$	$+\frac{1}{3}$	0
strange	s	$-\frac{1}{3}$	$+\frac{1}{3}$	-1

ANTIQUARKS

Name	Symbol	Charge	Baryon number	Strangeness
anti-up	$\bar{u}$	$-\frac{2}{3}$	$-\frac{1}{3}$	0
anti-down	$\bar{d}$	$+\frac{1}{3}$	$-\frac{1}{3}$	0
anti-strange	$\bar{s}$	$+\frac{1}{3}$	$-\frac{1}{3}$	$+1$

There are Three Other Types of Quark

1) **Evidence** for the **up**, **down** and **strange** quarks came in the 1960s, and **two more** quarks were detected in experiments in the 1970s — the **bottom** and **charm** quarks.

2) Most of the **quarks** and **leptons** that had so far been discovered came in **pairs** (the up and down quark, the electron and electron neutrino etc). It was therefore **predicted** from the **symmetry of the model** that there was a **sixth** quark — the bottom quark's **partner**. This sixth quark was called the **top** quark and wasn't detected **until 1995**.

3) The last three quarks to be detected are all quite **unstable** though, so you don't come across them very often.

The **top (t)**, **bottom (b)** and **charm (c)** quarks and some of their properties are shown in the table:

Name	Symbol	Charge	Baryon number	Strangeness
top	t	$+\frac{2}{3}$	$+\frac{1}{3}$	0
bottom	b	$-\frac{1}{3}$	$+\frac{1}{3}$	0
charm	c	$+\frac{2}{3}$	$+\frac{1}{3}$	0

Quarks

Baryons are Made from Three Quarks

Evidence for quarks came from **hitting protons** with **high-energy electrons**. High-energy electrons have a **short de Broglie wavelength** (p.90) — which means they can be used to probe the **tiny distances** inside a proton. The way the **electrons scattered** showed that there were **three concentrations of charge** (quarks) **inside** the proton.

The **quark compositions** of protons, neutrons and their antiparticles are shown below.

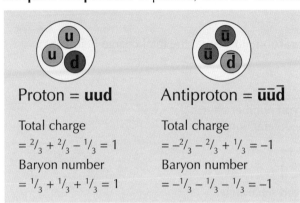

Proton = **uud**

Total charge
$= \frac{2}{3} + \frac{2}{3} - \frac{1}{3} = 1$
Baryon number
$= \frac{1}{3} + \frac{1}{3} + \frac{1}{3} = 1$

Antiproton = **ūūd̄**

Total charge
$= -\frac{2}{3} - \frac{2}{3} + \frac{1}{3} = -1$
Baryon number
$= -\frac{1}{3} - \frac{1}{3} - \frac{1}{3} = -1$

Neutron = **udd**

Total charge
$= \frac{2}{3} - \frac{1}{3} - \frac{1}{3} = 0$
Baryon number
$= \frac{1}{3} + \frac{1}{3} + \frac{1}{3} = 1$

Antineutron = **ūd̄d̄**

Total charge
$= -\frac{2}{3} + \frac{1}{3} + \frac{1}{3} = 0$
Baryon number
$= -\frac{1}{3} - \frac{1}{3} - \frac{1}{3} = -1$

Mesons are a Quark and an Antiquark

Pions are just made from combinations of **up**, **down**, **anti-up** and **anti-down** quarks.
Kaons have **strangeness** so you need to put in **s** quarks as well (remember, the **s** quark has a strangeness of S = −1).

Before we move on, it's worth mentioning that the π^- meson is just the **antiparticle** of the π^+ meson, the **K⁻** meson is the antiparticle of the **K⁺** meson, and the **antiparticle** of a π^0 meson is **itself**. It all makes sense when you look at the quark compositions to the right...

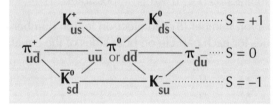

Physicists love patterns. Gaps in patterns like this predicted the existence of particles that were actually found later in experiments. Great stuff.

There's No Such Thing as a Free Quark

What if you **blasted** a **proton** with **enough energy** — could you **separate out** the quarks? Nope. Your energy just gets changed into more **quarks and antiquarks** — it's **pair production** again and you just make **mesons**. It's not possible to get a quark by itself — this is called **quark confinement**.

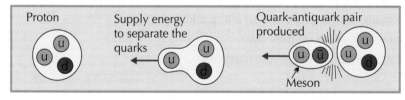

Simon was practising quack confinement.

You can Represent Particle Interactions with Equations

1) You've met a few **particle interactions** already (see p.122), but there are many more possible interactions, and they can all be represented with **equations**.

There's more on particle interaction equations in Topic 11 (see p.150).

2) You can either write the equations in terms of the **hadrons** involved, or the specific **quarks** (if one quark is **changing** into a different one).

3) For example, in **beta-minus decay**, a **neutron** decays into an **proton** (by way of a **down** quark turning into an **up** quark) and emits an **electron** and an **electron antineutrino**. This is shown in the equations:

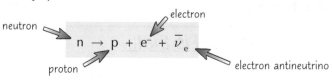

Quarks

There are Properties That Must be Conserved in Particle Interactions

Energy and Momentum are Always Conserved

In **any** particle interaction, there is **conservation of momentum** (p.92) and **conservation of energy** (p.36).

Charge is Always Conserved

In **any** particle interaction, the **total charge** after the interaction must equal the total charge before it.

Baryon Number is Always Conserved

Just like with charge, in **any** particle interaction, the **baryon number** after the interaction must equal the baryon number before the interaction.

Conservation of Lepton Number is a Bit More Complicated

The **different types** of lepton number have to be conserved **separately**.

1) For example, the interaction $\pi^- \rightarrow \mu^- + \bar{\nu}_\mu$ has $L_\mu = 0$ at the start and $L_\mu = 1 - 1 = 0$ at the end, so it's OK. Similarly, $n \rightarrow p + e^- + \bar{\nu}_e$ is fine. $L_e = 0$ at the start and $L_e = 1 - 1 = 0$ at the end.

2) On the other hand, the interaction $\nu_\mu + \mu^- \rightarrow e^- + \nu_e$ can't happen. At the start $L_\mu = 2$ and $L_e = 0$, but at the end $L_\mu = 0$ and $L_e = 2$.

Example: Is the interaction $p \rightarrow n + e^- + \nu_e$ possible?

To see if charge, baryon number (B) and electron lepton number (L_e) are conserved, write out their values for each particle on both sides of the equation:

	p		n	+	e^-	+	ν_e
Charge	+1	≠	0	+	−1	+	0
L_e	0	≠	0	+	+1	+	+1
B	+1	=	+1	+	0	+	0

You could stop after considering charge — an interaction can't happen if any one conservation law isn't obeyed.

Charge and electron lepton number are not conserved, so the interaction **is not** possible.

Practice Questions

Q1 What is a quark? State the quarks that make up a neutron.
Q2 Explain why high-energy particles are needed to probe the structure of protons.
Q3 Which type of particle is made from a quark and an antiquark?
Q4 Explain why quarks are never observed on their own.
Q5 List seven quantities that are conserved in particle reactions.

Exam Questions

Q1 A lambda particle Λ_0 is a baryon with no charge and strangeness −1. Write down its quark composition given that it's made up of a combination of any of: u, $\bar{u}$, d, $\bar{d}$, s and $\bar{s}$ quarks. [2 marks]

Q2 a) A neutron decays into a proton and emits an electron and one other particle. Show that this particle is an electron antineutrino using the conservation laws. [3 marks]

b) Write down the equation (in terms of hadrons) for this decay. [1 mark]

c) Explain how the quark composition is changed when a neutron decays into a proton. [2 marks]

Q3 A K^+ particle is a hadron with the quark composition $u\bar{s}$. Give one reason why the reaction $p + p \rightarrow p + K^+$ does not happen. [1 mark]

A physical property called strangeness — how cool is that...

Learn as much as you can from this three-page topic, then go back to page 119, and work back through to here.

Detecting Particles

Luckily for us, charged particles affect atoms as they pass by — which means we can see what's going on...

Charged Particles Leave Tracks

When a charged particle passes through a substance it causes **ionisation** — electrons are knocked out of atoms. The particle leaves a **trail of ions** as it goes.

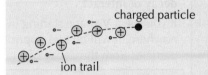

charged particle

ion trail

The easiest way to **detect** the particle is if you somehow make the **trail of ions show up** and then take a **photo**.

Cloud Chambers and Bubble Chambers detect Charged Particles

1) **Cloud chambers** work using a **supercooled vapour** — that's something that's still a gas below its usual condensation temperature. The ions left by particles make the vapour **condense** and you get "**vapour trails**" (a bit like the ones left by jet planes). Heavy, **short** tracks mean lots of ionisation, (these tracks could be caused by, e.g. α-**particles**, see p.148). Fainter, **long** tracks are from particles that cause less ionisation (e.g. β-**particles**).

2) **Bubble chambers** are a bit like cloud chambers in reverse. Hydrogen is kept as a **liquid** above its normal **boiling point** by putting it under **pressure**. If the pressure is suddenly **reduced**, **bubbles of gas** will start to form in the places where there is a trail of ions. You have to take the photo **quickly** before the bubbles grow too big.

3) Both chambers only show up **charged particles**.

A cloud chamber photograph from an alpha source might look like this:

(The thin line is a cosmic ray particle.)

Charged Particles are Deflected by a Magnetic Field

1) A **charged particle** moving in a **magnetic field** will experience a **force** — making the particle follow a **curved track**.

You derived this equation on p.116.

The radius, r, of a charged particle's curved track is given by the equation:
The **larger** the curve **radius**, the **greater** the particle's **momentum**.

$$r = \frac{p}{BQ}$$

where p is the particle's momentum, B is the magnetic flux density and Q is the charge on the particle.

2) Positive and negative particles curve **opposite** ways — you can find out which is which using **Fleming's** left-hand rule (see p.106).

3) You don't see neat circular patterns, but instead see **spirals**, as interactions with the detector decrease the kinetic energy (and so the momentum) of the particle.

4) You can also use this equation to find the magnetic field you need to keep a charge in a particular radius of circular path — very handy when you're dealing with **particle accelerators** (see p.116).

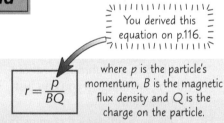

Two oppositely charged particles in a magnetic field

radius of path decreases as particle loses kinetic energy

The deflection of charged particles by magnetic fields is used in **mass spectrometers** to analyse chemical samples: **Ions** (charged particles) with the **same velocity, v**, are made to enter a **magnetic field** which deflects them in a curved path towards a detector. The **radius of curvature** varies between ions according to their **mass (m) to charge ratio** — $r = \frac{p}{BQ} = \frac{mv}{BQ}$, and v and B are constant, so r only varies with $\frac{m}{Q}$. This means that by measuring **where** the ion is detected, its radius of curvature and therefore its mass to charge ratio can be calculated. From this, the **identity** of the ion can be deduced.

Detecting Particles

And now for the best bit — the pretty pictures...

Neutral Particles Only Show Up When They Decay

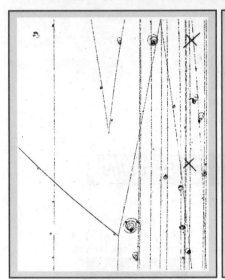

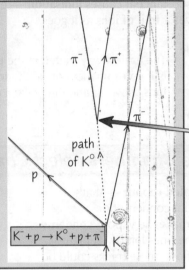

path of K⁰

π^- π^+

π^-

p

$K^- + p \rightarrow K^0 + p + \pi^-$ K^-

Here the particles have so much momentum that the tracks are almost straight.

Remember that **neutral** particles **don't** make tracks. You can only see them when they **decay** or **interact**.

If you see a **V** shape starting in the middle of nowhere, it will be two oppositely charged particles from the decay of a neutral particle.

This V comes from the decay $K^0 \rightarrow \pi^+ + \pi^-$

The **distance** from the **interaction point** to the V depends on the **half-life** of the neutral particle. Longer-lived particles travel **further** on average before they decay — but you have to be careful.

The particles are travelling **close to the speed of light** so they experience **relativistic time dilation**. That means that time seems to run **more slowly** for the moving particle than it does for you as a stationary observer — so they seem to **survive** for **much longer** than normal.

Real Bubble Chamber Photographs can be a bit Intimidating

At first sight the photo might look a bit of a mess with tracks everywhere. Don't panic — start by finding the incoming beam...

1) The **straight** lines are from the incoming beam. Several particles will go straight through without doing anything — you can just ignore them.

2) Look for a little spiral coming from one of the straight tracks. It shows a **knock-on electron** — an electron that's been kicked out of one of the hydrogen atoms. Knock-on electrons tell you **two** things — **which way** the particles are going and which way negative particles **curve**.

3) Here the particles are going **up** and **negative** ones curl **clockwise**.

4) Find a **point** with **several** curved tracks coming from it — that's a reaction. You can identify positively and negatively charged particles from the **way they curve**.

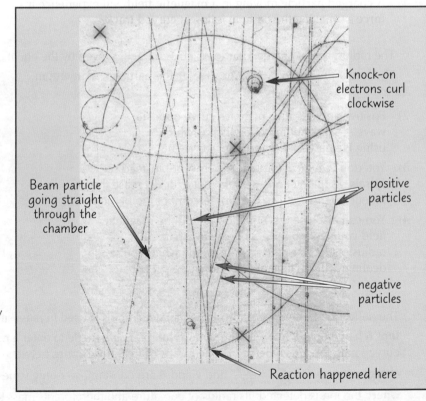

Knock-on electrons curl clockwise

Beam particle going straight through the chamber

positive particles

negative particles

Reaction happened here

Detecting Particles

You can Calculate the Particle's *Momentum*

From the **radius** of the track, you can find the **momentum** of a particle.

> **Example:** Particle X is an unstable neutral particle that quickly decays into a positron and an electron while in a bubble chamber. Both the electron and positron follow circular tracks perpendicular to a 1.2×10^{-4} T magnetic field with an initial radius of 260 m. Find the initial magnitude of the momentum of the electron ($e = 1.60 \times 10^{-19}$ C).

Using $r = \dfrac{p}{BQ}$, so $p = rBQ = 260 \times 1.2 \times 10^{-4} \times 1.60 \times 10^{-19} = 4.992 \times 10^{-21} = \mathbf{5.0 \times 10^{-21}}$ **kg ms⁻¹ (to 2 s.f.)**

Cloud Chambers and *Bubble Chambers* aren't used *Any More*

Nowadays, particle physicists use detectors that give out **electrical signals** that are sent **straight** to a **computer**. It's a bit easier than having a whole team of scientists squinting over thousands of photos. Modern detectors include **drift chambers**, **scintillation counters** and **solid state detectors**.

Meena insisted on making her own bubble chamber.

Practice Questions

Q1 Which particles don't leave tracks in bubble chambers and cloud chambers?

Q2 How does the track of an electron show that the electron is losing energy?

Q3 Explain why a positron and an electron will move in opposite directions in a magnetic field.

Q4 Write down the equation used to relate the radius of a circular path taken by a charged particle in a magnetic field to the particle's momentum.

Q5 Explain why particles moving close to the speed of light seem to survive for much longer than normal.

Exam Questions

Q1 Explain how the charges of particles can be found from their tracks in bubble chamber photographs. [3 marks]

Q2 Suggest one reason why antineutrinos are harder to detect than beta particles. [1 mark]

Q3 The reaction $\mathbf{p} + \mathbf{p} \rightarrow \mathbf{p} + \mathbf{n} + \boldsymbol{\pi}^+ + \boldsymbol{\pi}^0$ occurs in a bubble chamber.
Which products of this reaction will form tracks?
    A π^0 and n   **B** n and π^+ **C** π^+ and p   **D** All of them [1 mark]

Q4 A photon, travelling through a bubble chamber, is converted into an $e^- e^+$ pair.
Draw a sketch showing the tracks that would be formed by this reaction. [3 marks]

Q5 Particle Y decays to form an electron and a positron in a cloud chamber.
The electron leaves a track with an initial radius of 3.2 m in a magnetic field of 1.8×10^{-6} T.
Find the magnitude of the momentum of the electron. [2 marks]

Look, there's one... → ·

Cloud and bubble chambers might be a bit out-of-date now, but you can apply the principles behind why they work to other situations too. So, if you're given a detector you're not familiar with in the exam, just remember what you've learnt here and on pages 116-117 — charged particles are deflected if they pass through a magnetic field, and you can deduce some of their characteristics from the paths they take.

Internal Energy and Temperature

Everything's got internal energy. You might not believe it when your alarm goes off on a Monday morning, but it's true.

Internal Energy is the Sum of Kinetic and Potential Energy

1) All things (solids, liquids, gases) have **energy** contained within them. The amount of **energy** contained in a system is called its **internal energy** — it's found by **summing** the **kinetic** and **potential energies** of all the **molecules** within it.

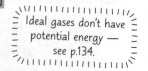
Ideal gases don't have potential energy — see p.134.

> **Total internal energy** is the **sum** of the **kinetic** and **potential energy** of the **molecules** within a system.

2) The kinetic and potential energies of molecules in a system that make up its internal energy are **randomly distributed**. This means **any** molecule could have any energy within the range of energies contained in the system.

3) The **kinetic energy** of a molecule depends on its **mass** and **speed**. Through **kinetic theory** (p.136), the average kinetic energy is proportional to **temperature** — the **hotter** the temperature, the **higher** the **average kinetic energy**.

4) This means that the **internal energy** of a system will **also** increase as its temperature increases.

5) **Potential energy** is caused by **interactions** between molecules and is based on their **positions** relative to each other. The **further apart** the molecules in a system are, the **higher** their potential energies.

There's an Absolute Scale of Temperature

The **Celsius scale** uses the **freezing** and **boiling points** of **water** (0 °C and 100 °C) to make a temperature scale which can be easily used for **day to day** activities. However, scientists use the **kelvin** scale (**the absolute scale of temperature**) for **all equations** in **thermal physics**.

It's also known as the **thermodynamic scale**, and it **does not depend** on the properties of any **particular substance**, unlike the **Celsius** scale.

Zero kelvins is the **lowest possible temperature** and is called **absolute zero***.

At **0 K** all molecules have the **minimum** possible **internal energy** — everything theoretically stops. At higher temperatures, molecules have more energy — the **higher** the **temperature** of a system, the **higher** the **average** kinetic energy of the molecules in the system (see page 137).

Equivalent temperatures	
373 K	100 °C
273 K	0 °C
0 K	−273 °C

*It's true. −273 °C is the lowest temperature theoretically possible. Weird, huh. You'd kinda think there wouldn't be a minimum, but there is.

1) The Kelvin scale is named after Lord Kelvin who first suggested it.

2) A change of **1 K** equals a change of **1 °C**.

3) To change from degrees Celsius into kelvins you **add 273** (or subtract 273 to go the other way):

$$T(\text{K}) \approx \theta(\text{°C}) + 273$$

Example: A baker needs his bread oven to be at a temperature of 175 °C. It is currently at 412 K. By how many degrees should he heat or cool his oven to reach the right temperature?

To convert from kelvins to degrees Celsius, subtract 273.

The current temperature of the oven in degrees Celsius = 412 − 273 = 139 °C.

So the temperature of the oven needs to increase by 175 − 139 = **36.0 °C**

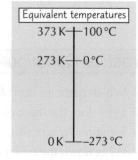

Revision tip number 42: De-stress by pummelling some bread dough in your revision breaks. Then you'll be nicely relaxed and have some tasty bread to enjoy later. Mmm, bread.

Internal Energy and Temperature

You can use a *Thermistor* in a *Potential Divider* Circuit as a *Thermostat*

1) **Thermostats** are used to **control** the temperature in a room. They contain a temperature-sensitive circuit, such as a **potential divider** (see p.54) containing an **NTC thermistor** (see p.47), to measure the temperature. The voltage across the thermistor, V_{out}, **varies** with temperature, which means the circuit can be used as a **heat sensor**. The V_{out} is then the supply for a heater which needs a **minimum voltage** to work, so that if the **temperature** is **too high**, V_{out} is too **low** and the heater **isn't turned on**.

2) The **circuit** needs to be **calibrated** so you know how the voltage across the thermistor, and therefore V_{out}, varies as the temperature changes. The experiment below shows how to do this:

Example: Calibration of a thermostat.

Here's a potential divider using an **NTC thermistor**.

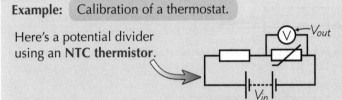

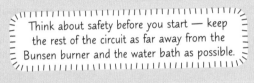
Think about safety before you start — keep the rest of the circuit as far away from the Bunsen burner and the water bath as possible.

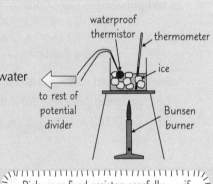

This kind of circuit could also form part of the circuit for an **electronic thermometer** (as well as a thermostat — see above). To **calibrate** the circuit, you can use the equipment shown on the right:

1) Set up the equipment as shown, then measure the **temperature** of the water using the **thermometer**, and record the **voltage** across the thermistor.

2) **Heat** the beaker **gently** using the Bunsen burner (make sure the water is well-stirred), and record the temperature and the voltage at **regular intervals** over a **suitable range** (e.g. at 5 °C intervals over a range of 0-100 °C).

3) Plot a **graph** of temperature against voltage from your results. This graph is the thermistor's **calibration curve**. You can use it to find the temperature of the thermistor from the voltage across it, without needing the thermometer — the thermistor and the calibration curve together are effectively **another thermometer**.

Pick your fixed resistor carefully — if its resistance is too high, V_{out} won't vary enough with temperature, and if it's too low, V_{out} might vary over a bigger range than your voltmeter can handle.

Practice Questions

Q1 What is internal energy?

Q2 Explain the difference between the Celsius and Kelvin scales.

Q3 State in degrees Celsius the lowest possible temperature that a substance could theoretically be cooled to and explain why it cannot be cooled any further.

Q4 Explain how kinetic energy and absolute temperature are linked.

Q5 Draw the circuit diagram for a potential divider that works as a temperature sensor in a thermostat, where the output p.d. decreases when the temperature increases.

Q6 Explain how to calibrate a potential divider circuit containing a thermistor to work as a temperature sensor.

Exam Questions

Q1 An unknown solution boils at 107 °C. Calculate its boiling temperature in kelvins.   [1 mark]

Q2 A student builds a thermostat using an NTC thermistor in a potential divider.

   a) Explain how this equipment and the thermistor's calibration curve can be used to measure changes in temperature.   [2 marks]

   b) Explain how the fixed resistor in the potential divider can affect the function of the thermostat.   [2 marks]

Thermistors — there's a weather joke there, but I can't see it in all this fog...

Celsius, I'm sorry — it's not you it's me, I just need someone more absolute and proportional, who is always positive. We'll still be friends and see each other in weather forecasts and ovens, we just can't be exclusive in thermodynamics...

Thermal Properties of Materials

This couple of pages has more heat than Guy Fawkes on bonfire night. Phwoar...

Specific Heat Capacity *tells you how much* Energy *it Takes to* Heat *Something*

When you heat something, the amount of energy needed to raise its **temperature** depends on its **specific heat capacity**.

> The **specific heat capacity** (*c*) of a substance is the amount of **energy** needed to **raise** the **temperature** of **1 kg** of the substance by **1 K** (or 1°C).

which gives: **energy change = mass × specific heat capacity × change in temperature**

in symbols: $\Delta E = mc\Delta\theta$ ⟵ ΔQ is sometimes used instead of ΔE for the change in thermal energy.

ΔE is the energy change in J, m is the mass in kg and $\Delta\theta$ is the temperature change in K or °C. Units of c are $J\,kg^{-1}\,K^{-1}$ or $J\,kg^{-1}\,°C^{-1}$.

Example: 0.580 kg of orange juice is pasteurised by heating it from 3.0 °C to 92 °C. Orange juice has a specific heat capacity of 3700 $J\,kg^{-1}\,K^{-1}$. Calculate the energy gained by the juice during this process.

Energy gained, $\Delta E = mc\Delta\theta$.
Change in temperature, $\Delta\theta = 85 - 3.0 = 82$ °C (or 82 K).
So $\Delta E = 0.580 \times 3700 \times 89 = 190\,994 = \mathbf{1.9 \times 10^5\ J\ (to\ 2\ s.f.)}$

Nev's new juicer was a little too big for his parents' kitchen.

The Three Phases of Matter *are Defined by the* Arrangement of Molecules

You'll remember these **three phases** (or states) **of matter** (**solid**, **liquid** and **gas**) from GCSE — but here's a quick recap just in case.

Solids

Molecules vibrate about fixed positions in a regular lattice. They're held in position by strong forces of attraction.

Liquids

Molecules are constantly moving around and are free to move past one another, but are attracted to each other.

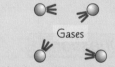

Gases

Molecules are free to move around with constant random motion.

The **potential energies** of the molecules **increase**, and the forces **between** the molecules **weaken**, as a substance moves from **solid** to **liquid** to **gas**. For an **ideal gas** (see p.134), there are **no forces** between the molecules at all.

The idea that solids, liquids and gases are made up of **tiny** moving or vibrating **molecules** is called the **kinetic model of matter**. It seems obvious now, but this **wasn't** always accepted by the scientific community. It took **several scientists** and **hundreds of years** to **develop** a **controversial idea** into an **accepted theory**.

A Change of Phase *Means a* Change of Internal Energy

1) When you **heat** a substance, you **increase** its **temperature** — thereby **increasing** the **kinetic energy** of the molecules within it and its **internal energy**.

2) When a substance **changes phase**, its **internal energy** changes, but its **kinetic energy** (and temperature) **doesn't**. This is because the change of phase is altering the bonds and therefore **potential energy** of the molecules.

3) For example, in a pan of **boiling water**, the **potential energy** of the water molecules **increases**, **breaking the bonds** between the water molecules and causing the molecules to move **further apart**. The water in **both** phases is at **100 °C**.

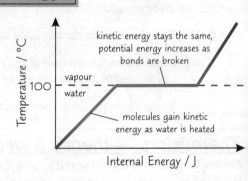

kinetic energy stays the same, potential energy increases as bonds are broken

vapour
water

molecules gain kinetic energy as water is heated

Temperature / °C

100

Internal Energy / J

Thermal Properties of Materials

Specific Latent Heat is the Energy Required to Change State per kg

To **melt** a **solid**, you need to **break the bonds** that hold the molecules in place. The **energy** needed for this is called the **latent heat of fusion**. Similarly, when you **boil or evaporate a liquid**, **energy is needed** to **free** the molecules **completely**. This is the **latent heat of vaporisation**.

The **larger** the **mass** of the substance, the **more energy** it takes to **change** its **state**.
That's why the **specific latent heat** is defined per kg:

> The **specific latent heat** (L) of **fusion** or **vaporisation** is the quantity of **thermal energy** required to **change the state** of **1 kg** of a substance.

which gives: | **energy change = specific latent heat × mass of substance changed** | or in symbols: | $\Delta E = L \Delta m$

Where ΔE is the energy change in J and Δm is the mass in kg. The units of L are $J\,kg^{-1}$.

You'll usually see the latent heat of vaporisation written L_v and the latent heat of fusion written L_f.

Measuring the Specific Latent Heat of a Solid or Liquid

For a **solid**, e.g. ice:

1) Put a **heating coil** and equal masses of ice in **two funnels** above **beakers**.

2) Turn on **one** heating coil for **three minutes**. Record the **energy transferred** in the three minutes with a **joulemeter**. **Don't** turn on the other coil — it's there as a reference so you can measure how much ice **melts** due to the **ambient temperature** of the room. (You add the coil to the reference funnel so that it's as similar as possible to the funnel being heated.)

3) At the end of the three minutes, **measure** the **mass of water** collected in each beaker. Subtract one from the other to get the mass of ice, m, that melted **solely** due to the energy from the **heater**.

4) $\Delta E = L\Delta m$, so to find the **specific latent heat of fusion** for water just **divide** the energy supplied by the mass of ice that melted: $L = \Delta E \div \Delta m$.

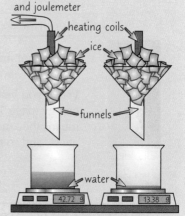
to power supply and joulemeter
heating coils
ice
funnels
water

For a **liquid**, you can do a very similar experiment — **boil** water in a **distilling flask** (a special sort of flask), **condense** the **vapour** given off and divide the energy transferred by the mass of condensed water collected.

If you don't have a joulemeter, you can measure the potential difference (V) and current (I) of your circuit containing the heating coil, and use the equation $E = VIt$ to calculate the energy supplied in $t = 3$ minutes.

Practice Questions

Q1 Define specific heat capacity.

Q2 Show that the thermal energy needed to heat 2 kg of water from 20 °C to 55 °C is ~300 kJ (c_{water} = 4180 $J\,kg^{-1}K^{-1}$).

Q3 Define the specific latent heats of fusion and vaporisation.

Q4 Describe an experiment to find the latent heat of fusion of water.

Exam Questions

Q1 A 2.0 kg metal cylinder is heated uniformly from 4.5 °C to 12.7 °C in 3.0 minutes.
The electric heater supplies energy at a rate of 90.0 Js^{-1}. Assuming that heat losses are negligible, calculate the specific heat capacity of the metal. State a correct unit for your answer. [3 marks]

Q2 A 4.0 kg metal block is heated to 100 °C (correct to 2 significant figures). It is then transferred into a container holding 2.0 kg of water (c_w = 4180 $J\,kg^{-1}\,K^{-1}$) at a temperature of 19 °C. The water and the metal block reach thermal equilibrium at 26 °C. Calculate an estimate for the specific heat capacity of the metal. [4 marks]

Q3 A 3.00 kW electric kettle contains 0.500 kg of water already at its boiling point.
Neglecting heat losses, calculate the length of time it will take to boil dry. (L_v (water) = 2.26×10^6 $J\,kg^{-1}$) [3 marks]

My specific eat capacity — 24 pies...

This stuff's a bit dull, but hey... make sure you're comfortable using those equations. Interesting(ish) fact for the day — the huge difference in specific heat capacity between the land and the sea is one of the causes of monsoons in Asia.

Ideal Gases

Well lah-de-dah, it's ideal gases. Guess bog-standard gases aren't good enough for them lofty thermodynamicists...

Ideal Gases Obey the Three Gas Laws

An ideal gas is a **theoretical** gas that **obeys** the gas laws (see below) and the **equation of state for an ideal gas** (see next page). Its internal energy only depends on the kinetic energy of its molecules — they have no potential energy.

The three gas laws were each worked out **independently** by **careful experiment**.
Each of the gas laws applies to a **fixed mass** of gas.

Boyle's Law: *pV* = constant

At a **constant temperature** the pressure *p* and volume *V* of a gas are **inversely proportional**.

E.g. if you **reduce** the volume of a gas, its molecules will be **closer together** and will **collide** with each other and the container more often, so the pressure will **increase**.

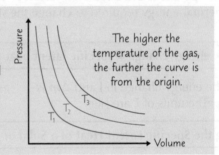

The higher the temperature of the gas, the further the curve is from the origin.

Charles's Law: *V/T* = constant

'Ello, 'ello...

At constant **pressure**, the **volume *V*** of a gas is **directly proportional** to its **absolute temperature *T***.

When you **heat** a gas, the molecules **gain** kinetic energy (page 130). At a constant pressure, this means they move **more quickly** and **further apart**, and so the **volume** of the gas **increases**.

For any ideal gas, the line meets the temperature axis at −273.15 °C — that is, absolute zero.

The Pressure Law: *p/T* = constant

At constant **volume**, the **pressure *p*** of a gas is **directly proportional** to its **absolute temperature *T***.

If you **heat** a gas, the molecules **gain** kinetic energy. This means they move **faster**. If the volume doesn't change, the molecules will **collide** with each other and their container more often and at higher speed, **increasing** the pressure inside the container.

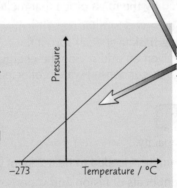

If you'd plotted these graphs in kelvins, they'd both have gone through the origin.

You can Carry Out an Experiment to Investigate Boyle's Law...

You can investigate the effect of **pressure** on **volume** by setting up the experiment shown. The **oil** traps a pocket of air in a sealed **tube** with **fixed dimensions**. A **tyre pump** is used to **increase** the pressure on the oil and the **Bourdon gauge** records the **pressure**. As the pressure increases, more oil will be pushed into the tube, the **oil level** will **rise**, and the air will **compress**. The volume occupied by air in the tube will **reduce**.

Measure the volume of air when the system is at **atmospheric pressure**, then gradually increase the pressure, keeping the **temperature constant**. Note down both the pressure and the volume of air as it changes. Multiplying these together at any point should give the **same value**.

If you plot a **graph** of *p* against $\frac{1}{V}$ you should get a **straight line**.

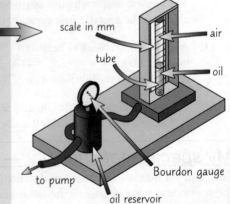

Ideal Gases

... and to **Investigate Charles's Law**

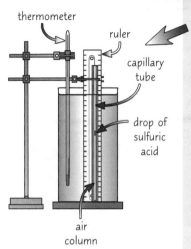

thermometer

ruler

capillary tube

drop of sulfuric acid

air column

You can investigate the effect of **temperature** on **volume** by setting up the experiment shown. A **capillary tube** is **sealed** at the bottom and contains a drop of **concentrated sulfuric acid** halfway up the tube — this traps a **column of air** between the bottom of the tube and the acid drop. The beaker is filled with **near-boiling water**, and the **length** of the trapped column of air increases. As the water cools, the length of the air column **decreases**.

Regularly record the **temperature** of the water and the air column **length** as the water cools. **Repeat** with fresh near-boiling water twice more, letting the tube adjust to the new temperature between each repeat. Record the length at the **same temperatures** each time and take an **average** of the three results.

If you plot your **average results** on a graph of **length** against **temperature** and draw a line of best fit, you will get a **straight line**. This shows that the length of the air column is **proportional** to the temperature. The volume of the column of air is equal to the volume of a cylinder, which is proportional to its length ($V = \pi r^2 l$), so the **volume** is also proportional to the temperature. This agrees with **Charles's law**.

The Gas Laws **Combine** to Give the **Equation of State** for an **Ideal Gas**

1) The gas laws from the previous page can be **combined** to give the equation: $\frac{pV}{T} = \text{constant}$.

2) The constant in the equation depends on the **amount** of gas present. It's equal to Nk, where N is the **number of molecules** in the gas and k is called **Boltzmann's constant**. The value of Boltzmann's constant is **1.38×10^{-23} JK^{-1}**.

3) Plugging Nk into the equation and rearranging gives:

$pV = NkT$ — the equation of state for an ideal gas

where p is pressure in Pa, V is volume in m^3, N is the number of molecules in the gas, k is Boltzmann's constant in Jk^{-1} and T is the temperature in kelvins.

This equation works well (i.e. a real gas approximates to an ideal gas) for gases at **low pressures** and fairly **high temperatures**.

Ideal gases obey Boyle's, Charles's and the pressure laws.

Practice Questions

Q1 State Boyle's law and Charles's law.

Q2 The pressure of a gas is 100 000 Pa and its temperature is 27 °C. The gas is heated — its volume stays fixed but the pressure rises to 150 000 Pa. Show that its new temperature is 177 °C.

Q3 Describe an experiment to demonstrate the effect of temperature on the volume of a gas when pressure is constant.

Q4 What is the equation of state of an ideal gas?

Exam Questions

Q1 a) A flask contains 3.00×10^{23} molecules of nitrogen gas. The flask has a volume of 0.0130 m^3 and its temperature is 27.2 °C. Calculate the pressure of the gas inside it. ($k = 1.38 \times 10^{-23}$ JK^{-1}) [2 marks]

b) Explain what would happen to the pressure inside the flask if the number of molecules of nitrogen in the flask were halved. [2 marks]

Q2 A gas expands from 2.42 m^3 to 6.43 m^3. The final temperature of the gas is 293 K. Calculate the initial temperature of the gas, assuming the pressure remains constant. [2 marks]

Q3 a) Describe an experiment to investigate the effect of pressure on the volume of a gas when temperature is constant. Include a description of your method and the relationship you would expect to see. [4 marks]

b) A parcel of air has a volume of 0.460 m^3 at 1.03×10^5 Pa. Calculate its volume at 3.41×10^5 Pa. Assume that the temperature does not change. [2 marks]

Equation of state for an ideal physics student: thermodynamics = learnt...

All this might sound a bit theoretical, but most gases you'll meet in the everyday world come fairly close to being 'ideal'. They only stop obeying these laws well when the pressure's too high or they're getting close to their condensation point.

Kinetic Theory and Internal Energy

Kinetic theory tries to explain the gas laws. It basically models a gas as a series of hard balls that obey Newton's laws.

You Need to be Able to **Derive** the **Pressure** of an **Ideal Gas**

Start by **Deriving** the **Pressure** on **One Wall** of a Box — in the x direction

Imagine a cubic box with sides of length *l* containing *N* molecules each of mass *m*.

This isn't an easy page. Work through it properly and make sure you understand it.

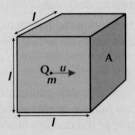

1) Say molecule **Q** moves directly towards **wall A** with velocity *u*. Its **momentum** approaching the wall is *mu*. It strikes wall **A**. Assuming the **collisions** are perfectly **elastic**, it rebounds and heads back in the opposite direction with momentum −*mu*. So the **change in momentum** is −*mu* − *mu* = −2*mu*.

2) Assuming **Q** suffers no collisions with other molecules, the **time between collisions** of **Q** and wall **A** is 2*l* ÷ *u*. The number of **collisions per second** is therefore *u* ÷ 2*l*.

Gases under pressure can be udderly delightful.

3) This gives the **rate of change of momentum** as −2*mu* × *u* ÷ 2*l*.

4) Force equals the rate of change of momentum (Newton's second law), so the **force exerted by the wall** on this one molecule = −2*mu²* ÷ 2*l* = −*mu²* ÷ *l*.

5) Particle **Q** is only one of many in the cube. Each molecule will have a different velocity u_1, u_2 etc. towards **A**. The total force, *F*, of all these molecules on wall **A** is:

$$F = \frac{m(u_1^2 + u_2^2 + \ldots)}{l}$$

This force is now positive as we're talking about the force on the wall.

6) You can define a quantity called the **mean square speed**, $\langle u^2 \rangle$ as: This is the mean of the squared speeds of the particles travelling horizontally. $\langle u^2 \rangle$ has units m²s⁻².

$$\langle u^2 \rangle = \frac{u_1^2 + u_2^2 + \ldots}{N}$$

7) If you put that into the equation above, you get:

$$F = \frac{Nm\langle u^2 \rangle}{l}$$

You might also see mean square speed written as $<u^2>$ or $\overline{u^2}$ — they mean the same thing.

8) So, the pressure of the gas on wall **A** is given by: where *V* = volume of the cube.

$$\text{pressure, } p = \text{force} \div \text{area} = \frac{Nm\langle u^2 \rangle}{l} \div l^2 = \frac{Nm\langle u^2 \rangle}{l^3}$$

$$= \frac{Nm\langle u^2 \rangle}{V}$$

...Then for the **General Equation** you need to think about **All 3 Directions** — x, y and z

A gas molecule can move in **three dimensions** (i.e. the *x*, *y* and *z* directions).

1) You can calculate its **speed**, *c*, from Pythagoras' theorem in three dimensions: $c^2 = u^2 + v^2 + w^2$ where *u*, *v* and *w* are the components of the molecule's velocity in the *x*, *y* and *z* directions.

2) If you treat all *N* molecules in the same way, this gives an **overall** mean square speed of: $\langle c^2 \rangle = \langle u^2 \rangle + \langle v^2 \rangle + \langle w^2 \rangle$.

3) Since the molecules move **randomly**: $\langle u^2 \rangle = \langle v^2 \rangle = \langle w^2 \rangle$ so $\langle c^2 \rangle = 3\langle u^2 \rangle$ and so $\langle u^2 \rangle = \frac{\langle c^2 \rangle}{3}$.

4) You can substitute this into the equation for pressure that you derived above and rearrange to give:

$$pV = \tfrac{1}{3}Nm\langle c^2 \rangle$$

Kinetic Theory and Internal Energy

A Useful Quantity is the **Root Mean Square Speed** or c_{rms}

1) $\langle c^2 \rangle$ is the average of the **square speeds** of **all** the molecules, so the square root of it gives you the typical speed.

2) This is called the **root mean square speed** or, usually, the **r.m.s. speed**. It's often written as c_{rms}. The **unit** is the same as any speed — ms^{-1}.

$$r.m.s.\ speed = \sqrt{mean\ square\ speed} = \sqrt{\langle c^2 \rangle} = c_{rms}$$

There's more on root mean squares on page 113.

3) So you can write the equation on the previous page as: $pV = \frac{1}{3}Nm(c_{rms})^2$.

Internal Energy is Proportional to **Absolute Temperature** for an Ideal Gas

1) All the **internal energy** (see page 130) of an **ideal gas** is due to the **kinetic energy** of its **molecules** (there's no potential energy).

2) You can get an expression for the **average kinetic energy of a molecule** in an ideal gas in terms of temperature by combining the **ideal gas equation** ($pV = NkT$, page 135), and the equation on the previous page, ($pV = \frac{1}{3}Nm\langle c^2 \rangle$):

- $\frac{1}{2}m\langle c^2 \rangle$ is the **average kinetic energy** of an **individual molecule** (because $E_K = \frac{1}{2}mv^2$).

- If you **equate** the equations in point 2) above, you get $\frac{1}{3}Nm\langle c^2 \rangle = NkT \Rightarrow \frac{1}{3}m\langle c^2 \rangle = kT$.

- If you multiply both sides by $\frac{3}{2}$ you get an expression for the average kinetic energy of a molecule: $\frac{1}{3}m\langle c^2 \rangle \times \frac{3}{2} = kT \times \frac{3}{2} \Rightarrow \frac{1}{2}m\langle c^2 \rangle = \frac{3}{2}kT$.

You can rearrange this equation to find the r.m.s. speed from the temperature, T.

$$\text{average energy per molecule} = \frac{1}{2}m\langle c^2 \rangle = \frac{3}{2}kT$$

k is the Boltzmann constant (1.38×10^{-23} JK^{-1}), T is the temperature (in K)

To get the **internal energy** of a whole gas, multiply this equation by N, the **number of molecules** it contains.

3) This means the **internal energy** of an ideal gas is **proportional** to its **absolute temperature** (or vice-versa — the temperature of a gas is proportional to the average energy per molecule). So...

A **rise** in **absolute temperature increases** the **kinetic energy** of each molecule, causing a rise in **internal energy**.

Practice Questions

Q1 What is the change in momentum when a gas molecule hits a wall of its container head-on?

Q2 What is the force exerted on the wall by this one molecule? What is the total force exerted on the wall?

Q3 What is the pressure exerted on this wall? What is the total pressure on the container?

Q4 Use kinetic theory to derive the equation $pV = \frac{1}{3}Nm\langle c^2 \rangle$.

Q5 What would cause a rise in the internal energy of an ideal gas?

Q6 Use the ideal gas equation and the equation you derived in Q4 to derive the equation $\frac{1}{2}m\langle c^2 \rangle = \frac{3}{2}kT$.

Exam Question

Q1 Some helium gas is contained in a flask of volume 7.0×10^{-5} m^3. Each helium atom has a mass of 6.6×10^{-27} kg, and there are 2.0×10^{22} atoms present. The pressure of the gas is 1.0×10^5 Pa.

    a) Calculate the root mean square speed of the atoms.   [2 marks]

    b) The absolute temperature of the gas is doubled. Use ideas about Newton's second law and molecule velocity and momentum to explain why the pressure of the gas will have increased.   [4 marks]

Help — these pages are de-riving me crazy...

Don't forget — mean square speed is the average of the squared speeds — i.e. square all the speeds, then find the average. Don't make the mistake of finding the average speed first and then squaring. No, no no...

Black Body Radiators

Black body radiators <u>perfectly</u> absorb and emit all EM radiation — they're the goody two-shoes of the world of physics.

A **Black Body Radiator** is a **Perfect Absorber** and **Emitter**

1) Objects emit **electromagnetic radiation** due to their **temperature**. At everyday temperatures this radiation lies mostly in the **infrared** part of the spectrum (which we can't see) — but heat something up enough and it will start to **glow**.

2) **Pure black** surfaces emit radiation **strongly** and in a **well-defined way**. We call it **black body radiation**.

3) A black body is defined as:

> A body that **absorbs all wavelengths** of electromagnetic radiation (that's why it's called a **black** body) and can **emit all wavelengths** of electromagnetic radiation.

4) The **radiation curve** of **intensity** against **wavelength** for a black body varies with **temperature**, as shown in the graph:

5) To a reasonably good approximation **stars** behave as **black bodies** and their black body radiation produces a **continuous spectrum**.

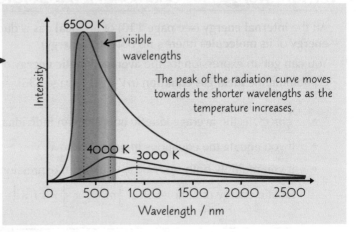

The peak of the radiation curve moves towards the shorter wavelengths as the temperature increases.

Energy is Quantised

1) You should remember from page 86 that electromagnetic radiation is emitted in **discrete packets** (quanta) called **photons**. This idea is called **quantisation of energy**.

2) You can **calculate** the **energy** of individual photons emitted by a black body radiator using the equation $E = hf = \frac{hc}{\lambda}$ (see page 86).

3) Higher temperature stars will emit **more** photons with **higher energies**. This means the **hotter** the star, the **shorter** the **wavelength** (and the **higher** the frequency) the peak of its black body radiation curve will be at.

The **Peak Wavelength** gives the **Temperature**

1) For each temperature, there is a **peak** in the radiation curve at a wavelength called the **peak wavelength**, λ_{max}.

2) λ_{max} is related to the object's **temperature** by **Wien's law**:

$$\lambda_{max}T = \text{constant} = 2.898 \times 10^{-3} \text{ mK}$$

where T is the temperature in kelvin and mK is a <u>metre-kelvin</u>.

The **Luminosity** of a Black Body Depends on **Temperature** and **Surface Area**

1) The **luminosity**, **L**, of a black body radiator (its **power output**) is the **total energy** it emits **per second** and is related to the **temperature** of the black body radiator and its **surface area**.

2) The luminosity is proportional to the **fourth power** of the black body radiator's **temperature** and is **directly proportional** to its **surface area**. This is the **Stefan-Boltzmann law**:

$$L = \sigma A T^4$$

where L is the luminosity of the black body radiator (in W), A is its surface area (in m²), T is its surface temperature (in K) and σ (a little Greek "sigma") is the Stefan-Boltzmann constant.

3) Measurements give the Stefan-Boltzmann constant as $\sigma = 5.67 \times 10^{-8}$ Wm⁻²K⁻⁴.

4) For a **spherical** black body radiator, like a star, you may not know the **surface area**. If you know the **radius** of the spherical black body radiator, you can **combine** the equation above with the equation for the surface area of a sphere, $A = 4\pi r^2$, to get:

$$L = 4\pi r^2 \sigma T^4$$

where L is the luminosity of the black body radiator (in W), r is its radius (in m), T is its surface temperature (in K) and σ (a little Greek "sigma") is the Stefan-Boltzmann constant.

Black Body Radiators

You Can Put the *Equations* Together to *Solve Problems*

Example: The star Sirius B has a surface area of 4.1×10^{13} m² and produces a black body spectrum with a peak wavelength of 115 nm. What is the luminosity of Sirius B? ($\sigma = 5.67 \times 10^{-8}$ Wm⁻²K⁻⁴)

First, find the **temperature of Sirius B**:

$\lambda_{max}T = 2.898 \times 10^{-3}$ mK, so $T = (2.898 \times 10^{-3}) \div \lambda_{max}$

$= (2.898 \times 10^{-3}) \div (115 \times 10^{-9})$

$= 25\ 200$ K

There's loads more on stars in the next topic.

Now, you can use the **Stefan-Boltzmann law** to find the **luminosity**:

$L = \sigma A T^4 = (5.67 \times 10^{-8}) \times (4.1 \times 10^{13}) \times (25\ 200)^4$

$= 9.37... \times 10^{23}$

$= \mathbf{9.4 \times 10^{23}}$ **W (to 2 s.f.)**

It's no time for joking — these bees are having a really sirius conversation.

Example: A spherical black body radiator of radius 5.00 m has a luminosity of 5.11×10^6 W. Calculate the peak energy of the photons emitted by the black body radiator.

First, find the **temperature** of the black body radiator:

$L = 4\pi r^2 \sigma T^4$, so $T = \sqrt[4]{\dfrac{L}{4\pi r^2 \sigma}} = \sqrt[4]{\dfrac{5.11 \times 10^6}{4 \times \pi \times 5.00^2 \times (5.67 \times 10^{-8})}} = 731.8...$ K

Next find the **peak wavelength** of the radiation:

$\lambda_{max}T = 2.898 \times 10^{-3}$ mK, so $\lambda_{max} = \dfrac{2.898 \times 10^{-3}}{731.8...} = 3.959... \times 10^{-6}$ m

Then find the **frequency** of radiation with this wavelength:

$c = f\lambda$ (which you met on p.66), so $f = \dfrac{c}{\lambda} = \dfrac{3.00 \times 10^8}{3.959... \times 10^{-6}} = 7.576... \times 10^{13}$ Hz

Remember that $h = 6.63 \times 10^{-34}$ (see page 86).

Finally, find the **energy** of photons of this frequency:

$E = hf = (6.63 \times 10^{-34}) \times (7.576... \times 10^{13}) = 5.022... \times 10^{-20} = \mathbf{5.02 \times 10^{-20}}$ **J (to 3 s.f.)**

Practice Questions

Q1 Define a black body radiator.

Q2 Give Wien's law, defining all variables.

Q3 What is the relationship between luminosity, surface area and temperature?

Exam Questions

Q1 A star, X, has a surface temperature of 4000 K and the same luminosity as the Sun (3.9×10^{26} W). The Sun has a surface temperature of 6000 K.

a) State which radiation curve represents this star — X, Y or Z. Explain your answer.

[2 marks]

b) State whether star X or the Sun is larger. Explain your answer.

[2 marks]

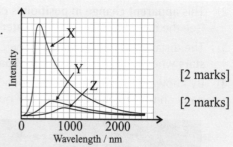

Q2 The star Procyon A, which has a luminosity of 2.3×10^{27} W, produces a black body spectrum with a peak wavelength of 436 nm. Calculate the surface area of Procyon A.

[3 marks]

Remember, black body radiators are nothing do to with gothic plumbing...

...and getting them muddled up won't earn you many marks — even though the examiners do seem to think black (ink) is very fashionable. So you'd better check you've learnt it all, especially that graph and those pesky equations.

Determining Astronomical Distances

Distances in astronomy are... well, astronomical. Astronomers use some pretty clever techniques to measure them...

Distances in the Solar System Can Be Measured in Astronomical Units (AU)

1) From **Copernicus** onwards, astronomers were able to work out the **distance** the **planets** are from the Sun **relative** to the Earth, using **astronomical units** (AU). But they could not work out the **actual distances**.

> One **astronomical unit** (**AU**) is defined as the **mean distance** between the **Earth** and the **Sun**.

2) The **size** of the AU wasn't accurately known until 1769 — when it was carefully **measured** during a **transit of Venus** (when Venus passed between the Earth and the Sun).

Another Measure of Distance is the Light-Year (ly)

1) All **electromagnetic waves** travel at the **speed of light**, c, in a vacuum ($c = 3.00 \times 10^8$ ms^{-1}).

> The **distance** that electromagnetic waves travel in **one year** is called a **light-year** (ly).

2) If we see the light from a star that is, say, **10 light-years away** then we are actually seeing it as it was **10 years ago**. The further away the object is, the further **back in time** we are actually seeing it.

3) **1 ly** is equivalent to about **63 000 AU**.

The Distance to Nearby Stars can be Measured by Trigonometric Parallax

1) You experience parallax every day.
Imagine you're in a **moving car**. You see that (stationary) objects in the **foreground** seem to be **moving faster** than objects in the **distance**:

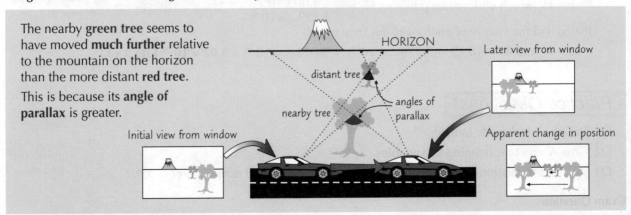

The nearby **green tree** seems to have moved **much further** relative to the mountain on the horizon than the more distant **red tree**.

This is because its **angle of parallax** is greater.

Initial view from window

Later view from window

Apparent change in position

HORIZON

distant tree

angles of parallax

nearby tree

2) This **apparent change in position** is called **parallax** and is measured in terms of the **angle of parallax** (see the diagram above). The **greater** the **angle**, the **nearer** the object is to you.

3) The distance to **nearby stars** can be calculated by observing how they **move relative** to **very distant stars** when the Earth is in **different parts** of its **orbit**. This gives a **unit** of distance called a **parsec** (**pc**).

4) By knowing the distance between the Sun and the Earth, and measuring the parallax angle, you can use **trigonometry** to work out the distance to a star. This is **trigonometric parallax**.

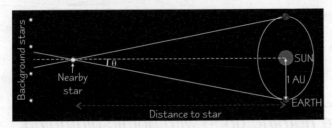

Background stars

Nearby star

θ

SUN

1 AU

EARTH

Distance to star

> A star is exactly **one parsec** (**pc**) away from Earth if the **angle of parallax**,
> $$\theta = 1 \text{ arcsecond} = \left(\frac{1}{3600}\right)^{\circ}$$

5) Parsecs are a popular **distance unit** among astronomers. 1 parsec $\approx 3.09 \times 10^{16}$ m.

Determining Astronomical Distances

The **Luminosity** of a Star Can Be Estimated from its **Intensity** and **Distance**

1) The **luminosity** of a star is the **total energy** it emits **per second** (i.e. its total power).

2) Stars are (approximately) **black body radiators** (p.138-139). This means you can estimate their luminosity from their temperature and their surface area using the **Stefan-Boltzmann law**:

$$L = \sigma A T^4$$

Where L is the luminosity of the star (in W), A is its surface area (in m^2), T is its surface temperature (in K) and σ (a little Greek "sigma") is the Stefan-Boltzmann constant. $\sigma = 5.67 \times 10^{-8}$ $Wm^{-2}K^{-4}$

3) To find the luminosity of a star, remember that stars are approximately **spheres**. You can find the luminosity of a star by substituting the surface area of a sphere, $4\pi r^2$, into the Stefan-Boltzmann law:

$$L = 4\pi r^2 \sigma T^4$$

where r is the radius of the star (or sphere)

4) From **Earth**, we can measure the **intensity**, I, of the radiation that reaches us from a star. The intensity is the **power** of radiation **per square metre** (see p.69), so as the radiation from the star spreads out and becomes **diluted**, the intensity **decreases**. If the energy has been emitted from a **point** or a **sphere** (like a star, for example) then it obeys the **inverse square law**:

$$I = \frac{L}{4\pi d^2}$$

where I is the intensity in Wm^{-2}, L is the luminosity of the star (in W), and d is the distance from the star (in m)

You Can Use **Standard Candles** to Find **Distances** to Galaxies

The distances to most stars and objects in space are **too big** to measure using trigonometric parallax (see previous page). You can often use **standard candles** to find their distance.

1) Standard candles are objects, such as supernovae and Cepheid variables, that have a **known luminosity**.

2) Because you know the luminosity of the standard candle, you can measure its intensity on Earth and use the **inverse square law** above to find its distance.

3) So, if you find a standard candle within a galaxy, you can work out how far that galaxy is from us. This is how **Hubble's constant** was worked out (see p.145).

Myles and Natasha thought their candle was anything but standard.

Practice Questions

Q1 What is meant by a) an astronomical unit, b) a light-year and c) a parsec?

Q2 What is meant by the luminosity of a star?

Q3 What is the relationship between the luminosity, surface area and temperature of a star?

Exam Questions

Q1 Type 1a supernovae are standard candles.

a) State what is meant by a standard candle. [1 mark]

b) The light from a type 1a supernova with a peak luminosity of 2×10^{36} W is detected on Earth. Given that the intensity of the radiation from this supernova is 1.5×10^{-13} Wm^{-2}, calculate how far away it is. [2 marks]

Q2 a) A star has a luminosity of 3.9×10^{26} W and a surface temperature of 5500 K. Calculate the surface area of the star. [2 marks]

b) The star has an angle of parallax of 3.66×10^{-3} arcseconds. Describe how you could use this value to calculate the how far away the star is. [2 marks]

So — using a ruler's out of the question then...

It's insane to think just how big the universe is. It's even bigger than this:
Make sure you understand the definition of a parsec — it's a bit of a weird one.

H-R Diagrams and the Life Cycle of Stars

Stars go through several different stages in their lives and move around the H-R diagram as they go.

Luminosity *vs* Surface Temperature — *the* H-R diagram

1) If you plot **stellar luminosity** against **surface temperature**, you don't just get a random collection of stars. The stars appear to group in **distinct areas** on the plot.

2) The distinct areas show the main stages of a star's life cycle: the **main sequence**, **red giants** and **white dwarfs**. This is called the **Hertzsprung-Russell diagram**.

3) The reason you can see these areas is because stars exist in these **stable** stages of their life cycle for **long periods of time**. You don't see groups of stars in any transitional period on the H-R diagram because they are unstable and happen **quickly** (compared with the life of the star).

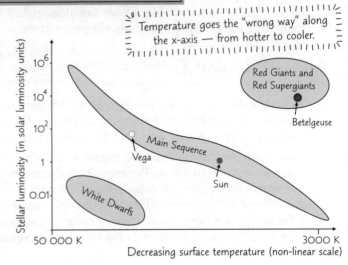

Temperature goes the "wrong way" along the x-axis — from hotter to cooler.

Stellar luminosity (in solar luminosity units)

10^6 10^4 10^2 1 0.01

Red Giants and Red Supergiants

Betelgeuse

Main Sequence

Vega

Sun

White Dwarfs

50 000 K — 3000 K

Decreasing surface temperature (non-linear scale)

Stars *Begin as* Clouds *of* Dust *and* Gas

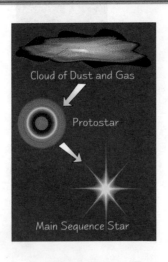

Cloud of Dust and Gas

Protostar

Main Sequence Star

1) Stars are born in a **cloud** of **dust** and **gas**, most of which was left when previous stars blew themselves apart in **supernovae**. The denser clumps of the cloud **contract** (very slowly) under the force of **gravity**.

Protostars move onto the main sequence from the right of the H-R diagram.

2) When these clumps get dense enough, the cloud fragments into regions called **protostars** that continue to contract and **heat up**.

3) Eventually the **temperature** at the centre of the protostar reaches a **few million degrees**, and **hydrogen nuclei** start to **fuse** together to form helium (see p.157).

4) This releases an **enormous** amount of **energy** and creates enough **pressure** (radiation pressure) to stop the **gravitational collapse**.

> The star has now reached the **MAIN SEQUENCE**, the **long diagonal band** on the H-R diagram. Stars will stay there in their long-lived **stable phase**, relatively **unchanged**, while they fuse hydrogen into helium.

Main Sequence *Stars become* Red Giants *when they* Run Out *of* Core Hydrogen

1) Stars spend most of their lives as **main sequence** stars. While on the main sequence, the **pressure** produced from **hydrogen fusion** (see p.157) in a star's **core balances** the **gravitational force** trying to compress it.

2) The position of a star in the main sequence on the **H-R diagram** depends on its size — **more massive stars are brighter and hotter**, so are found at the **top left** of the main sequence band. **Less massive stars** are **dimmer** and **cooler**, so are found at the **bottom right** of the main sequence.

3) When all the **hydrogen** in the **core** has been fused to helium, nuclear fusion **stops**, and with it the **outward pressure stops**. The helium core **contracts** and **heats up** under the **weight** of the star. The outer layers **expand** and **cool**, and the star becomes a **RED GIANT** or a **RED SUPERGIANT**.

4) The helium core continues to contract until, eventually, it gets **hot** enough and **dense** enough for **helium** to **fuse**. This releases a **huge** amount of energy, which **pushes** the **outer layers** of the star further outwards.

> When stars become red giants, they **move off** the main sequence and to the **top-right** corner of the H-R diagram.
>
> Red giants have a **high luminosity** and a relatively **low surface temperature**, so they must have a **huge** surface area (according to the **Stefan-Boltzmann law** on page 138).

H-R Diagrams and the Life Cycle of Stars

Lower Mass Red Giants form White Dwarfs

1) Once all the **helium** in the core of a **red giant** is fused, the star starts to collapse again under its own weight.

2) The core of a low mass star won't get up to high enough temperatures for any further **fusion**, and so it'll continue to **contract**.

3) Once the core has shrunk to about **Earth-size**, **electrons** will exert enough pressure to stop it collapsing any more. This is due to a quantum effect called **electron degeneracy** (fret not — you don't have to know about this).

4) As the core contracts, the outer layers become more and more **unstable**. The star **pulsates** and **ejects** its outer layers into space as a **planetary nebula**, leaving behind the dense core.

5) The star is now a very **hot, dense solid** called a **WHITE DWARF**. White dwarfs are stars at the **end** of their lives, where all of their fusion reactions have stopped and they are just **slowly cooling down**.

> White dwarfs have a **low luminosity** but a **high temperature**, so they must be very **small** (again, according to the Stefan-Boltzmann law). When a red giant becomes a white dwarf, it **moves** from the **top-right** to the **bottom-left** corner of the H-R diagram.

High Mass Stars have a Shorter Life and a more Exciting Death

1) Even though stars with a **large mass** have a **lot of fuel**, they use it up **more quickly** and spend **less time** in the **main sequence** than less massive stars.

2) **Really massive** stars can keep fusing elements until their core is made up of **iron**.

3) Nuclear fusion **beyond iron** isn't **energetically favourable** though, so once an iron core is formed then very quickly it's goodbye star.

4) The star explodes cataclysmically in a **SUPERNOVA**, leaving behind a **NEUTRON STAR** or (if the star was massive enough) a **BLACK HOLE**.

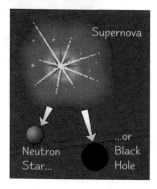

Massive Stars go out with a Bit of a Bang

1) When the core of a star runs out of fuel, it starts to **contract** — forming a white dwarf core.

2) If the star is **massive enough** though, it keeps contracting. This happens when the mass of the core is more than **1.4 times** the mass of the **Sun**.

3) The electrons get **squashed** onto the atomic **nuclei**, combining with protons to form **neutrons** and **neutrinos**.

4) The core suddenly collapses to become a **NEUTRON STAR**, which the outer layers fall onto.

5) When the outer layers **hit** the surface of the **neutron star** they **rebound**, setting up huge **shockwaves**, ripping the star apart and causing a **SUPERNOVA**. The light from a supernova can briefly outshine an **entire galaxy**.

> Neutron stars are incredibly **dense** (about 4×10^{17} kgm^{-3}). They're **very small**, typically about 20 km across, and they can **rotate very fast** (up to 600 times a second).

6) If the core of a star is **more than 3 times** the Sun's mass, the neutrons can't withstand the gravitational forces and the star collapses to form a **BLACK HOLE**.

> A black hole is an **infinitely dense point** in space. At this density, the normal **laws of physics** break down completely. Up to a certain distance away from a black hole, the gravitational pull is **so strong** that not even **light** can escape its grasp — hence the name.

Elle wasn't sure she wanted to be the star player anymore if this was how it would end...

7) Neutron stars and black holes **don't show up** on H-R diagrams. **Neutron stars** have very **low luminosity** because their surface area is so small, so you'd have to extend the luminosity axis massively to include them, and **black holes** have **no luminosity**, as they don't give off light.

H-R Diagrams and the Life Cycle of Stars

You can use H-R Diagrams to Age Stellar Clusters

1) You need to assume all the stars in a cluster formed at about the **same time**.
   In fact, the massive stars in a cluster form **before** lower mass stars, but this difference in time
   is so small compared to the life of the cluster that this is a reasonable assumption.

2) As you saw on page 143, the **bigger** a star is, the **more quickly** it runs out
   of fuel, and the **less time** it spends on the **main sequence**.

3) You also saw on page 142 that the **more massive** a star is, the **higher** its luminosity
   and the further up the **main sequence** region on a H-R diagram it will be.

4) The stars in the cluster leave the main sequence in order of luminosity (and therefore mass) — the most luminou‌s
   leave first and will move off to the right on a H-R diagram as they become **red giants** and **red supergiants**.

5) As the cluster gets **older**, lower mass stars will become red giants and supergiants, moving off the main sequence
   and the existing red giants and supergiants will dwindle to become **white dwarves** or explode in supernovae.

6) This means you can age of clusters of stars by plotting all the stars in a cluster on a
   H-R diagram and looking at which stars are left on the **main sequence**:

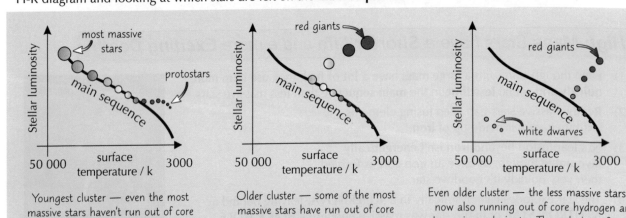

Youngest cluster — even the most massive stars haven't run out of core hydrogen to burn, so all the stars are on or joining the main sequence — the least massive stars are still protostars.

Older cluster — some of the most massive stars have run out of core hydrogen and moved off the main sequence, becoming red giants.

Even older cluster — the less massive stars are now also running out of core hydrogen and becoming red giants. The red giants formed from the more massive stars have exploded in supernovae or become white dwarves.

Practice Questions

Q1 What is an H-R diagram a plot of? Sketch a typical H-R diagram, labelling the areas where you would expect to find main sequence stars, red giants and supergiants, and white dwarfs.

Q2 Describe how the Sun was formed.

Q3 Outline the main differences between the evolution of high mass and low mass stars.

Q4 Describe how you can use the H-R diagram to compare the ages of clusters of stars.

Exam Question

Q1 The H-R diagram shows the three of the main stages of stellar evolution.

   a) Describe what occurs in the core of a low mass star as it evolves to become a red giant. Include a
      description of the star's luminosity and temperature, and its position on a H-R diagram.   [4 marks]

   b) Describe what happens to a low mass star at end of the red giant phase of its life cycle. Include a
      description of the star's luminosity and temperature, and its position on a H-R diagram.   [3 marks]

   c) When very high mass stars reach the end of their life, they collapse to form black holes.
      Explain why black holes aren't shown on H-R diagrams.   [2 marks]

Live fast — die young...

*Make sure you can describe how a star moves around the H-R diagram through its life cycle, and how this can be used
to age star clusters. Remember, the most massive stars fuse all of the hydrogen in their core so quickly that they only
live for a fraction of the Sun's lifetime — but when they go, they do it in style.*

Doppler Effect and the Fate of the Universe

Everyone's heard of the Big Bang theory — well here's some evidence for it. Plus some super-depressing stuff about the end of the universe. It's a laugh a minute, this physics...

The **Motion** of a Wave's **Source** Affects the **Observed Frequency**

1) You'll have experienced this effect **loads of times** with **sound waves**, e.g. the change in **pitch** of an ambulance siren as it passes you.

2) The diagram on the right shows an ambulance travelling **away** from **observer A** and **towards observer B**.

3) As the ambulance moves **towards observer B**, the sound waves from the siren bunch up in front of it — this effectively **increases** the **frequency** of the sound reaching observer B.

4) As the ambulance **moves away from observer A**, the sound waves **stretch** out behind the ambulance — this effectively **decreases** the **frequency** of the sound reaching observer A.

5) This change in **frequency** (and **wavelength**) is called the **Doppler shift**.

The **amount** the frequency (and wavelength) changes depends on the **velocity** of the **source** relative to the observer.

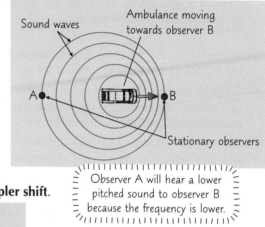

Sound waves. Ambulance moving towards observer B. A. B. Stationary observers.

Observer A will hear a lower pitched sound to observer B because the frequency is lower.

6) This happens with light too — when a **light source** moves **away** from us, the wavelengths become **longer** and the frequencies become lower. This shifts the light towards the **red** end of the spectrum and is called **redshift**.

7) When a light source moves **towards** us, the **opposite** happens and the light undergoes **blueshift**.

8) The amount of redshift or blueshift, **z**, is determined by the following formula:

$$\text{if } v \ll c \quad z = \frac{\Delta\lambda}{\lambda} \approx \frac{\Delta f}{f} \approx \frac{v}{c}$$

λ is the emitted wavelength, f is the emitted frequency, $\Delta\lambda$ and Δf are the differences between the observed and emitted wavelengths/frequencies, v is the velocity of the source relative to the observer and c is the speed of light. ($v \ll c$ means "v is much less than c".)

9) Velocity is measured **relative to the observer**, with motion **towards** the observer being the **positive** direction, and **away** from the observer being the **negative** direction. This means z is negative for objects with **blueshift**.

Redshift Shows That the **Universe is Expanding**

1) Until the early 20th century, cosmologists believed that the universe was **infinite** in both **space** and **time** (that is, it had always existed) and **static**. This seemed the **only way** it could be **stable**.

2) This changed when Edwin Hubble realised that the **spectra** from **galaxies** (apart from a few very close ones) all show **redshift** — so they're all **moving away** from us (and each other). The amount of **galactic redshift** gives the **recessional velocity** — how fast the galaxy is moving away.

3) Plotting **recessional velocity** against **distance** (found using Cepheid variables — see p.141) shows that they're **proportional** — i.e. the **speed** that **galaxies move away** from us depends on **how far** away they are.

4) This suggests that the universe is **expanding**, and gives rise to **Hubble's law**. If you can measure the recessional velocity (using the observed redshift), this allows you to measure **distances** on a **cosmological scale** (cosmological distances):

The light from stars doesn't form a completely continuous spectrum — there are lines in the spectra caused by the absorption of light at certain wavelengths (see p.87). These lines are redshifted or blueshifted (compared to lab spectra) in the light of galaxies moving relative to us.

Some nearby galaxies are moving towards us due to gravitational attraction. The light from these galaxies shows blueshift.

$$v = H_0 d$$

Where v = recessional velocity in kms^{-1}, d = distance in Mpc and H_0 = Hubble's constant in kms^{-1}Mpc^{-1}.

5) The **SI unit** for H_0 is s^{-1}. To get H_0 in SI units, you need v in ms^{-1} and d in m (1 Mpc $\approx$ 3.09 × 10^{22} m).

Since distance is very difficult to measure, astronomers used to **disagree** greatly on the value of H_0, with measurements ranging from 50 to 100 km s^{-1} Mpc^{-1}. It's now generally accepted that H_0 lies **between 65 and 80 km s^{-1} Mpc^{-1}** and most agree it's around the **mid to low 70s**. You'll be given a value to use in the exam.

Doppler Effect and the Fate of the Universe

The **Expanding Universe** gives rise to the **Hot Big Bang Model**

The universe is **expanding** and **cooling down**. So further back in time it must have been **smaller** and **hotter**. If you trace time back **far enough**, you get a **Hot Big Bang**:

> **THE HOT BIG BANG THEORY:** the universe started off **very hot** and **very dense** (perhaps as an **infinitely hot, infinitely dense** singularity) and has been **expanding** ever since.

1) According to the Big Bang theory, **before** the Big Bang, there was **no space or time** — space-time **began** with the Big Bang, (when time = 0 and the radius of the universe = 0) and has been expanding ever since.

2) The way cosmologists tend to look at this stuff, the galaxies aren't actually moving **through space** away from us. Instead, **space itself** is expanding and the light waves are being **stretched** along with it. This is called **cosmological redshift** to distinguish it from **redshift** produced by sources that **are** moving through space.

3) The formula on page 145 works for both types of redshift as long as v is much less than c. If v is close to the speed of light, you need to use a nasty, relativistic formula instead (you don't need to know that one).

The **Age** and **Observable Size** of the **Universe** Depend on H_0

1) If the universe has been **expanding** at the **same rate** for its whole life, the **age** of the universe is: $t = 1/H_0$ (time = distance/speed)
   This is only an estimate since the universe probably hasn't always been expanding at the same rate.

2) Unfortunately, since no one knows the **exact value** of H_0 we can only guess the universe's age. If $H_0 = 70$ kms⁻¹Mpc⁻¹, then the age of the universe $\approx 1/(2.2... \times 10^{-18}$ s⁻¹$) = 4.4... \times 10^{17}$ s = **14 billion years**.

3) The **absolute size** of the universe is **unknown** but there is a limit on the size of the **observable universe**. This is simply a **sphere** (with the Earth at its centre) with a **radius** equal to the **maximum distance** that **light** can travel during its **age**. So if $H_0 = 70$ kms⁻¹Mpc⁻¹ then this sphere will have a radius of **14 billion light years**. Taking into account the **expansion** of the universe, it is thought to be more like 46-47 billion light years.

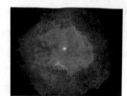

NB — 14 billion candles is too many to put on a birthday cake.

We **Can't Calculate** the **Age** of the Universe until we know its **Density**

1) All the **mass** in the universe is attracted together by **gravity**.
   This attraction tends to **slow down** the rate of expansion of the universe.

2) The **critical density**, ρ_c, is the density of mass in the universe that would mean gravity is **just strong enough** to stop the expansion at $t = \infty$. With a bit of mathematical jiggery-pokery you can get an equation for the critical density of the universe in terms of the **Hubble constant**, H_0:

$$\rho_c = \frac{3H_0^2}{8\pi G}$$

3) Because of the **controversy** over the value of the **Hubble constant**, H_0 (see previous page), we **don't know exactly** what the critical density of the universe is — it **depends** on the value of H_0. So cosmologists aren't sure whether the universe will **expand forever** or eventually begin **contracting**.

(G = gravitational constant,

4) If the **density of the universe**, ρ_0, is **less** than the critical density, gravity is **too weak** to stop the expansion. The universe would just keep **expanding for ever**.

5) If the density is greater than the critical density, gravity would be **strong enough** to stop the expansion and start the universe **contracting** again (ending up with a **Big Crunch**).

6) In fact if you look at the **graphs** of size against time, the **expansion rate** is **slowing down** in all three cases. So **all** three models suggest the universe was expanding **faster in the past** than it is now.

7) If that's true, then we've **overestimated** the time it's taken for the universe to get to the size it is now. The **more dense** the universe is, the **younger** it must be.

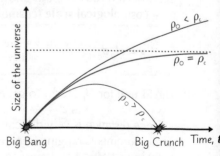

Doppler Effect and the Fate of the Universe

Dark Energy and Dark Matter Make Things More Complicated

1) Even if we knew the exact value of the Hubble constant, predicting the **ultimate fate** of the universe would still be a tricky business. This is because whether or not the universe will keep expanding forever also depends on its **density** (see previous page)

2) Working out the **density** of the universe **isn't easy**. Even if you manage to count up the total mass that you can see, like stars and galaxies, there's a lot of evidence for the existence of **dark matter**, which can't be observed directly.

> Dark matter is matter that we **can't see**, but which does have **mass** so is affected by **gravity**. Whilst the existence of dark matter is generally accepted, **no one knows** for sure what it is. It's been suggested that it could be very **dense normal matter** that doesn't give off light so is hard to detect (e.g. black holes), or **exotic quantum particles** that don't interact with EM radiation, but do interact with gravity. No one has ever observed these particles though, so they're purely theoretical.

3) If you include all the **dark matter** that's been detected **indirectly**, current **estimates** of the actual density aren't far off the **critical density**.

4) However, it looks like the situation might actually be even more **complicated** (as usual). Astronomers in the late '90s found evidence that the expansion is now **accelerating** — contrary to **all of the models** on page 146.

5) Cosmologists are trying to explain this acceleration using **dark energy** — a type of energy that fills the whole of space, creating a kind of **outward pressure** and accelerating the universe's expansion.

Black coffee — my dark energy of choice.

6) **No one** knows what dark energy **is**, and whether it's going to stay the same or change in the future. If dark energy carries on behaving as it is **now**, it could mean the universe carries on **expanding forever**. But it could **change its behaviour** in some way and start pulling in the same direction as gravity, leading to a **Big Crunch** — we just **don't know**.

Practice Questions

Q1 What is the Doppler effect?

Q2 Briefly state the Big Bang theory.

Q3 How is the fate of the universe affected by its density?

Q4 What is meant by 'dark matter'? What do physicists think dark matter might be?

Q5 Explain how dark matter and dark energy influence predictions of the ultimate fate of the universe.

Exam Question

> Assume $H_0 = 75 \ kms^{-1}Mpc^{-1}$. $1 \ year \approx 3.16 \times 10^7 \ s$, $1 \ pc \approx 3.09 \times 10^{16} \ m$, $c = 3.00 \times 10^8 \ ms^{-1}$.
>
> Q1 a) Calculate H_0 in SI units. [2 marks]
>
> b) Calculate an estimate of the age of the universe, and hence the radius of the observable universe, ignoring expansion. [3 marks]
>
> c) A galaxy has a redshift of 0.37. Estimate the speed at which it is moving away from the Earth. [1 mark]
>
> d) Use Hubble's law and your answer to part a) to estimate the distance (in light-years, ly) that the galaxy is from the Earth. [3 marks]
>
> e) With reference to the speed of the galaxy, explain why your answers to c) and d) are estimates. [1 mark]

The Big Crunch — taking a bite out of the Big Apple...

Well, not really, although a holiday to the States would be very welcome now I think about it. This stuff's tricky, so go back over it a few times to let it sink in. Then make yourself a cup of tea to take the edge off all that existential angst.

Radioactive Decay

You should recognise most of this stuff from GCSE — but that doesn't mean you can skip it. Make sure you know it.

Unstable Nuclei are Radioactive

1) If a nucleus is **unstable**, it will **break down** to **become** more stable. This **instability** could be caused by:

   - **too many neutrons**
   - **too few neutrons**
   - **too many nucleons** in total (it's **too heavy**)
   - **too much energy** in the nucleus

2) The nucleus **decays** by **releasing energy** and/or **particles**, until it reaches a **stable form** — this is called **radioactive** (or **nuclear**) **decay**.

3) Radioactive decay is **random** and **spontaneous** — it can't be predicted.

Dave's latest sound system was pumpkin' out the tunes, but it wasn't guaranteed against radio decay.

There are Four Types of Nuclear Radiation

You need to know all about the **four** different types of **nuclear radiation** — here's a handy **table** to get you started.

Radiation	Symbol	Constituent	Relative Charge	Mass (u)
Alpha	α	A helium nucleus — 2 protons & 2 neutrons.	+2	4
Beta-minus (Beta)	β or β^-	Electron	–1	(negligible)
Beta-plus	β^+	Positron	+1	(negligible)
Gamma	γ	Short-wavelength, high-frequency electromagnetic wave.	0	0

u stands for atomic mass unit — see p.155.

Remember from p.86 that EM radiation can also act as a particle (a photon).

The Different Types of Radiation have Different Properties

When radiation **hits** an **atom** it can **knock off electrons**, creating an **ion** — so, **radioactive emissions** are also known as **ionising radiation**.

Alpha, **beta** and **gamma** radiation can be **fired** at a **variety of objects** with **detectors** placed on the **other side** to see whether they **penetrate** the object.

Radiation	Symbol	Ionising Ability	Speed	Penetration/Range	Affected by magnetic field?
Alpha	α	Strong	Slow	Absorbed by paper or a few cm of air	Yes
Beta-minus (Beta)	β or β^-	Weak	Fast	Absorbed by ~3 mm of aluminium	Yes
Beta-plus	β^+	Annihilated by electron — so virtually zero range			
Gamma	γ	Very weak	Speed of light	Absorbed by many cm of lead, or several m of concrete	No

Radioactive Decay

Ionising Ability, Range and Penetration of Radiation are Related

1) **Alpha** particles are **strongly positive** — so they can **easily pull electrons** off atoms, **ionising** them.

2) Ionising an atom **transfers** some of the **energy** from the **alpha particle** to the **atom**. An alpha particle **quickly ionises** many atoms (about 10 000 ionisations per alpha particle) and **loses** all its **energy**. This means alpha particles **don't** travel very **far** (they have a low penetration).

3) **Beta**-minus particles have a **lower mass** and **charge** than alpha particles, but a **higher speed**. This means they can still **knock electrons** off atoms. Each **beta** particle will ionise about 100 atoms, **losing energy** at each ionisation.

4) This **lower** number of **ionisations** means that beta radiation travels **further** than alpha radiation in materials — it has a higher penetration.

5) Gamma radiation is even more **weakly ionising** than beta radiation, because it has no charge or mass. This means it has a very **high penetration**.

We're Surrounded by Background Radiation

Put a Geiger counter **anywhere** and it will click — it's detecting **background radiation**. When you take a **reading** from a radioactive source, you need to **measure** the **background radiation** separately and **subtract** it from your **measurement**. There are many **sources** of background radiation:

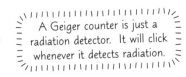
A Geiger counter is just a radiation detector. It will click whenever it detects radiation.

1) **The air:** Radioactive **radon gas** is released from **rocks**. It emits alpha radiation. The concentration of this gas in the atmosphere varies a lot from place to place, but it's usually the largest contributor to the background radiation.

2) **The ground and buildings: All rock** contains radioactive isotopes.

3) **Cosmic radiation:** Cosmic rays are particles (mostly high-energy protons) from **space**. When they collide with particles in the upper atmosphere, they produce nuclear radiation.

4) **Living things:** All plants and animals contain **carbon**, and some of this will be the radioactive isotope **carbon-14**.

5) **Man-made radiation:** In most areas, radiation from **medical** or **industrial** sources makes up a tiny, tiny fraction of the background radiation.

Practice Questions

Q1 Give four reasons that can make a nucleus unstable.

Q2 What is meant by the statement 'radioactive decay is random'?

Q3 Name four types of nuclear radiation and give the constituents, the relative charge and the mass, in u, of each.

Q4 Explain the differences in the ionising and penetrating powers of alpha, beta-minus and gamma radiation.

Q5 Give three sources of background radiation.

Exam Question

Q1 a) A student carries out an experiment to find out what type of radiation a radioactive source produces. He finds that the radiation coming from the source passes easily through paper but is blocked by a few mm of aluminium. State what type of radiation the source produces. [1 mark]

b) The student is using a radiation detector to measure the count rate close to the source. Explain why his results might be higher than expected and how he should correct for this error. [2 marks]

Radioactive emissions — as easy as α, β, γ...

You need to learn the different types of radiation and their properties. Remember that alpha particles are by far the most ionising and so have the lowest penetration. Gamma rays are the least ionising, so they can go for quite a while without ionising an atom and giving up energy. And don't forget — there is always background radiation around you.

More Radioactive Decay

Nope, not decay that's more radioactive — just more about radioactive decay...

You Can **Represent Nuclear Decay** Using **Equations**

1) When writing equations, you usually write particles in **standard notation** (see page 115) so you can see exactly what happens to the **protons** and **neutrons**.

2) For example, the decay of americium-241 to neptunium-237 looks like this: ⟹ $^{241}_{95}\text{Am} \longrightarrow {}^{237}_{93}\text{Np} + {}^{4}_{2}\alpha$

3) Decay equations need to be **balanced** — in every nuclear reaction, including fission and fusion (p.155-157), **charge** and **nucleon number** must be **conserved**.

4) In this example, there are 241 nucleons **before** the decay (in the americium-241 atom), and 241 nucleons **after** the decay (237 in the neptunium-237 atom and 4 in the alpha particle), so **nucleon number** is conserved.

5) You can see that **charge** is conserved by looking at the **proton number** (the blue numbers in the example above) — there are 95 protons before the decay and 95 after it.

6) Some particles have a **negative** charge. E.g. beta-minus particles are written with a **negative proton number** ($^{0}_{-1}\beta$).

7) **Energy** and **momentum** are also conserved in **all** nuclear reactions. Mass, however, **doesn't** have to be conserved — the **mass** of an alpha particle is **less** than the **individual masses** of **two protons** and **two neutrons**. The difference in mass is called the **mass deficit** (p.155), and the **energy released** when the nucleons **bind together** to form the alpha particle accounts for the missing mass. More on that later.

α **Emission** Happens in **Heavy Nuclei**

1) **Alpha emission** only happens from the nuclei of **very heavy** atoms like **uranium** and **radium**.

2) The **nuclei** of these atoms are **too massive** to be stable.

> When an alpha particle is emitted, the **proton number decreases by two**, and the **nucleon number decreases** by **four**.

Example: $238 = 234 + 4$ — nucleon numbers balance

$$^{238}_{92}\text{U} \longrightarrow {}^{234}_{90}\text{Th} + {}^{4}_{2}\alpha$$

$92 = 90 + 2$ — proton numbers balance, so charge is conserved

β⁻ **Emission** Happens in **Neutron-Rich** Nuclei

1) **Beta-minus** (β⁻) decay is the emission of an **electron** from the **nucleus** along with an **antineutrino** (p.122).

2) β⁻ decay happens in isotopes that are 'neutron rich' (have many more **neutrons** than **protons** in their nucleus).

3) One of the **neutrons** in the nucleus **decays** into a **proton** and ejects a beta-minus particle (an electron) and an antineutrino.

Example: $188 = 188 + 0 + 0$ — nucleon numbers balance

$$^{188}_{75}\text{Re} \longrightarrow {}^{188}_{76}\text{Os} + {}^{0}_{-1}\beta + {}^{0}_{0}\overline{\nu}$$

$75 = 76 - 1 + 0$ — proton numbers balance, so charge is conserved

> When a beta-minus particle is emitted, the **proton number increases by one**, and the **nucleon number stays the same**.

In **beta-plus emission**, a **proton** gets **changed** into a **neutron**, releasing a **positron** and a **neutrino**. The **proton number decreases by one**, and the **nucleon number stays the same**.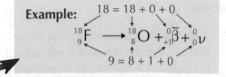

Example: $18 = 18 + 0 + 0$

$$^{18}_{9}\text{F} \longrightarrow {}^{18}_{8}\text{O} + {}^{0}_{+1}\beta + {}^{0}_{0}\nu$$

$9 = 8 + 1 + 0$

γ **Radiation** is Emitted from **Nuclei** with **Too Much Energy**

Gamma rays can be emitted from a nucleus with **excess energy** — we say the nucleus is **excited**. This energy is **lost** by emitting a **gamma ray**.

This often happens after an **alpha** or **beta** decay has occurred.

> During **gamma emission**, there is **no change** to the nuclear constituents — the nucleus just **loses excess energy**.

More Radioactive Decay

You Can **Investigate** the Absorption of **Gamma Radiation** by **Lead**

1) Choose a radioactive source that emits gamma radiation, e.g. cobalt-60. Set up the equipment as shown in the **diagram**, leaving out the **source** and the **lead sheet** at first.

2) As you will be increasing the thickness of lead by adding more lead sheets to the setup, your lead sheets should all be the **same thickness**. Use a micrometer to **measure** their thickness and **verify** this.

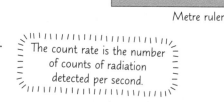

Stand (placed behind lead, not between source and tube)   Clamp
Geiger counter   Sheet of lead   Radioactive source
Metre ruler

3) Turn on the Geiger counter and take a reading of the **background count rate** (in counts per sec). Do this **three** times and take an **average**. You'll need to subtract this from your count rate measurements to get the **corrected count rate**.

The count rate is the number of counts of radiation detected per second.

Radioactive sources can be dangerous. Make sure you know how to handle them carefully to minimise your exposure.

4) Carefully place the radioactive source at a distance of about 15 cm from the tube — use the metre ruler. Don't move either again until your experiment is finished.

5) Place a piece of **lead** in the clamp. Make sure it is **perpendicular** to the Geiger counter and source, and that it **completely** blocks the straight line between the source and counter. **Record** the count rate for this thickness of lead. Do this **three** times and take an **average**.

6) Add a sheet of **lead** to the clamp to increase the **thickness** of lead between the source and Geiger counter.

7) Take three readings of the **count rate** for this **combined thickness** of lead, and take an **average**.

8) **Repeat** step 6 and step 7 until you have added all the sheets you can (about ten is a good amount).

9) Once the experiment is finished, put away your source **immediately** — you don't want to be exposed to more radiation than you need to be.

10) Correct your data for **background radiation** (p.149). Then plot a graph of **corrected count rate** against **thickness** of lead. You should see that the count rate reduces with each sheet of lead. This means the **absorption** increases.

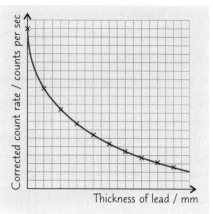

Practice Questions

Q1 Describe the changes that happen in the nucleus during alpha, beta-minus, and gamma decay.

Q2 Copy and complete the following equation for beta-plus decay: $^{10}_{6}C \rightarrow {}^{10}_{5}B + \square\square + \square\square$

Q3 Describe an experiment you could carry out to investigate how the absorption of gamma radiation changes for different thicknesses of lead.

Exam Question

Q1 a) Radium-226 (Ra, proton number 88) decays to radon (Rn) by emitting an alpha particle. Write a balanced nuclear equation for this reaction. [3 marks]

b) Potassium-40 (K, proton number 19) decays to calcium (Ca) by emitting an electron. Write a balanced nuclear equation for this reaction. [3 marks]

Nuclear decay — just one small typo away from being totally unclear...

Don't mess around with that experiment — you need to make sure you follow all instructions and handle the source carefully to stay safe. But then you can go brag about how you're a real nuclear physicist to those poor whatsits stuck in art class — they probably had to spend their morning staring at an arrangement of intriguingly mouldy fruit...

Exponential Law of Decay

Different radioactive isotopes emit radiation at different rates. Enter the decay constant and his sidekick half-life...

The **Rate of Radioactive Decay** is Measured by the **Decay Constant**

Radioactive decay is random (p.148), but for any radioactive sample, you can **predict** how many nuclei will decay in a given amount of time. The **activity** — the **number** of nuclei that **decay each second** — is **proportional** to the **size of the sample**. Activity is measured in **becquerels** (Bq). An activity of 1 Bq means that 1 nucleus decays per second (s^{-1}).

The **decay constant** (λ) is the **probability** that a given nucleus will **decay** each second — the **bigger** the value of λ, the faster the rate of decay. Its unit is s^{-1}.

Don't get λ confused with wavelength.

So you can write the activity as:

| **activity = decay constant × number of undecayed nuclei** |

Or in symbols: $A = \lambda N$

Because the activity, A, is the number of nuclei that decay each second, it is equal to minus the rate of change in the number of undecayed nuclei $\frac{dN}{dt}$. So you can write:

$$A = -\frac{dN}{dt} = \lambda N$$

The number of undecayed nuclei (N) is decreasing, so dN/dt is negative. A negative sign must be put in front of it to make sure A is positive.

Example: A sample of a radioactive isotope contains 3.0×10^{19} nuclei. Its activity is measured to be 2.4×10^{12} Bq. Calculate the isotope's decay constant.

Rearrange $A = \lambda N$ to give: $\lambda = A/N = (2.4 \times 10^{12}) \div (3.0 \times 10^{19}) = \mathbf{8.0 \times 10^{-8}\ s^{-1}}$

You can **Model Radioactive Decay** using a **Spreadsheet**

Radioactive decay is an **iterative** process (the number of nuclei that decay in one time period controls the number that are available to decay in the next). The rate of change of N, $\frac{dN}{dt}$, is close to the change in N, ΔN, divided by the change in t, Δt, provided that Δt is small. So you can model radioactive decay as: $-\frac{\Delta N}{\Delta t} = \lambda N$.

With this formula, you can use a **spreadsheet** to model how a sample of an isotope will decay if you know λ and N_0:

1) Set up a spreadsheet with column headings for **total time** (t), ΔN, and N, and data input cells for Δt and λ.

2) Decide on a Δt that you want to use — this is the **time interval** between the values of N that the spreadsheet will calculate. The most sensible time interval will depend on your decay constant.

3) You can then enter formulas into the spreadsheet to calculate the number of undecayed nuclei left in the sample after each time interval. You'll need to use $\Delta N = -\lambda \times N \times \Delta t$ (rearranged from above).

t in s	ΔN (from equation above)	N
$t_0 = 0$		$N_0 =$ initial number of nuclei in sample
$t_1 = t_0 + \Delta t$	$(\Delta N)_1 = -\lambda \times N_0 \times \Delta t$	$N_1 = N_0 + (\Delta N)_1$
$t_2 = t_1 + \Delta t$	$(\Delta N)_2 = -\lambda \times N_1 \times \Delta t$	$N_2 = N_1 + (\Delta N)_2$
$t_3 = ...$	$(\Delta N)_3 = ...$	$N_3 = ...$

$\lambda\ (s^{-1}) = $ e.g. 1×10^{-4}
$\Delta t\ (s) = $ e.g. 1000

Be careful when you refer to these in your formulas — make sure the cell references don't change when you autofill in new rows (iterations).

4) If you plot a graph of the number of undecayed nuclei against time, it should look like this: (You may have to fiddle with your value for Δt to get a graph with a nice shape.) This is an **exponential** graph (p.153).

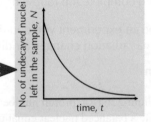

No. of undecayed nuclei left in the sample, N / *time, t*

You Need to Know the **Decay Equations**

This is the equation of the line generated from the spreadsheet above.

1) As you know, the **number of undecayed nuclei remaining**, N, depends on the **number originally present**, N_0, the **decay constant**, λ, and how much **time** has passed, t. There's an equation for this, too:

$$N = N_0 e^{-\lambda t}$$

Here t = time, measured in seconds.

2) And there's an equation for how a sample's **activity** goes down as it decays:

$$A = A_0 e^{-\lambda t}$$

A is the activity at time t, and A_0 is the initial activity (at $t = 0$ s). Both are measured in Bq.

Exponential Law of Decay

All Radioactive Isotopes have a Half-Life

The **half-life** ($t_{1/2}$) of an **isotope** is the **average time** it takes for the **number of undecayed nuclei** to **halve**.

Measuring the **number of undecayed nuclei** isn't the easiest job in the world.

In practice, half-life isn't measured by counting nuclei, but by measuring the **time it takes** the **activity** or **count rate** to **halve**.

The **longer** the **half-life** of an isotope, the **longer** it stays **radioactive**.

> The count rate is the number of decays detected per second (it's lower than the activity).

Jenny's count rate was pretty low since she lost her calculator.

The Half-Life can be Found from an Exponential Graph

You can use a **graph** of N against t to find the **half-life** of an isotope:

1) Read off the original number of undecayed nuclei (when $t = 0$).
2) Go to half the original value of N.
3) Draw a horizontal line to the curve, then a vertical line down to the x-axis.
4) The half-life is where this line meets the x-axis.
5) It's always a good idea to check your answer. Repeat steps 1-3 for a quarter of the original value of N, and divide the time where the line meets the x-axis by two. That will also give you the half-life. You can do the same for an eighth of the original value (divide the time by 3), and a sixteenth of the original value. Check that you get the same answer each way.

> You can also find the half-life using the same method from a graph of count rate against time or activity against time.

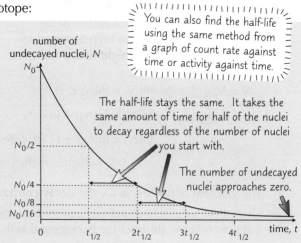

The half-life stays the same. It takes the same amount of time for half of the nuclei to decay regardless of the number of nuclei you start with.

The number of undecayed nuclei approaches zero.

You can Measure the Half-life of a Radioactive Material

You're most likely to do this using the isotope **protactinium-234**.
Protactinium-234 is formed when **uranium** decays (via another isotope).
You can measure protactinium-234's decay rate using a **protactinium generator** — a bottle containing a uranium salt, the decay products of uranium (including protactinium-234) and two solvents, which separate out into layers, like this:

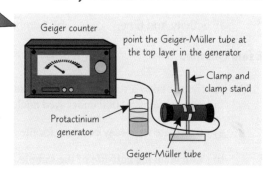

1) **Shake the bottle** to mix the solvents together, then add it to the equipment shown on the right.
2) Wait for the liquids to **separate**. The protactinium-234 will be in solution in the top layer, and the uranium salt will stay in the bottom layer. Then you can point the Geiger-Müller tube at the top layer to measure the activity of the protactinium-234.
3) As soon as the liquids separate, record the count rate (e.g. how many counts you get in 10 seconds). Re-measure the count rate at sensible intervals (e.g. every 30 seconds).
4) Once you've collected your data, leave the bottle to stand for at least ten minutes, then take the count rate again. This is the **background count rate** corresponding to background radiation (you could also do this at the beginning of the experiment, before shaking the bottle).
5) **Subtract this value** from your measured count rates, then plot a graph of count rate against time. It should look like the graph on the right. You can use this graph to find the **half-life** in exactly the same way as above. In this case the half-life is the time taken for the count rate to halve.

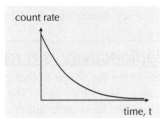

Exponential Law of Decay

You can **Calculate** the **Decay Constant** from the **Half-Life**

The equation for calculating the decay constant from the half-life is:

$$\lambda = \frac{\ln 2}{t_{1/2}}$$

Where ln is the natural log, λ is the decay constant in s^{-1}, and $t_{1/2}$ is the half-life in seconds.

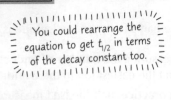
You could rearrange the equation to get $t_{1/2}$ in terms of the decay constant too.

It **Helps** to Take **Logs** of the **Exponential Decay Equations**

1) If you plot a **graph** of the **number of undecayed nuclei**, N, in a radioactive sample against **time**, t, you get an **exponential curve**.

2) But, if you plot the **natural log** (ln) of the number of **undecayed nuclei** against **time**, you get a **straight line**. To find the **natural log** of a number, just use the **ln button** on your calculator.

3) You get a straight line because the **decay equation**, $N = N_0 e^{-\lambda t}$, can be **rearranged** to the **general form** of a **straight line**: $y = mx + c$:

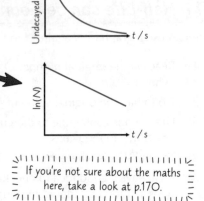

$$N = N_0 e^{-\lambda t} \implies \ln(N) = \ln(N_0 e^{-\lambda t})$$

$$\ln(N) = \ln(N_0) + \ln(e^{-\lambda t})$$

$$\ln(N) = \ln(N_0) + (-\lambda t) \implies \ln(N) = -\lambda t + \ln(N_0)$$

which is in the form: $y = mx + c$

If you're not sure about the maths here, take a look at p.170.

4) The **gradient** of the line is $-\lambda$ (the **decay constant**). From this you can **calculate** the **half-life**, $t_{1/2}$, of the sample.

5) This works for graphs of **activity** against **time** too. $A = A_0 e^{-\lambda t}$ becomes $\ln(A) = -\lambda t + \ln(A_0)$. But remember to **subtract** the **background activity** from any measurements first.

Practice Questions

Q1 Define the activity of a radioactive source.

Q2 Write down equations relating activity to:
   a) the decay constant,   b) the rate of change of the number of undecayed nuclei.

Q3 Sketch a general radioactive decay graph showing activity against time and write an equation for this relationship.

Q4 Define the term 'half life' and give an equation relating half-life and decay constant.

Q5 Describe an experiment to measure the half-life of protactinium-234.

Q6 Derive an equation that could be used to plot a straight line from the following quantities during radioactive decay:
   a) activity and time,   b) number of undecayed nuclei and time.

Exam Question

Q1 A scientist takes a reading of 750 Bq from a pure radioactive source. The radioactive source initially contains 50 000 undecayed nuclei, and background activity in the lab is measured as 50 Bq.

   a) Calculate the decay constant for the sample.   [2 marks]

   b) Calculate the half-life of the sample.   [1 mark]

   c) Calculate how many undecayed nuclei of the radioactive source will be left after 300 seconds.   [1 mark]

Radioactivity is a random process — just like revision shouldn't be...

Remember the shape of that graph — whether it's count rate, activity or number of nuclei plotted against time, the shape's always the same. The maths is a bit of a pain, but I think the experiment's pretty good. Protactinium generator, sounds like something out of a film that's on at 2 o'clock in the morning...

Nuclear Fission and Fusion

Turn off the radio and close the door, 'cos you're going to need to concentrate hard on this stuff about binding energy...

The **Mass Deficit** is **Equivalent** to the **Nuclear Binding Energy**

1) The **mass** of a **nucleus** is **less than** the mass of its **constituent parts** — the difference is called the **mass deficit**. Mass and energy are **equivalent**, according to Einstein's equation:

$$\Delta E = c^2 \Delta m$$

ΔE is the change in energy in J
c is the speed of light in a vacuum
Δm is the change in mass in kg

2) As nucleons join together, the total mass **decreases** — this '**lost**' mass is **converted** into energy and **released**. You can calculate this energy using the equation above, where Δm is the mass deficit.

You met $\Delta E = c^2 \Delta m$ in Topic 8 (see p.122).

3) The amount of **energy released** is **equivalent** to the **mass deficit**.

4) If you **pulled** the nucleus completely **apart**, the **energy** you'd have to use to do it would be the **same** as the energy **released** when the nucleus formed.

> The energy needed to **separate** all of the nucleons in a nucleus is called the **nuclear binding energy** (measured in **MeV**), and it is **equivalent** to the **mass deficit**.

Nuclear binding energy is often just called binding energy.

5) Atomic mass is usually given in atomic mass units (u), where 1 u = 1.66×10^{-27} kg. To convert from kg to u, divide the mass in kg by 1.66×10^{-27}. To go the other way and convert u to kg, multiply the mass in u by 1.66×10^{-27}.

> **Example:** Calculate the binding energy of the nucleus of a lithium atom, $^6_3$Li, given that its mass deficit is 0.0343 u.
>
> *$c = 3.00 \times 10^8$ ms^{-1} — this will be given in your data and formulae booklet.*
>
> 1) Convert the mass deficit into kg: Mass deficit = $0.0343 \times (1.66 \times 10^{-27}) = 5.6938 \times 10^{-29}$ kg
> 2) Use $\Delta E = c^2 \Delta m$ to calculate the binding energy: $\Delta E = (3.00 \times 10^8)^2 \times (5.6938 \times 10^{-29}) = 5.12442 \times 10^{-12}$ J
> 3) Convert your answer into electronvolts: $(5.12442 \times 10^{-12}) \div (1.60 \times 10^{-19}) = 32027625$ eV
>
> $$1 \text{ eV} = 1.60 \times 10^{-19} \text{ J (p.117)} \qquad = \textbf{32.0 MeV (to 3 s.f.)}$$

6) The **binding energy per unit of mass deficit** can also be calculated. Using the example above:

$$\frac{\textbf{binding energy}}{\textbf{mass deficit}} = \frac{32.0 \text{ MeV}}{0.0343 \text{ u}} \approx 930 \text{ MeVu}^{-1} \text{ (to 2 s.f.)}$$

7) This means that a mass deficit of **1 u** is equivalent to about **930 MeV** (to 2 s.f.) of binding energy. You can use this **approximation** to check your final answer.

The **Binding Energy Per Nucleon** is at a **Maximum** around **N = 50**

A useful way of **comparing** the binding energies of different nuclei is to look at the **binding energy per nucleon**.

$$\textbf{Binding energy per nucleon (in MeV)} = \frac{\textbf{Binding energy } (B)}{\textbf{Nucleon number } (A)}$$

So, the binding energy per nucleon for $^6_3$Li (in the example above) is 32.0 ÷ 6 = 5.3 MeV.

1) If you plot a **graph** of **binding energy per nucleon** against **nucleon number**, for all elements, the line of best fit shows a **curve**. A **high** binding energy per nucleon means that **more energy** is needed to **remove** nucleons from the nucleus.

2) In other words the **most stable** nuclei occur around the **maximum point** on the graph — which is at **nucleon number 56** (i.e. **iron**, Fe).

3) **Combining nuclei** is called nuclear **fusion** (p.157) — this **increases** the **binding energy per nucleon** dramatically, which means a lot of **energy is released** during nuclear fusion.

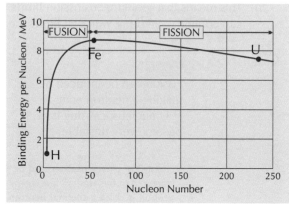

4) **Fission** is when **nuclei** are **split in two** (see next page) — the **nucleon numbers** of the two **new nuclei** are **smaller** than the original nucleus, which means there is an **increase** in the binding energy per nucleon. So, energy is also **released** during nuclear fission (but not as much energy per nucleon as in nuclear fusion).

Nuclear Fission and Fusion

The *Change* in *Binding Energy* Gives the *Energy Released*

The **binding energy per nucleon graph** can be used to **estimate** the **energy released** from nuclear reactions.

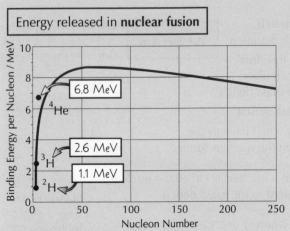

Energy released in **nuclear fusion**

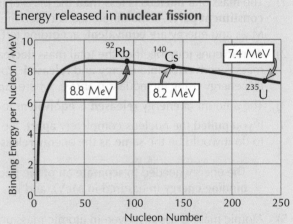

Energy released in **nuclear fission**

If ^{2}H and ^{3}H nuclei **fuse** together to form ^{4}He (and a neutron):

1) The binding energy before the fusion is:
binding energy ^{2}H + binding energy ^{3}H
$= (2 \times 1.1) + (3 \times 2.6) = $ **10 MeV**

2) The binding energy after the fusion is:
binding energy ^{4}He $= 4 \times 6.8 = $ **27.2 MeV**

3) So the **energy released** is:
$27.2 - 10 = 17.2 = $ **17 MeV (to 2 s.f.)**

If a ^{235}U nucleus **splits** into ^{92}Rb and ^{140}Cs (plus a few neutrons) during nuclear **fission**:

1) The binding energy **before** the fission is:
binding energy ^{235}U $= 235 \times 7.4 = $ **1739 MeV**

2) The binding energy **after** the fission is:
binding energy ^{92}Rb + binding energy ^{140}Cs
$= (92 \times 8.8) + (140 \times 8.2) = $ **1957.6 MeV**

3) So the **energy released** is:
$1957.6 - 1739 = 218.6$
$= $ **220 MeV (to 2 s.f.)**

Fusion gives you more energy per nucleon, but fission generally gives you more energy per reaction.

Fission Limits the *Size* of Nuclei

1) Fission happens because **heavy nuclei** (e.g. uranium), are **unstable**. This means some can randomly **split** into two **smaller** nuclei (and sometimes several neutrons).

2) This process is called **spontaneous** if it just happens **by itself**, or **induced** if we **encourage** it to happen.

3) **Energy is released** during nuclear fission because the new, smaller nuclei have a **higher binding energy per nucleon** (see p.155) and a lower total mass.

4) The **larger** the nucleus, the more **unstable** it will be — so large nuclei are **more likely** to **spontaneously fission**.

5) This means that spontaneous fission **limits** the **number of nucleons** that a nucleus can contain — in other words, it **limits** the number of **possible elements**.

Nuclear power stations generate electricity from nuclear fission reactions.

Example:

Fission can be induced by making a neutron enter a ^{235}U nucleus, causing it to become very unstable.

Only low energy neutrons can be captured in this way. A low energy neutron is called a **thermal neutron**.

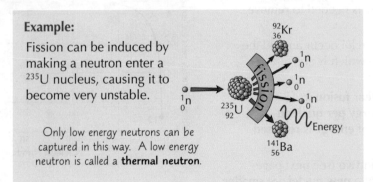

This season's fashion had a high blinding energy.

Nuclear Fission and Fusion

Nuclear Fusion Needs High Temperatures and a High Density of Matter

1) As you saw on p.155 and p.156, nuclei can fuse together, increasing the binding energy per nucleon and releasing a lot of energy. This is **nuclear fusion**.

2) All nuclei are **positively charged** — so there will be an **electrostatic** (or Coulomb) **force** of **repulsion** between them.

3) Nuclei can only **fuse** if they **overcome** this electrostatic force and get **close** enough for an attractive force called the **strong interaction** to hold them together.

4) Typically they need about **1 MeV** of kinetic energy — and that's **a lot of energy**. This means that fusion can only happen at **very high temperatures**.

5) There must be a **high density of matter** for fusion to occur — higher densities increases the likelihood of collisions between nuclei.

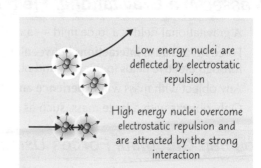

Low energy nuclei are deflected by electrostatic repulsion

High energy nuclei overcome electrostatic repulsion and are attracted by the strong interaction

Fusion Happens in the Core of Stars

1) The **energy** emitted by the **Sun** and other stars comes from nuclear **fusion** reactions.

2) Fusion can happen because the **temperature** in the **core of stars** is so **high** — the core of the Sun is about 10^7 K.

3) At these temperatures, **atoms don't exist** — the negatively charged electrons are **stripped away**, leaving **positively charged nuclei** and **free electrons**. The resulting mixture is called a **plasma**.

4) A lot of **energy** is released during nuclear fusion because the new, heavier nuclei have a **much higher binding energy per nucleon**. This helps to **maintain the temperature** for further fusion reactions to happen.

Example

In the Sun, **hydrogen nuclei** fuse in a series of reactions to form **helium**:

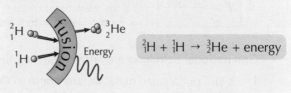

$$^2_1H + ^1_1H \rightarrow ^3_2He + \text{energy}$$

Practice Questions

Q1 Define the term 'binding energy per nucleon'.
Q2 Which element has the highest value of binding energy per nucleon?
Q3 What is spontaneous fission?
Q4 How can fission be induced in ^{235}U?
Q5 Describe the conditions in the core of a star. Why are these conditions necessary for fusion?

Exam Questions

Q1 The following equation represents a nuclear reaction that takes place in the Sun:
$^1_1p + ^1_1p \rightarrow ^2_1H + ^0_{+1}\beta + \text{energy released}$, where p is a proton and β is a positron.
a) State the type of nuclear reaction shown. [1 mark]
b) Given that the binding energy per nucleon for a proton is 0 MeV and for a ^2H nucleus it is approximately 1.11 MeV, estimate the energy released by this reaction. [2 marks]

Q2 This equation shows the reaction between deuterium (^2H) and tritium (^3H): $^2_1H + ^3_1H \rightarrow ^4_2He + ^1_0n + \text{energy}$
Deuterium nucleus = 2.013553 u, tritium nucleus = 3.015501 u, helium nucleus = 4.001505 u and neutron = 1.008665 u.
a) Calculate the total mass deficit for this reaction. [2 marks]
b) Calculate how much energy is released in this reaction in MeV. [3 marks]

If anyone asks, I've gone fission... that joke never gets old....

There's lots to take in on these three pages — you've got concepts like fission and fusion, a smattering of graphs and even a new unit to get to grips with. Make sure you're bezzers with the binding energy calculations and so down with the mass deficit you sound like a politician — they're exam faves (the binding energy and mass deficit, not politicians).

Gravitational Fields

Gravity's all about masses attracting each other.

Masses in a **Gravitational Field** Experience a **Force of Attraction**

1) A gravitational field is a force field — a **region** where an object will experience a **non-contact force**.

2) Force fields cause **interactions** between objects or particles — e.g. **static** or **moving charges** interact through **electric** fields (p.98-100) and objects with **mass** interact through **gravitational** fields.

3) Any object with mass will **experience an attractive force** if you put it in the **gravitational field** of another object.

4) Only objects with a **large** mass, such as stars and planets, have a significant effect.

You can **Calculate Forces** Using **Newton's Law of Universal Gravitation**

1) The **force** experienced by an object in a gravitational field is always **attractive**. It's a **vector** which depends on the **masses** involved and the **distance** between them.

2) The diagram shows the force acting on **mass m_1** due to **mass m_2**. (The force on m_2 due to m_1 is equal but in the opposite direction.)

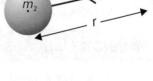

3) A **point mass** is a theoretical object that has a mass but no dimensions — so all its mass acts at a single point. If m_1 and m_2 are **uniform spheres**, you can assume they behave like point masses — as if all their mass is concentrated at their **centres**. To work out the **force** experienced by a **point mass** in a **gravitational field**, you just put the numbers into **Newton's law of universal gravitation**:

$$F = \frac{Gm_1m_2}{r^2}$$

where F is the force acting on mass m_1 due to mass m_2, G is the gravitational constant — 6.67×10^{-11} Nm²kg⁻² and r is the distance (in metres) between the two masses.

For uniform spheres, the distance r is the distance between the centres of the two spheres.

Gravitational field lines are arrows showing the **direction of the force** a mass would feel in a gravitational field:

1) If you put a small mass, m, anywhere in the Earth's gravitational field, it will always be attracted **towards** the Earth.

2) The Earth's gravitational field is **radial** — the lines of force meet at the centre of the Earth.

3) If you move mass m further away from the Earth — where the **lines** of force are **further apart** — the **force** it experiences **decreases**.

4) The small mass, m, has a gravitational field of its own. This doesn't have a noticeable effect on the Earth though, because the Earth is so much **more massive**.

5) Close to the Earth's surface, the field is (almost) uniform — the **field lines** are (almost) **parallel** and **equally spaced**. You can usually **assume** that the field is perfectly uniform.

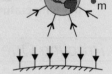

Newton's Law of Universal Gravitation is an **Inverse Square Law**

The law of universal gravitation is an **inverse square law** so:

1) If the distance r between the masses **increases** then the force F will **decrease**.

2) If the **distance doubles** then the **force** will be one **quarter** the strength of the original force.

$$F \propto \frac{1}{r^2}$$

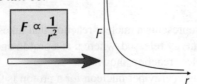

If you plotted a graph of F against $\frac{1}{r^2}$, it would be a straight line.

The **Field Strength** is the **Force per Unit Mass**

1) Gravitational field strength, g, is the **force per unit mass**:

$$g = \frac{F}{m}$$

Where F is the force on the mass (in N) and m is the mass (in kg). g has units of newtons per kilogram (Nkg⁻¹)

The value of g depends on **where you are in** the field. The **value** of g at the **Earth's surface** is approximately **9.81 Nkg⁻¹** (or 9.81 ms⁻², p.18).

2) g is a **vector** quantity, always pointing towards the centre of the mass whose field it's describing. Depending on the direction **defined** to be positive, it **could** be negative.

3) As the gravitational field is **almost uniform** at the Earth's surface, assume g is a **constant** if you don't go too **high**.

4) g is the **acceleration** of a mass in a gravitational field (as $F = ma$). It's often called the **acceleration due to gravity**.

Gravitational Fields

In a *Radial Field*, g is *Inversely Proportional* to r²

1) You know from the previous page that the force experienced by a point mass (m_1) in the gravitational field of another point mass (m_2) is given by $F = \frac{Gm_1m_2}{r^2}$.

2) You also know from the previous page that the force per unit mass experienced by a mass m is given by: $g = \frac{F}{m}$, so for the point mass m_1 in the gravitational field of m_2, $g = \frac{F}{m_1}$.

3) If you **combine** the two equations and **rearrange** a bit, you get an equation for how the **gravitational field strength** around mass m_2 changes with distance: $g = \frac{Gm_2}{r^2}$.

4) As the gravitational strength of mass m_2 doesn't depend on m_1, this is generally written as:

$$g = \frac{Gm}{r^2}$$

Where m is the mass of the object generating the gravitational field.

This equation works for **point masses**, and for the **area around uniform spheres** (which approximate as point masses). It doesn't, however, work for **inside** a uniform sphere — e.g. beneath the Earth's crust. For the area inside a uniform sphere, g is **zero** at the **centre** of the sphere, and **increases linearly** with distance from the centre of the sphere.

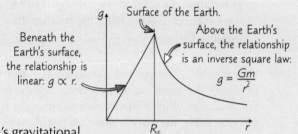

Beneath the Earth's surface, the relationship is linear: $g \propto r$.

Surface of the Earth.

Above the Earth's surface, the relationship is an inverse square law: $g = \frac{Gm}{r^2}$

The graph on the right shows how the strength of the Earth's gravitational field, g, varies with distance, r, from the centre of the Earth (assuming that the Earth has uniform density).

Example: The graph shows how the gravitational field strength, g, varies with distance, r, from the centre of the planet Mars, assuming that Mars has uniform density. The radius of Mars is approximately 3.4×10^3 km. Estimate the mass of Mars.

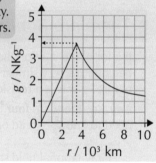

You can see from the graph that the value of g at the surface of Mars is about 3.7 Nkg⁻¹.

Rearrange the formula $g = \frac{Gm}{r^2}$ for m (and don't forget to convert to standard units first).

So, $m = \frac{gr^2}{G} = \frac{3.7 \times (3.4 \times 10^6)^2}{6.67 \times 10^{-11}} = 6.412... \times 10^{23} = \mathbf{6.4 \times 10^{23}}$ **kg (to 2 s.f.)**.

Practice Questions

Q1 Draw a diagram showing the Earth's gravitational field close to its surface. State the assumption made.

Q2 Define gravitational field strength and write an equation for it in terms of force.

Q3 Derive the equation that shows how the gravitational field strength around an object varies with distance.

Exam Questions

Acceleration due to gravity on Earth g = 9.81 ms⁻²

Q1 Define what is meant by the gravitational field of an object. [1 mark]

Q2 The Moon has a mass of 7.35×10^{22} kg and a radius of 1740 km.
a) Calculate the value of g at the Moon's surface. [1 mark]
b) Calculate the gravitational force on a 25 kg object 10 m (to 2 s.f.) above the surface of the Moon. [2 marks]

Q3 A satellite is orbiting Earth and experiences a gravitational field strength of $g = 4$ Nkg⁻¹. The radius of its orbit is then increased until it experiences a gravitational field strength of $g = 2$ Nkg⁻¹. Choose the option which describes the factor by which the radius of orbit has been increased, correct to 2 s.f.
A 1.2   B 1.4   C 1.6   D 1.8 [1 mark]

If you're really stuck, put 'Inverse Square Law'...

Clever chap, Newton, but famously tetchy. He got into fights with other physicists, mainly over planetary motion and calculus... the usual playground squabbles. Then he spent the rest of his life trying to turn scrap metal into gold. Weird.

More Gravitational Fields

Fee fi fo fields. Yep, more on gravitational fields — something Jack would have had to consider when growing beanstalks.

Gravitational Potential is the Work Done to Move a Unit Mass from 'Infinity'

1) The **gravitational potential**, V_{grav}, at a point is the **gravitational potential energy per unit mass** at that point.

2) It is also the **work done** in moving a **unit mass** from **infinity** to that **point**.

3) In a **radial field** (like the Earth's), the equation for gravitational potential is:

$$V_{grav} = \frac{-Gm}{r}$$

V_{grav} is gravitational potential (Jkg^{-1}), G is the gravitational constant, m is the mass of the object causing the gravitational field (kg), and r is the distance from the centre of the object (m).

Gravitational potential is **negative** — you have to **do work against** the gravitational field to move an object out of it. The **further** you are from the centre of a radial field, the **smaller** the magnitude of V_{grav}. At an **infinite distance** from the mass, the gravitational potential will be **zero**.

Work against gravity — best done with ropes.

4) If a mass, M, is moved but the distance, r, from the mass m is kept **the same**, **no work** is done against **gravity**. For example, when a **planet** moves around a star in a **circular orbit**, **no work is done** on the planet by the gravitational force because the distance, r, from the star is **constant**.

STAR

PLANET

The distance between the star and the planet is constant, so no work is done against gravity.

There are Similarities between Gravitational and Electric Fields...

If a lot of the stuff on the previous couple of pages sounded strangely familiar, it could be because it's very similar to the stuff on electric fields (or it could be because you've learnt it before — this is a revision book after all).

See pages 98-100 for more on electric fields.

Anyway, there are **four** big **similarities** between **electric** and **gravitational fields** that you need to know — read on.

Gravitational field strength, g, is **force** per **unit mass**.	Electric field strength, E, is **force** per **unit positive charge**.
Newton's law of universal gravitation for the **force** between two point masses is an **inverse square law**.	Coulomb's law for the electric **force** between two point charges is also an **inverse square law**.
The **field lines** for a point mass (or a uniform spherical mass)... 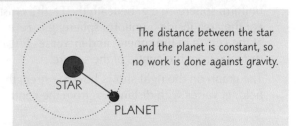	The **field lines** for a **negative** point charge (or a uniform spherical charge)...
Gravitational potential, V_{grav}, is **potential energy** per **unit mass** and is **zero** at **infinity**.	Electric potential, V, is **potential energy** per **unit positive charge** and is **zero** at **infinity**.

... and Three Differences too

Gravitational and electric fields aren't all the same — you need to know the **three main differences**:

1) Gravitational forces are always **attractive**. Electric forces can be either **attractive** or **repulsive**.

2) Objects can be **shielded** from **electric** fields, but not from gravitational fields.

3) The size of an **electric** force depends on the **medium** between the charges, e.g. plastic or air. For gravitational forces, this makes no difference.

More Gravitational Fields

The**The *Speed* of an Orbit depends on its *Radius* and the Mass of the *Larger Body***

1) Earth feels a force due to the gravitational 'pull' of the **Sun**. This force is given by Newton's law of universal gravitation...

$$F = \frac{Gm_1m_2}{r^2}$$

(see p.158)

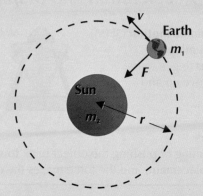

2) The Earth has velocity *v*. Its linear speed is constant but its **direction** is not — so it's accelerating. From Newton's First Law, an accelerating object must be experiencing a force (see p.28). The **centripetal force** (p.97) causing this acceleration is:

$$F = \frac{m_1v^2}{r}$$

3) The **centripetal force** on the Earth must be a result of the **gravitational force** due to the Sun, and so these forces must be **equal**:

$$\frac{m_1v^2}{r} = \frac{Gm_1m_2}{r^2} \quad \text{and rearranging...} \quad v = \sqrt{\frac{GM}{r}}$$

v is orbital speed (ms⁻¹), *G* is the gravitational constant, 6.67×10^{-11} Nm²kg⁻², *M* is the mass of the object being orbited (kg), *r* is the distance from the centre of the object being orbited to the centre of the orbiting object (m).

And the *Period* does too

The **time** taken **for one orbit** is called the **period, *T***. For circular motion $T = \frac{2\pi r}{v}$ (see p.96).

Substitute $v = \sqrt{\frac{GM}{r}}$ into the equation for *T* and rearrange:

$$T^2 = \left(\frac{4\pi^2}{GM}\right)r^3$$

T is the period in s.

Remember — the mass M in this equation is the mass of the object being orbited.

Practice Questions

Q1 What is gravitational potential? Write an equation for it.

Q2 Explain why no work is done against gravity when a planet moves in a circular orbit.

Q3 Derive an equation for the period, *T*, for an object orbiting a mass *M* at a distance of *r* metres from the centre of *M*.

Exam Questions

$G = 6.67 \times 10^{-11} Nm^2kg^{-2}$

Q1 State two similarities and one difference between gravitational and electric fields. [3 marks]

Q2 A 300 kg probe is sent to an asteroid to collect rock samples before returning to Earth. The asteroid has a mass of 2.67×10^{19} kg. The gravitational potential, V_g, at the surface of the asteroid is -1.52×10^4 Jkg⁻¹. Calculate the radius of the asteroid. [2 marks]

Q3 a) A satellite orbits 200.0 km above the Earth's surface. Given that the mass of the Earth is 5.98×10^{24} kg, and the Earth's radius is 6400 km, calculate the period of the satellite's orbit. [2 marks]

   b) Calculate the linear speed of the satellite. [1 mark]

Q4 The Sun has a mass of 2.0×10^{30} kg, but loses mass at a rate of around 6×10^9 kgs⁻¹. Discuss whether this will have had any significant effect on the Earth's orbit over the past 50 000 years, supporting your answer with calculations. [2 marks]

All this talk of orbits is putting my head in a spin...

Kepler is sometimes proclaimed as the first science fiction writer. He wrote a tale about a fantastic trip to the Moon, where the book narrator's mum asks a demon the secret of space travel, to boldly go where — oh wait, different story. Unfortunately Kepler's book might have sparked an actual witch-hunt on Kepler's mum, whoops-a-daisy...

Simple Harmonic Motion

Something simple at last — I like the sound of this. And colourful graphs too — you're in for a treat here.

SHM is Defined in Terms of Acceleration and Displacement

1) An object moving with **simple harmonic motion** (SHM) oscillates to and fro, either side of a **midpoint**. **Pendulums** and **mass-spring systems** (e.g. a mass hanging on a spring that's free to move up and down) are two examples.

Midpoint

Small displacement, therefore small force. Large displacement, therefore large force.

2) The distance of the object from the midpoint is called its **displacement**.

3) There is always a **restoring force** pulling or pushing the object back **towards** the **midpoint**. The **size** of the **restoring force** depends on the **displacement**, and the force makes the object **accelerate** towards the midpoint.

Condition for SHM: an object will move with SHM if the **restoring force** acting on it is **directly proportional** to the object's **displacement** from the **midpoint**, in the **opposite** direction to the displacement (i.e. **towards** the **midpoint**).

In symbols: $\boxed{F = -kx}$

where F is the restoring force, x is the displacement and k is a constant.

The Restoring Force Makes the Object Exchange PE and KE

1) The **type** of **potential energy** (E_p) depends on **what is** providing the **restoring force** — e.g. **gravitational potential energy** for pendulums or **elastic strain energy** (see p.58) for masses on springs moving horizontally.

2) As the object moves **towards the midpoint**, the restoring force **does work on** the object and so **transfers** some E_p to E_k. When the object is moving **away from the midpoint**, the object's E_k is transferred **back to** E_p again.

3) As the object passes the **midpoint**, its E_p is **zero** and its E_k is **maximum**.

4) At the **maximum displacement** (the **amplitude**) on both sides of the midpoint, the object's E_k is **zero** and its E_p is at its **maximum**.

Energy

$E_p + E_k$

E_p

E_k

left-hand side   right-hand side   Displacement

5) The **sum** of the **potential** and **kinetic** energy is called the **mechanical energy** and **stays constant** (as long as the motion isn't damped — see p.166-167).

6) The **energy transfer** for one complete cycle of oscillation is: E_p to E_k to E_p to E_k to E_p... and then the process repeats...

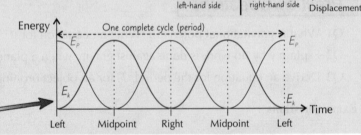

Energy   One complete cycle (period)

E_p E_p

E_k E_k → Time

Left   Midpoint   Right   Midpoint   Left

You can Draw Graphs to Show Displacement, Velocity and Acceleration

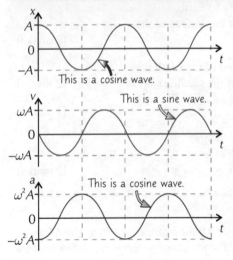

This is a cosine wave.

This is a sine wave.

This is a cosine wave.

Displacement, **x**, varies with time, **t**, as a cosine (or sine) wave with a maximum value, **A** (the amplitude).

Velocity, **v**, is a **quarter of a cycle** in front of the **displacement** (a phase difference of $\pi/2$) and has a maximum value of ωA. The **gradient** of a **displacement-time** graph at a given time gives the **velocity** at that time.

Acceleration, **a**, has a maximum value of $\omega^2 A$, and is in **antiphase** with the **displacement**. The **gradient** of a **velocity-time** graph at a given time gives the **acceleration** at that time.

The **period**, **T**, of an oscillator is the time taken for one oscillation, in s, and the **frequency**, **f**, is the number of oscillations per second, in s^{-1} or Hz (see next page). They are related by the equation: $\boxed{T = \dfrac{1}{f}}$

ω is the **angular frequency** of the oscillation (in rad s^{-1}):

$\boxed{\omega = 2\pi f}$

If you combine these equations, you get: $\boxed{T = \dfrac{2\pi}{\omega}}$

Simple Harmonic Motion

The **Frequency** and **Period** Don't Depend on the **Amplitude**

From **maximum positive displacement** (e.g. maximum displacement to the right) to **maximum negative displacement** (e.g. maximum displacement to the left) and **back again** is called a **cycle** of oscillation.

> In SHM, the **frequency** and **period** are independent of the **amplitude** (they're constant for a given oscillation), so a **pendulum clock** will keep ticking in **regular** time **intervals** even if its swing becomes very **small**.

Learn the SHM Equations

Make sure your calculator is set to radians before you use these equations.

1) The **displacement** of an object moving with SHM varies with time according to the equation: $\boxed{x = A\cos(\omega t)}$ where A is the amplitude of the oscillation (the maximum displacement)

2) If the displacement of an object over time is a **cosine wave**, then **velocity** is a **sine wave**. In fact, the velocity of an object moving with SHM is given by the equation: $\boxed{v = -A\omega\sin(\omega t)}$

3) According to the definition of SHM (p.162), the **restoring force** is **directly proportional** to the **displacement**, x. As $F = ma$ (p.28), this means that the **acceleration**, a, is also directly proportional to the displacement. So $a \propto x$, and the **constant of proportionality** is equal to $-\omega^2$. There's a minus sign here because the restoring force and therefore the acceleration is always in the **opposite direction** to the displacement.

These equations (and the graphs on p.162) all apply if you start timing when the oscillator is at its maximum displacement. If you started the timer at the midpoint of the oscillation (when x = 0) you'd need to swap round all the sines and cosines (and some of the minus signs).

Acceleration: $\boxed{a = -\omega^2 x}$ so: $\boxed{a = -A\omega^2 \cos(\omega t)}$

You can also find an expression for the **angular frequency**, ω, in terms of the **constant k**:

- If $F = ma$ and $F = -kx$, then $ma = -kx$. Rearranging this gives $a = -\dfrac{k}{m}x$
- You know from above that $a = -\omega^2 x$. This means that $\dfrac{k}{m} = \omega^2$, so $\omega = \sqrt{\dfrac{k}{m}}$.

k will vary depending on what the system is.

Practice Questions

Q1 Sketch a graph to show how both the kinetic and potential energy vary with displacement for an object oscillating with simple harmonic motion.

Q2 Sketch graphs to show how the displacement, velocity and acceleration of an object oscillating with SHM vary with time.

Q3 Give the relationships between: a) time period and frequency   b) time period and angular frequency.

Exam Questions

Q1 a) Define simple harmonic motion, and give an equation for the restoring force in terms of displacement. [3 marks]
   b) Explain why the motion of a ball bouncing off the ground is not simple harmonic motion. [1 mark]

Q2 A pendulum is pulled 0.050 m to the left and released.
   It oscillates with simple harmonic motion with a frequency of 1.5 Hz. Calculate:
   a) its displacement 0.10 s after it is released, [2 marks]
   b) the magnitude of its maximum velocity, [2 marks]
   c) the time it takes for its acceleration to first reach a magnitude of 0.70 ms⁻² after it is released. [2 marks]

Q3 Two pendulums, P and Q, are oscillating with simple harmonic motion. Pendulum P has the same maximum displacement as pendulum Q, but twice the angular frequency. Which option correctly describes the maximum acceleration of pendulum P with respect to pendulum Q?
   A half   B the same   C double   D quadruple   [1 mark]

"Simple" harmonic motion — hmmm, I'm not convinced...

Don't let all the 'ω's confuse you, this stuff's actually not too bad. Make sure you can remember the shapes of all the graphs on page 162. And make sure you're comfortable with all the formulas on these pages too.

Investigating Simple Harmonic Motion

There are a couple more equations to learn on this page I'm afraid. But the experiments are pretty fun at least...

A *Mass* on a *Spring* is a *Simple Harmonic Oscillator (SHO)*

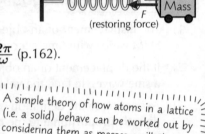

1) You know from page 162 that, for an object undergoing simple harmonic motion, the **restoring force** is proportional to the **displacement**, x, so $F = -kx$.

2) You also know from **Hooke's law** (see p.56), that if a spring is stretched or compressed by a displacement x, it will experience a restoring force equal to kx, where k is the **spring constant**. So mass-spring systems are an example of a simple harmonic oscillator.

3) You saw on page 163 that for an object experiencing SHM, the **angular frequency** of the oscillations, $\omega = \sqrt{\dfrac{k}{m}}$.

4) Finally, you know that the **time period** of a simple harmonic oscillator, $T = \dfrac{2\pi}{\omega}$ (p.162).

5) If you **stick all this together**, you get this **equation** for the time period of a mass-spring system oscillating with simple harmonic motion:

$$T = 2\pi\sqrt{\frac{m}{k}}$$

T = period of oscillation in seconds
m = mass in kg
k = spring constant in Nm⁻¹

A simple theory of how atoms in a lattice (i.e. a solid) behave can be worked out by considering them as masses oscillating on springs (see p.46). So there you go.

You Can Use this Formula to find the *Spring Constant*

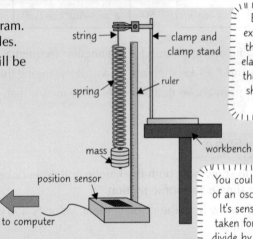

1) Set up the equipment as shown in the diagram. Weigh the masses using a set of digital scales.

2) **Pull** the masses down a set amount, this will be your initial **amplitude**. Let the masses go.

3) The masses will now oscillate with **simple harmonic motion**.

4) The **position sensor** measures the **displacement** of the mass over **time**.

5) Connect the position sensor to a computer and create a **displacement-time** graph. Read off the period T from the graph.

6) Rearrange the equation $T = 2\pi\sqrt{\dfrac{m}{k}}$ to get $k = \dfrac{4\pi^2 m}{T^2}$. Then substitute in your values of T and m to find the **spring constant**.

Because the spring in this experiment is hung vertically, the potential energy is both elastic and gravitational. For the horizontal spring system shown above, the potential energy is just elastic.

You could also measure the period of an oscillation using a stopwatch. It's sensible to measure the time taken for e.g. five oscillations, then divide by the number of oscillations to get an average, as it'll reduce the random error in your result.

You Can Also *Investigate Factors* Which Affect the *Period*

You can use this setup to test how changing different things causes the period to change.

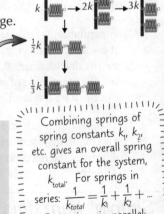

1) Change the **mass**, m, by loading more **masses** onto the spring.

2) Change the **spring constant**, k, by using different combinations of springs.

3) Change the **amplitude**, A, by pulling the masses down by different distances.

You'll get the following **results:**

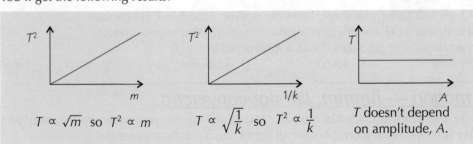

$T \propto \sqrt{m}$ so $T^2 \propto m$

$T \propto \sqrt{\dfrac{1}{k}}$ so $T^2 \propto \dfrac{1}{k}$

T doesn't depend on amplitude, A.

Combining springs of spring constants k_1, k_2, etc. gives an overall spring constant for the system, k_{total}. For springs in series: $\dfrac{1}{k_{total}} = \dfrac{1}{k_1} + \dfrac{1}{k_2} + \ldots$ For springs in parallel: $k_{total} = k_1 + k_2 + \ldots$

Investigating Simple Harmonic Motion

The **Simple Pendulum** is the **Classic Example** of an **SHO**

The **formula for the period of a pendulum** is:
where T = period of oscillation in seconds,
l = length of pendulum (between pivot and
centre of mass of bob) in m and
g = gravitational field strength in Nkg^{-1}.

$$T = 2\pi\sqrt{\frac{l}{g}}$$

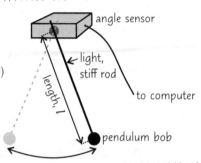

This formula works for situations where you can assume the bob acts as a point mass, and the rod (or string) of the pendulum has no mass. It only works for small angles of oscillations (up to about 10° from the equilibrium point).

You can use this to **estimate** the value of g:

1) Attach a **pendulum** to an **angle sensor** connected to a **computer**. Measure the length, l of the pendulum.

2) **Displace** the pendulum from its rest position by a small angle (less than 10°) and let it go. The pendulum will oscillate with **simple harmonic motion**.

3) The angle sensor measures how the bob's **displacement** from the **rest** position varies with **time**.

4) Use the computer to plot a **displacement-time** graph and read off the **period**, T, from it. Make sure you calculate the average period over **several oscillations** (at least 5) to reduce the **percentage uncertainty** in your measurement (see p.10).

5) Rearrange the formula $T = 2\pi\sqrt{\frac{l}{g}}$ to get $g = \frac{4\pi^2 l}{T^2}$.
Then plug in your values of l and T to calculate g.

You can also do this experiment by hanging the pendulum from a clamp and timing the oscillations using a stop watch. Use the clamp stand as a reference point so it's easy to tell when the pendulum has reached the mid-point of its oscillation.

You Can **Investigate Factors** Which Affect the **Period** for a Pendulum Too

You could change the **mass** of the pendulum bob, m, the **amplitude** of displacement, A, and the **length** of the rod, l, independently to see how they affect the **period**, T. Your results should look like this:

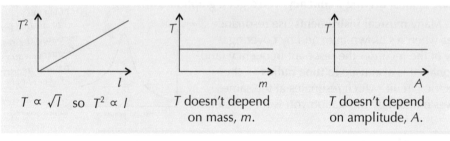

$T \propto \sqrt{l}$ so $T^2 \propto l$ | T doesn't depend on mass, m. | T doesn't depend on amplitude, A.

Bob hung around waiting for the experiment to start.

Practice Questions

Q1 Write down the formula for calculating the period of a simple pendulum displaced by a small angle.
Q2 Describe an experiment to estimate the value of g using a simple pendulum.

Exam Questions

Q1 A spring is suspended from a stand and clamp. A mass of 0.10 kg is attached to the bottom and the spring. The mass is pulled down and released, so it oscillates with simple harmonic motion, with a period of 0.72 s.

a) Calculate the spring constant of the spring in Nm^{-1}. [2 marks]

b) Calculate the mass needed to make the period of oscillation twice as long. [2 marks]

Q2 Two pendulums of different lengths were released from rest at the top of their swing. It took exactly the same time for the shorter pendulum to make five complete oscillations as it took the longer pendulum to make three complete oscillations. The shorter pendulum had a length of 0.20 m. Show that the length of the longer one was 0.56 m. [3 marks]

Go on — SHO the examiners what you're made of...

The most important things to remember on these pages are those two period equations. You'll be given them in your exam, but you need to know what they mean and be happy using them. So go and practise using them for a bit.

Free and Forced Oscillations

Resonance... tricky little beast. The Millennium Bridge was supposed to be a feat of British engineering, but it suffered from a severe case of the wobbles caused by resonance. How was it sorted out? By damping, of course — read on...

Free Oscillations — No Transfer of Energy To or From the Surroundings

1) If you stretch and release a mass on a spring, it oscillates at its **natural frequency**.

2) If **no energy's transferred** to or from the surroundings (i.e. it isn't damped — see below), it will **keep** oscillating with the **same amplitude forever** — this is because of the **principle of conservation of energy** (p.36).

3) In practice this **never happens**, but a spring oscillating in air is called a **free oscillation** (or vibration) anyway.

Forced Oscillations Happen when there's an External Driving Force

1) A system can be **forced** to oscillate (or vibrate) by a periodic **external force**.

2) The frequency of this force is called the **driving frequency**.

Resonance Happens when Driving Frequency = Natural Frequency

1) As the **driving frequency** approaches the **natural frequency**, the system gains more and more energy from the driving force and so oscillates with a **rapidly increasing amplitude**.

2) When this **energy transfer** is at a **maximum**, the system is **resonating**. The frequency that the system oscillates at is its **resonant frequency**. For an **undamped oscillator**, resonance occurs when the **driving frequency** equals the **natural frequency**.

3) You can **investigate resonance** using the equipment shown on the right. If you adjust the **driving frequency** of the vibration generator by adjusting the signal generator, the **amplitude** of the oscillations of the mass will vary — they will **increase** as the driving frequency gets **closer** to the natural frequency.

4) If you were to plot **amplitude** against **driving frequency**, you'd get a graph like this:

5) Resonance is **everywhere**. Many **musical instruments** use resonance — e.g. a recorder resonates when it's blown into, and by covering different holes on the body of the recorder the resonant frequency (and so the note) changes. Resonance is also used to **tune radios** — the tuning dial controls an electric circuit, which resonates at the same frequency as the radio waves emitted by the station you want to listen to.

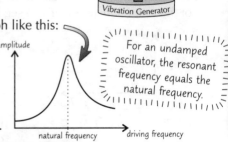

Mass oscillates | Mass
Signal Generator
Frequency
Vibration Generator

amplitude

For an undamped oscillator, the resonant frequency equals the natural frequency.

natural frequency   driving frequency

Damping Happens when Energy is Lost to the Surroundings

1) For an ideal, **undamped** oscillator, it's total energy will stay **constant** (p.162). In practice though, **any** oscillating system **loses energy** to its surroundings. This is usually down to **frictional forces** like air resistance (see p.30).

2) These **damping forces** are why a mass on a spring won't go on oscillating forever — **energy** is **transferred** away from the oscillator into other forms (like heat), and the oscillation **dies away** (unless there's a driving force). Energy is still **conserved overall** though — the energy of the oscillator **decreases**, but the energy of the surroundings **increases**.

3) Systems are often **deliberately damped** to **stop** them oscillating or to **minimise** the effect of **resonance**. The **degree** of damping can vary from **light** damping (where the damping force is small) to **overdamping**.

4) Damping **reduces** the **amplitude** of the oscillation over time. The **heavier** the damping, the **quicker** the amplitude is reduced to zero.

5) **Critical damping** reduces the amplitude (i.e. stops the system oscillating) in the **shortest possible time**.

6) Car **suspension systems** and **moving coil meters** (which control the arm in analogue voltmeters and ammeters) are critically damped so that they **don't oscillate** but return to equilibrium as quickly as possible.

7) Systems with **even heavier damping** are **overdamped**. They take **longer** to return to equilibrium than a critically damped system.

8) **Plastic deformation** of ductile materials (see p.56) **reduces** the **amplitude** of oscillations in the same way as damping. As the material changes shape, it **absorbs energy**, so the oscillation will become smaller.

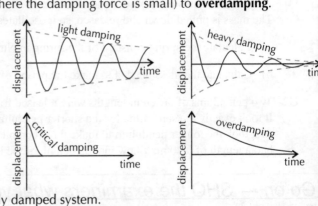

light damping — displacement vs time
heavy damping — displacement vs time
critical damping — displacement vs time
overdamping — displacement vs time

Free and Forced Oscillations

Damping Affects Resonance

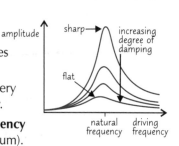

1) **Lightly damped** systems have a **sharp** resonance peak. Their amplitude only increases dramatically when the **driving frequency** is **very close** to the **natural frequency**.

2) **Heavily damped** systems have a **flatter response**. Their amplitude doesn't increase very much near the natural frequency and they aren't as **sensitive** to the driving frequency.

3) The **resonant frequency** of a damped system is generally **lower** than its **natural frequency** (which makes sense — a pendulum will take longer to swing in water than in a vacuum).

You can Investigate the Effect of Mass on Resonance

The natural frequency of a mass-spring system depends on mass (p.164), so you can use resonance to **estimate** the size of an unknown mass, m_u.

If the masses are quite small, you can assume the air resistance on them is negligible, so you can approximate this as an undamped system (so resonant frequency = natural frequency, p.166).

1) You'll need the equipment shown on the right, and a **set of masses** that you know the values of.

2) Attach a **known mass**, m, to the spring, and adjust the **frequency** of the **signal generator** until the mass **resonates** — this is when the **output** of the **position sensor** shows the **amplitude** of the oscillation appearing to reach its **maximum**. Record the **frequency** shown by the signal generator — this is the **resonant frequency** of the mass.

3) **Repeat** this for **different** known **masses** and record each of their resonant frequencies.

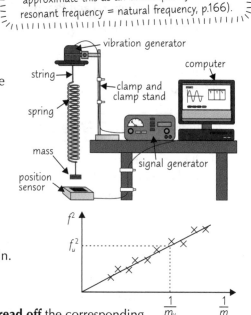

4) Getting the resonant frequency exactly right is tricky, as the amplitude will be **quite large** for a **range of frequencies** around the resonance peak (see page 166). You can reduce the effect of this on your results by **repeating** your measurement of the resonant frequency at least three times for each mass and taking an **average**.

5) Plot a graph of the **square** of **resonant frequency**, f^2, against $\frac{1}{m}$, and draw a **line of best fit**. This should be a straight line through the origin.

6) Attach your **unknown mass**, $m_{u'}$ to the spring, and find the **resonant frequency**, $f_{u'}$ as you did for the known masses.

7) **Square** this value to get f_u^2. Find this value of f^2 on your **graph**, and **read off** the corresponding value of $\frac{1}{m}$. Use this to **calculate** an estimate of the value of your mass ($m_u = 1 \div \frac{1}{m_u}$).

Since the resonant frequency of this system is approximately equal to its **natural frequency** (see above), you could also do this experiment by letting each mass vibrate freely with **SHM** (using the method on p.164), recording the **time period** of the oscillation for each mass, and using this to calculate the frequency using $f = \frac{1}{T}$.

If you're confused about the axes here, have a look at the equation for the period of a mass-spring system on p.164. T is proportional to $\sqrt{m}$, so f^2 is proportional to $\frac{1}{m}$.

Practice Questions

Q1 Define the following: a) a free oscillation   b) a forced oscillation   c) resonance.

Q2 Explain how plastic deformation of ductile materials affects oscillations in SHM.

Q3 Describe an experiment to estimate the value of a mass using a set of known masses and a signal generator.

Exam Questions

Q1 a) Draw a diagram to show how the amplitude of a lightly damped system varies with driving frequency. [2 marks]
   b) On the same diagram, show how the amplitude of the system varies with driving frequency when it is heavily damped. [1 mark]
   c) If a mass on a spring oscillates at its natural frequency underwater, the oscillation will quickly die away. Explain why this happens in terms of the transfer of energy. [2 marks]
   d) Describe how energy is conserved in the example in part c). [1 mark]

Q2 Define critical damping and state a situation where it is used. [2 marks]

Physics — it can really put a damper on your social life...

Resonance can be really useful (radios, organ pipes, swings — yay) or very, very bad...

Exam Structure and Technique

Good exam technique can make a big difference to your mark, so make sure you read this stuff carefully.

Get Familiar With the **Exam Structure**

For A-level Physics, you'll be sitting **three papers**. Find out your **exam timetable** and use the info below to **plan** your revision carefully.

You'll also do a Practical Endorsement as part of your A-level. It'll involve doing practicals throughout the course, and will be reported separately from your exam results.

Paper 1 — Advanced Physics I **1 hour 45 minutes**	**90** marks	**30%** of your A-level	Covers material from **topics 1–3 and 6–8** of this book.
Paper 2 — Advanced Physics II **1 hour 45 minutes**	**90** marks	**30%** of your A-level	Covers material from **topics 1, 4, 5 and 9–13** of this book.
Paper 3 — General and Practical Principles in Physics **2 hours 30 minutes**	**120** marks	**40%** of your A-level	It can cover material from **all topics (1–13)** of this book.

All three papers include a combination of **calculations** and **wordy** questions. The wordy questions will include a **range** of questions from **short-answer** to **extended writing** questions. Papers 1 and 2 also contain **multiple choice** questions.

If you're taking AS Physics, you'll do different exams altogether, so this information isn't relevant to you.

Make Sure You **Read the Question**

1) It sounds obvious, but it's really important you read each question **carefully**, and give an answer that matches what you've been asked.

2) Look for **command words** in the question — they'll give you an idea of the **kind of answer** you should write. Commonly used command words for written questions are **state**, **describe**, **discuss** and **explain**:

- If a question asks you to **state** something, you just need to give a **definition**, **example** or **fact**.
- If you're asked to **describe** what happens in a particular situation, don't waste time explaining why it happens — that's not what the question is after.
- For **discuss** questions, you'll need to include more **detail** — depending on the question you'll probably need to **identify** what's going on, **explore all sides** and provide a **reasoned conclusion**.
- If a question asks you to **explain** why something happens you must give **reasons**, not just a description. You **can** include **calculations** as part of your explanations.

3) Look at **how many marks** a question is worth before answering. It'll tell you roughly **how much information** you need to include. See the next page for more about **wordy questions**.

Manage Your *Time* Sensibly

1) The **number of marks** tells you roughly **how long** to spend on a question — you've got just over a minute per mark in the exam. If you get stuck on a question for too long, it may be best to **move on** so you don't run out of time for the others.

2) The **multiple choice questions** are only worth **one mark each**, so it's not worth stressing over one for ages if you get stuck — **move on** and come back to it later.

3) You don't have to work through the paper **in order** — you could leave questions on topics you find harder until last.

Don't be **Put Off** if a Question Seems **Strange**

1) You may get some weird questions that seem to have nothing to do with anything you've learnt. **DON'T PANIC.** Every question will be something you can answer **using physics you know**, it just may be in a new **context**.

2) Answering these **trickier questions** will get you **top marks**, but make sure you get the **easier marks** in the bag first.

3) All of the A-level exams could **pull together** ideas from different parts of physics, so check the question for any **keywords** that you recognise. For example, if a question talks about acceleration, think about the rules and equations you know, and whether any of them apply to the situation in the question.

Exam Structure and Technique

Watch out for *Practical Questions*...

1) Each paper could test anything in topic 1 (on working as a physicist). You may have to **describe an experiment** to investigate something, or **answer questions** on an experiment you've been given.

2) These could be experiments you've **met before**, or they could be **entirely new** to you. All the questions will be based on physics that you've **covered**, but may include bits from different topics put together in ways you haven't seen before. Don't let this put you off, just **think carefully** about what's going on.

3) Make sure you know the difference between **precision**, **accuracy** and **validity** (p.12). Learn what **uncertainty**, **random errors** and **systematic errors** are (p.10-12) and make sure you can give some examples of where each might come from.

4) You need to be able to **calculate errors** and **plot** and **interpret graphs** too.

> Knowing how to answer practical questions is particularly important for Paper 3, but make sure you're comfortable with answering them for Papers 1 and 2 as well.

...and *Wordy Ones*

For some questions, you'll need to write a slightly longer answer, where the '**quality** of your **extended response**' will be taken into account. You'll need to make sure you can develop a **clear** and **logical**, **well-structured line of reasoning**, backed up with **relevant information**.

You can avoid losing marks in these questions by making sure you do the following things:

1) Think about your answer before you write it. Your answer needs to be **logically structured** to get the top marks — your points should, where appropriate, follow on from each other clearly.

2) Make sure your answer is **relevant** to the question being asked and that you **explain** your ideas or argument **clearly**. It's dead easy to go off on a tangent.

3) Back up your points with **evidence** or **explanation**. You'll lose marks if you just make statements without supporting them.

4) Write in **whole sentences** and keep an eye on your **spelling**, **grammar** and **punctuation**. It'll help make sure your answer is clear and easy to read.

> Questions like this will be marked in some way in the exam — e.g. with an asterisk (*). Check the instructions on the front of your paper to find out.

Example: A large group of people walk across a footbridge. When the frequency of the group's footsteps is 1 Hz, the bridge noticeably oscillates.

Describe the phenomenon causing the bridge to oscillate, and suggest what engineers could do to solve this problem.

[6 marks]

Good Answer

The pedestrians provide a driving force on the bridge, causing it to oscillate. At around 1 Hz, the driving frequency from the pedestrians is roughly equal to the natural frequency of the bridge, causing it to resonate. The amplitude of the bridge's oscillations when resonating at 1 Hz will be greater than at any other driving frequency. The oscillations at this frequency are large enough to be noticed by pedestrians. Engineers could fix this problem by critically damping the bridge to stop any oscillations as quickly as possible. They could also adjust the natural frequency of the bridge so that it was not so close to a known walking frequency of large groups of people.

Bad Answer

resonance
driving frequency = natural frequency
damping

> There's nothing fundamentally wrong with the physics in the bad answer, but you'd miss out on some nice easy marks just for not bothering to link the physics with the context given and not putting your answer into proper sentences.

The penultimate joke in the book better be good... here goes... *Oh, I've run out of space...*

Making sure you're prepared for what the exams will be like, reading questions carefully and managing your time all sounds like pretty basic advice, but you'd be surprised how many people don't follow it. Make sure you do...

Maths Skills

At least 40% of the marks up for grabs in A-level Physics will require maths skills, so make sure you know your stuff. As well as being given some tricky calculations, you could be asked to work with exponentials and logarithms and work out values from log graphs. And it's easy when you know how...

Be **Careful** With **Calculations**

1) In calculation questions you should always **show your working** — you may get some marks for your **method** even if you get the answer wrong.

2) Don't **round** your answer until the **very end**. A lot of calculations in A-level Physics are quite **long**, and if you round too early you could introduce errors to your final answer.

3) Be careful with **units**. Lots of formulas require quantities to be in specific units (e.g. time in seconds), so it's best to **convert** any numbers you're given into these before you start. And obviously, if the question **tells** you which units to give your **answer** in, don't throw away marks by giving it in different ones.

There's more on quantities and their units on p.4-5.

4) You should give your final answer to the same number of **significant figures** as the data that you use from the question with the **least number** of significant figures. If you can, write out the **unrounded answer**, then your **rounded** answer with the number of significant figures you've given it to — it shows you know your stuff.

Many Relationships in Physics are **Exponential**

A fair few of the relationships you need to know about in A-level Physics are **exponential** — where the **rate of change** of a quantity is **proportional** to the **amount** of the quantity left. Here are a couple that crop up in the A-level course (if they don't ring a bell, go have a quick read about them)...

Charge on a capacitor — the decay of charge on a discharging capacitor is proportional to the amount of charge left on the capacitor: $Q = Q_0 e^{-t/RC}$ (see p.104)

There are also exponential relationships for I and V and for charging capacitors.

Radioactive decay — the rate of decay of a radioactive sample is proportional to the **number of undecayed nuclei** in the sample: $N = N_0 e^{-\lambda t}$ (see p.152)

The activity of a radioactive sample behaves in the same way.

You can **Plot** Exponential Relations Using the **Natural Log, ln**

1) Say you've got two variables, x and y, which are related to each other by the formula $y = ke^{-ax}$ (where k and a are constants).

2) The **natural logarithm** of x, **ln** x, is the power to which e (the base) must be raised to to give x.

A logarithm can be to any base you want. Another common one is 'base 10' which is usually written as 'log$_{10}$' or just 'log'.

3) So, by definition, $e^{\ln x} = x$ and $\ln(e^x) = x$. So far so good... now you need some **log rules**:

$$\ln(AB) = \ln A + \ln B \qquad \ln\left(\frac{A}{B}\right) = \ln A - \ln B \qquad \ln x^n = n \ln x$$

These log rules work for all logs (including the natural logarithm). You won't be given them in the exam — so make sure you learn them.

4) So, for $y = ke^{-ax}$, if you take the natural log of both sides of the equation you get:

$$\ln y = \ln(ke^{-ax}) = \ln k + \ln(e^{-ax}) \implies \boxed{\ln y = \ln k - ax}$$

5) Then all you need to do is plot (ln y) against x, and Eric's your aunty:

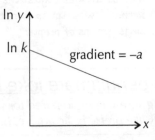

You get a **straight-line graph** with (**ln k**) as the **vertical intercept**, and **–a** as the **gradient**.

Maths Skills

You Might be Asked to find the **Gradient** of a Log Graph

This log business isn't too bad when you get your head around which bit of the log graph means what.

Example: The graph shows the radioactive decay of isotope X.

a) Find the initial number of undecayed nuclei, N_0, in the sample.

You know that the number of undecayed nuclei in a sample, N, is related to the initial number of undecayed nuclei, N_0, by the equation $N = N_0 e^{-\lambda t}$.

So: $\ln N = \ln N_0 - \lambda t$

The y-intercept of the graph is $\ln N_0 = 9.2$

$N_0 = e^{9.2} = 9897.129... = $ **9900 nuclei (to 2 s.f.)**

b) Find the decay constant λ of isotope X.

$-\lambda$ is the gradient of the graph, so: $\lambda = \dfrac{\Delta \ln N}{\Delta t} = \dfrac{9.2 - 7.8}{30.0 \times 60 \times 60} = $ **1.3×10^{-5} s^{-1} (to 2 s.f.)**

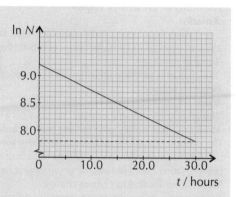

You can Plot **Any Power Law** as a **Log-Log Graph**

You can use logs to plot a straight-line graph of **any power law** — it doesn't have to be an exponential.

Say the relationship between two variables x and y is:

$$y = kx^n$$

Take the **log** (base 10) of both sides to get:

$$\log y = \log k + n \log x$$

So **log k** will be the **y-intercept** and **n** will be the **gradient** of the graph.

When it came to logs, Geoff always took time to smell the flowers...

Example:

The graph shows how the intensity of radiation from the Sun, I, varies with distance from the Sun, d. I is related to d by the power law $I = kd^n$.
Find n.

$\log I = \log (kd^n) = \log k + \log d^n$
$\qquad = \log k + n \log d$

So n is the gradient of the graph.
Reading from the graph:

$$n = \frac{\Delta \log I}{\Delta \log d} = \frac{5.4 - 15.4}{10 - 5} = -2$$

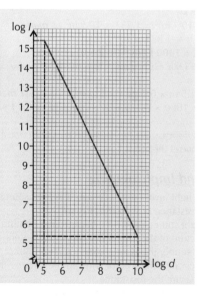

Lumberjacks are great musicians — they have a natural logarhythm...

Well, that's it folks. Crack open the chocolate bar of victory and know you've earned it. Only the tiny detail of the actual exam to go... ahem. Make sure you know which bit means what on a log graph and you'll pick up some nice easy marks. Other than that, stay calm, be as clear as you can and good luck — I've got my fingers, toes and eyes crossed for you.

Answers

Topic 1 — Working as a Physicist

Page 3 — The Scientific Process

1   *A maximum of two marks can be awarded for structure and reasoning of the written response:*
2 marks:
The answer is coherent and constructed logically, and displays clear reasoning and links between points throughout.
1 mark:
The answer is partially logical, with some reasoning and links between points.
0 marks:
The answer has no structure and no links between points.
Here are some points your answer may include:

- The proposed power station would produce electricity without producing greenhouse gases, and so replacing a nearby coal-fired power station could benefit the environment by helping to limit human contribution to climate change.
- As the proposed power station generates energy renewably, it won't use up resources, which will also benefit the environment.
- However, the power station could have a negative effect on the natural environment in the local area (for example by interfering with local habitats or through pollution during its construction).
- As well as damaging the environment, if the power station spoils the scenic coastline it may be unpopular with local people.
- As the coastline is important for tourism in the area, this could also damage the local economy.
- Building the new power station (and closing down the coal-fired power station) may be expensive.
- If the proposed power station causes a coal-fired power station to close, people there could lose their jobs.
- On the other hand, building a new power station could create other new jobs in the area.
[4 marks — 4 marks if 6 points mentioned including social, environmental, and economic factors, 3 marks if 4-5 points mentioned, covering at least two aspects of the question, 2 marks if 2-3 points mentioned, 1 mark if 1 point mentioned.]

Page 5 — Quantities and Units

1 a) SI base unit of mass = kg.
SI derived unit of volume = [SI base unit of length]^3 = m^3.
$\rho = m / V$, so in SI base units ρ = kg / m^3 = **kg m^{-3}** *[1 mark]*
  b) $m = 9.8$ g $= 9.8 \times 10^{-3}$ kg
$V = (11$ mm$)^3 = (11 \times 10^{-3}$ m$)^3 = 1.331 \times 10^{-6}$ m^3 *[1 mark]*
$\rho = m / V = (9.8 \times 10^{-3}) \div (1.331 \times 10^{-6})$
        $= 7362.88... = $ **7400 kg m^{-3} (to 2 s.f.)** *[1 mark]*
You could also have worked this out in g mm^{-3} then converted your answer, but this way is much easier.
  c) A bath tub is roughly 1.5 m × 0.5 m × 0.5 m = 0.375 m^3 *[1 mark]*
$\rho = m / V$, so $m = \rho V = 1000 \times 0.375 = 375$ kg ≈ **400 kg (to 1 s.f.)** *[1 mark]*
If you correctly calculated the mass using a volume between 0.2 m^3 and 0.8 m^3 you can award yourself the marks.

Page 7 — Planning and Implementing

1 a) Independent variable: light level / distance from the light source, dependent variable: resistance of the LDR *[1 mark]*.
  b) Any two of: e.g. the light source used / the background lighting in the room / the temperature of the room/LDR/wires / the potential difference / the power supply the LDR is connected to / the length of wires in the circuit / the type of wires in the circuit / the multimeter used to measure the resistance.
[2 marks available — 1 mark for each correct answer.]

Page 9 — Analysing Results

1 a)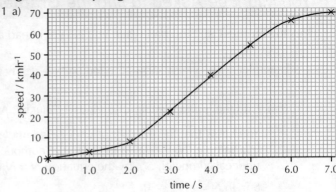
[1 mark for both axes drawn to a sensible scale, 1 mark for labelling both axes correctly, 1 mark for all the points drawn correctly and 1 mark for a sensible line of best fit.]
  b) The graph is linear between 2 and 5 seconds *[1 mark]*.
Accept an answer of 6 s as the upper limit if the graph in part a) agrees.
  c) The maximum acceleration is the value of the steepest gradient, which is the linear portion of the graph *[1 mark]*:
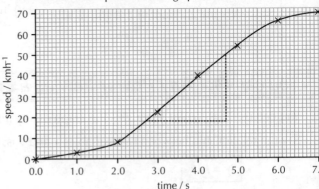
change in speed = 50 − 18 = 32 km hr^{-1} = 32 ÷ (60 × 60)
              = 0.0088... km s^{-1} *[1 mark]*
change in time = 4.7 − 2.7 = 2.0 s *[1 mark]*
acceleration = 0.0088... ÷ 2.0 = 0.0044... km s^{-2}
              = **0.0044 km s^{-2} or 57 000 km hr^{-2} (to 2 s.f.)** *[1 mark]*
Accept an answer in the range 0.0040-0.0046 km s^{-2} or 54 000-60 000 km hr^{-2}.

Answers

ge 11 — Measurements and Uncertainties

a) $(0.02 \div 0.52) \times 100 = 3.846... = $ **4% (to 1 s.f.)** *[1 mark]*

b) $(0.02 \div 0.94) \times 100 = 2.127... = $ **2% (to 1 s.f.)** *[1 mark]*

c) acceleration = change in velocity / time = $(0.94 - 0.52) \div 2.5$
$= 0.168$ ms^{-2} *[1 mark]*
Absolute error in change of velocity = $0.02 + 0.02 = 0.04$ ms^{-1}
Percentage uncertainty in
change of velocity: $(0.04 \div (0.94 - 0.52)) \times 100 = 9.523...\%$
[1 mark]
Percentage uncertainty in time taken = $(0.5 \div 2.5) \times 100 = 20\%$
Percentage uncertainty in acceleration = $9.523...\% + 20\%$
$= 29.523...\%$ *[1 mark]*
Absolute error in acceleration = $0.168 \times (29.523... \div 100)$
$= 0.0496$ ms^{-2}
So the acceleration = **0.17 ± 0.05 ms^{-2} (to 2 s.f.)** *[1 mark]*

ge 13 — Evaluating and Concluding

a) $t = 0.32$ seconds, $v = 2.0$ ms^{-1} *[1 mark]*

b) E.g. The results do not support this conclusion *[1 mark]*, because the student has only collected data for a small range of times so he cannot draw conclusions about times longer than those he measured *[1 mark]* / because the student has only investigated one object so he cannot draw conclusions about other objects *[1 mark]*.

pic 2 — Mechanics

ge 15 — Scalars and Vectors

Weight 75 N
Resultant force, F
Wind 20.0 N

$F^2 = 20.0^2 + 75^2 = 6025$
So $F = 78$ N (to 2 s.f.)
$\tan \theta = 20.0 / 75 = 0.266...$
So $\theta = \tan^{-1} 0.266... = 15°$ (to 2 s.f.)
The resultant force on the rock is **78 N (to 2 s.f.)** *[1 mark]* at an angle of **15° (to 2 s.f.)** *[1 mark]* to the vertical.
Make sure you know which angle you're finding — and label it on your diagram.

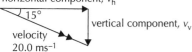

horizontal component, v_h
vertical component, v_v
velocity 20.0 ms^{-1}

horizontal component $v_h = 20.0 \times \cos 15.0°$
$= $ **19.3 ms^{-1} (to 3 s.f.)** *[1 mark]*
vertical component $v_v = 20 \times \sin 15.0°$
$= $ **5.18 ms^{-1} (to 3 s.f.)** *[1 mark]*

3 E.g. current, $v_{river} = 0.20$ ms^{-1}

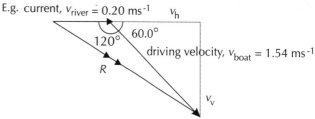

driving velocity, $v_{boat} = 1.54$ ms^{-1}

horizontal component $v_{river} = 0.20$ ms^{-1}
vertical component $v_{river} = 0$ ms^{-1}
horizontal component $v_{boat} = 1.54 \times \cos 60.0 = 0.77$ ms^{-1}
vertical component $v_{boat} = 1.54 \times \sin 60.0 = 1.333...$ ms^{-1}
So, horizontal $v_{resultant} = 0.20 + 0.77 = 0.97$ ms^{-1} *[1 mark]*
vertical $v_{resultant} = 0 + 1.333... = 1.333...$ ms^{-1} *[1 mark]*
Combine the vertical and horizontal components of R.

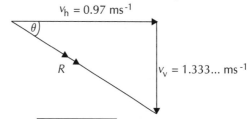

$v_h = 0.97$ ms^{-1}
$v_v = 1.333...$ ms^{-1}

$v_{resultant} = \sqrt{0.97^2 + 1.333...^2} = 1.649...$ ms^{-1}
$= $ **1.6 ms^{-1} (to 2 s.f.)** *[1 mark]*

$\tan \theta = 1.333... \div 0.97 = \tan^{-1} 1.374...$ so $\theta = $ **54° (to 2 s.f.)**
So the resultant velocity of the boat is 1.6 ms^{-1} at an angle of 54° to the current *[1 mark]*.

Page 17 — Motion with Uniform Acceleration

1 a) $a = -9.81$ ms^{-2}, $t = 5.0$ s, $u = 0$ ms^{-1}, $v = ?$
use : $v = u + at$
$v = 0 + 5.0 \times -9.81$ *[1 mark]*
$v = -49.05 = $ **–49 ms^{-1} (to 2 s.f.)** *[1 mark]*.
NB: *It's negative because she's falling downwards and we took upwards as the positive direction.*

b) Use: $s = \dfrac{(u + v)t}{2}$ or $s = ut + \frac{1}{2} at^2$
$s = \dfrac{-49.05 \times 5.0}{2}$ $s = 0 + \frac{1}{2} \times -9.81 \times 5.0^2$ *[1 mark]*
$s = -122.625$ m $s = -122.625$ m
So she falls **120 m (to 2 s.f.)** *[1 mark]*

2 a) $v = 0$ ms^{-1}, $t = 3.2$ s, $s = 40$ m, $u = ?$
use: $s = \left(\dfrac{u + v}{2}\right)t$
$40 = 3.2u \div 2$ *[1 mark]*
$u = 80 \div 3.2 = $ **25 ms^{-1}** *[1 mark]*

b) Use: $v^2 = u^2 + 2as$
$0 = 25^2 + 80a$ *[1 mark]*
$-80a = 625$
$a = -7.81... = $ **–7.8 ms^{-2} (to 2 s.f.)** *[1 mark]*
You could also have solved this using $v = u + at$.

3 a) Take upstream as negative: $v = 5$ ms^{-1}, $a = 6$ ms^{-2}, $s = 1.2$ m, $u = ?$
use: $v^2 = u^2 + 2as$
$5^2 = u^2 + 2 \times 6 \times 1.2$ *[1 mark]*
$u^2 = 25 - 14.4 = 10.6$
$u = -3.255... = $ **–3 ms^{-1} (to 1 s.f.)** *[1 mark]*
The negative root is taken because the boat is pushed upstream at the start, which we've taken to be the negative direction.

b) From furthest point: $u = 0$ ms^{-1}, $a = 6$ ms^{-2}, $v = 5$ ms^{-1}, $s = ?$
use: $v^2 = u^2 + 2as$ *[1 mark]*
$5^2 = 0 + 2 \times 6 \times s$
$s = 25 \div 12 = 2.083... = $ **2 m (to 1 s.f.)** *[1 mark]*

Answers

Page 19 — Free Fall

1 a) The student needs the computer to record:
The time for the first strip of card to pass through the beam
[1 mark]
The time for the second strip of card to pass through the beam
[1 mark]
The time between these events *[1 mark]*.

b) Average speed of first strip while it breaks the light beam =
width of strip ÷ time to pass through beam *[1 mark]*
Average speed of second strip while it breaks the light beam =
width of strip ÷ time to pass through beam *[1 mark]*
Acceleration = (second speed – first speed)
÷ time between light beam being broken *[1 mark]*

c) E.g. the device will accelerate while the beam is broken by the strips *[1 mark]* / The device will experience air resistance, which will slow it down *[1 mark]*.

2 a) You know $s = 5.0$ m, $a = -g$, $v = 0$
You need to find u, so use $v^2 = u^2 + 2as$
$0 = u^2 - 2 \times 9.81 \times 5.0$ *[1 mark]*
$u^2 = 98.1$, so $u = 9.90... = $ **9.9 ms⁻¹ (to 2 s.f.)** *[1 mark]*

b) You know $a = -g$, $v = 0$ at highest point, $u = 9.90...$ ms⁻¹
You need to find t, so use $v = u + at$
$0 = 9.90... - 9.81t$ *[1 mark]*
$t = 9.90.../9.81 = $ **1.0 s (to 2 s.f.)** *[1 mark]*

c) Her velocity as she lands back on the trampoline will be
−9.9 ms⁻¹ (to 2 s.f.). *[1 mark]*
She has a negative velocity because she's moving downwards and the same magnitude as her initial speed because no energy has been lost due to air resistance.

Page 21 — Projectile Motion

1 a) You only need to worry about the vertical motion of the stone.
$u = 0$ ms⁻¹, $s = -560$ m, $a = -g = -9.81$ ms⁻², $t = ?$
You need to find t, so use: $s = ut + \frac{1}{2}at^2$
$-560 = 0 + \frac{1}{2} \times -9.81 \times t^2$
$t = \sqrt{\dfrac{2 \times (-560)}{-9.81}}$ *[1 mark]*
$t = 10.68... = $ **11 s (to 2 s.f.)** *[1 mark]*

b) You know that in the horizontal direction:
$v = 20$ m/s, $t = 10.68...$ s, $a = 0$, $s = ?$
$s = v \times t = 20 \times 10.68...$ *[1 mark]*
$s = 213.69... = $ **210 m (to 2 s.f.)** *[1 mark]*

2 **C** *[1 mark]*
Use $v^2 = u^2 + 2as$ to find the vertical displacement when $v = 0$. The arrow was fired from 1.0 m above the ground so don't forget to include the extra metre in your calculations.

Page 23 — Displacement-Time Graphs

1 Split graph into four sections:

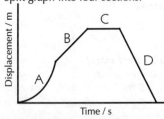

A: acceleration *[1 mark]*
B: constant velocity *[1 mark]*
C: stationary *[1 mark]*
D: constant velocity in opposite direction to A and B *[1 mark]*

2 a)

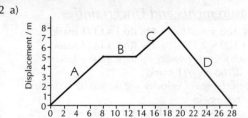

[4 marks — 1 mark for each section correctly drawn]

b) At A: $v = s \div t = 5 \div 8 = 0.625 = $ **0.6 ms⁻¹ (to 1 s.f.)**
At B: $v = $ **0 ms⁻¹**
At C: $v = 3 \div 5 = $ **0.6 ms⁻¹**
At D: $v = -8 \div 10 = $ **−0.8 ms⁻¹**
[2 marks for all correct or just 1 mark for 2 or 3 correct]

Page 25 — Velocity-Time and Acceleration-Time Graphs

1 a)

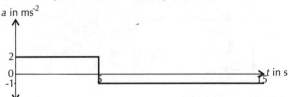

[1 mark for drawing a correctly labelled pair of axes, with a straight line between $v = 0$ ms⁻¹, $t = 0$ s and $v = 10$ ms⁻¹, $t = 5$ s. 1 mark for correctly drawing a straight line between $v = 10$ ms⁻¹, $t = 5$ s and $v = 0$ ms⁻¹, $t = 15$ s.]

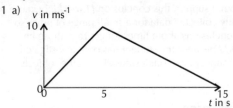

[1 mark for drawing a correctly labelled pair of axes, with a straight line between $a = 2$ ms⁻², $t = 0$ s and $a = 2$ ms⁻², $t = 5$ s. 1 mark for correctly drawing a straight line from $a = 2$ ms⁻², $t = 5$ s and $a = -1$ ms⁻², $t = 5$ s, and a straight line between $a = -1$ ms⁻², $t = 5$ s and $a = -1$ ms⁻², $t = 15$ s.]

b) Distance travelled is equal to the area under v-t graph between $t = 0$ and $t = 5$ *[1 mark]* $= 0.5 \times 5 \times 10 = $ **25 m** *[1 mark]*

Answers

Page 27 — Forces

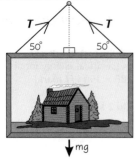

The picture is in equilibrium, so the forces are balanced.
Resolving vertically:
Weight = vertical component of tension × 2
$8 \times 9.81 = 2T \sin 50°$ *[1 mark]*
$78.48 = 0.7660... \times 2T$
$102.448... = 2T$
$T = 51.224... =$ **50 N (to 1 s.f.)** *[1 mark]*

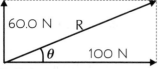

By Pythagoras:
$R = \sqrt{100^2 + 60.0^2} = 116.619... =$ **117 N (to 3 s.f.)** *[1 mark]*
$\tan \theta = (60.0 \div 100)$
so $\theta = \tan^{-1} 0.6 = 30.96... =$ **31.0° (to 3 s.f.)** *[1 mark]*

Page 29 — Newton's Laws of Motion

a) Force perpendicular to river flow = 500 − 100 = 400 N *[1 mark]*
Force parallel to river flow = 300 N
Resultant force = $\sqrt{400^2 + 300^2} =$ **500 N** *[1 mark]*
b) $\Sigma F = ma$ so $a = \Sigma F \div m = 500 \div 250 =$ **2 ms^{-2}** *[1 mark]*
B *[1 mark]*
The overall acceleration is a, so ma must be equal to the resultant force, which is the force John is pushing with minus the resistance caused by friction. So $F_{John} - F = ma$, and $F_{John} = ma + F$.
The only force acting on each of them is their weight = mg *[1 mark]*. Since $\Sigma F = ma$, this gives $ma = mg$, or $a = g$ *[1 mark]*. Their acceleration doesn't depend on their mass — it's the same for both of them — so they reach the water at the same time *[1 mark]*.

Page 31 — Drag and Terminal Velocity

1 a) The velocity increases at a steady rate, which means the acceleration is constant *[1 mark]*.
Constant acceleration means there must be no atmospheric resistance (atmospheric resistance would increase with velocity, leading to a decrease in acceleration). So there must be no atmosphere *[1 mark]*.
b)
[2 marks — 1 mark for drawing a graph that still starts from the origin, 1 mark for showing the graph curving to show the velocity increasing at a decreasing rate until the velocity is constant.]
Your graph must be a smooth curve which levels out. It must NOT go down at the end.
c) The graph becomes less steep because the acceleration is decreasing *[1 mark]* and because air resistance increases with speed *[1 mark]*. The graph levels out because air resistance has become equal to weight *[1 mark]*.
If the question says 'explain', you won't get marks for just describing what the graph shows — you have to say <u>why</u> it is that shape.

Page 33 — Momentum

1 a) total momentum before collision = total momentum after *[1 mark]*
$(0.60 \times 5.0) + 0 = (0.60 \times -2.4) + 2.0v$
$3 + 1.44 = 2v$ *[1 mark]*
So $v = 2.22 =$ **2.2 ms^{-1} (to 2 s.f.)** *[1 mark]*
b) $F = \dfrac{\Delta(mv)}{\Delta t} = \dfrac{(0.60 \times 5.0) - (0.60 \times -2.4)}{0.0055}$ *[1 mark]*
$= 807.27... =$ **800 N (to 2 s.f.)** *[1 mark]*
2 momentum before = momentum after *[1 mark]*
$(0.7 \times 0.3) + 0 = 1.1v \Rightarrow 0.21 = 1.1v$ *[1 mark]*
So: $v = 0.190... =$ **0.2 ms^{-1} (to 1 s.f.)** *[1 mark]*

Page 35 — Work and Power

1 a)
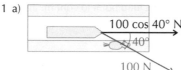

Force in direction of travel = $100 \cos 40° = 76.6...$ N *[1 mark]*
$\Delta W = F\Delta s = 76.6... \times 1500 = 114\,906...$
$= $ **100 000 J (to 1 s.f.)** *[1 mark]*
b) Use the equation for power:
$P = \dfrac{W}{t} = \dfrac{114\,906...}{31 \times 60}$ *[1 mark]*
$= 61.77... =$ **60 W (to 1 s.f.)** *[1 mark]*
2 a) Use $\Delta W = F\Delta s$
$\Delta W = 20.0 \times 9.81 \times 3.0$ *[1 mark]* $= 588.6$
$=$ **590 J (to 2 s.f.)** *[1 mark]*
Remember that 20.0 kg is not the force — it's the mass. So you need to multiply it by 9.81 Nkg^{-1} to get the weight.
b) First find the time taken to lift the load 3.0 m:
Use $v = \dfrac{\Delta s}{t}$ and rearrange for time:
$t = \dfrac{\Delta s}{v} = \dfrac{3.0}{0.25} = 12$ s *[1 mark]*
Substitute this into the equation for power:
$P = \dfrac{W}{t} = \dfrac{588.6}{12}$ *[1 mark]* $= 49.05 =$ **49 W (to 2 s.f.)** *[1 mark]*

Answers

Page 37 — Conservation of Energy and Efficiency

1 a) Use $E_k = \frac{1}{2}mv^2$ and $\Delta E_{grav} = mg\Delta h$ **[1 mark]**
$\frac{1}{2}mv^2 = mg\Delta h$
$\frac{1}{2}v^2 = g\Delta h$
$v^2 = 2g\Delta h = 2 \times 9.81 \times 2.0 = 39.24$ **[1 mark]**
$v = \sqrt{39.24} = 6.264... = $ **6.3 ms^{-1} (to 2 s.f.) [1 mark]**
'Negligible friction' allows you to assume that the changes in kinetic and potential energy will be the same.

b) 2.0 m — no friction means the kinetic energy will all change back into potential energy, so he will rise back up to the same height as he started **[1 mark]**.

c) Put in some more energy by actively 'skating' / 'pumping the board' **[1 mark]**.

2 a) If there's no air resistance, $E_k = \Delta E_{grav} = mg\Delta h$ **[1 mark]**
$E_k = 0.020 \times 9.81 \times 8.0 = 1.5696 = $ **1.6 J (to 2 s.f.) [1 mark]**

b) If the ball rebounds to 6.5 m, it has gained gravitational potential energy:
$\Delta E_{grav} = mg\Delta h = 0.020 \times 9.81 \times 6.5 = 1.2753$ J **[1 mark]**
So $1.5696 - 1.2753 = 0.2943 = $ **0.29 J (to 2 s.f.)** is converted to other forms **[1 mark]**.

You could also work out the loss of E_p from the difference in height —
$E_p = 0.020 \times 9.81 \times (8.0 - 6.5) = 0.29$ J (to 2 s.f.).

3 Use efficiency $= \dfrac{\text{useful output energy}}{\text{total input energy}}$
$= (140 - 65) \div 140 = 0.535... = $ **0.54 (to 2 s.f.) [1 mark]**

Page 39 — Mass, Weight and Centre of Gravity

1 B **[1 mark]**
$W = mg$, so $m = W/g = X/g$.

2 a) Hang the object freely from a point so that it hangs vertically. Hang a plumb bob from the same point, and use it to draw a vertical line down the object **[1 mark]**. Repeat for a different point and find the point of intersection **[1 mark]**.
The centre of gravity is halfway through the thickness of the object (by symmetry) at the point of intersection **[1 mark]**.

b) E.g. Source: the object and/or plumb line might move slightly while you're drawing the vertical line **[1 mark]**.
Reduced by: hang the object from a third point to confirm the position of the point of intersection **[1 mark]**.

Page 41 — Moments

1 Moment = force × distance
$60 = 0.40F$ **[1 mark]**, so $F = $ **150 N [1 mark]**

2 Clockwise moment = anticlockwise moment
$W \times 2.0 = T \times 0.3$
[1 mark for either line of working]
$60 \times 9.81 \times 2.0 = T \times 0.3$
$T = 3924 = $ **4000 N (to 1 s.f.) [1 mark]**
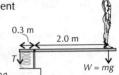
The moments caused by the tension in the spring and the force exerted by the diver on the spring are equal and opposite.

Topic 3 — Electric Circuits

Page 43 — Charge, Current and Potential Difference

1 Time in seconds $= 10 \times 60 = 600$ s
$I = \Delta Q / \Delta t = 4500 / 600 = 7.5 = $ **8 A (to 1 s.f.) [1 mark]**

2 Energy transferred to water $= 0.88 \times$ electrical energy input so the energy input will be $308 / 0.88 = 350$ J **[1 mark]**
$V = W/Q$ so $Q = W / V$
$Q = 350 \div 230 = 1.521... = $ **1.5 C (to 2 s.f.) [1 mark]**
The heat energy that the kettle transfers to the water is less than the electrical energy input because the kettle is less than 100% efficient.

3 $I = nqvA$ so $v = I / nqA$
so $v = 13 \div ((5.0 \times 10^{-6}) \times (1.0 \times 10^{29}) \times (1.60 \times 10^{-19}))$ **[1 mark]**
$= 1.625 \times 10^{-4} = $ **1.6 × 10^{-4} ms^{-1} (to 2 s.f.) [1 mark]**

Page 45 — Resistance and Resistivity

1 Area $= \pi r^2 = \pi (d/2)^2$ and $d = 1.0 \times 10^{-3}$ m
so area $= \pi \times (0.5 \times 10^{-3})^2 = 7.853... \times 10^{-7}$ m^2 **[1 mark]**
$R = \rho L / A = (2.8 \times 10^{-8} \times 4.0) \div 7.853... \times 10^{-7}$ **[1 mark]**
$= 0.1426... = $ **0.14 Ω (to 2 s.f.) [1 mark]**

2 a) $R = V / I = 7.00 \div (9.33 \times 10^{-3}) = 750.267...$
$= $ **750 Ω (to 3 s.f.) [1 mark]**

b) For $V = 3.00$ V, $R = 3.00 \div (4.00 \times 10^{-3}) = 750$ Ω
for $V = 11.00$ V, $R = 11.00 \div (14.67 \times 10^{-3}) = 749.82...$ Ω **[1 mark]**
The component is an ohmic conductor (for the range considered) **[1 mark]**, because there is no significant change in resistance for different potential differences **[1 mark]**.

Page 47 — I-V Characteristics

1 a)
Current / A

P.d. / V

[1 mark]

b) E.g. Increasing the voltage increases the current, which increases the temperature of the filament bulb **[1 mark]**. This causes the ion lattice in the wire filament to vibrate more, causing the charge carrying electrons to collide with it more frequently, reducing their kinetic energy and thus their mean drift velocity **[1 mark]**. As current is proportional to mean drift velocity **[1 mark]**, this reduces the current for a given potential difference, thus increases the filament bulb's resistance **[1 mark]**.

c) A temperature increase releases more charge carriers as more electrons have energy to escape their atoms **[1 mark]**. An increase in charge carriers means the current will also increase ($I = nqvA$) **[1 mark]**. As a result, the resistance will decrease (because $R = V/I$) **[1 mark]**.
Remember, even though increasing the temperature increases the vibration of the lattice making it harder for the current to flow, this effect is dwarfed by the release of more charge carriers.

Answers

Page 49 — Electrical Energy and Power

a) $I = P / V = 920 \div 230 = \textbf{4.0 A}$ *[1 mark]*
b) $I = V / R = 230 \div 190 = 1.210... = \textbf{1.2 A (to 2 s.f.)}$ *[1 mark]*
c) $P_{motor} = VI = 230 \times 1.210... = 278.421...$ W *[1 mark]*
Total power = motor power + heater power
$= 278.421... + 920 = 1198.421...$ W $= \textbf{1.2 kW (to 2 s.f.)}$
[1 mark]
You could also answer this question by calculating using
$P_{total} = V_{total}I_{total}$ where $V_{total} = 230$ V (the source p.d.) and
$I_{total} = 4.00 + 1.210...$ A.
a) Energy transferred $= W = VIt = 12 \times 48 \times 2.0$
$= 1152 = \textbf{1200 J (to 2 s.f.)}$ *[1 mark]*
b) Energy wasted in wires $= W = I^2Rt = 48^2 \times 0.010 \times 2.0 = 46.08$
$= \textbf{46 J (to 2 s.f.)}$ *[1 mark]*

Page 51 — E.m.f. and Internal Resistance

a) $\varepsilon = I (R + r)$ so $I = \varepsilon / (R + r)$
$= 24 / (4.0 + 0.8) = \textbf{5 A}$ *[1 mark]*
b) $V = IR = 5 \times 4.0 = \textbf{20 V}$ *[1 mark]*
You could also have used $\varepsilon = V + Ir$.
C *[1 mark]*
$\varepsilon = I(R + r)$, but since there are two cells in series replace r with $2r$, and ε
with 2ε, then rearrange to find I.

Page 53 — Conservation of Charge & Energy in Circuits

a) Resistance of parallel resistors:
$1/R_{parallel} = 1/6.0 + 1/3.0 = 1/2$
$R_{parallel} = 2.0\,\Omega$ *[1 mark]*
Total resistance:
$R_{total} = 4.0 + R_{parallel} = 4.0 + 2.0 = \textbf{6.0}\,\Omega$ *[1 mark]*
b) $V = I_3R_{total}$ so rearranging $I_3 = V / R_{total} = 12 / 6.0$
$= \textbf{2.0 A}$ *[1 mark]*
c) $V = IR = 2.0 \times 4.0 = \textbf{8.0 V}$ *[1 mark]*
d) E.m.f. = sum of p.d.s in circuit, so $12 = 8.0 + V_{parallel}$
$V_{parallel} = 12 - 8.0 = \textbf{4.0 V}$ *[1 mark]*
e) $I = V/R$, so
$I_1 = 4.0 / 3.0 = \textbf{1.3 A (to 2 s.f.)}$ *[1 mark]*
$I_2 = 4.0 / 6.0 = \textbf{0.67 A (to 2 s.f.)}$ *[1 mark]*
You can check your answers by making sure that $I_3 = I_2 + I_1$.

Page 55 — The Potential Divider

Parallel circuit, so p.d. across both sets of resistors is 12 V.
a) There are two equal resistors in the top branch of the circuit. The
p.d. between points A and B is equal to the potential difference
across one of these resistors:
$V_{AB} = \frac{1}{2} \times 12 = \textbf{6.0 V}$ *[1 mark]*
b) There are three equal resistors in the bottom branch of the
circuit. The p.d. between points A and C is equal to the potential
difference across two of them:
$V_{AC} = \frac{2}{3} \times 12 = \textbf{8.0 V}$ *[1 mark]*
c) $V_{BC} = V_{AC} - V_{AB} = 8 - 6 = \textbf{2.0 V}$ *[1 mark]*
a) $V_{AB} = 50/80 \times 12 = \textbf{7.5 V}$ *[1 mark]*
(ignore the 10 Ω — no current flows that way)
b) Total resistance of the parallel circuit:
$1/R_T = 1/50 + 1/(10 + 40.0) = 1/25 \Rightarrow R_T = \textbf{25}\,\Omega$ *[1 mark]*
p.d. over the whole parallel arrangement = 25/55 × 12 = 5.45... V
[1 mark]
p.d. across AB = 40.0/50 × 5.45...
= 4.36... V = **4.4 V (to 2 s.f.)** *[1 mark]*
current through 40.0 Ω resistor = V/R
= 4.36.../40.0 = **0.11 A (to 2 s.f.)** *[1 mark]*

Topic 4 — Materials

Page 57 — Hooke's Law

1 a) Force is proportional to extension. The force is 1.5 times as great,
so the new extension will also be 1.5 times the original extension.
new extension = 1.5 × 4.0 mm = **6.0 mm** *[1 mark]*
b) $\Delta F = k\Delta x$ and so $k = \Delta F/\Delta x$
$k = 10.0 \div (4.0 \times 10^{-3}) = \textbf{2500 Nm}^{-1}$ or **2.5 Nmm^{-1}** *[1 mark]*
c) Any one from e.g. the string now stretches much further for small
increases in force *[1 mark]*. / When the string is loosened it is
longer than at the start *[1 mark]*.
2 The rubber band does not obey Hooke's law *[1 mark]* because
when the force is doubled from 2.5 N to 5.0 N, the extension
increases by a factor of 2.3. *[1 mark]*.
Or you could show that k is different for 2.5 N and 5.0 N.

Page 59 — Stress, Strain and Elastic Strain Energy

1 a) Area $= \pi r^2$ or $\pi\left(\frac{d}{2}\right)^2$
So area $= \pi \times \frac{(1.0 \times 10^{-3})^2}{4} = 7.853... \times 10^{-7}$ *[1 mark]*
Stress, $\sigma = \frac{F}{A} = 300 \div (7.853... \times 10^{-7}) = 3.819... \times 10^8$
$= \textbf{3.8} \times \textbf{10}^8$ **Nm^{-2} (or Pa) (to 2 s.f.)** *[1 mark]*
b) Strain, $\varepsilon = \frac{\Delta x}{x}$
$= (4.0 \times 10^{-3}) \div 2.00 = \textbf{2.0} \times \textbf{10}^{-3}$ *[1 mark]*
2 a) $\Delta F = k\Delta x$ and so rearranging $k = \Delta F \div \Delta x$ *[1 mark]*
$k = 50.0 \div (3.0 \times 10^{-3}) = 1.666... \times 10^4$
$= \textbf{1.7} \times \textbf{10}^4$ **Nm^{-1} (to 2 s.f.)** *[1 mark]*
b) Elastic strain energy, $\Delta E_{el} = \frac{1}{2}F\Delta x$
$= \frac{1}{2} \times 50.0 \times (3.0 \times 10^{-3})$
$= \textbf{7.5} \times \textbf{10}^{-2}$ **J** *[1 mark]*
You could also use $\Delta E_{el} = \frac{1}{2}k\Delta x^2$ and substitute in your value of k.

3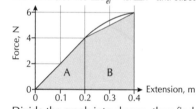

Divide the graph into shapes, then find the area of each:
Area A = 0.5 × base × height = 0.5 × 0.2 × 4 = 0.4 J
Area B = 0.5 × (a + b) × h = 0.5 × (4 + 6) × 0.2 = 1 J
*[1 mark for sensibly splitting the area under the graph up and
correctly calculating at least one of these areas]*
Total elastic strain energy stored = 0.4 + 1
= **1.4 J** *[1 mark]*
Shape B is a trapezium. The area of a trapezium is given by
$A = \frac{1}{2}(a + b) \times h$, where a is the length of the first side, b is the length
of the second side and h is the width of the strip. You won't be given
this formula in your exam, so if you get stuck you can always break the
trapeziums up into rectangles and triangles.
You could also calculate this area by estimating the number of grid squares
the area under the graph covers. The area of each grid square is equal to
2 × 0.1 = 0.2 J. There are approximately 7 grid squares under the graph,
so the total energy stored is approximately 7 × 0.2 = 1.4 J.
4 The force needed to compress the spring is:
$\Delta F = k\Delta x = 40.8 \times 0.05 = 2.04$ N *[1 mark]*
The elastic strain energy in the spring is then:
$E = \frac{1}{2}F\Delta x = \frac{1}{2} \times 2.04 \times 0.05 = 0.051$ J *[1 mark]*
Assume all this energy is converted to kinetic energy in the ball.
$E = E_{kinetic} = \textbf{0.051 J}$ *[1 mark]*.
You could also begin by using Hooke's law to replace F in the formula for
elastic strain energy, to give $\Delta E_{el} = \frac{1}{2}k\Delta x^2$, and then substituting into this.

Answers

Page 61 — The Young Modulus

1   Cross-sectional area $= \pi r^2$ or $\pi\left(\frac{d}{2}\right)^2$

So area $= \pi \times \frac{(0.60 \times 10^{-3})^2}{4} = 2.827... \times 10^{-7}$ m^2 *[1 mark]*

Stress, $\sigma = \frac{F}{A} = 80.0 \div (2.827... \times 10^{-7})$

$= 2.829... \times 10^8$ Nm^{-2} *[1 mark]*

Strain, $\varepsilon = \frac{\Delta x}{x} = (3.6 \times 10^{-3}) \div 2.50$

$= 1.44 \times 10^{-3}$ *[1 mark]*

Young modulus, $E = \frac{\sigma}{\varepsilon} = (2.829... \times 10^8) \div (1.44 \times 10^{-3})$

$= 1.964... \times 10^{11}$

$= \textbf{2.0} \times \textbf{10}^{\textbf{11}}$ **Nm^{-2} (to 2 s.f.)** *[1 mark]*

2   $E = \frac{\sigma}{\varepsilon} = \frac{F}{A} \div \frac{\Delta x}{x} = \frac{Fx}{\Delta x A}$. Force, original length and extension are
the same for both wires, so $E \propto \frac{1}{A}$.
The wire B has half the cross-sectional area of the wire A. So the
Young modulus of wire B (E_B) must be twice that of the wire A
[1 mark].
$E_B = 2 \times (7.0 \times 10^{10}) = \textbf{1.4} \times \textbf{10}^{\textbf{11}}$ **Nm^{-2}** *[1 mark]*

3 a) Young modulus, $E = \frac{\sigma}{\varepsilon}$

$\varepsilon = \frac{\sigma}{E} = (2.6 \times 10^8) \div (1.3 \times 10^{11})$ *[1 mark]*

$= \textbf{2.0} \times \textbf{10}^{\textbf{-3}}$ *[1 mark]*

b) $\sigma = \frac{F}{A}$ and so $A = \frac{F}{\sigma} = 100 \div (2.6 \times 10^8)$ *[1 mark]*

$= 3.846... \times 10^{-7}$

$= \textbf{3.8} \times \textbf{10}^{\textbf{-7}}$ **m^2 (to 2 s.f.)** *[1 mark]*

c) Strain energy per unit volume

$= \frac{1}{2} \times \sigma \times \varepsilon = \frac{1}{2} \times (2.6 \times 10^8) \times (2.0 \times 10^{-3})$ *[1 mark]*

$= \textbf{2.6} \times \textbf{10}^{\textbf{5}}$ **Jm^{-3}** *[1 mark]*

Give the mark if answer is consistent with the value calculated for strain in
part a).

Page 63 — Stress-Strain and Force-Extension Graphs

1   E.g.

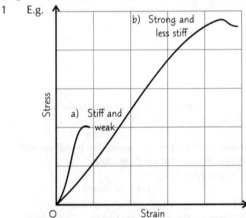

*[1 mark for a stiff and weak curve that stops at a low stress and a
low strain. 1 mark for a strong and less stiff curve that stops at a
high stress and a high strain]*

2 a) Yield stress = 900 MNm^{-2} *[1 mark]*

b) Energy per unit volume = area under the graph
Limit of proportionality = 800 MNm^{-2} *[1 mark]*

$= (800 \times 0.2) \div 2 = \textbf{80 MJm}^{\textbf{-3}}$ **(or 8 $\times$ 10^7 J m^{-3})** *[1 mark]*

Page 65 — Density, Upthrust and Viscosity

1 a) Stokes's law gives viscous drag, $F = 6\pi\eta rv$, where η is the viscosity
of the fluid (Nsm^{-2} or Pas), r is the radius of the object (m) and v is
the speed the object is moving at (ms^{-1}) *[1 mark]*.

b) Any three of: The object moving through the fluid must be small
[1 mark] / spherical *[1 mark]* / moving through the fluid with
laminar flow *[1 mark]* / moving slowly through the fluid *[1 mark]*

c) Weight – drag – upthrust = 0 *[1 mark]*
So you can work out the weight by calculating the drag and
upthrust acting on the ball bearing.
Upthrust = weight of fluid displaced $= m_{liquid} \times g$

$m_{liquid} = \rho_{liquid} \times V_{liquid}$

$= 1400 \times \frac{4}{3}\pi (3.0 \times 10^{-3})^3 = 1.583... \times 10^{-4}$ kg *[1 mark]*

So upthrust $= m_{liquid} \times g = 1.583... \times 10^{-4} \times 9.81$

$= 1.553... \times 10^{-3}$ N *[1 mark]*

Drag $= F = 6\pi\eta rv = 6\pi \times 3.0 \times (3.0 \times 10^{-3}) \times 0.040$

$= 6.785... \times 10^{-3}...$ N *[1 mark]*

So weight $= (1.553... \times 10^{-3}) + (6.785... \times 10^{-3}) = 8.339... \times 10^{-3}$

$= \textbf{8.4} \times \textbf{10}^{\textbf{-3}}$ **N (to 2 s.f.)** *[1 mark]*

Topic 5 — Waves and Particle Nature of Light

Page 67 — The Nature of Waves

1 a) The gain is set to 2.0 volts/div and the trace
has a maximum amplitude of 2 divisions.
So, the maximum voltage $= 2 \times 2.0 = \textbf{4.0 V}$ *[1 mark]*

b) One cycle spans 3 divisions, so
$T = 3 \times 3.0$ ms = 9.0 ms = 9.0×10^{-3} s *[1 mark]*
$f = 1/T = 1/9.0 \times 10^{-3}$ *[1 mark]*
$f = 111.1... = \textbf{110 Hz}$ **(to 2 s.f.)** *[1 mark]*
$v = f\lambda$ so $\lambda = v/f$
$\lambda = 280/111.1...$ *[1 mark]*
$\lambda = 2.52$ m = $\textbf{2.5 m}$ **(to 2 s.f.)** *[1 mark]*

Page 69 — Types of Wave

1 a) $I = P \div A = 10.0 \div 0.002 = \textbf{5000 Wm}^{\textbf{-2}}$ *[1 mark]*

b) D *[1 mark]*

Page 71 — Polarisation of Waves

1 a) They are at right angles to one another (90°, 270° etc.) *[1 mark]*.

b) It would be half of the intensity of the original light *[1 mark]*.
This is because at 45° the vertical and horizontal contributions are equal, so
the intensity is halved between them.

Page 73 — Ultrasound Imaging

E.g. A transducer is used to send pulses of ultrasound waves into the patient's body *[1 mark]*. Waves are partially reflected and partially transmitted when they meet an interface, with the proportion reflected increasing with the difference in density between the media *[1 mark]*. A gel is put on the patient's skin with a similar density to tissue, to increase the amount of ultrasound transmitted into the patient's body *[1 mark]*. When the ultrasound waves meet an interface in the patient's body, for example between different tissues, some of the ultrasound waves are reflected back, which are then detected by the transducer *[1 mark]*. From the time taken for the signals to return, a computer attached to the transducer can work out the location of different tissue boundaries, and build up an image of inside the patient's body *[1 mark]*.

a) Sound waves with short wavelengths diffract less than sounds waves with long wavelengths *[1 mark]*. So decreasing the wavelength means that the waves spread out less, which improves the precision of the location of tissue surfaces *[1 mark]*. This means the image produced is of a higher quality *[1 mark]*.

b) The shorter the pulse length, the less likely it is that a reflected ultrasound wave will reach the transducer whilst it is still transmitting the pulse *[1 mark]*. The transducer cannot receive the reflected waves whilst it is transmitting, so if this did happen, data would be lost *[1 mark]*. A longer time between the pulses means a reflected ultrasound wave is less likely to reach the transducer after it has transmitted the next pulse *[1 mark]*. If this did happen, the computer would not be able to distinguish which transmitted wave corresponded with which reflected wave, and so image quality would be lost *[1 mark]*.

Page 75 — Superposition and Coherence

a) The frequencies and wavelengths of the two sources must be equal *[1 mark]* and the phase difference must be constant *[1 mark]*.

b) Interference will only be noticeable if the amplitudes of the two waves are approximately equal *[1 mark]*.

B *[1 mark]*

Page 77 — Stationary (Standing) Waves

Rearrange $v = \sqrt{\frac{T}{\mu}}$ for μ:

$\mu = \frac{T}{v^2} = \frac{3.2}{16^2} = 0.0125$ kgm^{-1} *[1 mark]*

$\mu = \frac{M}{l}$, so $M = \mu l = 0.0125 \times 2.8 = $ **0.035 kg** (= 35 g) *[1 mark]*

a) The length of the string for a stationary wave oscillating at its first harmonic frequency is half the wavelength of the wave *[1 mark]*, so $\lambda = 2 \times 1.2 = $ **2.4 m** *[1 mark]*.

b) $f_{new} = \frac{1}{2l}\sqrt{\frac{2T}{\mu}} = \sqrt{2} \times \left(\frac{1}{2l}\sqrt{\frac{T}{\mu}}\right) = \sqrt{2} \times f_{original}$ *[1 mark]*

$f_{new} = \sqrt{2} \times 10$ *[1 mark]* = 14.142...
= **14 Hz (to 2 s.f.)** *[1 mark]*

c) When the string forms a standing wave, its amplitude varies from a maximum at the antinodes to zero at the nodes *[1 mark]*. In a progressive wave all the points vibrate at the same amplitude *[1 mark]*.

Page 79 — Refractive Index

1 a) $n_{diamond} = c / v = (3.00 \times 10^8) / (1.24 \times 10^8) = 2.419...$
= **2.42 (to 3 s.f.)** *[1 mark]*

b) $n_{air} \sin \theta_1 = n_{diamond} \sin \theta_2$, $n_{air} = 1$
So, $n_{diamond} = \sin \theta_1 / \sin \theta_2$ *[1 mark]*
$\sin \theta_2 = \sin 50 / 2.419... = 0.316...$
$\theta_2 = \sin^{-1}(0.316...) = 18.459... = $ **18.5° (to 3 s.f.)** *[1 mark]*
You can assume the refractive index of air is 1, and don't forget to write the degree sign in your answer.

2 a) When the light is pointing steeply upwards some of it is refracted and some reflected — the beam emerging from the surface is the refracted part *[1 mark]*.
However when the beam hits the surface at more than the critical angle (to the normal to the boundary) refraction does not occur. All the beam is totally internally reflected to light the tank, hence its brightness *[1 mark]*.

b) The critical angle is 90° – 41.25° = 48.75° *[1 mark]*.
$n_{water} = 1 / \sin C$
= 1 / sin 48.75°
= 1 / 0.7518... = 1.3300... = **1.330 (to 4 s.f.)** *[1 mark]*
The question talks about the angle between the light beam and the floor of the aquarium. This angle is 90° minus the incident angle — measured from a normal to the surface of the water.

Page 81 — Lenses

1 a) Rays meeting the lens parallel to the principal axis converge at the principle focus. *[1 mark]*

b) $\frac{1}{v} = -\frac{1}{u} + \frac{1}{f}$ so $\frac{1}{v} = -\frac{1}{0.2} + \frac{1}{0.15} = \frac{5}{3}$ *[1 mark]*,
so $v = \frac{3}{5} = $ **0.6 m** *[1 mark]*

2 a) $m = \frac{\text{size of image}}{\text{size of object}} = \frac{47.2}{12.5} = 3.776 = $ **3.78 (to 3 s.f.)** *[1 mark]*

b) $m = \frac{v}{u}$, giving $v = m \times u$ *[1 mark]*
$v = 3.776 \times 4.0 = 15.104 = $ **15 mm (to 2 s.f.)** *[1 mark]*

c) $P = \frac{1}{f} = \frac{1}{u} + \frac{1}{v}$ *[1 mark]*, so $P = \frac{1}{0.004} + \frac{1}{0.015104} = 316.20...$
= **320 D (to 2 s.f.)** *[1 mark]*

d) $P_{total} = \frac{1}{f} = \frac{1}{0.0022} = 454.5...$ D *[1 mark]*
Rearrange $P_{total} = P_1 + P_2$ to give:
$P_2 = P_{total} - P_1 = 454.5... - 316.20... = 138.33...$
= **140 D (to 2 s.f.)** *[1 mark]*

Answers

Page 83 — Diffraction

1   When a wavefront meets an obstacle, the waves will diffract round the corners of the obstacle. When the obstacle is much bigger than the wavelength, little diffraction occurs. In this case, the mountain is much bigger than the wavelength of short-wave radio. So the "shadow" where you cannot pick up short wave is very long *[1 mark]*.

[1 mark]

When the obstacle is comparable in size to the wavelength, as it is for the long-wave radio waves, more diffraction occurs. The wavefront re-forms after a shorter distance, leaving a shorter "shadow" *[1 mark]*.

2   E.g. Set up a ripple tank, using an oscillating paddle to create straight, parallel waves. Place two objects into the water, creating a barrier with a gap in the middle *[1 mark]*. Vary the sizes of the objects to increase and decrease the gap width. Observe the amount of diffraction of the water waves as the gap width varies *[1 mark]*. The most diffraction will be seen when the gap is roughly the same size as the wavelength of the water waves *[1 mark]*.

Page 85 — Diffraction Gratings

1 a) Use $\sin \theta = n\lambda / d$
    For the first order, $n = 1$
    So, $\sin \theta = \lambda / d$ *[1 mark]*
    No need to actually work out d. The number of lines per metre is 1 / d.
    So you can simply multiply the wavelength by that.
    $\sin \theta = 6.00 \times 10^{-7} \times 4.0 \times 10^5 = 0.24$
    $\theta = \sin^{-1}(0.24) = 13.8865... = $ **14° (to 2 s.f.)** *[1 mark]*
    For the second order, $n = 2$ and $\sin \theta = 2\lambda / d$. *[1 mark]*
    You already have a value for λ / d. Just double it to get sin θ for the second order.
    $\sin \theta = 0.48$
    $\theta = \sin^{-1}(0.48) = 28.685... = $ **29° (to 2 s.f.)** *[1 mark]*

  b) No. Putting $n = 5$ into the equation gives a value of $\sin \theta$ of 1.2, which is impossible *[1 mark]*.

2   $\sin \theta = n\lambda / d$, so for the 1st order maximum, $\sin \theta = \lambda / d$
    $\sin 14.2° = \lambda \times 3.70 \times 10^5$ *[1 mark]*
    $\lambda = $ **663 nm (or 6.63×10^{-7} m) (to 3 s.f.)** *[1 mark]*.

Page 87 — Light — Wave or Photon?

1 a) i) E (eV) $= V = 12.1$ eV *[1 mark]*
    ii) E (J) $= E$ (eV) $\times (1.60 \times 10^{-19}) = 12.1 \times (1.60 \times 10^{-19})$
          $= $ **1.94×10^{-18} J (to 3 s.f.)** *[1 mark]*

  b) i) The movement of an electron from a lower energy level to a higher energy level by absorbing energy *[1 mark]*.
    ii) $-13.6 + 12.1 = -1.5$ eV. This corresponds to $n = 3$ *[1 mark]*.
    iii) $n = 3 \rightarrow n = 2$: $-1.5 - (-3.4) = $ **1.9 eV** *[1 mark]*

    $E = hf$, so $f = \dfrac{E}{h} = \dfrac{1.9 \times 1.60 \times 10^{-19}}{6.63 \times 10^{-34}} = 4.5852... \times 10^{14}$ Hz
               $= $ **4.6×10^{14} Hz (to 2 s.f.)** *[1 mark]*
    $n = 2 \rightarrow n = 1$: $-3.4 - (-13.6) = 10.2$ eV
                      $= $ **10 eV (to 2 s.f.)** *[1 mark]*

    $f = \dfrac{E}{h} = \dfrac{10.2 \times 1.60 \times 10^{-19}}{6.63 \times 10^{-34}}$
        $= 2.4615... \times 10^{15}$ Hz
        $= $ **2.5×10^{15} Hz (to 2 s.f.)** *[1 mark]*
    $n = 3 \rightarrow n = 1$: $-1.5 - (-13.6) = 12.1$
                  $= $ **12 eV (to 2 s.f.)** *[1 mark]*

    $f = \dfrac{E}{h} = \dfrac{12.1 \times 1.60 \times 10^{-19}}{6.63 \times 10^{-34}}$
        $= 2.9200... \times 10^{15}$ Hz
        $= $ **2.9×10^{15} Hz (to 2 s.f.)** *[1 mark]*

Page 89 — The Photoelectric Effect

1   $\phi = 2.9$ eV $= 2.9 \times (1.60 \times 10^{-19})$ J $= 4.64 \times 10^{-19}$ J *[1 mark]*
    $f = \dfrac{\phi}{h} = \dfrac{4.64 \times 10^{-19}}{6.63 \times 10^{-34}} = 6.99... \times 10^{14}$
    $= $ **7.0×10^{14} Hz (to 2 s.f.)** *[1 mark]*

2 a) $E = hf$
       $= (6.63 \times 10^{-34}) \times (2.0 \times 10^{15}) = 1.326 \times 10^{-18}$ J *[1 mark]*
    1.326×10^{-18} J $= \dfrac{1.326 \times 10^{-18}}{1.60 \times 10^{-19}}$ eV
                  $= 8.2875 = $ **8.3 eV (to 2 s.f.)** *[1 mark]*

  b) $hf = \phi + \frac{1}{2}mv^2$, where $\frac{1}{2}mv^2$ is the maximum kinetic energy, so this can rearranged to give:
    $E_{k \, (max)} = hf - \phi$
            $= 8.2875 - 4.7 = 3.5875$ *[1 mark]*
            $= $ **3.6 eV (to 2 s.f.)** (or 5.7×10^{-19} J to 2 s.f.) *[1 mark]*

3   An electron needs to gain a certain amount of energy (the work function energy) from one photon before it can leave the surface of the metal *[1 mark]*.
    If the energy carried by each photon is less than this work function energy, no electrons will be emitted *[1 mark]*.

Page 91 — Wave-Particle Duality

a) Electromagnetic radiation can show characteristics of both particles and waves *[1 mark]*.

b) $\lambda = \frac{h}{p}$

so $p = \frac{h}{\lambda}$ *[1 mark]*

$= \frac{6.63 \times 10^{-34}}{590 \times 10^{-9}} = 1.123... \times 10^{-27}$

$= \mathbf{1.1 \times 10^{-27}\ kg\,ms^{-1}}$ **(to 2 s.f.)** *[1 mark]*

a) $\lambda = \frac{h}{p} = \frac{h}{mv}$

$\lambda = \frac{6.63 \times 10^{-34}}{9.11 \times 10^{-31} \times 3.50 \times 10^{6}}$ *[1 mark]*

$= 2.079... \times 10^{-10}$

$= \mathbf{2.08 \times 10^{-10}\ m}$ **(to 3 s.f.)** *[1 mark]*

b) Either $\lambda = \frac{h}{p} = \frac{h}{mv}$

So $v = \frac{h}{m\lambda} = \frac{6.63 \times 10^{-34}}{1.673 \times 10^{-27} \times 2.079... \times 10^{-10}}$ *[1 mark]*

$= 1905.85... = \mathbf{1910\ ms^{-1}}$ **(to 3 s.f.)** *[1 mark]*

Or momentum of protons = momentum of electrons

so $m_p \times v_p = m_e \times v_e$

$v_p = v_e \times \frac{m_e}{m_p} = 3.50 \times 10^{6} \times \frac{9.11 \times 10^{-31}}{1.673 \times 10^{-27}}$ *[1 mark]*

$= 1905.85... = \mathbf{1910\ ms^{-1}}$ **(to 3 s.f.)** *[1 mark]*

c) The proton has a larger mass, so it will have a smaller speed, since the two have the same kinetic energy *[1 mark]*. Kinetic energy is proportional to the square of the speed, while momentum is proportional to the speed, so they will have different momenta *[1 mark]*. Wavelength depends on the momentum, so the wavelengths are different *[1 mark]*.

This is a really hard question. If you didn't get it right, make sure you understand the answer fully. Do the algebra if it helps.

B *[1 mark]*

Topic 6 — Further Mechanics

Page 93 — Momentum and 2D Collisions

total momentum before collision = total momentum after

$(0.145 \times 1.94) + 0 = (0.145 \times -0.010) + 0.148v$ *[1 mark]*

$0.2813 + 0.00145 = 0.148v$, so $v = 1.910...$

$= \mathbf{1.9\ ms^{-1}}$ **(to 2 s.f.)** *[1 mark]*

Resolving all the velocities in the horizontal direction:

Total momentum before

$= (1.00 \times 1.20 \times \cos 20) + (m_B \times 3.50 \times \cos 30)$

Total momentum after

$= (1.00 \times 6.21 \times \cos 45) + (m_B \times 1.54 \times \cos 25)$

Put these equations equal to each other and rearrange so that all terms with m_B are on one side:

$(m_B \times 3.50 \times \cos 30) - (m_B \times 1.54 \times \cos 25)$

$= (1.00 \times 6.21 \times \cos 45) - (1.00 \times 1.20 \times \cos 20)$ *[1 mark]*

Take out a factor of m_B on the left hand side and rearrange:

$m_B = \frac{(1.00 \times 6.21 \times \cos 45) - (1.00 \times 1.20 \times \cos 20)}{(3.50 \times \cos 30) - (1.54 \times \cos 25)}$

$= 1.9955...$

$= \mathbf{2.0\ kg}$ **(to 2 s.f.)** *[1 mark]*

You can also do this question by resolving the velocities in the vertical direction. Be careful if you do though — you'll need to pick either vertically up or vertically down to be the negative direction.

Page 95 — Force, Impulse and Energy

1 $F\Delta t = \Delta p$ so $F\Delta t = m\Delta v$

rearrange to find m:

$m = \frac{F\Delta t}{\Delta v} = (9.8 \times 0.47) \div 29$ *[1 mark]*

$= 0.1588 = \mathbf{0.16\ kg}$ **(to 2 s.f.)** *[1 mark]*

2 a) $E_k = \frac{p^2}{2m} = \frac{16\,000^2}{2 \times 12\,000} = 10\,666.6... = \mathbf{11\,000\ J}$ **(to 2 s.f.)** *[1 mark]*

b) total momentum before = total momentum after

$16\,000 = (12\,000 + 15\,000)v$ *[1 mark]*

So $v = 16\,000 \div 27\,000 = 0.592... = \mathbf{0.59\ ms^{-1}}$ **(to 2 s.f.)** *[1 mark]*

c) To answer this question, you must first calculate the kinetic energy after the collision:

$E_k = \frac{1}{2}mv^2 = 0.5 \times 27\,000 \times (0.592...)^2 = 4740.74...\ J$ *[1 mark]*

The collision is inelastic, as the total kinetic energy after the collision is less than the total kinetic energy before it *[1 mark]*.

Page 97 — Circular Motion

1 a) $\omega = \frac{\theta}{t}$, so $\omega = \frac{2\pi}{3.2 \times 10^{7}}$ *[1 mark]*

$= 1.9634... \times 10^{-7}$

$= \mathbf{2.0 \times 10^{-7}\ rad\ s^{-1}}$ **(to 2 s.f.)** *[1 mark]*

b) $v = \omega r = 1.9634... \times 10^{-7} \times 1.5 \times 10^{11}$ *[1 mark]*

$= 2.9452... \times 10^{4}$

$= \mathbf{2.9 \times 10^{4}\ ms^{-1}}$ **(to 2 s.f.)** *[1 mark]*

c) $F = mr\omega^2 = 6.0 \times 10^{24} \times 1.5 \times 10^{11} \times (1.9634... \times 10^{-7})^2$ *[1 mark]*

$= 3.4697... \times 10^{22}$

$= \mathbf{3.5 \times 10^{22}\ N}$ **(to 2 s.f.)** *[1 mark]*

d) Towards the Sun *[1 mark]*

2 a) $a = v^2 \div r = 15^2 \div 12 = 18.75 = \mathbf{19\ ms^{-2}}$ **(to 2 s.f.)** *[1 mark]*

b) Since $a = \omega^2 r$, $\omega^2 = \frac{a}{r} = \frac{18.75}{12}$,

so $\omega = 1.25 = \mathbf{1.3\ rad\ s^{-1}}$ **(to 2 s.f.)** *[1 mark]*

$\omega = 2\pi \div T$, so $T = 2\pi \div \omega = 5.026... = \mathbf{5.0\ s}$ **(to 2 s.f.)** *[1 mark]*

Topic 7 — Electric and Magnetic Fields

Page 100 — Electric Fields

1 Charge on alpha particle, $Q_1 = +2e = 2 \times 1.60 \times 10^{-19}$

$= 3.20 \times 10^{-19}\ C$

Charge on gold nucleus, $Q_2 = +79e = 79 \times 1.60 \times 10^{-19}\ C$

$= 1.264 \times 10^{-17}\ C$ *[1 mark for both]*

$F = \frac{1}{4\pi\varepsilon_0} \frac{Q_1 Q_2}{r^2} = \frac{1}{4\pi\varepsilon_0} \frac{3.20 \times 10^{-19} \times 1.264 \times 10^{-17}}{(5.0 \times 10^{-12})^2}$ *[1 mark]*

$= 1.4548... \times 10^{-3} = \mathbf{1.5 \times 10^{-3}\ N}$ **(to 2 s.f.)** *[1 mark]*

The force is directed away from the gold nucleus *[1 mark]*

2 a) $E = V/d = 1500/(4.5 \times 10^{-3}) = 3.33... \times 10^{5}$

$= \mathbf{3.3 \times 10^{5}\ Vm^{-1}}$ **(to 2 s.f.)** *[1 mark]*

The field is perpendicular to the plates *[1 mark]*.

b) $d = 2 \times (4.5 \times 10^{-3}) = 9.0 \times 10^{-3}\ m$

$E = V/d \Rightarrow V = Ed = 3.33... \times 10^{5} \times 9 \times 10^{-3} = \mathbf{3000\ V}$ *[1 mark]*

Answers

Page 103 — Capacitors

1 a) $W = \frac{\frac{1}{2}Q^2}{C} = \frac{\frac{1}{2}(1.5 \times 10^{-6})^2}{250 \times 10^{-6}} = \mathbf{4.5 \times 10^{-9}}$ **J** *[1 mark]*

b) $W = \frac{1}{2}QV$ so $V = \frac{2W}{Q} = \frac{2 \times 4.5 \times 10^{-9}}{1.5 \times 10^{-6}}$ *[1 mark]*
$= 6.0 \times 10^{-3} = \mathbf{6.0}$ **mV** *[1 mark]*

You could also use $V = Q/C$ to answer this question.

c)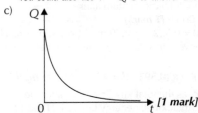
[1 mark]

2 The current decreases exponentially because as charge builds on the plates of the capacitor, it becomes harder and harder to overcome the electrostatic repulsion and deposit electrons onto the plate *[1 mark]*.

3 C *[1 mark]*
From $W = \frac{1}{2}CV^2$, as the potential difference doubles, the energy stored will quadruple.

Page 105 — Discharging Capacitors

1 a) The charge falls to 37% after RC seconds *[1 mark]*,
so $\tau = 1000 \times 2.5 \times 10^{-4} = \mathbf{0.25}$ **seconds** *[1 mark]*

b) $Q = Q_0 e^{-t/RC}$, so after 0.7 seconds:
$Q = Q_0 e^{-0.7/0.25} = Q_0 \times 0.060...$ *[1 mark]*

So **6%** (to 1 s.f.) of the initial charge is left on the capacitor after 0.7 s *[1 mark]*.

c) The total charge stored doubles: V is proportional to Q *[1 mark]*. The time taken to discharge the capacitor wouldn't change, as the discharging time depends only on the capacitance of the capacitor and the resistance of the circuit, which don't change *[1 mark]*.

Page 108 — Magnetic Fields and Forces

1 C *[1 mark]*

2 a) $F = BIl\sin\theta$ so $\theta = \sin^{-1}\left(\frac{F}{BIl}\right)$
$= \sin^{-1}\left(\frac{1.20 \times 10^{-6}}{(2.00 \times 10^{-5}) \times 3.00 \times 0.0400}\right)$ *[1 mark]*
$= \mathbf{30.0°}$ *[1 mark]*

b) The force is zero *[1 mark]* because there is no component of the current that is perpendicular to the external magnetic field *[1 mark]*.

3 $F = Bqv\sin\theta$
So $v = \frac{F}{Bq\sin\theta} = \frac{4.91 \times 10^{-15}}{1.10 \times (1.60 \times 10^{-19}) \times \sin 30.0}$ *[1 mark]*
$= 55\,795.4... = \mathbf{55\,800}$ **ms⁻¹ (to 3 s.f.)** *[1 mark]*

Page 111 — Electromagnetic Induction

1 a) $s = v\Delta t$
so the distance travelled by the plane in 1 second is:
$148 \times 1 = 148$ m
and the area cut by the plane's wings in 1 second is:
$148 \times 33.9 = 5017.2$ m²
$\phi = BA$ so the flux cut in 1 second is:
$(6.00 \times 10^{-5}) \times 5017.2 = 0.301...$ Wb *[1 mark]*
$\varepsilon = \frac{d(N\phi)}{dt} = \frac{d\phi}{dt}$ (as $N = 1$)
$= \frac{\Delta\phi}{\Delta t}$, as the plane's velocity is constant and the magnetic field is uniform, so the rate of flux cutting is constant *[1 mark]*.
$\varepsilon = 0.301... \div 1 = \mathbf{0.301}$ **V (to 3 s.f.)** *[1 mark]*

b)
[1 mark]

2 a) $N\phi = BAN = 0.92 \times 0.010 \times 550 = \mathbf{5.06}$ **Wb** *[1 mark]*

b) Flux linkage after movement
$= BAN \cos\theta$
$= 0.92 \times 0.010 \times 550 \times \cos 90° = 0$ Wb *[1 mark]*
$\varepsilon = -\frac{d(N\phi)}{dt} = -\frac{0 - 5.06}{0.5} = 10.12 = \mathbf{10}$ **V (to 2 s.f.)** *[1 mark]*

3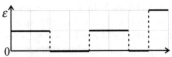

[1 mark for first step and third step the same,
1 mark for second and fourth step both equal to zero,
1 mark for fifth step twice the size of the first and third step].

Page 113 — Alternating Currents

1 a) i) $\frac{n_s}{n_p} = \frac{V_s}{V_p}$ so, $n_s = \frac{V_s \times n_p}{V_p} = \frac{45.0 \times 158}{9.30}$
$= 764.51... = \mathbf{765}$ **turns** *[1 mark]*

ii) $\frac{n_s}{n_p} = \frac{V_s}{V_p}$, so $V_s = V_p \times \frac{n_s}{n_p} = 9.30 \times \frac{90.0}{158}$
$= 5.297... = \mathbf{5.30}$ **V (to 3 s.f.)** *[1 mark]*

b) $\frac{I_p}{I_s} = \frac{n_s}{n_p}$ so, $I_s = I_p \times \frac{n_p}{n_s} = 1.50 \times \frac{158}{90.0} = 2.6333...$
$= \mathbf{2.63}$ **A (to 3 s.f.)** *[1 mark]*

2 a) $I_{rms} = \frac{I_0}{\sqrt{2}} = \frac{9.13}{\sqrt{2}} = 6.4558... = \mathbf{6.46}$ **A (to 3 s.f.)** *[1 mark]*

b) $V_{rms} = \frac{V_0}{\sqrt{2}}$ so $V_0 = V_{rms} \times \sqrt{2} = 119 \times \sqrt{2} = 168.29...$ *[1 mark]*
$V_{peak\,to\,peak} = 2 \times V_0 = 2 \times 168.29... = 336.58...$
$= \mathbf{337}$ **V (to 3 s.f.)** *[1 mark]*

Answers

Topic 8 — Nuclear and Particle Physics

Page 115 — Atomic Structure

a) The nuclear model states that an atom consists of a positive nucleus containing protons and neutrons *[1 mark]*, surrounded by orbiting negative electrons *[1 mark]*. The nucleus makes up a tiny proportion of the volume of an atom, but most of its mass *[1 mark]*.

b) E.g. Most alpha particles passed straight through the foil, so there must be a lot of empty space in an atom *[1 mark]*. Some alpha particles were deflected through large angles, so the centre of the atom must have a large positive charge to repel them — the nucleus *[1 mark]*. Very few particles were deflected by more than 90 degrees (and most went straight through), so the diameter of the nucleus must be tiny compared to the diameter of the atom *[1 mark]*. Some of the alpha particles were deflected by more than 90 degrees, which is only possible if they are scattered by something more massive than themselves, so most of the mass must be in the nucleus *[1 mark]*.

Proton number = 57, so there are **57 protons** and **57 electrons**.
Nucleon number = no. of protons + no. of neutrons = 139
so no. of neutrons = 139 – 57 = **82 neutrons**
[2 marks for all correct, 1 mark for two correct]

Page 118 — Particle Accelerators

$F = BQv = 0.770 \times 1.60 \times 10^{-19} \times 5.00 \times 10^6$ *[1 mark]*
$= \mathbf{6.16 \times 10^{-13}}$ **N** *[1 mark]*

$r = \dfrac{p}{BQ} = \dfrac{mv}{BQ} = \dfrac{(9.11 \times 10^{-31}) \times (2.3 \times 10^7)}{(0.60 \times 10^{-3}) \times (1.60 \times 10^{-19})}$ *[1 mark]*

$= 0.218... = \mathbf{0.22}$ **m (to 2 s.f.)** *[1 mark]*

Page 121 — Classification of Particles

Mesons are hadrons but the muon is a lepton *[1 mark]*.
The muon is a fundamental particle but mesons are not. Mesons are built up from simpler particles *[1 mark]*.
You need to classify the muon correctly first and then say why it's different from a meson because of what it's like.
The correct answer is **B** *[1 mark]*.
Protons and neutrons are both baryons, which are a type of hadron. Electrons are leptons.

Page 123 — Antiparticles

The creation of a particle of matter requires the creation of its antiparticle. In this case no antineutron has been produced *[1 mark]*. / Because baryon number is not conserved *[1 mark]*.
The electron and positron are destroyed and two photons are produced *[1 mark]*. This is called annihilation *[1 mark]*.
The antineutron has the same mass as the neutron, so the combined mass is 2 × 0.939375 = 1.87875 GeV/c^2 *[1 mark]*.
So the minimum energy of the photon required in pair production is **1.87875 GeV** *[1 mark]*.
This is true because $\Delta E = c^2 \Delta m$,
so $\Delta E = c^2 \times 1.87875$ GeV/$c^2 = 1.87875$ GeV
The energy of each particle is equal to $\Delta E = c^2 \Delta m$ (assuming kinetic energy is negligible)
When the proton and the antiproton annihilate, two photons are produced. So $2E_\gamma = 2c^2 m$ or $E_\gamma = c^2 m$.
$E_\gamma = hf$ and equating, $c^2 m = hf$,
so $f = \dfrac{c^2 m}{h}$ *[1 mark]*

$= \dfrac{(3.00 \times 10^8)^2 \times (1.67 \times 10^{-27})}{(6.63 \times 10^{-34})}$ *[1 mark]*

$= 2.266.. \times 10^{23}$
$= \mathbf{2.27 \times 10^{23}}$ **Hz (to 3 s.f.)** *[1 mark]*

Page 126 — Quarks

1   It must have 3 quarks, 0 charge and strangeness –1 *[1 mark]*, so the quark composition is uds *[1 mark]*.

2 a) Call the particle x, and write out the values of each of baryon number, charge and electron lepton number on both sides.

Give x the values needed to balance each equation (otherwise the interaction can't happen).

	n	→	p	+	e⁻	+	x
Charge:	0	→	+1	+	–1	+	0
B:	+1	→	+1	+	0	+	0
L_e:	0	→	0	+	+1	+	–1

So, particle x has an electron lepton number of –1, so it must be an antilepton, and it has no charge, so it must be an electron antineutrino.
[3 marks available — 1 mark for correctly working out the charge using conservation, 1 mark for correctly working out the electron lepton number using conservation, and 1 mark for saying that the only particle that has these properties is an electron antineutrino.]

b) $n \rightarrow p + e^- + \bar{\nu}_e$ *[1 mark]*

c) A down quark is converted into an up quark (plus an electron and an electron-antineutrino) *[1 mark]*.
The neutron (udd) becomes a proton (uud) *[1 mark]*.

3   The baryon number changes from 2 to 1, so baryon number is not conserved *[1 mark]*.

Page 129 — Detecting Particles

1   Charged particles follow curved tracks in a magnetic field *[1 mark]*. +ve and –ve particle tracks curve in opposite directions *[1 mark]*. You can identify the direction of curvature for negative particles by looking for knock-on electrons OR by applying Fleming's left-hand rule *[1 mark]*.

2   Antineutrinos are neutral and so will not leave tracks in many standard detectors. Beta particles are charged and so will ionise particles and leave a track, and so are more easily detected *[1 mark]*.

3   The proton and the positive pion give tracks but the neutron and the neutral pion do not. So the correct answer is **C** *[1 mark]*.

4

[1 mark for two tracks of similar size and shape going in opposite directions, 1 mark for not showing a track for the photon, 1 mark for tracks spiralling inwards.]

5   $r = \dfrac{p}{BQ}$ so $p = rBQ = 3.2 \times 1.8 \times 10^{-6} \times 1.60 \times 10^{-19}$ *[1 mark]*
$= 9.216 \times 10^{-25}$
$= \mathbf{9.2 \times 10^{-25}}$ **kgms⁻¹ (to 2 s.f.)** *[1 mark]*

Answers

Topic 9 — Thermodynamics

Page 131 — Internal Energy and Temperature

1   107 + 273 = **380 K** *[1 mark]*
2 a) The resistance of the thermistor changes with temperature, so the potential difference across it changes *[1 mark]*. The temperature can be obtained by comparing the output voltage across the thermistor to the thermistor's calibration curve *[1 mark]*.
   b) The fixed resistor ensures the output voltage is within a range that can be recorded by a voltmeter *[1 mark]*. If its resistance is too high, V_{out} won't vary enough with temperature, and if it's too low, V_{out} might vary over a bigger range than your voltmeter can handle *[1 mark]*.

Page 133 — Thermal Properties of Materials

1   Electrical energy supplied: $E = 90.0 \times (3.0 \times 60)$
                                       = 16 200 J *[1 mark]*
The temperature rise is 12.7 – 4.5 = 8.2 °C

$E = mc\Delta\theta$, so $c = \dfrac{E}{m\Delta\theta}$

so $c = \dfrac{16\,200}{2.0 \times 8.2} = 987.8... = $ **990 Jkg⁻¹°C⁻¹ (to 2 s.f.)**

[1 mark for correct number, 1 mark for correct unit.]
You need the right unit for the third mark — Jkg⁻¹K⁻¹ would be right too.

2   $\Delta E = mc\Delta\theta$
The heat transferred to the water is equal to the heat transferred from the block, so:
$m_w c_w \Delta\theta_w = m_b c_b \Delta\theta_b$.
Rearranging for c_b gives: $c_b = \dfrac{m_w c_w \Delta\theta_w}{m_b \Delta\theta_b}$ *[1 mark]*

The water heats up from 19 °C to 26 °C,
so $\Delta\theta_w = 26 - 19 = 7$ °C
The block cools down from 100 °C to 26 °C,
so $\Delta\theta_b = 100 - 26 = 74$ °C
[1 mark for calculating both temperature changes]

So $c_b = \dfrac{2.0 \times 4180 \times 7}{4.0 \times 74}$ *[1 mark]*
        = 197.7... = **200 J kg⁻¹ K⁻¹ (to 2 s.f.)** *[1 mark]*

3   Total amount of energy needed to evaporate all the water:
$\Delta E = L\Delta m = (2.26 \times 10^6) \times 0.500 = 1.13 \times 10^6$ J *[1 mark]*
3.00 kW means you get 3000 J in a second, so
time in seconds = $(1.13 \times 10^6) \div 3000$ *[1 mark]*
                = 376.6... = **377 s (to 3 s.f.)** *[1 mark]*

Page 135 — Ideal Gases

1 a) $pV = NkT$, so $p = \dfrac{NkT}{V}$. $T = 27.2 + 273 = 300.2$ K *[1 mark]*
   $p = \dfrac{(3.00 \times 10^{23}) \times (1.38 \times 10^{-23}) \times 300.2}{0.0130}$
      = 95 602.15...
      = **95 600 Pa (to 3 s.f.)** *[1 mark]*
   b) The pressure would also halve *[1 mark]* because it is proportional to the number of molecules — $pV = NkT$ *[1 mark]*.
2   $V_1 = 2.42$ m³, $V_2 = 6.43$ m³, $T_2 = 293$ K.
   Charles's Law: $\dfrac{V}{T}$ = constant so $\dfrac{V_2}{T_2} = \dfrac{6.43}{293} = 0.02194...$ *[1 mark]*
   $T_1 = \dfrac{V_1}{\text{constant}} = \dfrac{2.42}{0.02194...} = 110.273...$
                                        = **110 K (to 3 s.f.)** *[1 mark]*
3 a) E.g. Connect a tube containing only oil and air to a Bourdon gauge and a bike pump *[1 mark]*. Measure the dimensions of the tube and the depth of the oil, then increase the pressure in the tube using the bike pump *[1 mark]*. Note down the pressure from the Bourdon gauge and measure the depth of the oil again *[1 mark]*. Repeat for different pressures then use your measurements to calculate the volume of the air in the tube. The results should show that as pressure increases, air volume decreases by the same proportion, and vice versa — i.e. pV = constant *[1 mark]*.
   b) $V_1 = 0.460$ m³, $p_1 = 1.03 \times 10^5$ Pa, $p_2 = 3.41 \times 10^5$ Pa.
   $p_1 \times V_1$ = constant
   $(1.03 \times 10^5) \times 0.460 = 47\,380$ *[1 mark]*
   V_2 = constant $\div p_2 = 47\,380 \div (3.41 \times 10^5)$
        = 0.13894... = **0.139 m³ (to 3 s.f.)** *[1 mark]*

Page 137 — Kinetic Theory and Internal Energy

1 a) $pV = \frac{1}{3}Nm\langle c^2 \rangle$ so $\langle c^2 \rangle = \dfrac{3pV}{Nm} = \dfrac{3 \times (1.0 \times 10^5) \times (7.0 \times 10^{-5})}{(2.0 \times 10^{22}) \times (6.6 \times 10^{-27})}$
                                        = 159 090.90... *[1 mark]*
   $\sqrt{\langle c^2 \rangle} = \sqrt{159\,090.90...} = 398.86...$
                                = **400 ms⁻¹ (to 2 s.f.)** *[1 mark]*
   b) The increase in temperature will increase the average speed and therefore momentum of the gas particles *[1 mark]*. This means that as the particles hit the walls of the flask there will be a greater change in momentum, and from Newton's second law this means they will exert a greater force on the walls of the flask *[1 mark]*. As the particles are travelling faster they will also hit the walls (and exert a force) more frequently *[1 mark]*. This leads to an increase in pressure (as pressure = force ÷ area) *[1 mark]*.

Page 139 — Black Body Radiators

1 a) According to Wien's law $\lambda_{max}T = 2.898 \times 10^{-3}$, so for this star
   $\lambda_{max} = (2.898 \times 10^{-3}) \div 4000 = 7.245 \times 10^{-7}$ m *[1 mark]*
   Curve Y peaks at around 700 nm (= 7×10^{-7} m), so could represent the star *[1 mark]*.
   b) Star X is larger *[1 mark]*.
   From $L = \sigma A T^4$, power output is proportional to temperature (T^4) and to area. Given that the power output of both stars is the same, if one star has a higher temperature than the other, it must have a smaller surface area. The Sun has a higher temperature than star X, so it must have a smaller surface area *[1 mark]*.
2   $\lambda_{max}T = 2.898 \times 10^{-3}$
   So $T = (2.898 \times 10^{-3}) \div (436 \times 10^{-9}) = 6646.78...$ K *[1 mark]*
   $L = \sigma A T^4$, so $A = \dfrac{L}{\sigma T^4} = \dfrac{2.3 \times 10^{27}}{(5.67 \times 10^{-8}) \times (6646.78...)^4}$
                            = 2.07... $\times 10^{19}$
                            = **2.1 × 10¹⁹ m² (to 2 s.f.)** *[1 mark]*

Answers

Topic 10 — Space

Page 141 — Determining Astronomical Distances

a) A standard candle is an object in space with a known luminosity from which its distance can be calculated *[1 mark]*.

b) $I = \dfrac{L}{4\pi d^2}$ so $d = \sqrt{\dfrac{L}{4\pi I}} = \sqrt{\dfrac{2 \times 10^{36}}{4\pi \times (1.5 \times 10^{-13})}}$ *[1 mark]*

   $= 1.030... \times 10^{24} = \mathbf{1 \times 10^{24}}$ **m (to 1 s.f.)** *[1 mark]*

a) $L = \sigma A T^4$ so $A = \dfrac{L}{\sigma T^4} = \dfrac{3.9 \times 10^{26}}{(5.67 \times 10^{-8}) \times 5500^4}$ *[1 mark]*

   $= 7.516... \times 10^{18}$

   $= \mathbf{7.5 \times 10^{18} \ m^2}$ **(to 2 s.f.)** *[1 mark]*

b) You could use the observed trigonometric parallax of the star and the distance between the Earth and the Sun to make a right-angled triangle *[1 mark]*. The distance to the star could then be found using trigonometry *[1 mark]*.

Page 144 — H-R Diagrams and the Life Cycle of Stars

a) Once the hydrogen in the core runs out, the core of the star starts to collapse *[1 mark]*. The outer layers of the star expand and cool, and the star becomes a red giant *[1 mark]*. Red giants have a higher luminosity than main sequence stars and a lower surface temperature *[1 mark]*, so the star moves off the main sequence to the top right-hand part of the H-R diagram *[1 mark]*.

b) At the end of a low mass star's red giant phase, the helium in its core runs out and the star collapses to form a white dwarf *[1 mark]*. White dwarfs have a lower luminosity and a higher surface temperature than main sequence stars *[1 mark]*, so when a star becomes a white dwarf it moves to the bottom left-hand part of the H-R diagram *[1 mark]*.

c) Because black holes are so dense that not even light can escape them *[1 mark]* so they have no luminosity *[1 mark]*.

Page 147 — Doppler Effect and the Fate of the Universe

a) $H_0 = v / d = 75 \ \text{kms}^{-1} / 1 \ \text{Mpc}$
   $75 \ \text{kms}^{-1} = 75 \times 10^3 \ \text{ms}^{-1}$ and $1 \ \text{Mpc} = 3.09 \times 10^{22} \ \text{m}$
   So $H_0 = (75 \times 10^3 \ \text{ms}^{-1}) \div (3.09 \times 10^{22} \ \text{m})$
   $= 2.427... \times 10^{-18} \ \text{s}^{-1}$
   $= \mathbf{2.4 \times 10^{-18} \ s^{-1}}$ **(to 2 s.f.)**
   [1 mark for the correct value, 1 mark for the correct unit]

b) $t = 1/H_0$ so $t = 1 \div (2.427... \times 10^{-18}) = 4.12 \times 10^{17} \ \text{s}$ *[1 mark]*
   $(4.12 \times 10^{17}) \div (3.16 \times 10^7) = 1.303... \times 10^{10}$
   $= \mathbf{13 \ billion \ years}$ **(to 2 s.f.)** *[1 mark]*
   So the observable universe has a radius of
   13 billion light-years (to 2 s.f.) *[1 mark]*.

c) $z \approx v/c$ so $v \approx 0.37 \times (3.00 \times 10^8) \approx 1.11 \times 10^8$
   $= \mathbf{1.1 \times 10^8 \ ms^{-1}}$ **(to 2 s.f.)** *[1 mark]*

d) $v = H_0 d$ so $d = \dfrac{v}{H_0} = (1.11 \times 10^8) \div (2.427... \times 10^{-18})$
   $= 4.5732 \times 10^{25} \ \text{m}$ *[1 mark]*
   distance = speed × time so $1 \ \text{ly} = (3.00 \times 10^8) \times (3.16 \times 10^7)$
   $= 9.48 \times 10^{15} \ \text{m}$ *[1 mark]*
   $(4.5732 \times 10^{25}) \div (9.48 \times 10^{15}) = 4.824... \times 10^9 \ \text{ly}$
   $= \mathbf{4.8 \ billion \ ly}$ **(to 2 s.f.)** *[1 mark]*

e) $z \approx v/c$ is only valid if $v \ll c$ — it isn't in this case *[1 mark]*.

Topic 11 — Nuclear Radiation

Page 149 — Radioactive Decay

1 a) Beta-minus radiation *[1 mark]*

b) When measuring the count rate from the radioactive source, the student will also be detecting background radiation *[1 mark]*. To correct this error, the student should measure the background radiation separately before the experiment begins, without the source. Then he should subtract this from any measurements taken *[1 mark]*.

Page 151 — More Radioactive Decay

1 a) $^{226}_{88}\text{Ra} \rightarrow \ ^{222}_{86}\text{Rn} + \ ^{4}_{2}\alpha$ *[3 marks available — 1 mark for alpha particle, 1 mark each for proton and nucleon number of radon]*

b) $^{40}_{19}\text{K} \rightarrow \ ^{40}_{20}\text{Ca} + \ ^{0}_{-1}\beta + \ ^{0}_{0}\bar{\nu}$ *[3 marks available — 1 mark for beta particle and antineutrino, 1 mark each for proton and nucleon number of calcium]*

Page 154 — Exponential Law of Decay

1 a) Activity, A = measured activity – background activity
   $= 750 - 50 = 700 \ \text{Bq}$ *[1 mark]*
   $A = \lambda N$, so $\lambda = A \div N = 700 \div 50\,000 = 0.014$
   $= \mathbf{0.01 \ s^{-1}}$ **(to 1 s.f.)** *[1 mark]*

b) $\lambda = (\ln 2) \div t_{1/2}$, so $t_{1/2} = (\ln 2) \div \lambda = (\ln 2) \div 0.014 = 49.510...$
   $= \mathbf{50 \ s}$ **(to 1 s.f.)** *[1 mark]*

c) $N = N_0 e^{-\lambda t} = 50\,000 \times e^{-0.014 \times 300} = 749.77...$
   $= \mathbf{700}$ **(to 1 s.f.)** *[1 mark]*

Page 157 — Nuclear Fission and Fusion

1 a) Fusion *[1 mark]*

b) The increase in binding energy per nucleon is about 1.11 MeV *[1 mark]*. There are 2 nucleons in ^{2}H, so the increase in binding energy is about 2.22 MeV — so about 2.22 MeV is released (ignoring the positron) *[1 mark]*.

   You can ignore the positron because it isn't bound to anything, so it has no binding energy — it's just a particle by itself like the protons on the left of the equation. There's more on positrons on p.122.

2 a) mass deficit = mass before – mass after *[1 mark]*
   $= (2.013553 + 3.015501) - (4.001505 + 1.008665)$
   $= \mathbf{0.018884 \ u}$ *[1 mark]*

b) Covert the mass deficit to kg:
   $0.018884\text{u} = 0.018884 \times (1.66 \times 10^{-27})$
   $= 3.134... \times 10^{-29} \ \text{kg}$ *[1 mark]*
   $\Delta E = c^2 \Delta m = (3.00 \times 10^8)^2 \times (3.134... \times 10^{-29})$
   $= 2.821... \times 10^{-12} \ \text{J}$ *[1 mark]*
   $2.821... \times 10^{-12} \div (1.60 \times 10^{-19}) = 1.763... \times 10^7 \ \text{eV}$
   $= \mathbf{17.6 \ MeV}$ **(to 3 s.f.)** *[1 mark]*

Answers

Topic 12 — Gravitational Fields

Page 159 — Gravitational Fields

1 The gravitational field of an object is the region around it where a mass will experience an attractive force. *[1 mark]*

2 a) $g = \dfrac{Gm}{r^2} = \dfrac{6.67 \times 10^{-11} \times 7.35 \times 10^{22}}{(1740 \times 10^3)^2}$
$= 1.619... = \textbf{1.62 Nkg}^{-1}$ **(to 3 s.f.)** *[1 mark]*

  b) $F = \dfrac{Gm_1m_2}{r^2} = \dfrac{6.67 \times 10^{-11} \times 7.35 \times 10^{22} \times 25}{((1740 \times 10^3) + 10)^2}$ *[1 mark]*
$= 40.4... = \textbf{40 N}$ **(to 2 s.f.)** *[1 mark]*

3 $\dfrac{Gm}{r_1^2} = 4$ and $\dfrac{Gm}{r_2^2} = 2$ so $4r_1^2 = 2r_2^2$
so $r_2 = \sqrt{2}r_1$
If g decreases until it's at half of its original value, r will increase by a factor of $\sqrt{2} \approx 1.4$.
So the answer is **B** *[1 mark]*

Page 161 — More Gravitational Fields

1 Similarities — Any two from: Both gravitational and electric field strengths are forces per unit — gravitational field strength, g, is force per unit mass and electric field strength, $E_{electric}$, is force per unit positive charge. / Both gravitational and electric potentials are potential energy per unit — gravitational potential, V_{grav}, is potential energy per unit mass and electric potential, $V_{electric}$, is potential energy per unit positive charge. / Both gravitational and electric fields are zero at infinity. / The force between two point masses is an inverse square law, and so is the force between two point charges. / The field lines for a point mass and the field lines for a negative point charge are the same. *[2 marks — 1 mark for each correct similarity]*
Differences — Any one from: Gravitational forces are always attractive, whereas electric forces can be attractive or repulsive. / The size of an electric force depends on the medium between the charges, e.g. plastic or air. For gravitational forces, this makes no difference. / Objects can be shielded from electric fields, but not from gravitational fields. *[1 mark for one correct difference]*

2 At the surface:
$V_{grav} = \dfrac{-Gm}{r}$ so $r = \dfrac{-Gm}{V_{grav}}$
$r = \dfrac{-6.67 \times 10^{-11} \times 2.67 \times 10^{19}}{-1.52 \times 10^4}$ *[1 mark]*
$= 117\,163.8... = \textbf{117 000 m}$ **(to 3 s.f.)** *[1 mark]*

3 a) $T^2 = \left(\dfrac{4\pi^2}{Gm}\right)r^3$
so $T = \sqrt{\dfrac{4\pi^2 r^3}{Gm}} = \sqrt{\dfrac{4\pi^2((6400 + 200.0) \times 10^3)^3}{6.67 \times 10^{-11} \times 5.98 \times 10^{24}}}$ *[1 mark]*
$= 5334.3...$ seconds
$= \textbf{5300 seconds or 1.5 hours}$ **(to 2 s.f.)** *[1 mark]*

  b) $v = \sqrt{\dfrac{Gm}{r}} = \sqrt{\dfrac{6.67 \times 10^{-11} \times 5.98 \times 10^{24}}{(6400 + 200.0) \times 10^3}}$
$= 7773.9...\ \text{ms}^{-1} = \textbf{7800 ms}^{-1}$ **(to 2 s.f.)** *[1 mark]*

4 50 000 years is $50\,000 \times 365 \times 24 \times 3600 = 1.57... \times 10^{12}$ s
This means the sun will have lost:
$1.57... \times 10^{12} \times 6 \times 10^9 = 9.46... \times 10^{21}$ kg of mass *[1 mark]*.
This is less than 5×10^{-7} % of the Sun's mass, so will not have caused any significant change in the Earth's orbit *[1 mark]*.

Topic 13 — Oscillations

Page 163 — Simple Harmonic Motion

1 a) Simple harmonic motion is an oscillation in which the restoring force acting on an object is directly proportional to its displacement from the midpoint *[1 mark]*, and is directed towards the midpoint *[1 mark]*.
The force, F, is given by: $F = -kx$ *[1 mark]*
  b) The force acting on a ball bouncing off the ground is not a restoring force that is proportional to displacement, so the motion is not SHM. *[1 mark]*

2 a) $x = A\cos(\omega t) = A\cos(2\pi ft) = 0.050 \times \cos(2\pi \times 1.5 \times 0.10)$ *[1 mark]*
$= 0.0293... = \textbf{0.029 m}$ **(to 2 s.f.)** *[1 mark]*
  b) $v = -A\omega \sin(\omega t)$
$v_{max} = \pm A\omega$ (since v is maximum when $\sin(\omega t) = 1$ or -1) *[1 mark]*
You're only looking for the magnitude of v, so you can ignore the minus.
$v_{max} = A \times (2\pi f)$
$= 0.050 \times 2\pi \times 1.5 = 0.4712...$
$= \textbf{0.47 ms}^{-1}$ **(to 2 s.f.)** *[1 mark]*
  c) $a = -A\omega^2\cos(\omega t) = -A(2\pi f)^2\cos(2\pi ft)$
Again, we're only looking for the magnitude of acceleration, so we can ignore the minus sign.
$\dfrac{a}{A(2\pi f)^2} = \cos(2\pi ft)$
$\cos^{-1}\left(\dfrac{a}{A(2\pi f)^2}\right) = 2\pi ft$
$\cos^{-1}\left(\dfrac{a}{A(2\pi f)^2}\right) \div (2\pi f) = t$
$t = \cos^{-1}\left(\dfrac{0.70}{0.050 \times (2\pi \times 1.5)^2}\right) \div (2\pi \times 1.5)$ *[1 mark]*
$= 0.149... = \textbf{0.15 s}$ **(to 2 s.f.)** *[1 mark]*
Don't forget to put your calculator in radian mode when you're solving questions on SHM — it's an easy mistake to make.

3 $a = -\omega^2 x$
$x_{max} = A$, acceleration is maximum when displacement is maximum, so $a_{max} = -\omega^2 A$
$\omega_P = 2\omega_Q$
$a_{max,\,P} = -\omega_P^2 A = -(2\omega_Q)^2 A = -4\omega_Q^2 A$
$a_{max,\,Q} = -\omega_Q^2 A$
So $a_{max,\,P} = 4a_{max,\,Q}$
D *[1 mark]*

Answers

age 165 — Investigating Simple Harmonic Motion

a) $T = 2\pi\sqrt{\frac{m}{k}}$ so $k = \frac{4\pi^2 m}{T^2} = \frac{4\pi^2 \times 0.10}{0.72^2}$ *[1 mark]*

$\qquad\qquad = 7.615... = \textbf{7.6 Nm}^{-1}$ **(to 2 s.f.)** *[1 mark]*

b) $m \propto T^2$ so if T is doubled, T^2 is quadrupled
and m is quadrupled *[1 mark]*.
So mass needed $= 4 \times 0.10 = \textbf{0.40 kg}$ *[1 mark]*

E.g. $5T_{\text{short pendulum}} = 3T_{\text{long pendulum}}$ *[1 mark]* and $T = 2\pi\sqrt{\frac{l}{g}}$
Let length of long pendulum $= l$

So $5\left(2\pi\sqrt{\frac{0.20}{g}}\right) = 3\left(2\pi\sqrt{\frac{l}{g}}\right)$ *[1 mark]*

Dividing by 2π and squaring gives: $25 \times \frac{0.2}{g} = 9 \times \frac{l}{g}$
Which simplifies to $5 = 9l$
So length of long pendulum $= 5 \div 9 = 0.555...$

$\qquad\qquad = \textbf{0.56 m}$ **(to 2 s.f.)** *[1 mark]*

age 167 — Free and Forced Oscillations

a) E.g.

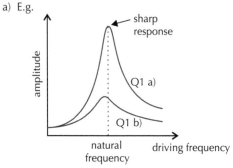

*[1 mark for showing a peak at the natural frequency, 1 mark for
a sharp peak.]*

b) *[See graph in part b). 1 mark for a smaller peak at the natural
frequency.]*
The peak will actually be slightly to the left of the natural frequency
due to the damping, but you'll get the mark if the peak is at the same
frequency as your diagram in part a).

c) The mass-spring system is being heavily damped *[1 mark]*.
Energy is transferred away from the mass-spring system, causing
the oscillations to die away *[1 mark]*.

d) The energy lost from the mass-spring system is transferred to
the water, so the energy of the water increases and energy is
conserved overall *[1 mark]*.
A system is critically damped if it returns to rest in the shortest
time possible when it's displaced from equilibrium and released
[1 mark]. It is used in e.g. car suspension systems *[1 mark]*.

Index

Index

Index